Academic Librarianship

Academic Librarianship

SECOND EDITION

G. EDWARD EVANS
STACEY GREENWELL

ALA
Neal-Schuman

CHICAGO :: 2018

© 2018 by G. Edward Evans and Stacey Greenwell

Extensive effort has gone into ensuring the reliability of the information in this book; however, the publisher makes no warranty, express or implied, with respect to the material contained herein.

ISBNs
978-0-8389-1563-9 (paper)
978-0-8389-1668-1 (PDF)
978-0-8389-1667-4 (ePub)
978-0-8389-1669-8 (Kindle)

Library of Congress Cataloging-in-Publication Data
Names: Evans, G. Edward, 1937- author. | Greenwell, Stacey, author. | Alire, Camila A. Academic librarianship.
Title: Academic librarianship / G. Edward Evans, Stacey Greenwell.
Description: Second edition. | Chicago : ALA Neal-Schuman, an imprint of the American Library Association, 2018. | Revised edition of: Academic librarianship / Camila A. Alire and G. Edward Evans. [2010]. | Includes bibliographical references and index.
Identifiers: LCCN 2017043130| ISBN 9780838915639 (print : alk. paper) | ISBN 9780838916674 (epub) | ISBN 9780838916681 (pdf) | ISBN 9780838916698 (kindle)
Subjects: LCSH: Academic libraries—United States—Administration. | Academic librarians. | Libraries and colleges.
Classification: LCC Z675.U5 A427 2018 | DDC 025.1/977—dc23
LC record available at https://lccn.loc.gov/2017043130

Cover design by Kimberly Thornton; imagery © Adobe Stock. Text design and composition by Karen Sheets de Gracia in the Cardea and Acumin Pro typefaces.

♾ This paper meets the requirements of ANSI/NISO Z39.48-1992 (Permanence of Paper).

Printed in the United States of America
22 21 20 19 18   5 4 3 2 1

CONTENTS

LIST OF TABLES *xi*

PREFACE TO THE SECOND EDITION *xiii*

FOREWORD *xv*

ACKNOWLEDGMENTS *xvii*

---

1   Context *1*

Higher Education Variations *2*

The Future of Higher Education and Its Libraries *5*

   Student Debt 5

   Worth of a Degree 7

   Immediacy versus Long-Term 7

   Degrees versus Badges 8

   Socioeconomic Gap among Students and Graduates 9

   Funding Challenges, Doing More with Less, and Amenities 10

What Makes an Academic Library Academic? *12*

Academic Library Challenges *13*

Why Bother Studying the Subject If Everything Will Change? *17*

References *17*

---

2   Higher Education's Historic Legacy *19*

Where It All Began *20*

Italian Influence *21*

French Influence *21*

English Influence *22*

German Influence *23*

How the Transplants Took Root in the United States (1636–1770) *24*

Post–War of Independence to 1865 *27*

1860s to World War II *29*

Wars and Higher Education *32*

Retrenchment and Realignment (1960–1990) *34*

1990s to the Present *38*

    The Rise and Decline of For-Profit Education 38

    New Emphasis on an Old Concept 40

References *41*

3 **Faculty** *43*

Faculty Responsibilities *44*

    Service 45

    Teaching 48

    Research 52

The Ladder and Tenure *57*

    Part-Time/Adjunct Faculty 59

    Climbing the Ladder 60

Diversity *60*

Key Points to Remember *61*

References *61*

4 **Students** *63*

Student Thoughts on Higher Education *64*

Recruitment and Admissions *66*

Financial Aid *69*

Retention *71*

Student Services *73*

Student Groups *75*

Collegiate Sports *77*

Graduation and Beyond *79*

Key Points to Remember *79*

References *80*

5 **Curriculum** *83*

What Is General Education? *83*

Debating the Curriculum *86*

Modifying the Curriculum *90*

Continuing Education *92*

Distance Education *95*

Key Points to Remember *99*

References *99*

6 **Governance** *101*

Role of the State *102*

Those Who Establish Guidelines *103*

Those Who Administer *107*

Those Who Do *111*

Concluding Thoughts on Campus Governance *114*

Key Points to Remember *116*

References *116*

7 **Funding** *119*

Higher Education Finances *119*

Grants and Research *121*

Endowments *123*

The Budget Process *124*

    The Budget as a Control Device 125

    The Budget Cycle 127

    Budget Preparation 127

    Presenting and Defending the Budget Request 129

Income Generation *132*

Planning and Budgeting *137*

Key Points to Remember *138*

References *139*

8 **Facilities** *141*

How Academic Libraries Differ from Other Campus Buildings *143*

Planning for Renovations *144*

Managing the Facility *148*

    Housekeeping Matters 149

    Managing Risk and the Unexpected 149

Health, Safety, and Security *150*

Crime 152

Disaster Management 153

Deferred Maintenance *155*

Trends in Library Spaces *156*

Key Points to Remember *157*

References *158*

9   Technology *159*

Academic Libraries and Information and Communication Technology *163*

Long-Term Technology Planning *164*

Controlling Technology Costs *167*

Staff Training *170*

Future Directions *170*

Key Points to Remember *171*

References *171*

10   The Academy, Accreditation, and Accountability *173*

Accreditation *173*

Information Literacy and Accreditation *178*

Beyond Accreditation *181*

Benchmarking 184

Quality Management 185

Six Sigma–Lean Six Sigma 186

Balanced Scorecard 186

Cost Analysis 187

Work Analysis 187

Library Value and User Studies *188*

Key Points to Remember *189*

References *190*

11   Collections *193*

Past and Present Practice *194*

Impact of World War II and Association of Research Libraries Cooperative Projects *196*

Developing Academic Library Collections *198*

Assessing Needs 199

Collection Policy 199

Selection Resources 200

Collection Balance 200

Collection Funding 201

Acquisition Procedures 202

Assessment 203

Remote Storage 204

Preservation Issues 206

Licensing Considerations *209*

Key Points to Remember *210*

References *211*

12   Services *213*

Customer Service *214*

Reference Services *216*

Instructional Services *219*

Circulation Services *219*

Handling Confrontational Situations 220

Confidentiality 221

Interlibrary Loan and Document Delivery 222

Reserve Services 222

Library Liaison Services *224*

Key Points to Remember *226*

References *226*

13   Staffing *229*

Librarians *231*

Support Staff *234*

Other Full-Time Staff *235*

Student Employees *237*

The Staffing Process *238*

Recruitment and Selection 239

Orientation 239

Retention 240

Training and Staff Development 240

Performance Appraisal *241*

Key Points to Remember *243*

References *244*

14 Career Development *247*

From Student to Academic Librarian *248*

    Marketing Yourself with a CV and Cover Letter 248

    The Search Committee 253

    Selecting the Pool 254

    The Interview 254

Adjusting to the Position *258*

Starting Your Career Development Plan *260*

    Mentors 261

    Self-Assessment of Knowledge and Skills 262

Changing Views of a Career *264*

    Career Breaks 264

    Work-Life 265

Moving Forward *265*

Key Points to Remember *266*

References *267*

ABOUT THE AUTHORS *269*

ABOUT THE COAUTHOR OF THE FIRST EDITION *271*

ABOUT THE ADVISORY BOARD *273*

INDEX *275*

TABLES

TABLE 1.1   Topics discussed by essay contributors in the first edition of *Academic Librarianship* 15

TABLE 2.1   Early college transplants to the United States 25

TABLE 2.2   Summary of U.S. higher education before 1865 30

TABLE 2.3   Developments in U.S. higher education from 1865 to 1940 33

TABLE 2.4   Post–World War II assumptions about the academy 35

TABLE 2.5   Post-1970s issues in U.S. higher education 36

TABLE 5.1   Differences between general education and liberal education 86

TABLE 9.1   Key information and communication technology planning issues 168

TABLE 10.1   U.S. regional accreditation associations 175

PREFACE

TO THE SECOND EDITION

Academic institutions may be among the oldest ongoing organizations in Europe and the Americas, but they do change. In today's world, any organization must rethink and reimagine itself in order to survive, and the academic institution is no exception. Everyone knows change is part of their lives. The same is true for academic libraries, and the same is true for textbooks. Thus, a second edition of *Academic Librarianship* was developed.

In this edition, we hope we retained all the highly praised material from the first edition, revised the dated discussions, and deleted the less useful ones. The world of higher education has changed considerably since 2009 when the first edition when into production. This edition of *Academic Librarianship* reflects those changes. Along with those changes comes a new coauthor, Stacey Greenwell, who brings a fresh perspective to the book.

We continue the tradition of employing sidebars to provide real-world examples of academic librarianship as experienced by the authors and members of the Advisory Board. Additional new sidebars provide suggestions for in-depth reading about the topic under discussion rather than appending a long list without context at the end of each chapter.

Although the core principles of academic librarianship remain the same, much has changed in the world of higher education since the previous edition appeared. As a result, academic librarians deliver information, offer services, and provide learning spaces in new ways to better meet the needs of today's students, faculty, and other communities of academic library users. This edition of *Academic Librarianship* includes revisions addressing such changes in higher education and the responses of academic librarians. We provide guidance on finding the most current higher education expenditure information online. Our increased emphasis on staying current in higher education is evident throughout the text with a focus on updated resources in each chapter as well as links to additional resources. We enhanced the material related to academic librarian careers with even more practical advice and expanded the chapter on career development, seeking advice from recent graduates about which topics would be most helpful. Although for space considerations we dropped the final chapter of the first edition ("Leaders Look Toward the Future"), we look at trends and consider the future as appropriate throughout the text.

We updated chapters 3–6 to reflect a variety of topics and include some discussion of what the future might hold in these areas given current conditions. The concept of faculty status in general, and particularly for librarians, is facing growing challenges in the media along with institutional concerns about librarian status, and we address this issue in chapter 3 ("Faculty"). Students (chapter 4) continue to be more vocal on campus with higher expectations akin to customers of the university—shades of the early days of higher education. Student debt and the high cost of higher education are ongoing issues. In terms of curricular matters (chapter 5), colleges and universities continually try to address demands to demonstrate employability of students. That concern, in turn, raises questions about the balance between general education requirements and applied courses. In chapter 6 ("Governance"), we explore current and future trends in campus collaborations, particularly the growing tension on some campuses between faculty and administration.

We shifted focus in chapter 7 ("Funding"). Rather than providing detailed higher education expenditure data, we explain how to find such data online so that the most current information is easily accessible. Given the continued importance of philanthropic support, the section on development and advancement ("Income Generation") has been updated. We also addressed today's prevalent budget models and the implications for academic libraries. Finally, the chapter covers the increasing cost of scholarly communication, and more attention is given to alternative models of accessing scholarly resources in chapter 11 ("Collections").

Chapters 8 ("Facilities") and 9 ("Technology") consider current and future trends within these essential areas on campus. More campuses are constructing posh residence halls and elaborate amenities including fitness, entertainment, and recreational facilities. What does this mean for the academic library, and what opportunities do campus leaders have to take advantage of librarian expertise in developing classroom and common learning spaces around campus? Updates to chapter 9 consider the increasing trend in merging library and technology support services within the library as well as new technology services being developed within the library.

Chapter 10 ("The Academy, Accreditation, and Accountability") now touches on the trend to quantify library value and demonstrate the impact of library collections and services on retention and student success. Although most of these studies are currently correlational in nature, the chapter considers future opportunities for better making those connections. User experience is an important part of assessment, and the chapter addresses new opportunities for understanding user needs and satisfaction. Campuses are putting greater focus on return on investment, and, as a result, librarians are increasingly developing outcomes-based assessment to measure student learning as a result of information literacy instruction. We also cover the Information Literacy Framework of the Association of College and Research Libraries (ACRL) in terms of the assessment of information literacy instruction.

Chapter 11 ("Collections") describes changes in the scholarly publishing model through academic library-led outlets for publishing scholarly communication while retaining a strong foundation in collection development practices in any format. Chapter 12 ("Services") considers current trends in service delivery within physical spaces as well as how those services need to evolve given the increasing numbers of students completing coursework online. The chapter includes updates to redefining and expanding the library liaison role. Chapter 13 ("Staffing") reflects the need and possible resources for ongoing professional development.

This edition includes an enhanced focus on academic library careers throughout the text. Based on feedback from students, chapter 14 ("Career Development") includes more details on preparing application materials and participating in multiday, on-campus interviews. The text offers advice on preparing a vita as well as basic guidelines for conducting appropriate research in order to ask good questions at an interview. New and updated sidebars throughout the text provide even more support for career development.

Ultimately the second edition of *Academic Librarianship* serves as a guide to help you throughout your career, particularly in better understanding higher education institutions and how academic libraries support those institutions.

FOREWORD

I t is no surprise that libraries are transitioning in an ever-changing global environment, but we need to better understand the direction of our society and higher education in order to lay the groundwork today for our future. Libraries need visionary leaders who combine the ability to daily manage with forecasting skills in order to develop tactics that strategically place the library in a position for future success. In this updated edition of *Academic Librarianship,* Ed Evans and Stacey Greenwell provide relevant and practical guidance for individuals who desire to be successful academic librarians This text is unique because it provides a strong foundation for understanding the past and current states of higher education. Knowledge of the framework of higher education is essential to understanding the broader context of our academic libraries, enabling us to develop services and collections that contribute to the mission of our parent organization. No longer can academic libraries depend on the belief that libraries are a good thing or that individuals value libraries as a social good. Although the Pew library study (Horrigan 2016) noted that there is high regard for and trust in libraries, this attitude does not translate into the necessary financial support for libraries even within the higher education environment among educators who typically understand the role of the library as an extension of the classroom. No longer are university administrators concerned about how many books are checked out; rather, if students checked out books, are they better students who will be retained and will successfully graduate? Academic libraries must compete with other pressing and valid priorities for attention, funding, and support. It is up to librarians and library workers to align the mission of the library to the mission of the university or college and to constantly demonstrate, through data and stories, the contributions of the library to the goals of the institution. Strong leadership and excellent management within academic libraries are required in order to build trust and respect for the library within our universities and colleges, and the following chapters will enable librarians and library employees to understand the challenges and opportunities in higher education.

The grounding within the higher education framework provides the structure for discussions on academic library management. Academic libraries are complex, having different employee classifications requiring a variety of guidelines for hiring, training, professional development, discipline, and support. Librarians must consider these various aspects and develop skills that are effective for all types of employee classification. Traditional library services are shifting to virtual and online services that interact with library patrons on the desktop. Such changes require librarians to think more like commercial operators in developing responsive online services in a virtual environment. Academic librarians are deeply engaged with instruction, research, and liaison services combined with assessment metrics that link to the university or college mission, demonstrating relevance to the goals of student success, retention, time to degree, and productive careers. Ed and Stacey provide comprehensive overviews of all these areas plus more issues that academic librarians need to consider in order to understand their role, successfully manage a department, and lead an organization. Rounding out the text is an overview of continuing professional development and career development to ensure that librarians are attentive to continual growth and personal achievements.

This book serves as an introductory text to academic librarianship and a refresher for experienced librarians as well as a reference for all academic librarians who need to investigate specific issues. No one book could contain all that academic librarians need, so thankfully there are extensive curated reference lists that provide additional materials for consideration. Academic libraries have an important mission in educating and in serving higher education, thereby contributing to the advancement of education, economics, and culture in our society, but to do so, leaders must struggle with competing priorities, inadequate budgets, high expectations, and limited staffing. These circumstances call on academic library leaders to possess sophisticated political skills, financial competency, advanced personnel management abilities, and leadership talents. What follows will assist you on your journey in developing your librarianship to effectively contribute to the success of our academic libraries.

Maggie Farrell

Dean of Libraries, University of Nevada, Las Vegas

maggie.farrell@unlv.edu

Maggie is the author/editor of the quarterly column

"Leadership Reflections" in the *Journal of Library Administration.*

REFERENCE

Horrigan, John B. 2016, September. "Libraries 2016." Pew Research Center. www.pewinternet.org/2016/09/09/2016/Libraries-2016/.

ACKNOWLEDGMENTS

Our editorial advisory board deserves special recognition, and we give our profound thanks for all their reading, review, and comments:

Jim DelRosso
Digital Projects Coordinator, Catherwood Library
Cornell University
Ithaca, New York

Catherine Lavallée-Welch
Director, Murphy Library
University of Wisconsin–La Crosse

Leslie J. Reynolds
Interim Dean of University Libraries
University of Colorado Boulder

In seeking to make the text most relevant for those in the current job market, we particularly appreciate the comments and suggestions from two recent graduates:

Brittany Netherton
Knowledge and Learning Services Librarian
Darien Library
Darien, Connecticut

Fantasia Thorne-Ortiz
Assistant Professor and Librarian
Onondaga Community College
Syracuse, New York

We are grateful that Dr. Camila A. Alire, coauthor of the first edition, provided feedback on this edition. We also wish to thank Dr. Donna Weistrop and Dr. David Schaffer for their comments on the first two chapters.

CHAPTER 1

Context

The days in which the phrase *digital higher education* is meaningfully distinguishable from simply *higher education* are numbered. . . . That said, we have a legacy of infrastructure, particularly for broad-access institutions, built before the digital model existed.

—Anya Kamenetz (2015)

Yet while waves of change will come our way, one thing is certain and sure. The future of the academic library will be dependent on the future of learning. As the premier supporting service to learning, the library must chart its future in alignment with the direction of learning.

—Susan C. Curzon (2010, personal communication)

U.S. higher education institutions and their libraries have changed in many ways since the first edition of this book appeared, yet in other ways they remain as they were, as the Kamenetz quotation suggests. "The worldwide respect accorded to American higher education should be a source of satisfaction to many people, not least to those who work in the academy. Ironically, however, this newfound prominence has brought many problems in its wake. No longer are colleges and universities left to function as they please" (Bok, 2013, p. 2). The change Bok refers to arises from the fact that many stakeholders in higher education are demanding more accountability and transparency in how institutions operate as costs have escalated. People question the value for money spent. There are more demands by the public for accountability and transparency. There is a tendency to look at job placement numbers as well as how long a graduate must seek employment when thinking about the usefulness of a degree. We look at these and other factors throughout this text.

U.S. postsecondary education is a vibrant mix of institutions that is rather unusual from a global perspective. There are public (UCLA is one such) and private institutions (Harvard is the leading and oldest example) as well as for-profit organizations (University of Phoenix is one of the largest); some are gender-based (such as Wesleyan College), some are culturally oriented (such as Diné College, a Navajo college), some are faith-based (Biola University is an example), while others are vocational in character (Lincoln Technological Institute). The mix also employs a variety of pedagogical approaches to teaching, curriculums, completion requirements, and other operational matters. Equally varied are the degrees, certificates, and "badges" (more about badges later in the chapter) offered to an individual completing these institutions' programs.

Another distinctive trait of U.S. postsecondary education, compared to that of other countries, is the percentage of the population enrolled in the programs. The spring 2016 total enrollment was 18.3 million students, down slightly from 2015 (https://nscnews.org/

241000-fewer-college-students-over-age-24-enrolled-under-age-24-enrollments-remain
-steady/). That figure is about 5.5 percent of the total U.S. population at that time. The vast
majority of students enroll in an institution that is, at least partially, funded by a state or
local government (two- and four-year degree-granting bodies). Fewer than 7 percent enroll
in a for-profit program. For current enrollment data, visit https://nscresearchcenter.org/.

Almost all institutions share at least one commonality—the need to provide students
with resources to complete their assignments. More often than not that support is, in part,
in the form of library services. Libraries have been a part of U.S. higher education since
the first "college" was established in Cambridge, Massachusetts, in 1636. They have been,
and remain, a significant component in the process of providing education and training of
students, as we will demonstrate throughout this book.

HIGHER EDUCATION VARIATIONS

What constitutes U.S. academia? There is no short answer to this question. The mix of institutions is challenging when it comes to trying to generalize about U.S. higher education. The
fact of the matter is that organizational researchers have been trying to bring a structure to
the field for many years. Institutions are embedded in various political arrangements and
governance structures of remarkable diversity. Some are multicampus operations, in some
cases with each campus functioning more or less as an autonomous institution with its own
curriculum and admission standards. Others operate as a single entity, even if geographically dispersed. Some are single-purpose institutions—law schools, for example—while others
offer a wide range of subjects and degrees.

In light of the great diversity within U.S. postsecondary education, it is not surprising
that academic libraries are equally diverse. A survey conducted by the U.S. Department of
Education's National Center for Education Statistics (Institute of Education Sciences [IES],
2016) identified 3,700 entities meeting the following definition:

> An academic library is the library associated with a degree-granting institution of high-
> er education. Academic libraries are identified by the post-secondary institution of
> which they are a part and provide all of the following:
>
> 1. an organized collection of printed or other materials or a combination thereof;
> 2. staff trained to provide and interpret such materials as required to meet the
>   informational, cultural, recreational, or educational needs of clientele;
> 3. an established schedule in which services of the staff are available to clientele;
>   and
> 4. the physical facilities necessary to support such a collection, staff, and
>   schedule.

The IES survey employed both its own "level" categories and the "Carnegie Classification"
for grouping institutions and their libraries. The Carnegie Classification is a widely used
method of grouping "like" institutions. ("Like" is in quotation marks because it is difficult to
identify two completely identical institutions; if nothing more, the enrollment demographics will differ.) Nevertheless, the classification is better than any other and is therefore
widely employed when attempting to bring some structure to the diversity of U.S. colleges
and universities.

Because the classification system is dynamic and subject to change as circumstances change, we based the following discussion on information available as of 2015 on the website of the Carnegie Foundation for the Advancement of Teaching (http://carnegieclassifica tions.iu.edu/). Today there are thirty-three categories of institutions making up six broad groupings with subdivisions:

Associate colleges (often referred to as community colleges by the public) are those institutions whose highest degree is the two-year associate degree or who grant less than 10 percent of their total degrees as four-year bachelor's degrees. The majority of associate institutions are publicly funded.

Baccalaureate colleges offer more than 10 percent of their degrees as bachelor's and grant fewer than fifty master's degrees per year. The majority of institutions in this category are privately funded.

Master's colleges and universities award at least fifty master's degrees per year and fewer than twenty doctorates in addition to offering bachelor's degree programs. This grouping is a mix of public and private institutions.

Doctorate-granting universities award twenty or more doctoral degrees per year, not counting "first professional" degrees such as law or medicine. The doctorates must be research based (PhDs). As with master's institutions, there is a mix of public and private universities in this category.

Special-focus institutions are primarily private and offer undergraduate and graduate degrees in a single field; sometimes the "field" can be rather broad such as art, design, or music. This category includes stand-alone medical and law schools (nonprofit or for-profit institutions). Having a single focus (e.g., an art school) does not always mean granting just one type of degree. There might be a dozen or more degrees, such as a bachelor's in painting, another in ceramics, and the like, as well as a master of fine arts degree.

Tribal colleges constitute the final group. Institutions in this group must be members of the American Indian Higher Education Consortium. These institutions have funding from tribal, private, and federal sources. They generally offer only bachelor's degrees, although some have vocational programs, and a few grant a master's degree in a limited number of subjects.

We have structured our academic libraries courses by adopting a modified Carnegie approach: research universities, comprehensive universities, colleges, and community colleges. Research universities and their libraries (members of the Association of Research Libraries [ARL]) are the giants of U.S. higher education. They are considered giants in terms of staffing, enrollments, degrees granted (both in number and variety of subjects), funding, and public prestige. These institutions have programs for undergraduate, graduate, and postgraduate work. They normally have a variety of professional graduate schools—education, law, library and information science, and medicine, for example—that offer professional degrees as well as higher degrees. Often they are the "flagship" in a state's public higher education system. Their alumni are numerous and influential in public affairs. As giants, these institutions also dominate the direction and issues in higher education as well as best practices, including librarianship.

Comprehensive universities are, in many instances, striving to achieve research university status. (One of this book's authors retired from a university that was striving "to become the Georgetown of the West.") Research status is, in part, a function of numbers (such as degrees and overall size), but it is more complex than pure numbers, as we will discuss in later chapters. The primary differences between the two categories (comprehensive universities and research universities) are the research emphasis and the presence or lack of postgraduate programs. Comprehensive universities also offer fewer professional degrees and generally have fewer prize-winning faculty members. (In some state higher education systems, such as those of California, New York, and Texas, there may be both types of universities.)

Colleges offer the greatest range in size and degree programs. Enrollments vary from a few hundred to several thousand; a few are still single-gender institutions. They are undergraduate focused, although some offer a few master's-level programs. In terms of sheer numbers, colleges are the most numerous. Many are or were religion based, as we will discuss in the next chapter. Funding is always a critical issue for smaller colleges, and every year one or two close due to lack of money. Perhaps as many colleges in the United States have been created and have disappeared since 1636 as there are existing colleges and universities today. Generally the vast majority of their funding comes from the current tuition and fees of enrolled students. A shortfall in expected enrollment may lead to serious cutbacks in the current year's operations. Long-term low enrollments also result in low graduation numbers, which in turn means there are fewer alumni to turn to when fiscal problems arise.

Community colleges (Carnegie class "associate" and in the past referred to as junior colleges) provide a variety of two-year programs. They offer two broad categories of programs: "transfer" (articulated programs) and vocational degrees. Most of the community colleges (CCs) offer a two-year program that represents the equivalent of the freshman- and sophomore-level work (lower division) at colleges and universities. To be effective as a transfer program (that is, allowing the student to receive academic "credit" for such courses at a four-year institution), such programs *must* engage in a high level of collaboration with at least local if not statewide four-year institutions—that is, making certain that English 101 at the community college is the equivalent of English 101 at the four-year institutions. In the best case, a student will receive an associate degree from a community college and be able to enroll in a four-year institution as a junior. Such a level of cooperation takes time and effort on both sides but truly benefits the students. In the past, such programs primarily benefited students whose high school academic record did not achieve the level necessary for direct admission to a four-year program. Today, with the very high cost of higher education, many students opt for the lower cost community college lower division programs to cover their first two years of higher education. Needless to say, this option requires careful review by the student and family to make certain their transfer goals are fully realized.

The community colleges' vocational programs may be, along with high school programs, the key to the future of local economies. CCs by their nature can be more agile in

👥 FROM THE AUTHORS

Evans often employed the Carnegie Classification information using "comparable" institutions and libraries along with ACRL standards to seek more support for his operations. Keep in mind that *comparable* is a relative term when it comes to U.S. higher education, and everyone involved understands that fact. Sometimes the technique worked and sometimes it didn't. However, it worked often enough to keep the tactic in the budgetary tool kit.

responding to changing economic conditions, which allows them to adjust—add or drop—programs more quickly than can four-year institutions. (By law, a student who enters a four-year program has the right to complete that program, as outlined in the institution's bulletin for the year of entry. This requirement means that a two-year program can change more rapidly than one with a four-year commitment to a cohort of students.) The range of vocational programs is limited only by the current economy, projections of short-term needs (perhaps no more than two years ahead), and, perhaps, accreditation standards.

Opportunities for academic librarians are as diverse as the institutions that hire them. We firmly believe the future is bright, if challenging, for those who choose this career path.

THE FUTURE OF HIGHER EDUCATION AND ITS LIBRARIES

What follows is a rather long discussion of current higher education issues. Why devote space to such topics in a book about academic librarianship? It is our contention that you cannot truly understand academic librarianship without a sound understanding of higher education. So the first and most fundamental reason for the discussion is that when an organization faces challenges and issues, all its component parts will experience the associated pressures to a greater or lesser extent. The second reason is that these challenges and issues do have an impact on what the library can and cannot do in the way of service to campus.

Our earlier quotation from Derek Bok suggests that higher education institutions—and their libraries—face challenges. In truth, the academy has always faced challenges, public skepticism, and "crises" of one kind or another. Somehow, not always quickly, institutions found a solution and survived as a concept—certainly not every institution, but many.

What are some of today's most significant challenges? Some are as old as higher education itself, while others are quite new. One thing that ties all of them together, however, is money or the lack thereof. The following list contains what we think are some of the most pressing concerns for the present and the immediate future. Would the list have been different were it not for the Great Recession? Perhaps, perhaps not. Many of these issues have roots that go much farther back than 2008.

- Student debt—Cost of degrees
- Value of a degree
- Immediate employment versus critical thinking and problem solving
- Degrees versus badges
- Socioeconomic gap among members of student body
- Diversity and inclusion
- Retention and time to degree
- Funding challenges
- Doing more with less
- Amenities versus education

Student Debt

Long gone are the days of graduating with a four-year degree and being debt free. Yes, some lucky individuals manage to do so as a result of family wealth or scholarship awards. Rebecca Blank, chancellor of the University of Wisconsin-Madison, in an interview with a

University of Minnesota alumni magazine reporter, commented on her undergraduate degree days: "When I went to the University of Minnesota . . . it was not a problem for me to pay my way through college. It is almost impossible to do that now" (2015, p. 18). She was referring to being able to work and attend college and pay for the educational costs.

What is the debt load? In mid-2016, there were more than forty-three million graduates and enrolled students who owed well over $1.3 trillion. (Note that the forty-three million–plus U.S. debtors is larger than the population of two hundred countries, including Canada, Poland, and Australia.) By the time you read this, both the size of debt and the number of borrowers will be higher. The average student debt load was $30,000 in late 2016. In 2013 Thomas Mortenson wrote about working and college costs. His basic assumption was that employment opportunities for an undergraduate are limited to minimum wage positions. Using that assumption he calculated that a student in 2012 would have to work sixty-one hours per week for fifty-two weeks to cover the year's educational expenses. Mortenson's assumptions may be overly pessimistic; however, his primary point that it is almost impossible to work your way through college today is spot on.

One of the employment opportunities for undergraduates is on-campus jobs, especially through work-study programs. We will look at work-study employment in a later chapter because such positions are critical for most academic library operations. The point here is that work-study programs generally limit a student to twenty hours per week. Also hourly salaries are not far above the minimum wage.

For many debtors no longer in school, making the minimum monthly loan payment(s) can be a major challenge. This is especially true for those who have debt but dropped out before completing a degree. Default is a significant concern for the debtors, creditors, and society at large. The debtors in default find themselves in difficulty on several fronts. One issue is that some employers do credit checks of prospective hires. A person in default is often dropped from consideration because of a negative report. The debt size is increasing while entry-level salaries are barely increasing, making repayment more difficult. The interest rates on a loan can increase, at least for private-party loans, further magnifying repayment concerns. Defaulters in some states may lose their professional license that they worked so hard to earn. In at least one state, they can even lose their driver's license. Bankruptcy and even death are not always means of ending a student loan obligation, at least for nongovernment loans. One reason for this result is that often a family member was a cosigner on the loan agreement.

Who benefits from these loans? Certainly private lenders do well. What is often overlooked is that the federal government also does very well, even taking the default rate into consideration. In 2013, the Congressional Budget Office projected that the government would have a $50 billion return on student loans that year. That total was greater than the 2012 profits of ExxonMobil, the country's most profitable company (www.usatoday.com/story/news/2013/06/16/us-government-projected-to-make-record-50b-in-student-loan-profit/2427443/).

A final hopeful note about student debt: there is little doubt that debt load impacts an individual's spending patterns. Given the overall dollar amount due lenders, it is not surprising that there are impacts on the economy, such as fewer cars sold, fewer homes purchased, and so on. The hopeful news is that some companies are helping their employees with student loan repayment by offering matching funds. For example, in late summer 2016, Aetna announced a plan that could help employees with student loans by providing up to $10,000 in matching grants ($2,000 per year for up to five years; Cao, 2016). The employee must have graduated from an accredited institution within the past three years. The goal for companies offering such assistance is to retain younger employees who might be tempted by a higher salary elsewhere.

Worth of a Degree

Given the preceding, it is not too surprising to find many questioning the return on investment (ROI) of the monies spent. Questioning the value of higher education is not new; it seems highly probable that some people have always had doubts about the need for individuals to spend time "studying." In the early days, when the students were males only, the loss of labor was the main concern. What is different today is the cost of earning a degree and just what benefit the awardee gains.

There is a concern that organizations require a college degree for no valid reason. (We wonder if there may be some logic to the trend, given widespread doubts about the quality of secondary-school graduates.) A reflection of this concern appeared in an *Arizona Republic* editorial page essay in late 2015 by Robert Robb. He wrote, "Basically by default, a college degree became a necessary credential for a white-collar professional job. There is no logical reason for that" (p. 20A). On the other hand, another newspaper article from 2016 (Davidson) carried the headline, "No College? No Problem at More and More Jobs." Davidson, commenting about a tightening job market, quoted a director of the Center for Economic and Policy Research (Washington, D.C.) as stating that the current environment means "there is less of an advantage for people with a college degree" (p. 4B).

Generally, people believe, and data support that belief, that a person does earn more over a lifetime if she has a college degree. A pair of somewhat old surveys conducted by the Pew Research Center (2011) explored a number of issues related to higher education. One survey included more than two thousand people who were interviewed about the issues. A second online survey included 1,055 college and university presidents (public, private, and for-profit institutions). Some of the topics covered were the cost and value of a degree, the monetary payoff, why not college? and the mission of higher education. The public's view on value for the money was 57 percent negative, while 87 percent of those with a degree said it had been worth the investment. Not surprisingly, the presidents had a different view regarding the value, with 59 percent positive. What is surprising is that the presidents' percentage is so low. Clearly, the leaders of colleges and universities realize there is a significant cost problem that they must address.

As we stated earlier, the real question is the ROI of the degree. As the Pew Research Center reported in 2014, "On virtually every measure of economic well-being and career attainment—from personal earnings to job satisfaction to the share of employed full-time—young college graduates are outperforming their peers with less education" (p. 1). All the data regarding the economic benefits of being a college degree holder rest on broad averages. Something to keep in mind is that not all degrees are created equal. The benefit depends very much on the field. That fact relates to the next pressing issue—the purpose of the degree.

Immediacy versus Long-Term

The cost of getting a degree has obviously made employment opportunities upon graduating a primary concern for parents and students alike. (This concern also has been something of an issue in library education in the past—was the education for day one on the job or for a career?) Degrees in the "soft disciplines" such as literature, philosophy, and history (see chapter 3 for details about hard and soft disciplines) are thought to be poor choices when it comes to seeking employment.

In a very broad sense, higher education has always been about work (see chapter 2 for a detailed discussion of the changing purposes for postsecondary education). Social sciences and humanities degrees are not too often focused on a type of employment upon graduation, at least at the baccalaureate level. After 2008's economic downturn, individuals harboring doubts about higher education, especially legislators seeking every opportunity to reduce spending, looked at such degrees in a highly negative manner. They viewed the programs as very expensive to operate when the degree lacked immediate employment prospects. John Coleman, dean of the College of Liberal Arts at the University of Minnesota, wrote, "If we are not optimistic and enthusiastic for the liberal arts, we can't expect others to be . . . . The long-standing American tradition of a liberal arts education is more relevant than ever before. . . . We will be on the offense—and not the defense—when talking about the College and the importance of the liberal arts" (2015, p. 1).

There is a pressure on institutions to emphasize, at a minimum, employability. You can see this trend in the need to provide graduation rates, placement rates, and placement time frames. For-profit institutions have faced serious questions from the federal government regarding their outcomes in these areas. The U.S. Department of Education has made moves against some institutions, such as cutting off student loan funds, because of alleged misrepresentation of, if not fraudulent, job opportunities, placement rates, and the like. The closure of ITT Technical Institute campuses in 2016 is one such example.

The trend to emphasize employability was reflected in a statement by Secretary of Education John B. King (Kerr, 2016): "A college degree remains one of the best investments anyone can make in his or her future. But that's only true if it's a meaningful degree that helps you land a better job, not if it's a worthless piece of paper that's an artifact of deception rather than proof of accomplishment" (p. 10A). Certainly King's focus was on deception regarding employability; however, he implies that the purpose of a degree is to get a job. His comments also suggest that there is some immediacy for finding a job.

The Association of American Colleges and Universities (Humphreys and Kelly, 2014) undertook a survey of employers regarding graduates' employability and what those individuals actually learned. One finding was that 93 percent of the respondents indicated that critical thinking, the ability to communicate effectively, and the ability to resolve complex problems were of greater importance than a person's college major. Although we know many majors can provide those three abilities, we believe that the liberal arts are the most focused on such skills.

In our view, as well as that of others in higher education, there is a degree of shortsightedness in putting so much emphasis on immediate placement in the workforce. Problem solving, critical thinking, logical reasoning, and an understanding of the world are traits that are essential for maintaining a long-term career and being an informed citizen. All those traits arise in part from the liberal arts.

Degrees versus Badges

Concern is growing among employers about exactly what a college degree certifies—in particular, a bachelor's degree in a nonprofessional discipline such as history or sociology.

For years there have been concerns about the effectiveness of elementary and secondary schools in teaching the three Rs (reading, "'riting," and "'rithmatic"). Those concerns include the qualifications of people who go on to college. (Perhaps higher education teachers have had some such misgivings since the earliest days of the academy. It is just human nature to worry about the abilities of the next generation.)

What is different now is that employers are expressing serious qualms. Two other factors have added further reservations about what a college degree actually certifies. First, in the past, a "gentleman's C" was acceptable to many people, even a student. "Grade inflation" is now very much an issue within and without the academy. The second factor, and related to grades, is a fairly recent institutional concern with "retention"—that is, engaging in efforts to keep all enrollees in place (more advising, tutoring, counseling, and the like). Gone are the days when professors would warn, "Some of you will not pass this course." Institutions spend time and effort trying to determine why a student dropped out or left—money, academic ability, campus atmosphere, and so on. Certainly, colleges and universities have offered tutoring and remedial classes for the underprepared for a long time; however, there are some who believe the underprepared are now receiving degrees.

Badges have long been a method of "certifying" a person's skill in this or that area. Derek Bok, who served as president of Harvard University for almost twenty-five years, has in his various publications (such as *Our Underachieving Colleges: A Candid Look at How Much Students Learn and Why They Should Be Learning More* [Princeton University Press, 2009], and *Higher Education in America* [Princeton University Press, 2013]) made the point that college transcripts are a poor tool for assessing what a student has learned. As a result of doubts about transcripts, some universities have begun to issue badges.

Arne Duncan, then secretary of the U.S. Department of Education, noted in a speech in late 2011, "Badges can help speed the shift from credentials that simply measure seat time, to ones that more accurately measure competency" (www.ed.gov/news/speeches/digital-badges-learning). How widespread the notion may become is still unclear. However, it is one more reflection of the challenges facing today's academy. One university that has implemented the idea is Purdue, which suggests, "Digital badges, icons that represent academic achievements or skills smaller than a college degree, are an increasingly popular way for universities to acknowledge the breadth of student learning" (www.purdue.edu/newsroom/releases/2012/Q3/digital-badges-show-students-skills-along-with-degree.html). Two other well-known universities that employ the badge concept are New York University and the University of California–Davis. By the time you read this book, there may be a host of other institutions doing so.

Socioeconomic Gap among Students and Graduates

A cherished role of higher education is that of enhancing upward social mobility and economic well-being. As the cost of a degree escalates, there is a decline in the mobility outcome—not because the degree does not help, but because the cost is out of reach for more and more people. In 2006 Robert Haveman and Timothy Smeeding noted, "Indeed, since the 1970s students from lower-income families have increasingly become clustered in two-year postsecondary institutions which often turn out to be the end of their formal education" (p. 126). Nine years later, Goldie Blumenstyk (2015) reinforced the point by stating, "Meanwhile, for all the billions of dollars government does still put toward institution and student aid, higher education is failing as a force for social mobility" (p. 9). She went on to say, "While access to college is broader than ever, higher education is more stratified by income and race than it has been in two generations" (p. 9).

This is more than a higher education issue. It is a societal issue that will have very long-term consequences if not addressed effectively very soon.

Funding Challenges, Doing More with Less, and Amenities

Our last three concerns are interlinked. As we noted earlier, some of the pressing issues for higher education are far from new—there was and is never enough money to do all the desirable things an institution could do. Doing more with less is a somewhat newer concept, but it is not a product of the twenty-first-century environment. The amenities concerns are relatively recent. Certainly all three concerns have become more pressing as a result of the Great Recession. There are a variety of reasons for the ever-rising cost of a degree. No one factor is *the* reason; however, some of the factors are not directly related to instruction.

Public institutions have seen a drop in the percentage of funding coming from the government. Many inside and outside higher education blame the loss of government funding for the high cost of today's degrees. The problem of escalating degree costs predates the economic downturn. The institution certainly must make up the difference when there are shortfalls. Sometimes the shortfall results from not receiving the allocation requested, which is a very different issue than having a reduction from last year's allocation. Whatever the facts may be, there have been regular tuition increases and more and higher fees that add to students' costs and that exceed the economy's inflation rate.

In a 2015 *New York Times* Op-Ed essay, Paul Campos noted that, in 2009, state higher education appropriations were at a record high of $86.6 billion, adjusted for inflation. There was a drop during the recession; however, by 2014 the appropriations were at $81 billion, making for an overall decline of under 7 percent. Tuition increases averaged 5 percent. That lower rate of tuition increase may appear to be good news, but it is not.

The problem is that the cost of a degree goes far beyond tuition. There are "fees," some that all students pay and some that only some have to pay. For most institutions, tuition

---

▥ CHECK THIS OUT

The following resources more fully explore the topics discussed in this section; they supplement the articles and books we cited in the text. Of those items, we strongly recommend the Bok and Ginsberg titles. Another interesting title is *Remaking College: The Changing Ecology of Higher Education,* edited by Michael W. Kirst and Mitchell L. Stevens (Stanford, CA: Stanford University Press, 2015).

Some very good articles and reports are John R. Thelin's "Success and Excess: The Contours and Character of American Higher Education since 1960" (Society 50, no. 2 [2013]: 106–114); the Pew Charitable Trusts' Issue Brief *Federal and State Funding of Higher Education: A Changing Landscape* (June 11, 2015; www.pewtrusts.org/en/research-and -analysis/issue-briefs/2015/06/federal-and-state-funding-of-higher-education); and Peter C. Herman's "Administrative Bloat Comes to the CSU System" (*Times of San Diego,* October 31, 2014; http://timesofsandiego.com/opinion/2014/10/31/administrative-bloat-comes-csu -system/).

increases are debated and approved by the governing board. That is not the case for fees at many institutions (parking, athletic, health service, etc., etc.). Thus, institutions have found it easier to keep the tuition increase percentage low while being able to substantially increase fees as well as add new fees from time to time. For many students, room and board costs are almost as high as tuition; again, those costs may not require governing board approval. Assuming fees and residence costs increased by only 1 percent per year, a rather naive assumption, the increases at least match the losses in state funding.

From the students' perspective, there are other unavoidable costs, not the least of which is required course material. For many, there are the transportation costs and at least some campus food costs—if nothing more than cups of coffee. These costs also escalated, and the institution will get some additional income from such campus expenditures with the concessionaires (food service and bookstores are the most common concessionaires). In addition to dollar increases, many institutions actively seek to increase enrollment. Some institutions calculate a dollar value for each additional student that is larger than the basic tuition and fees level based on income from "auxiliary" services.

If the decline in government appropriations is only a small part of the cost problem, are the salaries of full-time tenured faculty the issue? Are they to blame? Or, for that matter, are staff salary increases the major issue? Increases in the number of faculty and nonadministrative staff as well as salary increases are modest and in line with the Consumer Price Index. The *New York Times* piece we cited earlier noted the following: "Today half of the postsecondary faculty members are lower-paid part-time employees, meaning the average salaries of the people who do the teaching in American higher education are actually quite a bit lower than they were in the 1970s" (Campos, 2015, p. SR4).

Benjamin Ginsberg (2011) discussed administrative "bloat" (administrators not directly involved in teaching) and noted that between 1975 and 2005 those positions had risen

👥 FROM THE AUTHORS

As practitioners as well as faculty members, we have dealt with the issue of work-study hours and library operation for many years. We explore this topic in some depth in chapter 4.

Evans has had experiences with most of the issues discussed in this section during his career. For example, at one institution, the university president informed him that although a new library was needed, the board had decided that a first-class student fitness center was essential for recruitment and retention. Further, the monies for the facility would be bond funds, whereas the library project would require a long fund-raising campaign. The same rationale was used when new residence halls took precedence over the library project and the much-needed new science building. Faculty and staff often referred to the new halls as the Club Med dorms. They were so nice that a new president chose to occupy one of the apartments rather than the "official" residence (certainly the view was much better).

Another example involved administrative bloat. During almost twenty years at one university, Evans succeeded in getting three additional FTEs for the library. Student enrollment more than doubled during that time in terms of head count. At the same time, the number of administrators at or above the dean level rose from 47 to 147.

Institutional issues do impact the library!

by 240 percent. Further, spending on instruction rose 22 percent during that time while administrative spending increased by 36 percent. In many institutions, barely 50 percent of all spending goes toward instruction. (That statistic is worrisome because library budgets are normally categorized as instructional.) The bloat is a recognized issue, but the literature suggests that almost nothing is being done to address the problem that is part of what drives up the cost of a degree.

The final factor is campus facilities, a necessary part of the brick-and-mortar campus. There has been a steady increase in campus construction over the past thirty years. In some cases, it is hard to find a year in which a campus does not have a major construction project under way. Best guesses are that 50 percent of such projects are academic in character. If you add in residence halls, the total is about 75 percent. However, as Goldie Blumenstyk (2015) stated, "That said, many of the fitness centers, student centers, and residence halls that account for the rest of the building boom seem pretty lavish" (p. 94). Many of these facilities use bond issue funds to cover the cost of construction. Bond issues can raise money, but they also entail a debt service obligation. Bond fund debt becomes part of the students' costs. Although the students may enjoy such amenities (usually constructed to attract more students and retain the current enrollees), if they had the option to reduce their educational costs by foregoing the "luxury," what would they do?

WHAT MAKES AN ACADEMIC LIBRARY ACADEMIC?

A book many managers find useful is *The Art of War* by Sun-Tzu (also called Sunzi). We certainly do not subscribe to the notion that the book can be a basic management guide; however, it does contain useful ideas. One of the more useful of these concepts appears in the first chapter: "Warfare is a great matter to a nation . . . it is the way of survival and of destruction and must be examined" (Sun-Tzu, n.d.). If you substitute *environment* for *warfare* and *organization* for *nation*, you have a key concept of our book—a library's operating environment is the fundamental factor in what it does and how it goes about doing the work. The answer to this section's heading is this: the organization of which the library is a part makes the library what it is.

That answer applies to almost all libraries—there are very few stand-alone libraries. Libraries are normally part of some larger organization, be it a government, a business, a school district, an academic institution. All libraries perform, in some manner, the same fundamental functions: selection, acquisition, organization, storage and preservation, and service and access. What differentiates the types is the "parent" organization's mission and goals. These factors are the key environment within which the library's functions are developed and put into operation. Without a sound understanding of this environment, one cannot consistently create and maintain appropriate information services for the parent group. Although it is always beneficial to understand the nature of the parent organizational environment and its culture regardless of library type, such an understanding is essential in order to have a successful academic library career.

Libraries exist in a tripartite environment. First, the library has an internal environment over which it has, or should have, reasonably good control and influence. Second, there is the environment within the parent organization, over which the librarians may have some, if small, influence. Finally, there is the environment beyond the parent institution over which the library has no control. All three environments require monitoring and responding to, if the library is to be successful. A good article that explores the reason for examining the environment of a nonprofit organization is by Andrews, Boyne, and Walker (2006).

Another element in becoming a successful librarian is learning the organizational culture. Every organization has a culture that its members learn, or should learn, in order to be effective. That culture plays a very significant role in how the organization operates. Typically staff members are unaware of its influence on their behavior and actions except when someone acts in a contrary manner. Essentially, "learning" the culture is an informal process whereby a newcomer picks up bits and pieces through observation. Both the library and its parent institution have a culture, and it is necessary to understand both. Often these cultures have significant differences, so being aware of which culture you are currently operating in is key to creating successful interactions with people and other units. Just what is "organizational culture"? As Kell and Carrott (2005) noted, "Corporate culture, like personal character, is an amorphous quality that exerts a powerful influence" (p. 22). They go on to note both the positive and negative aspects of organizational culture. Although we acknowledge that the concept is rather amorphous, some elements are generally agreed on. One such element is that the culture is shared (consciously or not) by members of the organization. They share a set of values, assumptions, and expectations regarding what the organization is "about," how things should be done, what is important and acceptable. People act on these views even though the culture is rarely articulated, much less recorded. One learns it as we learn social culture, through observation and the mistakes we make. Although it is an internal "environment," it can and does evolve as a result of changes in the external environment. Individuals who ignore this internal environment do so at their peril—understanding the culture can make all the difference when it comes time for the organization to make changes due to external factors.

ACADEMIC LIBRARY CHALLENGES

First and foremost, libraries are affected by the pressures on their parent organizations. There is a "trickle down" for all the institution's component parts. Those impacts are examined in some detail in the rest of this book's chapters. Here we look at the challenges that are library focused and long term. We begin by looking at some challenges that a number of academic library directors identified in the final chapter of the first edition of *Academic Librarianship*.

IIII **CHECK THIS OUT**

Every year, the Research Planning and Review Committee of the Association of College and Research Libraries (ACRL) assembles either a "Top Trends in Academic Libraries" report or an "Environmental Scan" of higher education to consider how academic libraries can respond to current trends in academia. A recent report included implications related to higher education costs, enrollment trends, information literacy issues, new forms of educational resources, open data, changes in scholarly communication, digital preservation, research metrics, collection assessment, and the role of libraries in social justice. These reports are well worth reviewing annually (see www.ala.org/acrl/issues/whitepapers).

Twenty-one library directors provided their assessment of the most important issues facing academic libraries at the end of the first decade of the twenty-first century. Table 1.1 is a summary of those comments. Almost all the topics remain as ongoing concerns. We explore these and other issues in the rest of the book.

We agree with David Lewis's (2007) assumptions about twenty-first-century academic libraries' major challenges and their character:

- Libraries are a means, not an end.
- Disruptive technologies can and will disrupt libraries.
- A small change here and there will not result in real change.
- There is time to make effective changes, if we do not wait too long.
  (pp. 419–420)

We think a fifth assumption is necessary to complete the picture: if libraries do not change, they will join the dinosaurs. Our opening quotation from Susan Curzon is a sound summary of why being flexible and agile in your approach to change is so important.

Everyone is in agreement that academic institutions, libraries, and librarians have changed, dramatically so when looking back over just the past twenty years. Even a cursory look at the history of the academy makes it clear that the institution and its various components are adaptable to changing circumstances and societal needs. Admittedly, the pace of change has often been rather slow, but change proceeds nonetheless.

Successful organizational transformations are seldom quick or painless. Thinking back to discussions in basic management courses about change and the change process—at its most basic level the process of unfreezing, change, freezing (Lewin, 1951)—it is clear that time is a key factor in moving from one organizational state to another. Another factor is that some organizations change more quickly than others. The agile ones tend to be the most successful in the long term.

Toni Carbo (2008) wrote about the future of academic libraries, the web, and change, exploring some of the negative views that some librarians and students hold about profit-oriented competitors such as Google. In particular, she expressed concern about such attitudes as for-profit information services being "money-grubbing," about a cavalier dismissal of "techies" in such organizations, and about oversimplifying complex ethical and policy issues. One of her central points was that thinking of information service competitors (the for-profits) as potential partners and seeking such partnerships will be more productive

---

▌▌ CHECK THIS OUT

A helpful approach to planning and managing in an academic library is to routinely review case studies from other institutions. We would be remiss if we did not mention a new collection of case studies—*Academic Library Management: Case Studies* (Dearie, Meth, and Westbrooks, 2017). This collection is unique because its authors were members of the UCLA Senior Fellows Class of 2014 (the UCLA program is one of the oldest immersive residency programs to prepare future academic library leaders).

The volume includes case studies on a variety of topics with a specific focus on the academic library environment: shared governance, strategic planning, funding, collection management, liaison services, succession planning, and more.

TOPIC DISCUSSED	Number of Essay Contributors Who Discussed the Topic
Radical change necessary	19
Effective adaptation of technology	18
Increase role in digitization	17
Library as place	13
Addressing financial challenges	13
Creating a positive user experience	13
Developing new skills for librarians and staff	13
Enhance/build better cross-institutional collaboration	12
More and better library advocacy	12
Build better connections with students	12
Strengthen mission focus	11
Essential to balance digital and print resources	10
Address the necessary and growing diversity of staff and student body	9
Improve students' research skills	9
Address the storage of legacy print collections	9
Engage in better collaboration with faculty	8
Take on greater campus leadership roles	8
Stay current with learning trends	8
Engage in deeper research into user needs	7
Become a campus agency of change	5
Disseminate campus research	4
Improve library distance education interface	4
Engage in efforts to truly become campus core	4
Vastly improve our business models	4
Be willing to change our organizational structure quickly	3
Be more supportive of faculty research	3
Help address need to make degrees more affordable	2
Increase awareness of librarians as teachers	2
Recognize and support the concept of the social side of libraries	2
Effectively address the changing relationship with information producers	2
Recognize the important role that community colleges play in higher education	2
Recognize the role of academic health science libraries	2
Recognize the value of archives	2

TABLE 1.1 Topics discussed by essay contributors in the first edition of *Academic Librarianship*

for everyone concerned. She mentioned the Open Content Alliance (https://archive.org/details/opencontentalliance) as an example of a collaborative project. Two ventures she did not mention are the Scholarly Publishing and Academic Resources Coalition (SPARC) and the Coalition for Networked Information (CNI). Her concluding comment was, "Sharing experiences, knowledge, and ideas and building a 'Bigger Us' can only help all of us prepare our future colleagues for tomorrow's academic libraries" (p. 100).

ACRL's Research and Scholarship Committee conducted a study of assumptions about the future of academic libraries and their staff (Mullins, Allen, and Hufford, 2007). The authors pointed out that their purpose was not to predict but to formulate statements intended to "encourage ACRL librarians to embrace changes and opportunities that are *already occurring* and to build into their libraries a culture that will continue to embrace change and opportunities that the future will bring" (p. 240). The ten assumptions, in a summary form, were the following:

- Digitization of print materials will accelerate, as will efforts to preserve digital archives and collections; likewise, there will be ever better methods of retrieval.
- Required staffing skills will adjust to changing demands of the service population (faculty, students, and others).
- End users will demand ever greater delivery speed and access.
- Intellectual property will be an ever more important issue for academic institutions and their libraries.
- Technological demands will require ever greater funding, likely at the expense of some services and collections.
- Colleges and universities will more and more approach their operations using "business" models.
- End users, especially students, will view themselves as customers of the institution and its library as tuition and fees increase. As a result, they will

---

▌▌▌▌ CHECK THIS OUT

A review of academic trends can be found in the ACRL Research Planning and Review Committee's "2016 Top Trends in Academic Libraries: A Review of the Trends and Issues Affecting Academic Libraries in Higher Education" (*College and Research Libraries News* 77, no. 6: 274–281).

One of the trends mentioned in the article is research data management. Ricky Erway, Laurence Horton, Amy Nurnberger, Reid Otsuji, and Amy Rushing prepared a study for the OCLC Research program that explores the topic is some detail—"Building Blocks: Laying the Foundation for a Research Data Management Program" (2016; www.oclc.org/research/publications/2016/oclcresearch-data-management-building-blocks-2016.html).

Another OCLC Research report (2015) explores how libraries can be more effective in providing realistic assistance to users based on what users actually do: "Shaping the Library to the Life of the User: Adapting, Empowering, Partnering, Engaging" (www.oclc.org/research/publications/2015/oclcresearch-shaping-library-to-life-of-user-2015.html).

expect and demand service of the highest level of quality.
- Virtual course work and degrees will represent a major component of academia's programs, if not the dominant aspect.
- Publicly funded research will be increasingly available to users at no cost.
- Privacy issues will be increasingly important and a challenge to handle.

Those assumptions remain valid today.

WHY BOTHER STUDYING THE SUBJECT IF EVERYTHING WILL CHANGE?

It may seem counterintuitive to spend time studying a subject when it is a "moving target" of sorts and always evolving. The first and foremost answer to the question is that everything changes, and one needs to understand what is good and what is not so good when deciding what to change. We firmly believe that it is by attending to the background (the past and present) that individuals and society are most likely to achieve new insights into what adjustments are necessary and desirable.

Another reason to study the subject is that you will be more effective in working with others in higher education when you have a broad understanding of its components. For example, it is easier to develop good working relationships with faculty when you understand most of the pressures under which they operate. Understanding the components of the institution and its fiscal requirements can help make your efforts to gain the financial support necessary for your service more successful. A library exists to provide services to its community of users, and knowing the "whats" and "hows" of that community allows you to identify and to implement the most useful and desired services. This knowledge will also assist you in establishing efficient policies and procedures from the library's and the users' perspective—something that is very important when funding is tight, as it almost always is.

REFERENCES

Andrews, Rhys, George Boyne, and Richard Walker. 2006. Strategy content and organizational performance. *Public Administration Review* 66, no. 1: 52–64.

Blank, Rebecca. 2015. Interview in "What's the future of higher education?" *Minnesota* 115, no. 1: 14–21.

Blumenstyk, Goldie. 2015. *American higher education in crisis? What everyone needs to know.* Oxford: Oxford University Press.

Bok, Derek. 2013. *Higher education in America.* Princeton, NJ: Princeton University Press.

Campos, Paul F. 2015. "The real reason college tuition costs so much." *New York Times,* April 4, SR4.

Cao, Athena. 2016. "Aetna to give its employees a break on student loans." *USA Today-Arizona Republic,* August 11, 5B.

Carbo, Toni. 2008. Them and us, or a bigger and better us? *Journal of Academic Librarianship* 34, no. 2: 99–100.

Coleman, John. 2015. *The state of the college.* Minneapolis: University of Minnesota, College of Liberal Arts.

Davidson, Paul. 2016. "No college? No problem at more and more jobs." *USA Today-Arizona Republic,* August 8, 4B.

Dearie, Tammy N., Michael Meth, and Elaine L. Westbrooks. 2017. *Academic library management: Case studies.* Chicago: ALA Neal-Schuman.

Ginsberg, Benjamin. 2011. *The fall of faculty: The rise of the all-administrative university and why that matters.* Oxford and New York: Oxford University Press.

Haveman, Robert, and Timothy Smeeding. 2006. The role of higher education in social mobility. *Future of Children* 16, no. 2: 125–150.

Humphreys, Debra, and Patrick Kelly. 2014. *How liberal arts and sciences majors fare in employment: A report on earnings, and long-term career paths.* Washington, DC: Association of American Colleges and Universities.

Institute of Education Sciences (IES). 2016. "Library statistics program: Academic libraries." https://nces.ed.gov/surveys/libraries/academic.asp.

Kamenetz, Anya. 2015. "DIY U: Higher education goes hybrid." In *Remaking college: The changing ecology of higher education,* edited by Michael W. Kirst and Mitchell L. Stevens. Stanford, CA: Stanford University Press.

Kell, Thomas, and Gregory Carrott. 2005. Culture matters most. *Harvard Business Review* 83, no. 5: 22.

Kerr, Jennifer. 2016. "Rule aims to prevent deception by colleges." *Arizona Republic,* June 14, 10A.

Lewin, Kurt. 1951. *Field theory in social sciences.* New York: Harper and Row.

Lewis, David. 2007. A strategy for academic libraries in the first quarter of the 21st century. *College and Research Libraries* 68, no. 5: 418–434.

Mortenson, Thomas G. 2013. "Income stratification of undergraduate enrollments by level and sector, 1998–2011." *Postsecondary Education Opportunity* (blog).

Mullins, James L., Frank R. Allen, and Jon R. Hufford. 2007. Top ten assumptions for the future of academic libraries and librarians. *College and Research Library News* 68, no. 4: 240–246.

Pew Research Center. 2011. *Is college worth it? College presidents, public assess value, quality, and mission of higher education.* Washington, DC: Pew Social and Demographic Trends. www.pewsocialtrends.org/2011/05/15/is-college-worth-it/.

Pew Research Center. 2014. *The rising cost of not going to college.* Washington, DC: Pew Social and Demographic Trends. www.pewsocialtrends.org/2014/02/11/the-rising-cost-of-not-going-to-college/.

Robb, Robert. 2015. "Are colleges now a societal detriment?" *Arizona Republic,* November 20, 20A.

Sun-Tzu. n.d. *The art of war.* Available at www.gutenberg.org/etext/132.

CHAPTER 2

Higher Education's Historic Legacy

When writers have tried to divine the future and how it will affect the library's role in society, a number of strong forces have come together. Their notions of the future have been shaped by how they understand the past.

—Hal B. Grossman, 2011

America's initial venture in the realm of higher learning gave no hint of future accomplishments. Nor could the handful of young men who arrived in Cambridge, Massachusetts, in 1638 to enter the nation's first college have had the faintest idea of what the future had in store for American universities.

—Derek Bok, 2013

The present is the living sum-total of the whole past.

—Thomas Carlyle, 1877

Higher education has a long history, and some of its institutions are among the oldest continuously operating organizations in the world. Twenty-one existing universities started prior to 1400. Harvard University is more than three hundred years old. That longevity suggests that societies have found higher education to be a valued institution that contributes to the overall social well-being. It also suggests that the institutions have changed along with their changing environments, albeit at a slow speed. Perhaps that speed reflects that, indeed, Thomas Carlyle's statement is a factor in understanding when and what to change as well as how fast to do so.

Today's higher education institutions in the United States, and in most of the rest of the world, owe more to the past than many people inside and outside higher education realize. Much of the structure, culture, basic purposes, and ceremonies have roots in the first days of university development in Europe. We know that you can operate an academic library without any thought to how we arrived at where we are in higher education; however, given the pervasive historic roots, we believe that some understanding of the past can be helpful and, on occasion, useful in planning for the future.

What, if any, lessons can the academy and its libraries learn from spending a few moments pondering the past? If nothing else, such consideration may provide a strong sense of hope for the future. That hope can arise from seeing how higher education has managed to adapt to a changing world, times of high social stress, variable economic conditions, and new technologies. Higher education has its roots in the arrival of a new millennium (AD 1000) when there was a general fear and great uncertainty that the world would survive the arrival date. Once 1000 came and went, European societies became optimistic about the future, and economic development rapidly increased. As the need for more and more people with some education grew, cathedral schools expanded. By 1200, some of these schools had transformed into the beginnings of what we think of today as higher education.

Looking at the past also demonstrates that some issues, at their most basic level, are enduring. They play a role in today's world just as they did in 1200, 1300, 1400, and onward. Certainly there is no guarantee they will remain so forever; however, it seems highly probable that higher education, as we know it, will continue to play a role for the foreseeable future, given its existence for more than eight hundred years.

WHERE IT ALL BEGAN

The roots of U.S. higher education lie in Western Europe. The four most influential countries in order of development of universities are Italy, France, England, and Germany. Each country contributed something to today's universities, just as they influenced one another during their developmental phases.

During its first one hundred–plus years, the university was not a "place." Rather, students and teachers or masters were international in character and highly mobile. Instruction was in Latin, the language of the church and learned nobility. The two groups sought communities that were teacher- and student-friendly and quickly moved on when they thought they could do better elsewhere. Thus, developments in one country were carried to other countries by the peripatetic students and teachers.

What we know as universities today grew out of the training process the Catholic Church had developed to educate those individuals who would prepare documents and help maintain the church's business. Parish priests provided some basic instruction for the local boys of nobility. A few boys went on to a secondary education at cathedrals where, at least in theory, they were educated in the seven "liberal arts": grammar, rhetoric, logic, arithmetic, geometry, astronomy, and music. These arts reflected the skills needed by the church to carry out its administrative and some religious activities—individuals who could prepare logical and grammatically correct documents, who could calculate dates for movable feasts, and who could help provide music for services.

Instruction in all the subjects was "in theory," because few cathedrals had individuals who were fully competent or interested in all the subjects. The differing interests and knowledge led to different cathedrals developing reputations for excellence in a few of the arts, which, in turn, attracted students who had a strong interest in the area(s) of strength. Learning was a matter of memorization because there were few books. Certainly no library was accessible to the students. Those books that were available were costly and kept under tight control. An instructional day would generally have a lecture, discussion of the lecture, repetition of the lecture's content, writing practice, and student recitation of the previous day's lecture. That pattern, at least the lecture and memorization, remained the standard for centuries (some critics of higher education might say it still has not changed all that much).

The mechanics of higher education—instruction by faculty in a formal course of study, examinations, commencements, and degrees—was established by the thirteenth century. Higher education remained the territory of the well-to-do male student for the better part of six centuries.

ITALIAN INFLUENCE

Italy had the first institutions we can identify as universities (Salerno and Bologna), and they served as the seedbeds for the rest of European higher education. Salerno was perhaps the earliest (circa AD 1050), but its focus on medicine restricted its influence on the schools with a broader focus. Had the Carnegie Classification existed at the time, Salerno would have been designated a "special-focus institution."

It is Bologna that most scholars consider the site of the development of higher education. It was also much larger than Salerno in terms of students and masters. Bologna gave rise to the term *university* (universitas). "University" has nothing to do with the universe of knowledge or universality of learning; rather, it referred to an organized group (a guild) that existed to establish standards as well as rules of behavior and activity and to protect the group's rights—for example, the rights of groups such as merchants, blacksmiths, weavers, masons, or students. Students in Bologna created their guild (universitas) to protect themselves from the townspeople (town-and-gown issues go back to the beginning), and later they added instructional rights (Hyde, 1988, pp. 18–19). Initially, student activism focused on the most immediate needs—setting room rents as well as the cost of food and other services provided by the city's people. There were no dormitories, food services, laundry facilities, or other amenities that today's students expect and consider their due, if they think much about such issues. Students' concerns about educational costs are clearly not new.

Once the universitas was established (it was a document that magistrates first looked to when handling a student-townsperson dispute), the students turned their attention to instructional expectations. Until there was a corporate institution of higher education, teachers and masters earned their income from fees they collected directly from individual students. Bologna student guilds created an employment contract that students could use to ensure some measure of learning opportunities. The contract covered such issues as how often a teacher might be absent from the lecture room and still receive a fee, the structure and length of instruction, and the quality of the instruction.

Clearly today's concern for the need to listen to and attend to students' voices as well as the students' desire to have a seat at the table grew out of the efforts of the Bologna student universitas. Many academic libraries today have advisory committees that include student representatives, an outgrowth of this early involvement of students. Students' evaluations of teaching, which are commonplace today, have their roots in the student-masters contracts.

FRENCH INFLUENCE

The leading French university during the early years was in Paris. *In* is an important word during the developmental period. We noted earlier that students and teachers were highly mobile. So it was a university *in* Paris, not the university *of* Paris. Several times in the 1200s and 1300s the Paris students and masters left the city for a variety of reasons, only to return later (Ferruolo, 1988, p. 23).

Teachers in Paris were among the first to form their own universitas in order to gain some protection and rights. Initially the masters' guild was a loose confederation of individuals who looked solely to their personal interests. However, relatively quickly they thought of themselves as a formal group (a faculty) and secured faculty rights such as establishing student admission standards and qualifications, determining the timing of examinations, and approving the granting of a degree. Often the prospective student had to pass an entrance exam before being allowed to attend lectures. The faculty's granting of a degree or license served to prove that the holder had the knowledge to teach others. Faculty reserved for themselves the right to decide what courses they would offer as well as when. (Faculty workloads and what days and times they will teach are issues that remain with us.)

About 1231, the university in Paris had four faculties, each with a dean and the beginnings of a sense of place. The four faculties were liberal arts, canon law, medicine, and theology. They, the faculties, elected a person to serve as rector—a person who represented the interests of all the faculties both internally and to the outside world. Later, the four groups (colleges) began to act like a corporation (university) that could hold property and control money for the good of all the students and faculties. Until then, lectures took place wherever a teacher could rent a room large enough for his class. Students and faculty rented living accommodations and took their meals wherever they could for the money they had. The college as physical place arose from the need for faculty to find reasonable accommodations. What started as a place to live and take meals soon grew into a gathering place for faculty and students. It was not too long before space was added or adjacent space rented to provide classrooms. Thus, the concept of *campus* began to form. At this time, the universities did not have libraries and depended on the book and manuscript collections of religious orders for what little access the teachers required.

French influence on higher education is seen in the structure of today's postsecondary campuses, faculties and their attendant rights, deans, rectors, and other administrators. It also led to a corporate institution. What started as a means of limiting local jurisdiction (the guild) soon led to a royal charter that protected the institution from local and papal interference or a papal charter that protected against local and royal requirements. The first higher education institution anywhere in the world to receive a legislative charter was Harvard in 1650 (Kivinen and Poikus, 2006).

ENGLISH INFLUENCE

Oxford and Cambridge (both of which were Puritan in orientation) developed the concept of campus and college beyond that of most continental universities. (A number of scholars of the history of higher education, at least in the United States, refer to them as Oxbridge to save space and emphasize their dual influence on each other and other institutions.) For the United States, they were, and to some degree still are, highly influential in terms of the symbols, forms, and vocabulary for undergraduate education. Essentially they represented the "ideal" institution for the United States until late in the nineteenth century; for some, they still represent what undergraduate education is, or should be, about.

What are some of the elements of that ideal? Having a residential educational experience with tutorial instruction in the liberal arts as the starting point, selective admission, an honors program, the "quad," attention to campus grounds, and the "gentleman scholar" (the "gentleman's C" grade)—all are legacies of Oxford and Cambridge. Other elements, such as elaborate extracurricular activities, sports (especially crew racing), pipe smoking, and tweed jackets with leather patches on the sleeves, when combined with the first list bring to mind Hollywood B movies about college life before the 1960s. Stereotypical or not, much of the foregoing is still what many people think of as a college or university (an ivory tower isolated from the real world).

In some ways that ideal influenced individuals like Clark Kerr when he formulated a master plan for California higher education in the mid-twentieth century. (One of his goals was to make a highly complex and large system appear less so by having a sequence or levels from community college to research university.) As late as 1970 the ideal served as the inspiration for St. Mary's College of Maryland's attempt to create a quality, public, and residential liberal arts education.

Not everyone believed the Oxford/Cambridge model was appropriate for the U.S. environment. The selective admission of primarily the sons of rich and influential families for an education in the liberal arts did not seem useful in a country that needed a population of workers and entrepreneurs. (The original meaning of the liberal arts was non-money making.) Johnson (1958), discussing the Oxbridge model and questioning its value, wrote,

> But it is applied to the education of sons of American farmers, store-keepers, plumbers, policemen, and street car conductors who have not inherited money and have made enough to send their boys to college only by years of intensive concentration on their jobs to the exclusion of purely intellectual interests. . . . Secondary education . . . has always been and is highly selective, restricted to an extremely small class. (p. 392)

Certainly the issue of diversity is still with us as we noted in the first chapter.

The value of the English model was a major issue for the U.S. public. Many doubted the need for and the value of higher education. Nevertheless, the English model was extremely influential during several hundred years of U.S. higher education.

GERMAN INFLUENCE

To a large extent, the Black Death's impact on the region's population caused German universities to get off to a slower start than elsewhere in Europe (Heidelberg University became operational in 1386). However, once begun, German universities quickly drew on what other European universities were doing and added elements of their own. They differed from their European colleagues in their heavy emphasis on scholarship. Teaching and scholarship (especially in the form of expanding knowledge) were seen as interlaced—good teachers added to the sum total of knowledge; they were not just dispensers of what already existed.

German universities also created two special rights, one for students and another for faculty. Students in the process of earning a degree had the right to attend lectures at any university. (The concept of taking classes at several institutions and having the work count toward a single degree, at least in terms of a person's major, is still not widely accepted in the United States.) The faculty right is one that plays a role today, which is the right to be allowed to "seek the truth" without interference from others (academic freedom).

Another contribution from the German universities was the creation of *institutes* for advanced study for a few select individuals (Thelin, 1982). Ultimately this concept led to the granting of degrees higher than the baccalaureate—the master's degree or doctor of philosophy or a general master's degree. Like their English counterparts, German institutions drew their students from aristocratic families. The curriculum was designed to build a cadre of men for government service. Thus, it was more overtly practical than the English model and the liberal arts curriculum that did not focus on that result. Nevertheless, most of the English graduates engaged in some form of professional or governmental work.

|||||| CHECK THIS OUT

The following will provide more details about European influences on the university:

Bender, Thomas. 1988. *The university and the city.* Oxford: Oxford University Press.
Clark, John Willis. 1968. *Libraries in the medieval and Renaissance periods.* Chicago: Argonaut Press.
Cobban, Alan B. 1975. *The medieval universities.* London: Methune.
Haskins, Charles H. 1940. *The rise of universities.* New York: P. Smith.
Thompson, James Westfall. 1939. *The medieval library.* Chicago: University of Chicago Press

---

From the outset, higher education faced questions about who should teach what to whom and where as well as how to pay for the process. We hardly mentioned libraries in the previous discussion of the early days of higher education. The nature of instruction (memorization) meant that, for students, there was little need for an institutional library; even where libraries did exist, students rarely had access. You gain a sense of the limited access from the following quotation taken from the medieval Oxford library regulations:

> Since in the course of time the great number of students using the library is in many ways harmful to the books and since the laudable purpose of these desiring to profit [by reading them] is often defeated by too much disturbance of noisy people, the university has ordered and decreed that only graduates and people in religious orders who have studied philosophy for eight years shall study in the library of the university. (Lucas, 1994, p. 56)

An additional factor limiting access was the mobile character of the university. Moving a library is never fun, and one can only speculate about the challenges of trying to move the books of the thirteenth and fourteenth centuries. Only when the Gutenberg revolution took hold did books become relatively affordable (students today may think books are still not affordable), and the prospect of real college and university libraries become necessary. Also, until about 1300 few new books were written—new in the sense of new content. Prior to that time, "new" books were basically copies of older works.

This brief review of early higher education in Europe merely highlights some of the antecedents of the form and function of today's postsecondary institutions. As you might expect, when the Europeans arrived in other parts of the world (especially in the Western Hemisphere), established colonies, and desired to have local higher education, the institutions they created were full transplants of what existed in their home countries.

HOW THE TRANSPLANTS TOOK ROOT IN THE UNITED STATES (1636-1770)

U.S. higher education, until the 1820s, was essentially a full transplant of the English and Scottish colleges whose classical curriculum was packaged in a theological framework. Between 1636 (Harvard) and 1769, nine colleges were established by several religious denominations (table 2.1). Although there were strong theological differences even within the same group (one Puritan group established Harvard and another Puritan group founded Yale), they all shared the same basic challenges: enrollments were low; it was hard to find teachers;

physical facilities were minimal; who should control what was to be taught was a frequent issue; town-and-gown relations were unpredictable, especially if money was involved; and funding was always touch and go.

You gain a sense of the low enrollments from the fact that by 1770 (134 years after the establishment of the first college), there had been only three thousand graduates (Vinton, 1878, p. 102). This number should not be too surprising given that the course of study was not about making money, unless one wished to become a minister. At that time, most people were concerned only with making it to tomorrow in a rather hostile country. What was socially important was creating settlements and a self-sustaining independent economy. Given the nature of a frontier society and its values, it is not surprising that few young men knew about, much less considered, attending college. Even those few who did had to look long and hard to find a local person who could teach the rudimentary skills necessary to be considered for college admission. The issues of practicality and relevance remain subjects of debate within academia and society.

Despite the challenges, as table 2.1 illustrates, the early transplants took root and survived, unlike many of the colleges created in the nineteenth century. What was different and all the more impressive is that they, unlike the colleges in Spanish America, did not serve the needs of a single religious group, the government, or a substantial wealthy aristocratic community. Another factor that encouraged taking root was that the English did not, as a matter of course, transplant colleges into their colonies as their empire grew. The mother country universities—Oxford, Cambridge, Dublin, and Edinburgh—had ample room for the "young men from the colonies" and thought that bringing them home would help ensure their loyalty to the mother country. We cannot but wonder how things might have changed had the U.S. colonies not founded their "home" colleges.

Perhaps one of the biggest factors in the Puritans' establishing of Harvard was the high concentration of Oxford and Cambridge graduates in New England, as many as one hundred by some estimates. A second factor was the desire to ensure and control the availability

FOUNDING NAME	FOUNDING DATE	CURRENT NAME	CHURCH AFFILIATION
Harvard	1636	Harvard	Puritan
William and Mary	1693	William and Mary	Anglican
Yale	1701	Yale	Puritan
Philadelphia College	1740	Pennsylvania	Quaker
College of New Jersey	1746	Princeton	Presbyterian
King's College	1754	Columbia	Anglican
Rhode Island College	1765	Brown	Baptist
Queen's College	1766	Rutgers	Dutch Reform
Moor's Indian Charity School	1769	Dartmouth	Congregational

TABLE 2.1 Early college transplants to the United States

and quality of the ministers for what the Puritans hoped would be a guiding set of moral values for the world. They also believed a college was an essential part of any good society. Apart from the number of English college graduates, most of the first colleges were created for basically the same reasons. Clearly there was a desire to use higher education as a means of achieving the religious ends of a particular denomination. All the colleges listed in table 2.1, except for what was to become Dartmouth, had as an early goal the training of ministers for a particular denomination (Stille, 1878, pp. 122–130).

Like European cities, larger communities in the United States viewed the presence of a college as a mark of prestige and status. Not that these attitudes translated into significant financial support. During the colonial period, no one thought in terms of "public" or "private" colleges; the college was just the college and was on its own when it came to funding. Such a distinction came later in terms of both funding and "ownership" in the nineteenth century.

Staying open was always a challenge. U.S. colleges did not, at least initially, meet the same social demand that those in England, Ireland, and Scotland did, beyond graduating a few ministers. What the latter institutions had that was lacking in the United States was a "market" of landed gentry whose sons required educating to be true gentlemen. Lacking such a market, there were few places to turn to for students and donations. There were a few families with ideas or pretensions of aristocracy, but they sent their sons "home" (meaning Europe) for their education. All of this translated into funding challenges.

College presidents then, as now, were always looking for opportunities to secure funding and donations to reduce financial uncertainty. (Today fund-raising has also become a part of any academic library director's life.) Two examples from the early years illustrate this point. Harvard is Harvard because of a gift from John Harvard. He was a Cambridge graduate, and when he died in 1638 he left his library (329 books) and half his estate (£780) to a then unnamed college (Carpenter, 1986, p. 2). Another "naming opportunity" (more about that concept and fund-raising in general in chapter 7) occurred when Elihu Yale, a wool merchant, donated £550 worth of cloth to another unnamed college in Connecticut (Handlin and Handlin, 1970, p. 39).

Then as now, all higher education institutions were dependent on student tuition to meet current expenses. (Certainly today there are some universities with huge endowment funds that take some of the fiscal pressure off, but this attribute does not keep them from raising tuition each year.) A different example of the financial troubles comes from what was to become the College of William and Mary. In 1619 the college had nine thousand acres to sell to raise the funds to create a college, but there were no takers. It tried again in 1660 to sell the land with the same result (Brubacher and Rudy, 1997, pp. 3–23). Obviously the effort to get started was long and frustrating; however, the founders kept trying, and William and Mary is now the second-oldest institution of higher education in the United States. As someone said about early colleges, they were short of money, faculty, and students, were searching for a public, and had befuddled policies, but they were convinced the future demanded their existence and growth. Sometimes faith can achieve surprisingly long-lasting results.

Slowly the notion developed in the United States, as it had in England, that there were two goals for colleges: to educate the clergy and to produce "lettered gentlemen." As early as 1647, President Dunster (Harvard) talked about the possibility of having students interested in going into all the professions (Handlin and Handlin, 1970, p. 29).

During these early years, academic libraries were small. The College of William and Mary in 1732 was the first college library recorded as being authorized to buy books. Before that, donations were the way the collections grew. As is so often the case with academic firsts, Harvard had the first U.S. academic librarian (The Keeper of the Books) in the person of Solomon Stoddard (Carpenter, 1986, p. 60). The Harvard library hired its first female employee in 1859 (Carpenter, 1986, p. 97), two years after the Boston Athenaeum became the first U.S. library to do so.

Not surprisingly, during this time, access to books for students was very limited, and most colleges had lists of prohibited books. Most of the prohibited works were deemed potentially dangerous to the denomination's beliefs and young men's minds. Other limited access items, just as today, were reference works, and no one could check them out. Not only were certain titles prohibited, but undergraduates could read a book only in the reading room while under the supervision of a tutor or teacher. As a final limitation, the libraries were open only a few hours two or three days a week, at least for students.

POST-WAR OF INDEPENDENCE TO 1865

Although the basics remained unchanged during the 1783–1865 period of development, some details were changing. First of all, there were many more colleges to choose from; between 1772 and 1802, state legislatures chartered nineteen new colleges, all of which have managed to survive.

Another aspect of this period was the slow but steady expansion of the curriculum beyond the liberal arts. Although Latin remained *the* language of most texts that were taught, Greek (humanistic works) and Hebrew (the language of the prophets) also began to be taught. "Natural history" appeared in some colleges, and overall there was a loosening of the theological requirements. As a result of French assistance in the War of Independence, some colleges added courses in the French language and French history. The trend was away from medieval scholarship toward a more practical and technological orientation. Perhaps the clearest indication of change was the establishment of West Point Military Academy in 1802, with its engineering curriculum, and the Philadelphia College of Apothecaries in 1821.

This period was also a time when governments began to seriously view higher education as something they should support. The first "public" college or university was the University of Virginia, established in 1819. Certainly there had been some funds from towns and legislatures earlier—Harvard received Charles River ferry tolls, and William and Mary had sporadic income from an export tax and the issuance of land surveyors' licenses. However, these revenue sources were small supplements to operating budgets, and no one thought the state should be the primary source of funding. Today both public and private institutions have a mix of funding sources.

The divide between public and private was not distinct. All the colleges had to receive a charter from the legislature. A few did receive some money from the state or local government. The real question was, who controlled the institution? It took the U.S. Supreme Court to settle the matter with a decision regarding Dartmouth College (a private school today). As is often the case today, the dispute started between the college president (John Wheelock, son of the founder) and the trustees. (We explore the issue of governance in more depth in chapter 6.) President Wheelock went public about the dispute in 1815 when he asked the New Hampshire legislature to investigate the affairs of the college. Needless to say, the trustees were less than happy with this request and voted to remove Wheelock from the board, the presidency, and his professorship. Seeing a political opportunity in the situation, the Republican Party took up Wheelock's cause and managed to win the 1816 elections using the case as a key element in the party's platform. The new governor (a Republican) and the legislature passed a law that would bring the college under state control on the grounds that the trustees perpetuated aristocratic rather than democratic values. In the court cases that followed and eventually were appealed to the U.S. Supreme Court, an unknown young Dartmouth graduate (Daniel Webster) presented the trustees' position. In a five to one decision (it became a landmark case), the Court ruled that Dartmouth was not a public institution because the state charter was a contract for a private venture.

That decision (*Trustees of Dartmouth College v. Woodward*, 17 U.S. 518) safeguarded private colleges from legislative interference. Another major outcome of the ruling made it clear that the governing board, not the faculty, students, or administrators, held overall control of the institution. A major outcome of the decision was phenomenal growth in the number of colleges created over the next thirty-plus years. Before the War of Independence there were nine colleges; by the start of the Civil War, there were 250. The result was that there were nearly as many colleges in existence as there were elementary schools. By comparison, in 1860, England, with a population of more than twenty-three million, had four universities; Ohio, with a population of about three million, had thirty-seven colleges and universities. Most of the new schools were located in rural settings, were small and underfunded, enrolled teenage males, offered a liberal arts–oriented curriculum, and used an "in loco parentis" (in the place of the parent) concept. Acting in the place of the parent was a constant challenge for the staff. One suspects the addition of organized sports to campus life was an attempt to burn off some of the boundless energy of teenage boys and keep them from causing trouble in the local communities. A common complaint of college presidents and faculty was the amount of time they had to devote to monitoring and controlling the boys' behavior. The expectation that the staff of the institution would control students' behavior has been long-standing and, as we will show later in this chapter, can have serious consequences for an institution.

Oberlin became the first institution to go coeducational when it admitted women in 1836. Georgia chartered the first women's college (Georgia Female College, which later became Wesleyan College) in 1836.

A rural setting did not mean life was peaceful. School violence is not a late twentieth-century, early twenty-first-century phenomenon; medieval students had brawls, sword fights, and more. Between 1800 and 1900 there were an average of four student deaths a year from fights or duels and at least one "student rebellion" per year from 1800 to 1875 (Brubacher and Rudy, 1997, pp. 59–119).

Underfunding was a perennial problem during this time and can be illustrated by the sad story of John W. Browne, founder of Miami University of Ohio. Browne went on a year-long trip to collect money and books for the library. At the end of his journey, he had $700 and a wagonload of books. Near the college, while crossing a river, the wagon tipped over, resulting in one dead John Browne and a load of lost books. Another example is Emory College, which "opened" on the basis of unpaid interest on unpaid pledges of support. At one point, when Bowdoin College (established in 1794) needed a classroom building, the college offered a Maine township (thirty-six square miles of land) to anyone who would build such a building and found no takers (Handlin and Handlin, 1970, pp. 56–91).

The liberal arts curriculum never had wide popular support, which was a significant factor in low enrollments. Three primary factors were behind the low public opinion regarding a college education, all related to labor. First, the cost was too high, perhaps not in terms of today's dollars but in terms of the expense of the schooling combined with the lost labor at home. During the nineteenth century, the lost labor had the much larger impact; even if the families did not calculate an actual labor cost, they understood the loss of a worker. Second, the colleges were seldom near home, resulting in substantial travel time. Often the distance was too great to return home during school holidays, meaning even those periods of potential labor were lost. Finally, there was the overriding fact that a liberal arts curriculum was not practical for the majority of people. Little if anything learned would translate into better production, less work, or improved income.

A key to the development of public higher education and an education with a practical emphasis was the Morrill Act of 1862, with its provision of either land or "scrip" for use in operating higher education institutions. The act, although not excluding "classical studies" or science, called for institutions to offer learning related to agricultural and mechanical arts. Although today a few universities retain "A&M" in their names, most such schools dropped that element from their name in the mid-twentieth century. Schools that started as, or existing schools that became, recipients of land or scrip are known as land-grant schools. A few of those schools still have some of the original tracts of land; however, the bulk of the land was sold to start or support one or more state-operated institution(s). The legislation provided for thirty thousand acres of public land per representative and senator or the equivalent in cash (scrip) for states in which there was little or no federal land. There are sixty-eight land-grant colleges and universities, almost all of them large research universities with names you probably know.

What was the status of academic libraries at the time? Libraries were small and still barely accessible to students, open perhaps one or two hours a week. Library staffs, such as there were, were charged with preserving the collection from unnecessary use. Almost always the person in charge of the library was one of the most respected faculty members who could be counted on to control collection access. There was little effort to organize the small collections beyond maintaining an alphabetical author order on the shelves. As late as the 1850s, most schools depended on book donations rather than purchases to build their collections.

Students responded to the lack of library access by creating literary societies, often away from campus, where they developed their own libraries to address their interests. Those libraries included newspapers and magazines, not just books that were housed in the campus libraries. Such societies were both social and intellectual. A favorite activity was debating, which called for a wide range of material. The library was open to any member any time, and outsiders might gain access with the permission of the members. Until the late 1800s, some of these student libraries had the broadest-based collections in a state.

The key issues associated with the development of higher education in the United States before 1865 are summarized in table 2.2.

1860s TO WORLD WAR II

The period from the end of the Civil War to the beginning of World War II was a time of growth, greater stability, and a continuation of the trends of the late 1850s. More coeducational opportunities were created, electives and majors became a staple, enrollments increased as the value of higher education was recognized, and the tension between the value of liberal/theoretical and practical became sharper (a tension that remains with us). The need to assure the public and the students' families of the quality of an institution led to accreditation boards (the first was the New England Association of Colleges and Preparatory

Schools in 1885). Social activities (especially Greek organizations) and athletics became standard features of college life.

One of the key developments at this time was the leading role that state universities took in expanding the subject options one could study. Two institutions, Cornell and the University of Wisconsin, were influential in this expansion. Cornell was created to be an all-purpose university. Its seal states, "I would found an institution in which any person can find instruction in any study" (Becker, 1943, p. 88). Essentially all subjects were to be equally valued, an idea that still receives lip service at most academic institutions but is often ignored

Student Body	• Small enrollment • Primarily white males 13–18 years old • Families better off than the average family • Tight control by the faculty and administrators • Campus is place of residence • First coeducational institution is Oberlin, in 1836 • Few higher education opportunities for women
Curriculum	• Primarily liberal arts and strong religious component • Fixed sequence of courses • Limited, if any, electives • Recitation and memorization of a few key books • Shift toward practical courses late in the 1850s
Faculty	• Primarily practicing or former ministers • Scholarship and research interests of little importance • High turnover due to low salary and dislike of acting as a father • Few have broad knowledge beyond what they learned in college
Governance	• Board of trustees or overseers and presidential control • Faculty have little say in operations • Students have no say—primary factor in "student rebellions" • Land-grant policy brings legislative oversight for those institutions
Facilities	• Few buildings but a campus setting • Libraries generally small with very limited student access—student literary societies fill the void • Lack of facilities often limits what the school can do
Funding	• Financial condition often so poor closure seems likely until passage of the Morrill Act (from 1862 until after 1960) • Fund-raising a constant challenge • Faculty and staff wait for months for their pay
Society's View	• Institutions mostly ignored during the earliest years • Interest increases after introduction of practical course work

TABLE 2.2 Summary of U.S. higher education before 1865

when it comes to funding and support. The "Wisconsin Idea" took shape in the early twentieth century as the concept that a college or university should address all the needs of a democratic society. The idea was a reflection of what the citizens of Wisconsin demanded, and they expected that the university would improve farming and industry. They did not want an "ivory tower" institution. Both of these concepts played important roles in the expansion of the curriculum for many colleges and universities.

Another important development during this period was the movement toward the German model of faculty advancing knowledge rather than just dispensing it. Johns Hopkins University, founded in 1876, is usually credited with being the first institution to fully achieve true university status. Within a few years, many other institutions were reorganizing themselves to offer graduate work and hire faculty who understood they were to be productive scholars. Today colleges and universities still have to address this orientation and desire. The expectation that faculty will engage in research had, and has, implications for teaching loads and the number of faculty required to maintain a desired teacher-student ratio. It also, at least in larger institutions, has an implication for who teaches which level course. For example, it is common that graduate student teaching assistants teach the lower division introductory classes and that full professors teach only upper-level courses. Also, the German concept of academic freedom became an issue, especially in the oldest institutions. Further research often required new buildings, especially for science and engineering activities, and overall more classrooms, offices, and dormitories were needed.

For academic libraries, the research emphasis and curriculum expansion had a profound influence on collections and collection building. Exploring new frontiers of knowledge calls for understanding what is already known as well as communicating what you have done recently. Collection depth and breadth had to increase dramatically to support the new curriculum and research activities. We will explore the research and scholarly communication issues in more depth in the next chapter.

Intercollegiate athletics had its roots in this period. What is now viewed by many as "big-time athletics" and the commercialization of college sports became an expected part of campus life. The first Rose Bowl football game took place in 1902. Today it is difficult to keep track of all the postseason bowl games on television. At the time probably few, if any, individuals would have thought these activities might one day be multimillion-dollar-a-year operations both as an expense and as income. We will explore this issue in more depth in chapter 4.

A new category of institution became part of U.S. higher education during this time—the junior community college. During the early years, the label was *junior college* (JC). In the last third of the last century, most changed their names to *community college* (CC). As a result of economic conditions at the start of the twentieth century, there were a number of advocates for creating an institution that handled the first two years of a baccalaureate degree. As reported by Sinwell (2008), "The mission of the original junior college was to provide passage to 4-year degrees for many young people who otherwise would have been denied access to higher education" (pp. 23–24). Sinwell also noted that the first JC owed its existence, in part, to William Rainey Harper, president of the University of Chicago, who signed an agreement to allow graduates of Joliet Junior College to have advanced standing on admission to the University of Chicago. This took place in 1901, and Joliet Junior College was the first two-year public institution of the new type.

For the first thirty years of their existence, community colleges focused on an articulated-transfer curriculum—that is, they offered the equivalent of the first two years of a baccalaureate degree. Enrollment was generally low, with no more than a few hundred students.

By the start of World War II, more than two hundred such schools had been established, a substantial increase from the twenty-five that existed in 1910 (American Association of Community Colleges, n.d.).

Community colleges shifted their focus during the 1930's depression to offering vocational education. Initially students appeared to be equally attracted to both curriculums, but in time the vocational aspect surpassed the transfer programs in popularity.

Community college students almost always lived off campus and often lacked some of the credentials for direct admission to a four-year institution. Often, unlike four-year institution students, they held part-time jobs while attending school. Faculty focused on teaching and attempting to ensure that the course quality was such that the work would meet transfer requirements.

Today the transfer program is once again coming to the forefront of CC programs. For example, after years of seeing themselves as competitors, the Coconino County Community College and the University of Northern Arizona announced in the summer of 2008 that they had entered into an agreement that would allow for easy transfer. The program, CCC2NAU, is a joint admission designed to meet the needs of students seeking a bachelor's degree ("CCC2NAU," 2008).

During this time faculty status for librarians became an issue because libraries faced challenges that should seem familiar to today's academic librarians. For the first time, individuals working in the libraries thought of themselves as professionals and wanted to be treated like faculty rather than clerks. There was not enough money to acquire all the materials the faculty and students wanted, and materials were not processed satisfactorily. Examples of complaints included inadequate classification or misclassification of books and excessive time for acquisition and binding of materials. Students and faculty also wanted more reading space, more service hours, and additional services. Harvard did not offer reference service until the late 1930s, the attitude being that if you were intelligent enough to attend or work at Harvard, you should be smart enough to find things without help. That may just be Harvard library folklore that gets passed on from one library staff to another; however, it is true that reference service was a long time in coming—students first made a formal request for such assistance in 1914 (Carpenter, 1986, p. 142). Collection growth also created space challenges. Harvard president Charles Eliot suggested in 1901 that rather than build additional library space on campus, the university should store "dead books" away from campus (Carpenter, 1986, p. 122). It was not until 1942 that a specially designed facility for such storage was built.

The developments in higher education from the mid-1860s to World War II are summarized in table 2.3.

WARS AND HIGHER EDUCATION

Wars are always disruptive to higher education. If nothing more, the young people are either in military service, preparing for such service, or preoccupied by what is happening. For the United States until the Civil War, these were the only issues.

Things began to change with the passage of the Morrill Act and the requirement that land-grant institutions include military tactics in the curriculum and with the use of a military service draft during the Civil War. World War I brought additional issues. Academic freedom, for example, became a subject of community concern—should faculty be required to actively support the war in their classrooms or be allowed to voice personal concerns? The Reserve Officers' Training Corps (ROTC) became a fixture at many institutions, even after the war was over. Some schools entered into contracts to provide military training as part of the degree program. Then there was the idea of exemptions from the military draft for certain classes of students, such as medicine and science majors and ROTC members.

World War II (WWII) had all those elements plus another feature that would have long-term consequences: contract research for the federal government. Universities' success in scientific problem solving greatly aided the war effort, and this type of work continued during the Cold War period. Government's real, and imagined, influence on institutional priorities often generated heated debates. The impact has been an ongoing sense of *haves*

Student Body	• Dramatic increase in numbers as the range of possible studies increases • Many coeducational institutions • Athletic opportunities begin to play a role in school selection • Family incomes closer to the national average • Less control by the faculty and administrators, but still important • Campus is residential in most cases • Invention of the automobile leads to new challenges for campus staff in terms of student control and community relations
Curriculum	• Liberal arts still present but great expansion in subjects • "Practical" courses come close to equaling the classical courses • Electives a normal part of a course of study
Faculty	• More often educated in the subjects taught—doctorate often a requirement • Scholarship and research become key factors in larger institutions • More stable faculty in terms of tenure of stay
Governance	• Board of trustees or overseers and presidential control • Faculty have more say in operations • Students have little say
Facilities	• New and often specialized buildings • Campuses become small cities in themselves • Libraries grow in size and hours of availability
Funding	• Larger enrollments lead to more stable funding • Broader course offerings and more students require more staffing and facilities • Sports complexes add new financial demands
Society's View	• Public institutions expected to improve life and solve problems • Value is seen in sending daughters and sons to schools with practical courses of study

TABLE 2.3 Developments in U.S. higher education from 1865 to 1940

(scientists) and *have-nots* (humanists and, to a lesser degree, social scientists) in terms of research funding sources outside the institution.

The successes of university researchers in solving defense challenges also led to a general belief that universities could resolve any problem, including long-standing social issues. When universities proved much less successful in these areas, public doubts began to grow about the worth of the institutions in the 1970s and 1980s.

Part of the war effort research even had an influence on libraries. The military activities were taking place in parts of the world that military planners had never thought much about. Academic library collections were scoured for maps and other data about little-known areas. Overall, the libraries did not have as rich collections in the lesser-studied areas as was desired. A postwar consequence of this situation was the creation of the Farmington Plan wherein academic research libraries across the country made an effort to collect everything printed in a country or subject. One product of the library WWII effort still exists—the Human Relations Area Files (HRAF; http://hraf.yale.edu/). HRAF is an outgrowth of efforts during the war to dissect the contents of books (paragraph by paragraph) and devise a sound retrieval system, especially for items relating to the Pacific and Southeast Asia for the U.S. Navy.

Perhaps two of the most significant outcomes of WWII, for academic institutions, were the G.I. (Government Issue) Bill of Rights and the 1947 President's Commission report on higher education's role in society (President's Commission on Higher Education, 1948). Essentially these two documents helped crystallize the idea that there should be a federal program to support higher education. Although the G.I. Bill provided federal funds for veterans for educational purposes, the commission recommended that higher educational opportunities for everyone capable of such work should have some federal support. The commission envisioned that enrollment in higher education would be 4.6 million by 1960, assuming economic, racial, and geographic barriers were removed (President's Commission on Higher Education, p. 101). Commission members also thought that free education should extend to two years beyond high school graduation. Needless to say, although the free aspect never materialized, the number of community colleges grew dramatically; ninety-two new institutions were founded between 1941 and 1950, and 497 between 1960 and 1970 (American Association of Community Colleges, n.d.). However, it was not until passage of the 1965 Higher Education Act that a broad permanent program of federal financial aid for both public and private colleges and their students was created.

Not only did CCs grow in number at this time but all colleges and universities began to plan for expansion as the G.I.s began to take advantage of the educational benefits available to them. Over the next twenty years, "instant" new colleges, including libraries, appeared across the country, and existing institutions added staff to handle the growing workload. It was a time of great optimism about the future of the academy. The American Library Association (ALA) publication *Books for College Libraries* was initially designed to help new libraries create "opening day" collections.

A summary of the assumptions regarding higher education after World War II appears in table 2.4.

RETRENCHMENT AND REALIGNMENT (1960-1990)

In some sense, the Vietnam War and the related campus protests against the conflict as well as protests about campus-based military and defense research ended an era of phenomenal growth. Unlike their nineteenth-century counterparts, students during the first sixty-plus years of the twentieth century did not engage in regular "student revolts." For the public, the return to such behavior might be expected from students in other countries but certainly not from U.S. students. As a result, doubts began to surface among the public, legislators, and even parents of students about faculty and administrators' control of the students along with concerns about what was being taught.

There were, of course, other factors operating that led to the decline in support of higher education at this time, primarily economic conditions. Taxpayer revolts in various guises (such as California's "Proposition 13," which passed in 1978) caused public institutions to engage in "belt tightening," such as deferring maintenance of buildings, reducing program size, and encouraging senior faculty to take early retirements. For private institutions, a major issue was maintaining enrollments because it became increasingly difficult for families to pay the escalating costs of private higher education.

Libraries faced midyear budget cuts, primarily in collection funds, as institutions faced budget shortfalls. There were years when all the available collection funds had to be used to pay for journal subscriptions, leaving nothing for new books. Hiring "freezes" occurred at the same time that more services were demanded. At best, institutions achieved a "steady state" status rather than losing ground.

Technology started to play a greater role at this time. Libraries were at the forefront of technological use and collaboration, a fact not always recognized outside the profession. One significant example is the Online Computer Library Center (OCLC), which was and is a highly successful library collaborative effort in the area of technology and services. When Wyman Parker was hired by the Ohio College Association in 1963 to develop a cooperative cataloging center, few people, if any, thought that it would in time become one of the world's largest library cooperatives. Perhaps Fredrick Kilgour had a grander vision in 1967 when he took the leadership of what by then was known as the Ohio College Library Center (OCLC). At one point, the organization was known as Online Computer Library Center Inc., which indicated its technological aspects as well as a much broader membership. By the 1970s, larger academic libraries were operating homegrown computer-based systems, and it was

ASSUMPTION	KEY ISSUES
Open to all	• More students • More classes • More extracurricular activities
Productive scholars	• Narrow fields of interest • Increased operating costs
Research justifies existence	• Results now • Outside grants key to support
Exists to serve society	• Extension and adult education programs • Facilities opened to community use
Will be supported indefinitely	• Little strategic or long-term planning

TABLE 2.4 Post–World War II assumptions about the academy

not much later that commercial systems were marketing "library automation" packages. Academic libraries were probably one of the first campus units to fully employ technology for almost all their daily operations.

Another area affected by technology was that of alternative educational programs (distance education). This technology has had major impacts on how academic libraries provide services and resources to students and faculty working remotely. For-profit programs started and offered almost unlimited flexibility for the student in how, when, and where she completed a degree. Again, this development had implications in terms of expectations for publicly supported academic libraries to provide services and resources to students and faculty who are not enrolled in the libraries' home institutions but who are paying tax dollars to support those institutions.

Before we end the discussion we need to mention two unique U.S. academic institutions: African American colleges (historically black colleges and universities [HBCUs]) and Native American tribal colleges. Both types of institutions play an important role in today's postsecondary educational system. Both types of institutions have faced, and are facing, the same challenges as the white institutions as well as some that are unique to their development, circumstances, and mission.

Issues associated with higher education during the 1970s and 1980s are summarized in table 2.5.

Looking back at table 2.1, you see that the first college for Native Americans was the institution that became Dartmouth. Although its initial purpose was to educate Native American preachers and it later dropped the Native American orientation, it was a college. Several hundred years elapsed between the establishment of Moor's Indian Charity School and what are today's tribal colleges (community colleges). From the time of Moor's start-up until the post–Civil War period, Native American education was handled by missionaries. Almost all of that education was at the primary level, and the focus was on "civilizing the savages." Although throughout U.S. history, relations between native peoples and the dominant society were a federal matter, the government asked that missionaries address education on its behalf. Needless to say, the instruction always took the slant of the teacher's religious orientation in the expectation that this approach would lead to the students joining that denomination. After Dartmouth changed its location, name, and "Indian" orientation, the first two higher education schools exclusively for Native American students were Bacone College, established in 1880 (a four-year college), and Pembroke State College, established in 1887 (now part of the University of North Carolina system). Even these institutions had an acculturation goal, with little or no recognition of the students' cultural heritage.

- Funding decreases for institution as a whole
- Costs increase for students and the institution
- Research into social issues fails to produce real results
- General public's view of the academy shifts from neutral to skeptical
- Value of higher education once again questioned
- Growing competition arises with alternative educational opportunities
- Pool of potential students decreases
- Technology presents both opportunities and financial challenges

TABLE 2.5 Post-1970s issues in U.S. higher education

▌▐ **CHECK THIS OUT**

The following titles provide a wealth of information about U.S. higher education history and academic libraries:

Battles, Mathew. 2003. *Library: An unquiet history.* New York: W. W. Norton.

Cohen, Arthur M., and Florence B. Brawer. 2003. *The American community college.* San Francisco, CA: Jossey-Bass.

Cremin, Lawrence Arthur. 1980. *American education: The national experience, 1783–1876.* New York: Harper and Row.

Eisenmann, Linda. 2006. *Higher education for women in postwar America: 1945–1965.* Baltimore: Johns Hopkins University Press.

Riddle, Phyllis I. 1989. *University and the state.* Stanford, CA: Stanford University Press.

Wiegand, Wayne A., and Donald Davies, eds. 1994. *Encyclopedia of library history.* New York: Garland Publishing.

In the 1960s, tribes began to push for tribally oriented higher education, and a series of tribal community colleges came into existence. Their curriculums are bilingual and bicultural in an effort to provide a balanced approach. "Native people, on the whole, have favored schools that teach their children non-Indian ways without forcing them to forget their Indian ways" (Reyhner and Eder, 2004, p. 330). More and more Native American students are enrolling and succeeding in all categories of higher education institutions. As of September 2016, the American Indian Higher Education Consortium had thirty-seven members.

Black colleges had some different challenges to overcome. Without a doubt the greatest challenge was the racial issue that existed and that still exists, although to a lesser extent. No colleges for blacks in the South existed until after the Civil War because southern states made it illegal to provide such opportunities. In the North, the first black colleges were Cheyney College in 1837 (now a university and part of the Pennsylvania State System of Higher Education), Lincoln College in 1854 (now a university and part of the Pennsylvania State System of Higher Education), and Wilberforce University in 1856 (a private institution located in Ohio). With the passage of the second land-grant Morrill Act (1890), the real growth in black colleges took place; today there are 106 such institutions.

The 1890 act's primary purpose was to create better endowments and physical facility maintenance of the white land-grant schools. A secondary outcome was the provision of land-grant funding for African American colleges. Essentially, the seventeen black colleges created after the Civil War became land-grant institutions, and some of their funding challenges became less severe (Harris and Worthen, 2004). "Black land grant institutions continue as a subgroup of the land grant system because of the economic and political forces that denied full citizenship to Africans freed from slavery after the Civil War" (p. 454).

Most academic libraries in these unique institutions have additional collection development requirements that include supporting their institutions' appropriate ethnic studies curriculum. This support includes maintaining special collections that reflect the uniqueness of those institutions' missions.

We also need to recognize that with this country's changing demographics there are an increasing number of Hispanic-serving higher education institutions (210) represented by the Hispanic Association of Colleges and Universities (HACU). Unlike the HBCUs and tribal colleges, many of the Hispanic-serving institutions did not set out with that particular goal in mind. However, as their community populations continued to change from predominantly white residents to emerging Hispanic populations, so did part of the mission of the institutions change.

1990s TO THE PRESENT

We examined some of the major post-1990s higher education concerns and changes in chapter 1. Here we will look at several other developments that are playing a role in today's academy environment and its libraries.

Perhaps the overarching developments are linked to technological advances. Certainly there was widespread use of computers on campus well before the 1990s. However, there was only modest networking, as we know it today, between institutions. The development and growth of the Internet has changed most aspects of postsecondary education to some degree. We believe that the opening quotation for chapter 1 perhaps is the best summarization of the post-1990s period: "The days in which the phrase *digital higher education* is meaningfully distinguishable from simply *higher education* are numbered" (italics in the original, Kamenetz, 2015, p. 39). In August 1991, the World Wide Web was opened to public access (www.internetsociety.org/internet/what-internet/history-internet/brief-history-internet). It probably comes as no surprise that this technology was the result of work by U.S. university researchers and that this development changed the way we do things personally today as well as how higher education operates.

The academy started using the Internet for a variety of purposes, from recruitment to instruction. The time- and place-shifting potential of the web made distance education a significant source of revenue for schools of any size and in any location. Certainly distance education was in place long before the Internet changed the environment; however, snail mail courses were not all that popular or revenue generating. The rapid growth in the variety of online programs in the United States as well as expansion globally generated concerns among accreditation agencies. (You will find an in-depth discussion of accreditation in chapter 10.) Their concerns focused on the quality of the offerings as well as student support issues. The global reach of brick-and-mortar and virtual campuses had implications for libraries and their support role for distant learners. (We explore distance education in more detail in chapter 5.) The potential gave rise to another type of postsecondary education, the for-profit organization.

The Rise and Decline of For-Profit Education

For-profit postsecondary education is far from new. Since the late 1890s, there have been small, local schools and businesses offering training in office work and other vocational

---

▌▌▌▌ CHECK THIS OUT

A good article on global library support is Harriett Green's 2013 "Libraries across Land and Sea: Academic Library Services on International Branch Campuses" (*College and Research Libraries* 74, no. 1: 9–23).

||||| **CHECK THIS OUT**

A very good title that covers everything we have discussed in this chapter, except in greater detail, is John R. Thelin's *A History of American Higher Education,* 2d ed. (Baltimore: Johns Hopkins University Press, 2011).

skills on a for-profit basis. They were, in a sense, the forerunners of today's community college vocational programs. They also drew on older adults seeking to expand their employment opportunities. Essentially that is the same market that today's major for-profit schools first focused on.

For-profit educational organizations' growth closely parallels the growth and speed of the Internet. A sense of the profitability of the market, as well as its challenges, is often found in the business sections of newspapers. Until 2000 the total enrollment was a small share of the total postsecondary enrollment—single-digit percentages. The peak enrollments occurred from 2010 to 2012 (the high point was just under 15 percent of total postsecondary enrollees). Certainly this growth was fueled, in part, by the recession. Other components of the growth were the for-profits' expansion of their marketing beyond older adults and the offering of student loans similar to those that traditional institutions could offer. You probably know some firms' names—for example, University of Phoenix, DeVry University, and Corinthian Colleges.

You might assign the start of the for-profits' decline to 2014, when Corinthian Colleges was forced to close and sell its assets as part of a settlement with the U.S. Department of Education. In chapter 1, we discussed student debt and repayment of student loans as one of the major challenges facing today's academy. Another starting point could be 2010 when the U.S. Office of Personnel Management released a report entitled *Federal Student Loan Repayment Program, Calendar Year 2009* (https://www.opm.gov/policy-data-oversight/pay-leave/student-loan-repayment/reports/2009.pdf). In that report, there were data indicating that only 22 percent of for-profit undergraduate degree seekers actually graduated (not-for-profit graduation rates ranged from 55 to 65 percent). Further, 46 percent of for-profit students with a federal loan were in default.

Because of the high dropout and default rates, as well as concerns about aggressive and misleading recruitment tactics, government bodies (federal and state) that provide student loans and grants cracked down on for-profit schools. One example appeared in a news article from the *Arizona Republic* (October 10, 2015, p. 15A) entitled, "Pentagon Bars College from Recruiting: University of Phoenix Cut Off from Revenue Source."

Since about 2014, such schools have dealt with ongoing problems with accreditation agencies, loan groups, and current and perspective students. The following are some newspapers' business section headlines from just one state that illustrate those problems:

- "Can It Rise Again? 82% Decline in Stock Price Since 2010, 70% Decline in Enrollment Since 2010, 40% Decline in Full-Time Staff Since 2010" (*Arizona Republic,* October 4, 2015, pp. 1A, 8A–9A). The article is about the University of Phoenix.
- "U of Phx Parent Aims to Go Private in $1.1B Sale" (Arizona Republic, February 9, 2016, pp. 1A, 12A)

- "ITT Tech Closes Campuses: Nationwide Shutdown Affects 1,300 Students in Phoenix, Tempe, and Tucson" (*Arizona Republic,* September 7, 2016, p.16A)

Other for-profit educational groups have to address similar issues as governments, especially the federal government, try to bring them under tighter control in terms of marketing, graduation rates, actual employment prospects, and loan repayment probabilities. Is this the "fall" of such institutions? Probably not, as they do provide a variety of educational options and approaches that few traditional institutions are inclined to follow.

Online degree for-profit businesses are not the only technology-focused companies that are affecting higher education and its libraries. Some college textbook publishers are staking claims in hosting online course material, and some companies now offer complete online courses. For example, Pearson Education offers more than seventy-five comprehensive online courses; McGraw-Hill's "Connect" is another example of a firm entering the online course field that is unaffiliated with a higher education institution ("learning company" is a frequently used label for such firms).

New Emphasis on an Old Concept

Another post-twentieth-century development is a reemphasis on the service aspect of higher education. There is a common notion within higher education that faculty members "sit" on a three-legged stool in terms of work performance—teaching, research, and service. Although that notion may be widespread, it is acknowledged that two of the legs—teaching and research—are given much more importance when it comes to compensation and promotion considerations. Service is a very distant third. Those three legs also support the institution as well as its staff, at least for public institutions. The idea that the institution has a responsibility to society at large that goes beyond effective education of students is a fact of life for publicly funded colleges and universities. However, during the last half of the twentieth century, institutional service was seldom a priority.

We don't know that there is a cause-and-effect factor currently operating in relation to the upswing in "engaging" the community. However, there seems to be a strong correlation between the upswing in institutional interest in service and outreach and the decline in public funding for colleges and universities. What is taking place currently is labeled "community engagement" rather than service. The belief that a public college or university has a

---

IIIII **CHECK THIS OUT**

The following are two bibliographies about community engagement:

Civic Engagement and Higher Education: Research Literature and Resources. http://blogs
.nd.edu/community-engagement-faculty-institute/files/2012/05/Community-Engage
ment-Literature-Review-Bibliography2.pdf.

Cohen, Laurie. *Community Engagement Bibliography.* www.honorscollege.pitt.edu/sites/
default/files/documents/community-engagement/Community%20Engagement%20
Bibliography.pdf.

duty to reach out to the citizens goes back at least as far as the "Wisconsin Idea" (the "idea" is more than 150 years old). Prior to the Civil War, the Wisconsin legislature pushed the thought that the University of Wisconsin should, indeed must, focus on "popular" needs. Essentially, the concept adopted by the university was that its limits lay at the state line. The university created a variety of "extension" programs and activities for citizens that went far beyond instructing students.

Today's community engagement concept even has a Carnegie Foundation classification program. The "certification" program began in 2006 and, as of 2015, had 361 actively engaged campuses. Engagement is widely interpreted by different schools. Perhaps the best description of what the term means in practice is this: developing outreach and partnerships with local and regional groups to address a social need. For example, finding cooperative methods to provide nontraditional learners with access to some form of postsecondary education would be engagement. A sense of what engagement means to a state university appeared in Meleah Maynard's 2016 interview with Andrew Furco, vice president for public engagement (University of Minnesota), in which he stated, "In the 25 years I have been studying this issue, there has been a dramatic shift in how community engagement is perceived, valued, and legitimized in higher education. . . . [C]ommunity-engaged work can be the key to strengthening relationships with the broader community" (p. 24).

There is little doubt that this trend will have an impact on libraries at engaged institutions. Just what that impact may be is unclear, but one potential is that community members may have access to more services and in greater numbers than in the past.

REFERENCES

American Association of Community Colleges. n.d. "About community colleges." www.aacc.nche.edu/AboutCC.

Becker, Carl L. 1943. *Cornell University: Founders and the founding.* Ithaca, NY: Cornell University Press.

Bok, Derek. 2013. *Higher education in America.* Princeton, NJ: Princeton University Press.

Brubacher, John S., and Willis Rudy. 1997. *Higher education in transition: A history of American colleges and universities.* New Brunswick, NJ: Transaction Publishers.

Carlyle, Thomas. 1877. *Characteristics.* Boston, MA: J. R. Osgood and Company.

Carpenter, Kenneth E. 1986. *The first 350 years of the Harvard University Library.* Cambridge, MA: Harvard University Library.

"CCC2NAU: Twice the value." 2008. *Arizona Daily Sun,* August 5, A1.

Ferruolo, Stephen C. 1988. "*Parisius-Paradisus:* The city, its schools, and the origin of the University of Paris." In *The university and the city,* edited by Thomas Bender, 22–41. Oxford: Oxford University Press.

Grossman, Hal B. 2011. A comparison of the Progressive era and the Depression years: Societal influences on predictions of the future of the library, 1895–1940. *Libraries and the Cultural Record* 46, no. 1: 102–128.

Handlin, Oscar, and Mary Handlin. 1970. *The American college and American culture.* New York: McGraw-Hill.

Harris, Rosalind, and Dreamal Worthen. 2004. Working through the challenges: Struggle and resilience within historically black land grant institutions. *Education* 124, no. 3: 447–455.

Hyde, J. K. 1988. "Universities and cities in medieval Italy." In *The university and the city,* edited by Thomas Bender, 13–21. Oxford: Oxford University Press.

Johnson, Gerald W. 1958. "Should our colleges educate?" In *The college years,* edited by Auguste C. Spectorsky. New York: Hawthorn Books.

Kamenetz, Anya. 2015. "DIY U: Higher education goes hybrid." In *Remaking college: The changing ecology of higher education,* edited by Michael W. Kirst and Mitchell L. Stevens. Stanford, CA: Stanford University Press.

Kivinen, Osmo, and Petri Poikus. 2006. Privileges of *universitas magistrorum et scolarium* and their justification in charters of foundation from the 13th to 21st centuries. *Higher Education* 52, no. 2: 185–213.

Lucas, Christopher J. 1994. *American higher education: A history.* New York: St. Martin's Press.

Maynard, Meleah. 2016. "Awesomely urban: The metropolitan setting of the Twin Cities campus is increasingly helping shape its mission and identity." *Minnesota Alumni* 116, no. 1: 22–29.

President's Commission on Higher Education. 1948. *Higher education for democracy: A report of the President's Commission on Higher Education.* New York: Harper and Brothers.

Reyhner, Jon, and Joanne Eder. 2004. *American Indian education: A history.* Norman: University of Oklahoma Press.

Sinwell, Carol A. Pender. 2008. "Post-transfer students' perception of a community college's institutional effectiveness in preparing them for persistence to baccalaureate attainment." Doctor of Education dissertation, University of Virginia Curry School of Education.

Stille, Charles J. 1878. "University of Pennsylvania." In *The college book,* edited by Charles F. Richardson and Henry A. Clark, 122–130. Boston, MA: J. R. Osgood and Company.

Thelin, John R. 1982. *Higher education and its useful past.* Cambridge, MA: Schenkman Publishing.

Vinton, Frederick. 1878. "The College of New Jersey." In *The college book,* edited by Charles F. Richardson and Henry A. Clark. Boston, MA: J. R. Osgood and Company.

CHAPTER 3

Faculty

How many of us have jobs that have great flexibility in work schedule, with rarely any two days alike, in which you must engage in lifelong learning, and it is often a pleasure to arrive at work? Among those with such good fortune are faculty in higher education. As we will discuss later in this chapter, it is quite challenging to secure a full-time, tenure-track position, but for those who do, the rewards are great.

Contrary to a widely held belief among the public, faculty members *do* work long hours, longer than anyone other than colleagues and family members realizes. Just doing a reasonably adequate job of preparing for each class session takes substantially longer than the public would believe possible. All good instructors regardless of level—from preschool to postdoctorate —devote large blocks of time just to staying current with developments in the subjects they teach. For excellent teachers, that time commitment is even greater.

In addition to the research responsibilities that necessitate keeping up to date, there is pressure that comes from students to be "current." For some students, anything older than tomorrow is out-of-date. There are probably few instructors or public services librarians who have not heard more than once some variation of the comment, "I couldn't find *any-thing* online about _____. It must not exist." As an example, and not an isolated incident, one academic library decided to place all its bound journals into remote storage due to space limitations. There was a fear from staff that retrieving these journals would lead to a significant workload increase during student term paper times. That problem never materialized. Students had long before ceased looking at journal back files. If they did not find what they needed online, they looked no further.

Perhaps this is the difference between what's good and what's good enough. For many undergraduates, finding a handful of sources online may be sufficient, but for faculty and graduate student research, it is essential to cast a much wider net to conduct thorough research. And as it turned out, the only complaints about the journal move came from senior faculty and some graduate students. Certainly, there are a host of ideas which are still

 KEEP IN MIND

One skill that academic librarians and staff need to develop is the ability to deal effectively with the occasional faculty member who has a rather strong sense of self-importance. At times, it is challenging to control the frustration at what seems to be, or is, a special privilege or service that no one else should receive. We touch on this type of "diplomacy" in the chapters on library services.

useful that someone long ago expressed, but continual student pressure for the "new" keeps faculty on their toes.

Other factors necessitating lifelong learning have been the ever-increasing cross-disciplinary nature of scholarship and the requirement for collaborative work. There has always been some degree of cross-fertilization; however, the rate of crossover research has been steadily growing for more than fifty years. This expansion requires one to have a sound understanding of one or more fields that were not the focus of one's original training. A good example of this development is archaeology. Fifty years ago, an archaeologist would normally excavate a site with a small crew of students and perhaps some volunteers. Today a field crew often consists not only of students and volunteers but also of several specialists (which could include a paleobotanist and perhaps a soil, a ceramics, or a lithics specialist) in addition to the archaeologist. A successful project requires the archaeologist to know enough about the other specialties and to understand the different agendas of each area to maintain a collaborative effort. It also calls for leadership and management skills that probably were not part of the archaeologist's academic course of study.

Today's archaeologist not only is required to stay current with many library databases in various disciplines but also needs to know how to access materials through various research institutional repositories, most often operated by the library. Theses repositories provide access to data sets that may be useful when engaging in fieldwork. For libraries, interdisciplinary collaboration expands the range of resources to which they must provide access and the type of services they offer to faculty and their students. We will explore collections and library services in much greater detail later in this book.

FACULTY RESPONSIBILITIES

Since the late nineteenth century, U.S. postsecondary institutions regardless of type have had three broad categories of faculty responsibility: teaching, research, and service. How much emphasis is placed on each category depends on the institutional type. As Burton Clark (1993) noted, "The academic profession is a multitude of academic tribes and territories" (p. 163). As a result, "disciplinary location and institutional locations together compose the primary matrix of induced and enforced similarities and differences among American academics" (p. 164). These factors play a role in how much emphasis the institution places on the preceding responsibilities.

Michelle Toews and Ani Yazedjian (2007) likened the handling of the responsibilities to the job of a circus ringmaster for which newcomers to the profession must master a sharp learning curve. Toews and Yazedjian suggested that the first two responsibilities are the main acts. Research and scholarly activities are akin to a high-wire performer or acrobats providing the "wow" factor that attracts the attention of colleagues and the public. Their suggestion that teaching is analogous to being an animal trainer may seem a tad harsh; however, anyone with teaching experience, at any level, recognizes that there is an element of truth in their view. Service, following the circus analogy, calls in the clowns: "They are a distraction between the main acts (research and teaching), but would be sorely missed if they were not part of the show" (p. 114).

Although life in academia is not really a circus, Toews and Yazedjian's analogy does suggest the challenges faculty face. Having experienced these pressures firsthand, we know one often feels like a juggler trying to keep four balls in motion—teaching, research, service, and, if one is lucky, something of a personal life. Randy Pausch (2007), a computer science professor at Carnegie Mellon whose "Last Lecture" gained worldwide attention before he died of pancreatic cancer, described the hard work it takes to be successful: "Junior faculty members used to come up to me and say, 'Wow, you got tenure early; what's your secret?' I said, 'It's pretty simple, call me any Friday night in my office at 10 o'clock and I'll tell you.'"

A faculty member in a doctorate-granting institution experiences heavy pressure to be equally effective in the entire triumvirate, but research had better be top-notch. Anything less will lead to an early departure. Master's institutions come closest to having a balance among the three obligations. Baccalaureate schools place their emphasis on teaching and service, with scholarly activity as an added bonus; it may even carry some institutional rewards. Associate degree organizations focus almost exclusively on teaching and service; any research performed is unexpected, not required, and likely uncompensated. As we will discuss later in this chapter, all types of institutions are increasingly relying on adjunct faculty positions, which are typically part-time, are temporary, and fill teaching needs only.

New faculty members must also recognize the needs of the institution and be able to adjust their focus appropriately, which can be somewhat overwhelming. We will discuss later in this chapter opportunities for new faculty to grow into their roles with the support of mentors as well as campus resources such as teaching and learning centers (TLCs). In talking about the future of campus faculty development initiatives, Austin and Sorcinelli (2013) describe the importance of helping faculty "learn to use technology in new ways, conduct more expansive and thorough assessments of student learning, connect their work more fully to the broader community, and find ways to be more productive and efficient in their efforts to deepen student learning" (p. 89). Thus, the three roles of teaching, research, and service are ever-expanding and evolving.

This chapter is not just background information about the faculty environment. When academic librarians have faculty status, they often face the same or similar performance expectations. We will explore the issue in more depth in chapter 13.

 KEEP IN MIND

Faculty status, or something similar to that status, for academic librarians carries with it all or almost all of the same requirements as for teaching faculty. Sometimes there is a tendency to think only of what are perceived to be the faculty "perks" when librarians seek to achieve a status similar to that of teaching faculty. A Chinese proverb goes something like this: "Be careful what you wish for because you might get it."

Service

We start our coverage of faculty responsibilities with the concept of service because it is probably the least understood outside higher education and because it receives the least credit within institutions. Although a necessary element of the faculty role, when it comes to promotion or compensation, service rarely carries much weight. As the title of Audrey Jaeger and Courtney Thornton's (2006) article aptly stated, "Neither Honor nor Compensation: Faculty and Public Service."

What is acceptable service from a college or university perspective? There is no simple answer to this question. There are both internal and external aspects to service that may or may not count toward promotion and tenure. In terms of external service, one can trace the expectation that university employees provide service to the community back to its roots in the land-grant institutions and the Wisconsin Idea that we mentioned in chapter 2. In the case of land-grant institutions, service to state citizens was mandated by the Morrill Act. Dan Butin (2007) stated that in terms of service at land-grant institutions, "the boundaries of the university are contiguous with the boundaries of the state" (p. 34). He went on to note that until rather recently even land-grant schools had been rather lax in providing much in the way of new community services. Certainly extension programs were created shortly after the institution was founded, but not too much more was done at that point. With public funds stretched thinner all the time and community members expecting greater accountability from institutions receiving public assistance, higher education institutions are more frequently giving back through community lectures and programs, sports and science camps, exhibits and performances, and other activities of benefit to the greater community. Sternberg (2014) emphasized the importance of strengthening the relationship between institutions and communities, particularly focusing on land-grants:

> Members of great land-grant institutions are connected to the communities in which they reside. They do not and cannot become "a world apart." If anything, a land-grant should be the opposite of an ivory tower. It should be an institution engaged with the world and actively seeking through its scholarship, teaching, and outreach to address the problems of the world. (p. 388)

It seems the recent emphasis on volunteerism has given rise to more community service. An increasing number of colleges and universities now require their students to engage in some volunteer work prior to graduation, often referred to as *service learning*. One now also sees community service mentioned on institutional websites and on the covers of alumni magazines.

However, in terms of compensation and promotion of faculty, this type of community service often does not count for much unless it is a priority of the institution, such as involving a greater number of students in service learning projects in the community. Even then, much more emphasis is still placed on the roles of teaching and research, which we will address in the following sections of this chapter.

One gray area when it comes to service is "consulting," which some faculty engage in fairly regularly. Is it a service (free) or a second job (fee)? Even a fee-based consultancy can,

 KEEP IN MIND

By *service*, we mean the activities that faculty and staff, including librarians, engage in outside their primary job responsibilities. Service activities that are of interest to the academy and that may carry modest weight when it comes to performance appraisal time tend to fall into two broad categories: institutional service and public or community service. Institutional service generally involves campus governance, a topic we explore in more depth in chapter 6. Community service takes many forms, which we'll discuss in this section.

FROM THE AUTHORS

Evans had a staff member who wanted the fact that he engaged in recycling listed as one of his services to the university. Needless to say, this did not happen. However, what if he had said that he was a Scout troop leader or that he was serving as a volunteer for a community organization? That might have warranted a notation in his personnel file, but it would not have been likely to impact his compensation or promotion prospects.

at times, be a service in the sense intended by the institution's community relations goals. Libby Morris (2007) identified some of the significant questions to think about when deciding what is and what is not community service:

> [D]o our students sense our respect for the clients and collaborators? . . . Do they see reciprocity in our service, who benefits and who gains? Do we take more than we give in community partnerships and applied research? . . . Are we enacting ethical behaviors from which our students learn? (pp. 248–249)

Morris's questions suggest that some faculty and administrators view service and consulting as enhancing the learning experience because each brings "real world" issues into their classrooms.

One might well ask what impact service could have on a library. There are a number of impacts, but two will serve as examples. First is the question of how much support the library should give service activities of individual faculty members. Second is the additional library services and resources required when faculty members engage in institutionally sponsored activities (a small-business assistance program, for example) that may call for both library services and resources.

Internal service is, in some ways, more important than external service. As we will explore in chapter 6, internal service is a critical element in university governance. The most common form of internal service is committee work. Committee work is often viewed as one of the major banes of the workplace in general; within academia, it is a part of the culture, like it or not. A significant problem arises, however, especially in doctorate-granting institutions. As Jaeger and Thornton (2006) stated, "Increased prominence of research enterprise and lack of rewards for public service leads to a socialization of faculty away from public service. . . . For these reasons, faculty at land grant institutions may receive mixed messages about their role in fulfilling the institution's articulated

KEEP IN MIND

All categories of library staff may be called on to serve on institutional committees from time to time. When librarians have something similar to faculty status, they will be called on for even greater service. Committee work takes time, and if the library does not factor such time consideration into planning workloads, especially for library faculty who have to staff reference desks, timely virtual reference, or reference by appointment, then library service performance problems may result.

public service mission" (p. 346). Although Jaeger and Thornton were writing about "public" service rather than institutional service, their point applies to either type of service.

Anyone spending any time in an academic institution will hear, with some regularity, complaints about having to serve on "yet another committee." This applies to almost all full-time university staff, not just teaching faculty, and is a common complaint of untenured faculty who often appear to be given more than an average committee workload. While on the tenure track, it can be hard to say no to the myriad requests to serve on committees that will likely come the way of the untenured faculty member. Seltzer (2015) offered some suggestions for women in particular, such as negotiating more and asking for help. The problem is that untenured faculty face serious time challenges when dealing with the "up or out" aspect of tenure. We will explore this concept and its time limits later in this chapter.

Teaching

Teaching, like service, is complex. Classroom time is a fraction of the total effort that goes into effective teaching at any educational level. Earlier in this chapter we noted the preparation time that any good teacher must engage in as well as the need to keep current with developments in his teaching areas. Further time demands include not only holding office hours (often a mandated amount based on classroom hours) but also advising, mentoring, preparing tests, and, last but not least, grading students' work.

Certainly it is possible to do some of these chores during office hours when not meeting with students. However, good teachers usually have a steady flow of students whose needs often exceed in-person or online office hours, so additional sessions are often scheduled at mutually acceptable times.

Another time commitment, especially at institutions offering graduate degrees, is working one-on-one with students on what might be broadly thought of as independent projects. The best teachers usually have a number of independent study requests every term. Rarely is this work thought of as part of the teaching load. Such work is taken into account in terms of promotion and compensation; however, given its unpredictable frequency, it normally would not reduce a faculty member's formal course load. Most baccalaureate institutions have honors or capstone requirements that may also call for one-on-one teaching. Thesis and dissertation advising activities are likewise not generally considered part of the teaching load, and, again, the best professors tend to have the greatest number of requests.

These factors should suggest that teaching load is a perennial issue at most institutions. Part of the problem lies in the fact that there is no national standard for "contact hours" for

 KEEP IN MIND

For libraries, the teaching of information literacy courses can raise some of the same workload issues, particularly given the importance of and increasing demand for information literacy instruction. Some institutions require an information literacy course or at least require components of information literacy to be taught within the general education curriculum. We will discuss this important topic in more depth in the chapter on library services.

any type of institution or discipline. Overall an institution may have some general guidelines, but there will be variations across disciplines. Another factor is that some professors are viewed by the students as more willing to take on independent student work. The process is similar to how students informally evaluate teaching and make efforts to avoid taking classes from teachers they believe are ineffective. Such factors play a role in departmental politics and can make a department chairperson's work of preparing balanced and effective teaching schedules more complex and frustrating. One has to strive for balance while recognizing that there will be performance differences that may impact assessment of departmental quality and result in staff resentment about workloads.

The foregoing suggests that not all faculty members are good, much less great, when it comes to teaching, both in and out of the classroom. Perhaps one reason is that there are a number of methods for handling a course—lecture, discussion, laboratory, case, fieldwork, small group, and workshop to mention a few—and some teachers are better at one or two options. Online courses bring a whole new set of challenges as well.

Since the 1960s, an increasing number of institutions have developed teaching and learning centers (TLCs) and related services to help individual faculty members assess and improve their teaching styles. Schumann and his colleagues (2013) described the collaboration of TLC personnel and faculty as a co-creation of value, specifically "faculty developers and stakeholders working together as a learning community with shared responsibility to design, implement, and assess the experiences necessary to encourage instructors to enhance their knowledge of learning and continuously improve their teaching skills" (p. 24). Ultimately, though, it is up to an individual faculty member to take advantage of such services.

For some faculty members, the idea that they might benefit from such services never crosses their minds; for others, it may be something akin to losing face by admitting they could use some assistance. More often than not, there is some mentoring effort within a department. A senior faculty member works with a junior member who is having trouble, but often even the best teachers do not realize just what makes their teaching special.

Another reality is that few graduate programs, especially at the doctoral level, offer courses in how to teach, much less require them. This is a rather interesting fact given that elementary and secondary school teachers receive extensive training in how to plan and present course material. This may account for the fact that the lecture is still the predominant teaching method, still rather like its medieval beginnings. Julia Hughes (2008) in writing about the teaching-research pressures made the following point:

> If demonstrated competence as a researcher is the predominant requirement of university faculty, then it should not be surprising that the lecture has remained the dominant pedagogical form. Within the traditional lecture, the speaker is expected to present his or her knowledge to those listening, something that most people with a Ph.D. should be more or less competent at doing. . . . Based on this assumption, the preparation of faculty for their teaching roles may be adequate. But is lecturing necessarily synonymous with teaching? (p. 52)

Understanding what method will work best for what group of individuals is essential for high-quality teaching. However, at graduate institutions, the research component tends to dominate the situation with almost no regard for teaching skills. Holding a teaching assignment while a graduate student does not necessarily translate into knowing how to be an effective teacher, particularly given all the pressures on graduate students to complete their own course work and work on their thesis or dissertation in addition to meeting the requirements of their teaching assignment.

Some critics of higher education teaching methods have a saying: "A teacher should be a guide at the side rather than a sage on the stage." Some teachers find this jingle insulting. Certainly anyone who has spent time in higher education has encountered the egotistic, self-important blowhard who does in fact act like the sage on the stage. However, for every egotist, there are hundreds of teaching faculty who do act the part of guide; these non-sages are the individuals who understand the linkage between teaching and learning. Mary Burgan (2006) made the point that "the opposition of saging and staging to teaching and learning derives from a set of pressing concerns in an age of rapid change in higher education. Among the most critical of these concerns are student diversity and the uses and possibilities of technology, each of which has played a part in re-centering higher education pedagogy from teachers to students" (p. 31).

To provide visual relief to lectures, many of us who teach or give presentations use software packages to create slide decks and other multimedia learning objects. These can be extremely time-consuming to prepare, if they are to look professional and relate directly to the course content. Unfortunately, few of us realize that slide packages in particular are presenter-oriented rather than audience-oriented. As a result, our slides tend to help the presenter stay on track rather than enhance the *content* of the presentation. We may have graphics, video, and perhaps some interactive elements, but have we added real information and value? It's important to not focus too heavily on the technology and instead use that technology as a communication tool to aid in learning. In addition to instructional design assistance available from campus TLCs (where applicable), there are numerous guides to creating and delivering more effective presentations, such as *Beyond Bullet Points* (Atkinson, 2011). Guides for moving course content online are available as well, notably *Teaching Online* (Ko and Rossen, 2010). These guides in no way replace the knowledge and experience that instructional designers and technologists can bring to designing course materials, but such guides can be quite helpful in making the transition to online teaching.

Certainly technology has changed teaching in significant ways over the past thirty years. It has radically changed the way in which institutions think about and deliver all courses, particularly those taught online. Technology has again played a role in allowing higher education to become less "place" oriented and more virtual in nature, somewhat like its earliest phases when "place" was transient, as we discussed in chapter 2.

Looking at in-person classes first, campuses are increasingly offering technology-equipped, learner-focused classrooms that allow for a variety of active learning and teaching methods as well as lectures. "Smart" classrooms, technology-enabled active learning (TEAL) classrooms, and other types of spaces that contain technology and easily rearranged furnishings are often collectively called *collaborative learning spaces*. The intention with these spaces is to create an environment that provides maximum flexibility to encourage inquiry learning among students. Beichner and Cevetello (2013) noted this aspect as well

---

‖‖‖ **CHECK THIS OUT**

Although it is some years old now, a good source for assistance in the use of presentation software as a teaching tool is E. R. Tufte's *Cognitive Style of PowerPoint* (Cheshire, CT: Graphic Press, 2006).

as some of the downsides to these spaces—namely, that faculty may need to develop new teaching methods, redesign teaching materials, and be comfortable with the technology. In this kind of environment, technical support is essential, and faculty should feel comfortable working with the campus TLC (where applicable) to develop appropriate learning strategies. Interestingly, in the most recent EDUCAUSE Center for Analysis and Research (ECAR) survey of undergraduate students and technology use, student respondents most preferred lecture as an in-person class learning activity over discussion, quizzes, group projects, and other interactive classroom activities (Dahlstrom et al., 2015). It will be interesting to see if this preference changes over time.

From a virtual point of view, technology has opened up new audiences for institutions as well as new revenue streams. An individual can earn a degree from a number of fully accredited institutions by successfully completing all or almost all the class work online. Being able to do the work whenever and wherever one desires has increased higher education opportunities for many individuals who otherwise would not have been able to physically go to campus and work within the institution's schedule.

👥 FROM THE AUTHORS

Greenwell has worked with several new librarians who never set foot on the campus where they earned their Master of Library and Information Science degree. Greenwell attended a conference with one new librarian who eagerly suggested they visit her alma mater for the first time. They did, and that new librarian proudly posted online some photos of herself visiting her campus library in person for the first time, though she had used it many times while acquiring her degree.

On a similar note, Greenwell has taught in a graduate program at an institution she has never seen in person, nor has she ever visited the city it is in.

Another opportunity the online environment presents is hybrid courses (i.e., courses that contain both online and in-person elements). This combination allows some material to be covered outside class time and makes possible a variety of formats for learning and responding. An increasing number of students are taking hybrid courses, and in the most recent ECAR survey of undergraduate student technology use and preferences, 79 percent of student respondents (n = 50,274) reported that they learn best in a hybrid environment (Dahlstrom et al., 2015). Of the faculty respondents (n = 13,276), 56 percent reported that they used blended teaching strategies that include in-person and online components (Brooks, 2015). It will be interesting to watch this trend over the next few years to see if more faculty introduce blended concepts into in-person courses; ECAR's annual surveys provide a good picture of how students and faculty use technology in relation to learning. For more information, see https://library.educause.edu/resources/2015/8/2015-student-and-faculty-technology-research-studies.

Since the previous edition of this book, more studies have been conducted to compare the time commitment for teaching the same course in online and in-person formats. In a thoroughly designed study, Cavanaugh (2006) found that his preparation time for the online version of the same course in the same term was ten times greater than that for the in-person class, and overall the online course took a total of ninety-three more hours. Van de Vord and Pogue (2012) examined twelve studies that looked at this same question, and the outcome was split roughly into thirds, with teaching online taking more time, teaching in person taking more time, or both being about the same. It's important to note that the time variation could of course be greater or lesser depending on the subject taught, the number of students, the level of students, the number of assessments, the amount of feedback, and so forth.

Udermann (2015) suggested that the perception of online teaching taking more time could have a variety of reasons. Faculty members are generally encouraged to completely develop an online course up front, whereas that approach is less common with an in-person course. If a faculty member hasn't prepped a new course in a number of years, she may have forgotten how time intensive it is to move even a familiar course into an online environment. In developing an online course, the faculty member might work with an instructional designer and be asked to evaluate all the learning outcomes, assessments, and instructional tools more thoroughly than perhaps was done in the past. If the faculty member is not comfortable with the technology being used for the online course, that lack of familiarity would create a time-consuming learning curve as well, though the same could be said for using new technologies for in-person teaching. Finally, some faculty feel the need to "check in" with the online course multiple times per day, which would not happen in an in-person environment. Faculty might feel the pressure to be "always on," and Udermann suggested setting boundaries by clearly defining expectations to students and managing one's schedule in such a way as to alleviate constant connectedness. Although time consumption likely is part perception and part reality, clearly such time differences have an impact on faculty workloads and need to be considered.

Online courses also raise the interesting question of intellectual property—who "owns" the course? No one worried about this question when a professor taught an in-person course. If you, as instructor, spend long hours putting together what turns out to be a highly successful online course, do you own the rights to that course, and could you make it available to other institutions for a fee that would not be shared by your home institution? Different institutions have different answers, but they tend to expect at least some ownership of the course material.

Successful teaching takes time that far exceeds the class time. Good instructors understand the linkage between teaching and learning, share their enthusiasm for the subject, mentor students, and make themselves available to students as much as possible. These points apply to any teaching, including instruction by librarians, which we will discuss in more detail in chapter 12.

 KEEP IN MIND

Online education programs, whatever their format, do present some service challenges for academic libraries. Online degree programs make the concept of 24/7 library service just a tad more complex. Accrediting agencies do look closely at how effectively the library serves online learners.

Research

Without question, the German academic model has played a major role in the development of U.S. higher education since the end of the nineteenth century. A rather unkind saying about academic research, but one containing more than a grain of truth, is that research leads to fewer and fewer people knowing more and more about less and less. The grain of truth has implications for academic libraries—more about these later in this chapter.

Today there is a generally accepted belief that research and teaching are complementary activities, the basic concept from the early German universities. New insights inform teaching and can lead to valuable developments for society in general. Teaching is what generates interest in some students to become the next generation of researchers, thus starting another cycle of research. Rosovsky (1990) discussed the need for both activities and explained why students should seek teachers who not only engage in research but also are good teachers. He contended that this situation (the good teacher-researcher) leads to the greatest learning opportunities—essentially such teacher-researchers are the best "guides" because they demonstrate the potential of research for the long-term benefit of society.

▓▓▓ CHECK THIS OUT

An outstanding book that every teacher should read is Kenneth Bain's *What the Best College Teachers Do* (Cambridge, MA: Harvard University Press, 2004).

At its most basic academic meaning, research is a process that either brings to light new information or revises a generally accepted conclusion. Research, in conjunction with new ways of thinking, is a special characteristic of academia. It is what attracts people to the academy and keeps them working hard to contribute something in return. By now you probably realize that few, if any, simple concepts exist in academia. So, no surprise, research not only is complex to carry out successfully but the manner of thinking about the activity is also complicated. This is not the book to explore the hundreds if not thousands of variations in research methodology. Creswell (2013) provided a solid overview of qualitative, quantitative, and mixed methods research for those who want to delve further into research methodology.

There is a widespread, if informal, accepted matrix that broadly categorizes academic research—pure versus applied and hard versus soft. These categories do provide a broad structure for thinking about academic research from a library point of view. Hard, pure research tends to be in the "hard sciences" (chemistry, for example) and tends to be journal-focused. Pure, soft research tends to be in the other sciences, which are also generally journal-focused. Hard, applied disciplines are a mix of sciences and social sciences; these researchers use a combination of journals and monographs in their work. Soft, applied research is generally found in the humanities and draws heavily on monographs and, to a

 KEEP IN MIND

Although many within higher education might publicly deny it, there is an informal pecking order when assessing academic research, at least when it comes to questions of promotion, compensation, and special recognition. If faced with the task of ranking research in terms of the matrix, the order would be pure-hard, applied-hard, pure-soft, and applied-soft among faculty at most institutions.

lesser degree, journals. Knowing who is doing what type of research is helpful in building library collections.

It is one thing to come up with new insights from one's research and another to have them accepted by one's peers. Until the late nineteenth century, the process of acceptance was slow and depended on many face-to-face discussions with one's peers. We see a remnant of this process in the thesis and dissertation defense. A final defense of one's thesis with the advisory committee is typical, and anyone knowing the time and place of the examination may attend and ask the candidate questions about the research. This is one example of what we now label *scholarly communication.*

 KEEP IN MIND

University presses' primary market is academic libraries. Without that market, many UPs would fold because there are generally too few individual buyers to generate the necessary income.

Daniel Coit Gilman, founder of Johns Hopkins University (1878), believed a major responsibility of universities was to advance humankind's knowledge *and* to disseminate that knowledge. At the time, the notion of disseminating new knowledge beyond the lecture hall was novel in the United States. Being a realist, Gilman knew that what was a thriving commercial publishing industry was most unlikely to undertake publishing research findings due to the limited market for such material—risks would be too high and sales too low to generate a profitable return. His solution to the dissemination challenge was to establish the Johns Hopkins University Press to fulfill the publisher's role. The press's first two publications were journals, which were later followed by monographs. The number of such presses grew along with the number of institutions offering doctoral degrees. University presses (UPs) stopped growing in the 1970s when institutional financial difficulties impacted their sales. Essentially, this curtailment occurred when a majority of libraries cut back on their book and journal purchases because academic libraries were the major customers of academic presses.

Since the first UPs began operating, most research and doctoral institutions have established similar operations. One special aspect of such presses is their nonprofit status. As a result, they are linked to the institution's mission of serving the general good rather than generating a maximum profit. As Pratt (2015) put it, UPs "are central to the grand theme

 KEEP IN MIND

There are many definitions of *scholarly communication.* At its most basic, it is the process by which scholars let others know about their research results. A sound definition comes from ALA's Association of College and Research Libraries:

Scholarly communication is the system through which research and other scholarly writings are created, evaluated for quality, disseminated to the scholarly community, and preserved for future use. The system includes both formal means of communication, such as publication in peer-reviewed journals, and informal channels, such as electronic listservs. (2003)

of things academic and their value cannot be measured by the spreadsheet alone" (p. 44). This is not to say that such presses do not hope that every title they publish will break even. Should a title do better than that, the added revenue goes toward putting out additional titles rather than increasing owner equity or shareholder dividends.

In summer 2016, Kirch reported that although only one UP was currently in danger of closing, others were managing to stay afloat largely because of their own revenue, unable to rely as heavily on institutional support, particularly in the form of public funding. To be successful, some UPs have gotten more creative, whether publishing scholarly titles that might generate slightly more popular interest or devising models to deal with electronic books. Fordham University Press's regional imprint, Empire State Editions, has contributed greatly to the press's growth in the past few years (Pratt, 2015). The University Press of Kentucky was rather innovative in launching a social media campaign in which owners of print editions could post a "selfie" with the book and receive free access to the e-book version in return. This campaign generated some free publicity as well as goodwill among the albeit small market of individuals interested in UP books (Rogers, 2013). Certainly there are opportunities for and examples of collaboration between UPs and their campus libraries as well, such as by making UP back file content available through a library repository. In some cases, the UP may be connected with the library organizationally, a trend that appeared on the rise at an Association of Research Libraries (ARL) summit of library deans and press directors in early 2016.

Publishing scholarly material, especially scientific items, is generally more costly than other categories. Not only do many scholarly titles require high-quality graphics, they often call for special characters and symbols. Scholarly publishers (UPs and professional associations) often employ a publishing subsidy fee to try to break even on their publications. A fairly common fee in the scientific journal area is an article processing charge (APC), also known as a page charge or a publication fee. Authors pay these fees to publishers, and the charges are rather significant.

Some might wonder about this cost control approach. Is it not the same as vanity publishing? Vanity publishing requires only that an individual have money enough to cover the printing and binding costs; there is no review of the manuscript by peers or the publisher and thus no quality control. There are at least two important differences between vanity and scholarly publishing subsidies. The most significant difference is that, unlike vanity publications, a scholarly manuscript undergoes a rigorous peer review process, or "refereed review." Reviewers are other academics who specialize in the field that the manuscript covers. They are asked to assess the content and its accuracy as well as its overall significance and, most important, whether it should be published. Thus the review process provides a measure of quality control—essentially a method of acting as an "honest broker" of the information put forth in the name of the dissemination of quality research. The subsidy comes into play only after the manuscript has been accepted for publication.

 KEEP IN MIND

Having a strong collection of refereed journals in the fields of faculty interest is an essential library service, though the rising cost of scholarly communication makes that function challenging.

The second difference is that the market for printed scholarly material is limited and production costs are high, even when the referees are not paid a reading fee. The high costs, again, are what drive the per-page charge. Serving on a scholarly publisher's editorial board is considered a form of service to higher education as well as a form of peer recognition of one's standing in the field. This suggests, and it is often the case, that reviewers are senior academics who have a track record of publishing. Refereeing does carry something of a quality stamp.

However, there is a danger, given who is selected to be a reviewer, that biases can impact the flow of new or contradictory research. Publishers typically attempt to control such influence by using an anonymous (double-blind) process—the author(s) name(s) and institutional information are redacted from the manuscript, and the reviewers' feedback goes to the author(s) without the name(s) of the reviewer(s). Overall, the process works well when dealing with broad topics, such as personnel management, academic librarianship, or information technology, for example. However, the system is not nearly as effective when it comes to very narrow topics (paleobotany in the Southwest, for example). The fact that advanced research results in fewer people knowing more about less leads to a tiny pool of potential authors and reviewers. The small pool means it is relatively easy to know who wrote what, as either author or reviewer, based on the content. Regardless of its shortcomings, refereeing nonetheless provides a measure of quality control.

An interesting outcome of scholarly publishers using a subsidy system was that a few commercial publishers saw an opportunity to enter the field, especially by working with professional associations in producing journals, memoirs, and conference proceedings. Academic libraries' materials budgets were rather quickly impacted by the change of publishers as the cost of the publications escalated. Journal subscription prices became at least dual, with one price charged for the individual and another, much higher price for the institution.

Today, the scholarly communication process is again undergoing significant changes, particularly with the growing open access (OA) publishing movement. Many of these publications are certainly of the quality of commercially published materials because they are often refereed to the same standards. The difference is that they are readily available to anyone. Some faculty, especially those undergoing the tenure process, remain skeptical of this movement, though it is a far more sustainable and equitable model for distributing scholarly research.

Technology of course makes it possible to disseminate information quickly at a modest cost. An early primary purpose of the Internet was to enhance and speed up scholarly communication. In today's online environment, it takes a reasonably sophisticated individual to sort out the good, the bad, the ugly, and the irrelevant material. For students in particular, this process can be particularly challenging, and we will address how academic librarians help when we discuss information literacy instruction in chapter 12.

▐▐▐ CHECK THIS OUT

For a brief but solid overview of the history of the open access movement, visit Peter Suber's website at http://legacy.earlham.edu/~peters/fos/overview.htm.

👥 FROM THE AUTHORS

Greenwell has had some lively debates with faculty, particularly those in her doctoral studies, over the merits of open access. Keep in mind that universities "pay" for scholarly content many times over, first by paying faculty, volunteer peer reviewers, and journal editors to research, write, and edit content and then by paying again to access that content from publishers. Without new models of access, the cost of scholarly communication becomes harder for libraries to bear. It will be a challenge for faculty to recognize that specific publications can be high quality even though they may be freely available online. Those publications must have the same level of rigor in acceptance, review, and editing, of course, but as the reputations of those publications rise, Greenwell argues that they should be just as acceptable for tenure as publishing in very expensive journals. It's likely a debate that won't end soon.

THE LADDER AND TENURE

Being a tenured faculty member has benefits not often found in other fields, such as a degree of job security, frequently an opportunity to take paid leave to engage in research (sabbatical), and flexible working hours. In the not-too-distant past, it was a good career choice for the academically inclined. Today the situation is rather different because the job market can be extremely competitive, as illustrated in a *Chronicle of Higher Education* article (June 2013) describing two job searches, one which yielded 117 applicants for a single position in the Ohio University English department, and another in which seventy-one applicants were interested in a single position in the University of Florida linguistics department. Along with fierce competition for jobs, faculty now face additional expectations, such as seeking grant funding or building relationships with donors or supervising staff. These responsibilities might make faculty work seem less palatable, but as we pointed out at the beginning of this chapter, there are not many jobs that are as satisfying.

There are few individuals outside higher education who fully understand the concept of tenure. In fact, many members of the public are highly suspicious of the practice. The suspicions are largely based on a lack of understanding of the concept. Some widely held negative ideas are that tenured faculty are accountable to no one, are lazy and overpaid, are guaranteed a lifetime job, and are getting away with something even if we do not know what that something is. And their teaching performance is almost always bad. Among college students, there is a belief that their favorite teachers are almost always denied tenure. Some untenured faculty harbor suspicions that they are brighter and better teachers than some of their tenured colleagues who may or may not grant them tenure.

None of these ideas is true, at least not most of the time. So what is tenure? It does provide some degree of job security, at least from indiscriminate dismissal. However, as many faculty members have learned, large numbers can be and have been dismissed when the institution declares a financial exigency. Entire departments can be and have been closed down, and in such cases tenure will do nothing to protect one's position.

Originally, tenure was intended to help preserve academic freedom and the German university notion that a professor should be free to explore ideas without outside interference. Thus, a professor may structure and present course content as he sees fit.

Other, less well-known factors supporting the use of tenure are (a) the process does provide a measure of quality control—the period of time before one gains tenure allows the institution to assess the individual's academic performance; (b) it provides a measure of stability in the core faculty—most people are disinclined to undergo a second tenure process, so they tend to stay at the institution that granted the tenure; and (c), to some degree, it helps balance out the higher income an individual might earn in the nonacademic sector by offering a measure of job security.

A general assumption on the part of the public is that anyone teaching at an academic institution is a "professor." Depending on what type of academic institution the teacher is affiliated with, this assumption has a greater or lesser chance of being correct. If the individual is from a baccalaureate institution, there is a good chance that she has a "ladder appointment" and a job title with the word *professor* in it. There are three levels to the ladder or tenure process: assistant professor, associate professor, and professor, sometimes called a full professor. At either graduate- or associate-level institutions (such as community colleges), there is a chance that the individual does not have a job title containing the word *professor*. If she does hold the title, it may be without a similar tenure process seen at doctorate institutions.

Graduate degree schools employ a number of job titles for those who engage in teaching. There are teaching assistants (TAs) at the lowest level of responsibility. They may assist by reading and grading student assignments or, at a slightly higher level of responsibility, monitor or run one or more "lab" sessions for a course. At some institutions, they may

👥 FROM THE AUTHORS

Evans worked at an institution that made no secret of the fact that less than 10 percent of the assistants had a real chance of becoming an associate, at least in that institution. Young PhDs chose to accept an assistant position knowing they would probably have to move on but believing that having the institution's name on their curriculum vitae was well worth the time and effort.

As the authors can attest from personal experience as ladder appointees and from experiences of library staff members who had faculty status, seven years seems generous at the time the "clock" starts ticking. However, the time seems to flash by at lightning speed, especially when one is a new PhD and really teaching for the first time. The first year is almost entirely devoted to trying to get one's courses structured and to understand the organizational culture of the department and college.

As an example from Evans's first year of teaching experience and with what the department called a "light" teaching load, the assignment consisted of two sections of one course for the fall term, two courses for the winter term, and two more courses for the spring term, one of which the department had never before offered. Needless to say, many late nights were spent trying to get the next morning's class material organized. There was precious little time for putting the final touches on the dissertation and getting something ready to submit for publication (naturally in a refereed journal). Certainly there was no time to engage in new research or think about submitting a grant proposal. This experience is not atypical for new assistant professors in their first year of a ladder appointment.

be expected to teach first-year undergraduate students. TAs are often first- or second-year graduate students, and their positions help cover some of their educational expenses. A more responsible teaching position is "instructor," held often by an advanced-level graduate student. Instructors have full responsibility for planning and teaching one or more courses. Another category is "adjunct," which we will discuss in more detail later in this chapter. Adjuncts might also be individuals with full-time jobs who occasionally teach part-time; a good example is the practitioner who works full-time in a library or related organization and teaches in library and information science programs. Somewhat similarly, there are specialists from outside higher education who may have a terminal degree in the field they are teaching—for example, a master of fine arts. Such appointments might be multiyear contracts and carry the title of lecturer. In addition to these standardized categories, some institutions have the additional category of faculty emeritus. The emeritus/emerita title is for the most part honorific and is intended to acknowledge outstanding service to the institution by a retired faculty member.

Associate degree institutions (community colleges) usually do not have the TA category because they do not have a pool of graduate students to draw on. They may, however, have a ladder similar to that of baccalaureate institutions that starts at the instructor rank and ends at professor. Associate degree institutions vary from their counterparts in two other ways: first, it may be possible for a faculty member to achieve the rank of professor without holding a doctorate in the field, and second, as mentioned previously, there likely will not be the same tenure requirements or procedures in place. These institutions may make more use of lecturers and adjunct teachers than other institutions but generally require lecturers and adjuncts to have the same qualifications as their full-time counterparts.

Part-Time/Adjunct Faculty

The part-time/adjunct category needs some fuller discussion because use has been increasing as institutions attempt to control personnel costs. Recent doctoral graduates often have to turn to adjunct or postdoctoral research appointments, something of a holding pattern, as they seek a tenure track appointment. A lesser trend is programs that employ practitioners to teach part-time; librarians serving as adjuncts to teach classes in library and information science master's programs are a good example of this. In the not-too-distant past, some institutions employed the adjunct category as a means of providing multiple course offerings without taking on more full-time teachers. Generally an adjunct position is part-time and provides no benefits beyond the course fee. Even the course fee is tenuous because it is paid only if the course "makes"—that is, it has a predetermined number of enrollees. Lacking the minimum number of enrollees, the class is canceled.

Accreditation bodies tend to take a dim view of what they consider excessive use of part-time appointments, and there are good reasons to worry about the overuse of part-time appointments. First and foremost are quality concerns. Although well-planned programs for part-time teachers can address many of the quality concerns, few institutions have well-planned operations. Part-timers are generally on their own; they seldom get to meet full-time faculty who may have taught the same course. At best the part-timer gets a copy of the course syllabus, which could be quite outdated. Mentoring is rarely in place, and the institution really only assesses course quality on the basis of student evaluation. No full-time staff sit in on a few class sessions of an adjunct's or other part-timer's course to assess the quality of the instruction. Adjuncts rarely are integrated into the department, much less asked to take part in curriculum discussions. They often know little or nothing about the content of other courses and are in no position to advise students. Today, many adjuncts are trying to make a living by teaching several courses at several institutions in the same term. Thus, they are rushing in and out of the classroom as they try to get through traffic from one institution to another.

Climbing the Ladder

Even those who obtain a tenure track appointment do not necessarily have job security. Those on the first rung of the ladder, the rank of assistant professor, may earn job security if all goes well. It is at the second rung, the rank of associate professor, that one usually receives tenure. One may be appointed an associate professor when coming from another institution without tenure but in the expectation that it will be granted rather quickly. This approach provides the department and institution an opportunity to see if there is a "fit."

The final rung is professor (or full professor); at some institutions this rank may have some additional levels, as does the associate rank, such as professor 1, 2, 3, 4, and 5. Promotion to such additional levels involves an assessment of performance rather similar to that of moving from assistant to associate and from associate to full professor. This type of system provides an additional level of quality control, motivation, and protection against becoming the "lazy faculty member" so popular in the public mind. It is also a system that most of the public does not realize exists. Some states require a post-tenure review of all levels of the professoriate. Usually the institution determines the process for the post-tenure review, with the faculty governing body leading the effort.

An assistant professor must prove her academic worth to the tenured faculty in the department in order to gain tenure. Having a ladder appointment as an assistant professor has some added performance pressures over and above the triad of faculty responsibilities. One added pressure in today's environment and especially in some fields such as the sciences is the expectation that the individual will be able to secure research grants from outside the institution. Furthermore, there is time pressure; generally the maximum time frame allowed is seven years. At the end of that time, one either gets tenure or has to leave the institution. There is no guarantee of obtaining tenure, and not everyone does.

Earlier we mentioned that the juggling of obligations and tasks that many faculty members engage in can almost be overwhelming for newcomers. By their third year, the time limit seems to be looming large, and worries something along the lines of "Will I get tenure? What will I do if I don't? What will family and friends think or say if I fail to get it?" begin to creep into their thoughts. We believe that, if one must prioritize library service to faculty—and this is necessary more often than librarians would like—assistant professors are the ones that should get the greatest assistance.

DIVERSITY

We cannot conclude a chapter about faculty and ignore the important issue of faculty diversity. Although women and nonwhite male students have been a growing part of the academic scene for more than 150 years, they make up a small percentage of faculty, tenure track or part-time. The overall picture is that white males continue to make up the majority of today's faculty members.

Given the preponderance of white males at the senior tenured level, most women and faculty of color face additional challenges in their efforts to achieve tenure, not to mention salaries (Bethea, 2015). There appear to be four broad, significant factors that are especially challenging—campus life and climate, tenure and promotion, discrimination, and teaching. As Stanley (2006) wrote, "Some of us believe that the academy is truly a meritocracy and culturally neutral. However, critical race theory shows that understanding truth and merit means challenging concepts that are socially constructed to reflect and benefit the majority" (pp. 724–725). Stanley's article contains seven and a half pages of recommendations to address the challenges, divided between what faculty members might do and what administrators might do. Reviewing the list today, there is still much work to be done.

Higher education must do more than just attempt to enroll an increasingly diverse and international student body. Higher education needs more faculty of color and of diverse backgrounds to serve as role models for students, as researchers, teachers, and colleagues who bring more perspectives and contributions to every conversation. Certainly this holds true for recruiting academic librarians as well.

🛈 KEY POINTS TO REMEMBER

- Faculty members have three broad responsibilities: teaching, research, and service.
- Institutional service in the form of committee work is a requirement of university governance.
- At some institutions—for example, land grant—there is a legal requirement to provide service to the community.
- Teaching loads vary substantially within an institution and by the type of institution.
- Research/scholarly activity is a major responsibility at graduate-level institutions and is considered important, but not required, at lower degree institutions.
- Scholarly work requires having access to large bodies of information about the area of interest as well as disseminating the results of one's own work.
- Research/scholarly activity is a key factor in planning and developing academic library services.
- The issues covered in this chapter may well apply to academic librarians in institutions in which they have a status identical or similar to teaching faculty.

REFERENCES

Association of College and Research Libraries. 2003. "Principles and Strategies for the Reform of Scholarly Communication 1." www.ala.org/acrl/publications/whitepapers/principlesstrategies.

Atkinson, Cliff. 2011. *Beyond bullet points: Using Microsoft PowerPoint to create presentations that inform, motivate and inspire*. Redmond, WA: Microsoft Press.

Austin, Ann, and Mary Dean Sorcinelli. 2013. "The future of faculty development: Where are we going?" In *The breadth of current faculty development: Practitioners' perspectives,* edited by C. William McKee, Mitzy Johnson, William F. Ritchie, and W. Mark Tew. Hoboken, NJ: Jossey-Bass.

Bain, Kenneth. 2004. *What the best college teachers do.* Cambridge, MA: Harvard University Press.

Beichner, Robert, and Joseph Cevetello. 2013. *7 things you should know about collaborative learning spaces.* EDUCAUSE. https://library.educause.edu/~/media/files/library/2013/1/eli7092-pdf.pdf.

Bethea, Dorine. 2015. A dollar short. *Chronicle of Higher Education* 61: 35-39.

Brooks, Christopher D. 2015. *ECAR study of faculty and information technology.* Louisville, CO: EDUCAUSE Center for Analysis and Research.

Burgan, Mary. 2006. In defense of lecturing. *Change* 38, no. 6: 30-34.

Butin, Dan W. 2007. Focusing our aim: Strengthening faculty commitment to community engagement. *Change* 39, no. 6: 34-37.

Cavanaugh, Joseph. 2006. Comparing online time to offline time: The shocking truth. *Distance Education Report* 10, no. 9: 8-9.

Clark, Burton R. 1993. "Faculty differentiation and dispersion." In *Higher education in America,* edited by Arthur Levine, 163-177. Baltimore: Johns Hopkins University Press.

Creswell, John. 2013. *Research design: Qualitative, quantitative, and mixed methods approaches.* New York: Sage.

Dahlstrom, Eden, with D. Christopher Brooks, Susan Grajek, and Jamie Reeves. 2015. *ECAR study of students and information technology.* Louisville, CO: EDUCAUSE Center for Analysis and Research.

Hughes, Julia C. 2008. Challenging the research teaching divide. *Education Canada* 48, no. 1: 52-57.

Jaeger, Audrey, and Courtney Thornton. 2006. Neither honor nor compensation: Faculty and public service. *Educational Policy* 20, no. 2: 345-366.

June, Audrey. 2013. The long odds of the faculty job search. *Chronicle of Higher Education.*

Kirch, Claire. 2016. University presses cope with budget cuts. *Publishers Weekly* 263, no. 23: 7-9.

Ko, Susan, and Daniel Rossen. 2010. *Teaching online: A practical guide.* New York: Routledge.

Morris, Libby. 2007. Faculty power and responsibility. *Innovative Higher Education* 31, no. 2: 81-82.

Pausch, Randy. 2007. *Randy Pausch's last lecture: Really achieving your childhood dreams.* Carnegie Mellon University. https://www.cs.cmu.edu/~pausch/Randy/pauschlastlecturetranscript.pdf.

Pratt, Darrin. 2015. Measuring success: The value of our work can't always be captured in a spreadsheet. *Journal of Scholarly Publishing* 47, no. 1: 44-59.

Rogers, Megan. 2013. Buy one, get one free. *Inside Higher Ed.* https://www.insidehighered.com/news/2013/11/05/university-press-uses-social-media-increase-brand-loyalty.

Rosovsky, Henry. 1990. *The university: An owner's manual.* New York: W. W. Norton.

Schumann, David W., John Peters, and Taimi Olsen. 2013. Cocreating value in teaching and learning centers. *New Directions for Teaching and Learning* 133: 21-32.

Seltzer, Rena. 2015. To find happiness in academe, women should just say no. *Chronicle of Higher Education* 61, no. 41: B12-B13.

Stanley, Christine A. 2006. Coloring the academic landscape. *American Educational Research Journal* 43, no. 4: 701-736.

Sternberg, Robert J. 2014. *The modern land-grant university.* West Lafayette, IN: Purdue University Press.

Suber, Peter. 2015. "Open access overview." Retrieved from http://legacy.earlham.edu/~peters/fos/overview.htm.

Toews, Michelle, and Ani Yazedjian. 2007. The three-ring circus of academia: How to become the ringmaster. *Innovative Higher Education* 32, no. 2: 113-122.

Tufte, E. R. 2006. *Cognitive style of PowerPoint.* Cheshire, CT: Graphic Press.

Udermann, Brian. 2015. Is online teaching more time intensive? *Distance Education Report* 19, no. 22: 3-7.

Van de Vord, Rebecca, and Korolyn Pogue. 2012. Teaching time investment: Does online really take more time than face-to-face? *International Review of Research in Open and Distance Learning* 13, no. 3: 132-146.

CHAPTER 4

Students

W hen academics discuss higher education issues, you are more likely to hear them talking in terms of faculty-student concerns rather than student-faculty concerns. This conception also applies to the order in which we have presented the material in this book. This arrangement is not meant to imply that students are of secondary importance; in fact, they are one of the main reasons that higher education exists! Rather, it is a function of time. The vast majority of students are in residence for four to five years or sometimes more while faculty members are part of the campus community for decades. Because being a student is transitory, and as a group their issues are often evolving, the faculty's long-term concerns tend to carry greater weight. Despite all of that, students ultimately are the primary concern, and it's important to keep that in mind. Likely you are currently a student, and you are our primary concern in writing this book.

We noted in chapter 2 how the post–World War II era radically changed U.S. higher education. The concept of "open to all" enlarged the pool of potential postsecondary students; the concept is particularly appropriate in terms of community colleges given the increasing enrollments there and at other two-year institutions such as technical schools. "Open to all" raised the expectation that higher education would in fact increase student body diversity in gender, race, nationality, and socioeconomic background—creating opportunities for many students to be the first in their family to attend college. "Open to all" brought about the first broad-scale, government-based financial support for undergraduate students. The effects of this concept have been significant; today's student body demographics are quite different from the homogeneous, largely male, and overwhelmingly white and Protestant composition of pre–World War II student bodies. In addition, international students, first-generation college students, and immigrants are increasing campus enrollments and bringing more diverse experiences and ideas to higher education.

If the library is the heart of the campus, there is no question that students are the lifeblood of the institution. Students are why postsecondary institutions exist, and certainly they are the primary source of most institutions' operating budget. Perhaps the greatest

 SOMETHING TO PONDER

How many academic libraries operating in institutions with strong teacher education programs and child-care centers see these preschool children as potential students? How many of them have thought of partnering with child-care centers to establish simple programs for these young children using the libraries' children's literature collection? How many have thought of partnering with schools of education to enlist these students as interns in their libraries? Are such programs expected only of public libraries?

issue facing nearly all students, potential students, and families today is the tremendous challenge in securing funding to begin or continue an education. An even greater challenge is to ultimately pay off what was borrowed. We know that you are likely all too familiar with that concept in your own experience.

The average age of students is changing, as more return to school for initial or second degrees. Many are independent from their parents, and an increasing number have dependents of their own. Some institutions have opened child-care centers for students and employees to help address this challenging issue. No matter their age, many students must commit more time to working at outside jobs to pay tuition and living expenses.

Academia, at least in the public sector, has a social contract with the community, which means enrolling eligible students regardless of socioeconomic status, partnering with secondary schools to ensure that graduates have the academic skills they will need to succeed at the next level, and offering academic programs relevant to society. These three elements raise some interesting challenges for "selective" public institutions, and we will discuss selectivity later in this chapter.

> **IIIII CHECK THIS OUT**
>
> Each fall since 1984, Beloit College in Beloit, Wisconsin, has released its "Mindset List" (www.beloit.edu/mindset/) for incoming freshmen. It is well worth a look each year and is a humbling reminder of how different your own experience likely was from that of today's incoming undergraduate students.

STUDENT THOUGHTS ON HIGHER EDUCATION

Although the student population continues to change, students' long-term objectives have remained fairly consistent. Given the widespread belief that college graduates have substantially higher lifetime incomes than do those who have no college degree, it is no surprise that the primary stated reason for attending college is some variation of securing a well-paying job. A National Center for Education Statistics (NCES) report notes that young adults who obtain a bachelor's degree or higher will earn on average 60 percent more than their counterparts who only completed high school (Kena et al., 2015). In a predictive analysis using data from 1991 through 2010, Carlson and McChesney (2015) found

> **IIIII CHECK THIS OUT**
>
> The UCLA Higher Education Research Institute's Cooperative Institutional Research Program (CIRP) conducts regular surveys of student attitudes and reasons for attending college. Periodically reviewing its findings can provide many insights about the changing student landscape and help in better understanding student needs and preferences. Such information can be highly useful in planning, adjusting, and promoting library services. Throughout this book, we mention many well-conducted annual surveys and reports that we encourage you to follow throughout your career in academic librarianship.

||||| CHECK THIS OUT

Founded in 2008, Project Information Literacy (PIL) conducts numerous research studies to better understand college life today, particularly in how students find, evaluate, and use information. The director, Alison J. Head, conducted several studies related to how recent graduates find, evaluate, and use information in the workplace. These studies help academic librarians better understand today's students as well as provide strong data for making the case for information literacy instruction and overall library support (see www .projectinfolit.org/publications.html).

---

that through 2030, the higher the level of education achieved, the more the person will earn, even during an economic downturn. Their findings led the researchers to suggest that, through 2030, buying power and standard of living will decline for education levels below a bachelor's degree. Although economic gain was a far cry from the original purpose of the liberal arts degree, it is now a major factor. Two other frequently mentioned reasons for college attendance are to become an authority in a subject field and to be able to help others and give back to the community. The academic library can help students be successful with all these goals.

The Cooperative Institutional Research Program (CIRP) at the Higher Education Research Institute at the University of California, Los Angeles (UCLA) has been conducting surveys of entering freshmen since 1966. As of 2015, more than fifteen million freshmen had completed the survey. Gathered from 1,900 baccalaureate institutions, the data provide an excellent sense of freshmen attitudes and behaviors. Not surprisingly, in the 2015 survey, 65 percent expressed concerns about being able to finance their education. Another worrisome finding, which could be an opportunity for the kind of library information literacy instruction that we'll discuss later, was that only 44 percent of respondents indicated that they considered the quality or reliability of information. Much more heartening, though, is that Eagan and his colleagues (2015) reported that 59 percent wanted to improve their understanding of other communities and cultures, and 75 percent felt it was very important to help those in difficulty. The CIRP report is an excellent one to review annually, and it will be interesting to see how freshman attitudes change over time.

👥 FROM THE AUTHORS

Greenwell has worked at a university that sets up rather elaborate recruiting receptions throughout the state. Representatives from every college within the university participate, as do personnel from financial aid, student affairs, dining services, residence life, and many other aspects of campus living. She has represented the library at these events and found it quite rewarding to talk with prospective students and their families. Another important aspect of library participation is involvement with the greater campus community to facilitate building relationships with other college and department personnel, even if that does include long bus trips across the state and too many fast-food dinners.

RECRUITMENT AND ADMISSIONS

Postsecondary institutions engage in an annual recruitment ritual that has become increasingly complex and costly. Admission staffs focus their activities where the institution has traditionally been most successful in recruiting students—visiting high schools, holding receptions, and inviting large numbers of students to come to the campus. A few have elaborate, weeklong, on-campus events for groups of potential students whom they most wish to enroll, such as merit scholars. Recruiting continues to expand its reach with more international recruiting efforts through various means, not to mention some institutions keeping permanent recruiting offices open for certain markets, such as large population centers in the region.

For some individuals within academia, the notion that the institution must market itself is repulsive and inappropriate. Like it or not, however, in today's environment institutions need to prove their worth to society as well as attract clients, customers, or users. Academic institutions compete with one another to at least maintain current enrollments, and competition becomes stronger every year. As noted earlier, enrollments drive revenue, and adequate revenue allows an institution to have greater control over its future.

Recruitment, admission, retention, and fiscal health are interrelated. The idea of student as customer becomes clear when you think about this relationship. Of course it's important to provide a quality educational and social experience to students, but the nationwide arms race over campus amenities is becoming quite extreme in some cases. Climbing walls, water parks, and other high-end recreation facilities are becoming more commonplace (Rubin, 2014), as are residence halls with fixtures and furnishings more lavish than students (or faculty) might find at home. However, this attention to the student experience can produce positive changes by simplifying complicated processes; for example, one university looked to a major grocery chain's customer service model to redesign its advising and registration system (Gardner, 2016).

At the risk of offending some friends working in enrollment management (the current umbrella label for those units that handle recruitment, admissions, and financial aid), we suggest that the financial side of acquiring a degree is somewhat akin to buying a car. Both have a sticker price, but no one expects that to be the final cost. Colleges and universities advertise an official tuition price; however, many students receive a financial aid package that includes some amount of institutional funds, such as a scholarship or grant. Thus, the tuition is "discounted" by some amount, similar to the trade-in amount

---

⦀ CHECK THIS OUT

See Camila Alire's "Word-of-Mouth Marketing: Abandoning the Academic Library Ivory Tower" (*New Library World* 106, no. 11/12 [2007]: 545–551). This article dispels the perception that academic libraries do not need to market their services and resources. It also acquaints readers with the concept of word-of-mouth marketing and its potential for academic libraries as well as provides an academic library marketing success story. Although the article was written before social media marketing became mainstream, the recommendations within it are not tool-dependent, and it is definitely worth a look. We will talk more about the importance of marketing library collections and services throughout this book.

KEEP IN MIND

At many publicly funded institutions, the library's funding is a function, to a significant degree, of enrollment. Very often it takes the form of so many dollars per full-time equivalent (FTE) student. One FTE student represents a person who is taking the number of credits per term that constitutes a full-time course load at that institution. Usually the FTE number is lower than "head count" because there are students who sign up for fewer credits than what constitutes a full load. We will explore this issue in chapter 12 when we discuss library services. As a long-time library director once said, "A half-time student never occupies half a chair in the library."

when buying an automobile. Also like a trade-in, the discount a student receives varies because of individual considerations; nevertheless, the institution has an average "discount rate."

This discount rate is rather controversial, given that some students pay more because they can afford to pay more, even in the form of loans. Out-of-state students are often highly desirable, given that their tuition is substantially higher, and they are attracted by various discounted offers (Hoover, 2016). Student fees that are part of each term's bill are the "taxes and license" that accompany the purchase of a car. Last but not least, there is a "cash price" for the educational package, which is the long-term cost that comes from borrowing some or all of the funds to pay the up-front costs. Most current and former students will be repaying student loans for many years after they graduate. They may not think of the process as a "cash price," but they experience it. As Zemsky, Shaman, and Shapiro (2001) noted, "A college education today is best understood as a private, even a consumer, good available to nearly everyone—although at radically different prices" (p. 13).

Some in higher education suggest that dependency on student revenue as well as the issue of attracting students is somehow new and worrisome. Is this dependency new? Not at all. Is it worrisome? Almost always. From day one, student fees have been central to the survival of higher education. As we noted in chapter 2, teachers initially collected their income directly from the students, and throughout its history, higher education has been dependent on such income. Lack of income from students is a serious issue. For some institutions with little in the way of endowments or alumni able or willing to donate to operating funds, insufficient enrollment and student tuition means closing. For public institutions, dwindling state support has a drastic impact as well, and we will discuss that issue in chapter 7.

As we prepared this chapter, three small colleges closed (Dowling College in New York, St. Catharine College in Kentucky, and Burlington College in Vermont), and others are certainly in danger (Biemiller, 2016). Some colleges finding themselves in financial trouble are fortunate to have a very powerful and passionate alumni base to offset diminishing student tuition dollars with fund-raising, as was the case with Sweet Briar College. The alumni and community came together to raise $12 million in three months to keep the college open, and one year later, they reported raising an additional $10 million (Svrluga, 2016). Institutions can clearly benefit from maintaining good relationships with alumni and the local community, particularly when the institution is a valued employer and cultural resource, and we will come back to these points many times.

KEEP IN MIND

Getting the library involved in campus recruiting activities helps raise awareness in prospective students about the value of the library to their academic careers. Even if this involvement is nothing more than one of the stops on a campus tour, there is an awareness value, not to mention the value to campus administration of the academic library participating in an important campus activity. Although there may be many such stops and a fair amount of time devoted to this activity, it is something for the academic library to consider. This is an excellent report:

Association of College and Research Libraries. 2010. *The value of academic libraries: A comprehensive research review and report.* Researched by Megan Oakleaf. Chicago: Association of College and Research Libraries.

On page 103, Oakleaf compiles a variety of examples that show how libraries contribute to student enrollment. Participating in these recruiting activities could very well be time well spent.

Often an institution will develop the coming year's budget based on a projected enrollment number. Failure to achieve that enrollment target causes stress and likely results in cuts in unit operating budgets. Because salaries are a large part of any operating budget and few institutions want to reduce staff, the first places budget officers tend to cut are those areas that appear less critical to the year's operations. One favorite area and one that seems easy to cut is the library budget, often the material acquisitions budget. A one-year reduction in acquisitions may not be too significant, but a series of annual cuts could be disastrous for student and faculty access to library collections and services. As we will discuss in chapter 11 and elsewhere in this book, subscriptions to journals and databases are essential for faculty and student research, and budget cuts have a drastic and lasting effect on those subscriptions. We will often point out how important it is to demonstrate the library's value to administrators and to build relationships with students and faculty to be advocates for the library's budget.

Of course institutions are not the only ones worrying about the admissions process. The applicants and their families are often in an even higher state of anxiety. Tensions can last for months—from January (early notification of admission) until April when the final letters go out.

A topic that has had some discussion in the popular media is student body diversity and "legacy" students. Legacies are applicants who have a parent, grandparent, or other relative who graduated from the institution and who, therefore, may receive special consideration in the admissions process. As Gasman and Vultaggio (2008) put it, "Yale has the Bushes, Basses and Whitneys. Harvard has the Astors, Roosevelts and Kennedys. Throughout the history of American higher education, the nation's most prestigious colleges and universities have employed legacy policies that preference the children of privileged alumni" (p. 24). The authors noted that a legacy applicant, on average, enjoys a 25 percent advantage over other applicants. In addition, they suggested that such advantages work against diversity goals, that legacies not only create "a potentially negative impact on students of color, but they also hurt the chances of admission for low-income and first generation students" (p. 24). We hope this situation is changing. A *Chronicle of Higher Education* analysis of student data at research universities and highly ranked liberal arts schools showed that the average "diversity index," a one-hundred-point scale measuring the likelihood that any two randomly chosen students from an institution will be of different races or ethnicities, increased seventeen points between 1992 and 2012 (Zweifler and Newman, 2013).

One can easily guess the primary reason for having a legacy admissions program: keeping alumni and potential donors happy with the institution. It is easier to accept that notion for small institutions that have difficulty meeting their enrollment targets and need all the alumni support they can get in order to survive, as we mentioned earlier about Sweet Briar College. It is not so easy to accept it in the case of institutions that have billions of dollars in endowments. We will cover the financial side of higher education in more detail in chapter 7, but in talking about students, we needed to discuss how recruitment and admission—which ultimately translate into tuition dollars, making up a significant part of the total budget—relate to the overall operation of the institution.

FINANCIAL AID

The issue of how financial aid packages are put together is complex and well beyond the scope of this book. One aspect of most financial aid offers that we believe requires some discussion is work-study because it plays a major role in library operations. Like some other elements of student aid programs (such as Pell Grants and Direct Loans), work-study is a federal program.

Work-study is a cost-sharing program wherein the institution contributes 25 percent of the hourly salary, with the balance coming from the federal government. Because

 KEEP IN MIND

From a library point of view, student employment is a major factor in daily operations. Summer session library operations can present some significant challenges as the pool of students is substantially lower. Most academic libraries would be hard-pressed to offer the variety and quality of service they do without either a major increase in permanent staff or maintenance of the number of work-study students. This is why work-study student employees are so critical to academic libraries. Libraries can stretch their student employment budgets much farther by hiring more work-study students than hourly students.

Greenwell has worked in several libraries where some effort went into keeping the best student employees on staff. Potlucks, minicompetitions, and small recognitions for longevity go a long way in keeping the best students. Greenwell particularly admires some colleagues who coordinate an annual event to honor graduating student employees. Each graduating student chooses a meaningful book in the library's collection that will bear that student's name on a bookplate and in the library catalog. Of course, there is a party with cake and pizza as well to celebrate.

Keep in mind, all library student employees benefit the library through covering shifts and helping keep the doors open, but they are still students, and providing a good learning experience for them is part of their overall success.

federal funding for the program has fallen and work hours available are often inconsistent (Dagher, 2016), more students are seeking employment opportunities off campus. This shift in turn has created some serious challenges for campus units such as the library that are highly dependent on work-study students for conducting daily operations. Another challenge is that as the federal minimum wage increases, the decline in federal dollars further reduces the number of hours an institution has available to allocate. Some states have minimum wage rates higher than the federal rate, and although the institution may use the federal rate, doing so often pushes more students off campus where they can earn much more per hour.

Even in the best of funding circumstances, there is a competition between on- and off-campus jobs at the lower wage rates. Businesses may offer some benefits that campus units cannot match, such as employee discounts and the potential for much higher pay for either outstanding performance or longevity. From the student's point of view, the only plus for work-study positions is that there is no impact on the financial aid package because the program is part of that package. In the case of off-campus work income, however, 50 percent of that income must be counted as covering educational expenses under federal guidelines. This requirement in turn can lead to a reduction in institutional aid in the following academic terms.

👥 FROM THE AUTHORS

Greenwell once collaborated on an orientation video that introduced "University 101" students to the campus libraries. The video addressed students' most basic questions— many students did not realize that there was more than one library on campus, for example—in a casual and humorous fashion. Students may find such videos lame attempts at librarians trying to be clever, but Greenwell's team worked with students in developing the concept, drafting the storyboard, and ultimately putting the project together. Library student employees can be quite helpful in advising about messages that resonate with other students.

Work-study students are limited in the number of hours they can work per week in order to keep their focus on the study side of the program. At most institutions, the allocation is to the student, not the academic unit. Thus, the student can "shop" for jobs, seeking positions that have ample opportunities to study and still get paid when things are slow. This circumstance can present a challenge for the library in which typically there is a never-ending stream of tasks to do. Another consideration is that the institution may choose to cap the allowable number of hours student workers can work per week in order to avoid paying for health benefits. Finally, there are usually some pay differentials on campus, so students tend to seek the highest possible pay, which the library may not be able to provide. As we'll discuss in the next section, as for student success and retention, students who work on campus rather than off campus tend to perform better academically, as several studies have shown (Weston, 2008).

RETENTION

Getting students enrolled is one issue; keeping them is a different matter. Offices focused on metrics, retention, and "student success" are increasingly found on campus in order to better understand retention issues and, it is hoped, rectify them. *Retention* (or *persistence*) *rate* is a term used to denote students staying enrolled in their academic program until they successfully graduate with their baccalaureate degrees. First-time college students have many adjustments to make in order to succeed, and the institution does all it can to help individuals make those adjustments. There are two broad categories of adjustment: academic and social integration. Both are important to retention and graduation, and the library can play a role in these processes.

On the academic side, retention has several components, including learning about academic expectations, getting assistance with basic academic skills, and receiving assistance in handling a particular subject area. For social integration, opportunities are available to get to know other students who share an interest in a topic or activity, to join a club or social organization, to get involved in the institution's governance, and to participate in intramural or intercollegiate sports.

Why do some students graduate and others do not? One key factor is their success in learning about their academic responsibilities. To do so requires grasping what their instructors' expectations are. Certainly, professors and advisors are willing to assist students, but students need to ask for assistance. In higher education, there is an expectation of a certain level of commitment to succeed on the students' part. This expectation can be quite challenging for some students, especially those who may be the first in their family to go to college. Almost all institutions of higher education try to address these needs with offices that provide various types of student assistance, from basic academic skills to the psychological adjustments necessary for life away from home.

One area that all students can benefit from is learning higher education study skills and time management. Some institutions have a mandatory orientation course designed to help new students successfully transition from high school to college, or back into college life in the case of individuals returning to school. These "College 101" or "University 101" courses typically include a variety of topics such as time management, study skills, and an introduction to campus resources, which is a great opportunity for the academic

---

▥ CHECK THIS OUT

Association of College and Research Libraries. 2015. *Academic library contributions to student success: Documented practices from the field.* Prepared by Karen Brown. Contributions by Kara J. Malenfant. Chicago: Association of College and Research Libraries.

This report describes more than seventy team-based assessment projects from campuses all over the United States to help show how academic libraries contribute to student learning, retention (persistence), and graduation. These projects were part of "Assessment in Action: Academic Libraries and Student Success," a three-year project sponsored by ACRL in partnership with the Association for Institutional Research and the Association of Public and Land-grant Universities and with funding from the U.S. Institute of Museum and Library Services.

library to get involved. The students who need the course most are not always the students who register for it, so some institutions put more effort into encouraging at-risk students to take it, if not require it.

Vincent Tinto (1993) provided a seminal framework for understanding the basic elements of retention—the academic and social integration we mentioned earlier. He suggested that one cure for attrition was to create a mixture of academic and social interaction by creating learning communities, or collaborative learning groups. Such groups of students share with one another tips for succeeding in a particular academic subject or campus interaction. These groups differ from the informal study groups that have probably existed since the beginning of higher education in that institutions encourage their formation.

Many institutions have further refined this concept through developing living-learning communities (LLCs), residence halls designed with a particular academic focus, such as engineering, theater, environmental issues, music, and so on. LLCs encourage students to build relationships among peers with common academic or creative interests. Some subject-focused classes may be held within the LLC, and faculty and other academic support personnel may hold regular office hours there. This is another opportunity for the academic library to consider getting involved.

Engstrom and Tinto (2008) found there was at least a 10 percent higher persistence rate for students in learning groups than for students on their own. Some of the factors the researchers identified as contributing to better retention were safety, support, and belonging. Students felt safer sharing ideas in the group and knew there would be support when they encountered problems. They also felt they belonged to both the group and the institution and could succeed. As for LLCs, the research literature has shown that living in one can help students have a greater sense of belonging (Spanierman et al., 2013), can instill greater academic confidence (Allen, 2011), and is a high-impact educational practice relative to student learning outcomes (Brower and Inkelas, 2010).

Once a student makes a successful transition to academic life, there is still more for the institution to do. Encouraging lifelong learning is a basic goal of higher education, and another is to recruit the next generation of scholars, if not to one's own field then perhaps elsewhere within higher education. A key to both endeavors is faculty-student interaction outside the classroom. Faculty-student research projects are a highly effective method for encouraging lifelong learning and gaining an appreciation of the value of

---

||||| CHECK THIS OUT

Some librarians are experimenting with ways to provide library services in living-learning communities (LLCs) and residence halls. Although it is a time-intensive and not easily scalable service, working with students in their residences at their point of need is convenient and appreciated. Here are some specific examples worth checking out:

Long, D. 2011. "Embedded right where the students live: A librarian in the university residence halls." In *Embedded librarians: Moving beyond one-shot instruction,* edited by C. Kvenild and K. Calkins, 99–211. Chicago: Association of College and Research Libraries.

Ngoc-Yen Tran. 2013. Making and shaping a library experience for students living in the residence halls: Designing a residence hall library and on-site librarian position at the University of Oregon libraries. *OLA Quarterly* 19, no. 2.

Strothmann, M., and K. Antell. 2009. The live-in librarian: Developing library outreach to university residence halls. *Reference and User Services Quarterly* 50, no. 1: 48–58.

academic research. At some institutions the process is informal, and in others it is highly structured. One example of the structured approach is a project that may begin in the first year and culminate with a substantial research project in the senior year. This is another opportunity for the academic library to be involved in marketing collections and services to students as well as offering research consultations and regular support to students and their faculty advisors.

Rona Wilensky (2007) summed up the situation for first-year students when she wrote about the gaps between students and professors from the professorial point of view, and this insight is quite relevant today:

> First, between what we value and what they value; second, between what we are good at and what the majority of them are good at; and third, between what we as professors thought students needed to know and what they might actually need in order to function well in the world that is not school. . . . The fundamental contradiction of college and university life is that professors want good students, while most of their students want good jobs. (p. B19)

STUDENT SERVICES

A key institutional unit in the retention process is "student affairs," "student life," "student services," or some other variant label. This unit may handle some of the services we mentioned in the previous section, as well as student government, student organizations, Greek life, and perhaps athletics. We will cover those later in this chapter.

First, let's briefly discuss another activity student affairs handles, a much less pleasant one—student discipline. Student discipline (*in loco parentis*) of the early days of higher education remains at the root of today's student affairs divisions, though the formalization and bringing together of student-related roles took place only in the early 1930s (Rentz, 1996). The ultimate base of the student affairs office goes back to the medieval German concept of student freedom. It also draws on early U.S. colleges' efforts to maintain order among unruly students away from home. During the nineteenth century, when colleges had a perceived need to provide more student guidance as degree programs became more numerous and electives more commonplace, the concept of student affairs flourished. By the late nineteenth century, another layer of institutional administration was added in the form of one or more deans—dean of men, dean of women, or dean of students, for example. This is not the place to explore the many facets of student affairs work; we will, however, touch on some highlights.

We mentioned in chapter 2 that there were frequent student revolts in the nineteenth century. Colleges also had to worry about town-and-gown relations, considering that the student body was composed almost entirely of boys away from home who generally had pranks on their minds, and occasionally pranks could escalate into significant property damage. There is no doubt that nineteenth-century professors and college presidents had their hands full with a rowdy student body. However, their challenges were minimal compared to those of a twenty-first-century campus dealing with sexual assaults, acts of terrorism, and many other threats to personal safety and well-being. There are some common student affairs issues between the nineteenth century and now; however, even the similar issues have become more complex, such as intellectual honesty, substance abuse, and interpersonal conflicts.

Intellectual honesty is more complex today given the great ease of copying and pasting from online sources or other students' work. Part of the challenge in this area is how students view online content and the general lack of understanding of copyright. The attitude of many seems to be, "If I find it online, I can use it however I wish." The opportunity for acquiring a term paper for a fee has become even easier, though plagiarism detection systems help in discouraging these practices. The library often plays a role in educating students about copyright and plagiarism, perhaps through online tutorials and other guides that could be used in orientation or first-year general education courses.

Today's student affairs professionals usually view discipline as development rather than punishment. In part, this approach arises from the fact that society now views the issue as lying on the boundary between community needs and individual liberties. Furthermore, many aspects of the activity involve legal requirements. Of major significance is the concept of due process and its application.

At least some library staff must understand how the institution handles due process. There are at least two reasons for the staff needing such knowledge. First, it is inevitable that there will be instances in which the library staff will have to deal with unacceptable student behavior. This conduct might take the form of vandalism, verbal confrontations with staff or students, harassment, or other unacceptable behaviors in the library. Handling the situation in accordance with the institution's due process procedures is essential. A second reason is that staff may likely be upset when they see a previous offender back in the library, and someone on staff should be able to explain the process.

Student affairs staff may likely have some responsibility for making sure that student demonstrations, protests, and other free speech activities are handled in accordance with

👥 FROM THE AUTHORS

Evans had an experience that involved a felony-level theft (at least in terms of the state's criminal code) from the library's special collections department. The young man was a work-study student assigned to sort through a donation of four "banker boxes" of baseball trading cards. The donor accumulated the cards over sixty years and believed some could be rather valuable. (As we learned, "star" cards often bring hundreds of dollars each.) One day a department staff member came to the director's office to say she believed that the young man was taking cards. After further inquiry, the chief of campus public safety became part of the discussion. An undercover officer was in the department when the young man next came to work and observed the student pocketing cards. This led to officers searching his dorm room where they found two thousand cards. The library was asked to get an appraisal of what was taken and what was left. The appraiser reported that the library had ten thousand cards worth an average of $0.65 each. Cards in the dorm room were valued at $3.00 to $4.00 each. Furthermore, the appraiser noted that it was strange that given the number of cards involved there were no star cards because he had heard that several hundred such cards had appeared in the local market recently.

You can imagine how upset the department staff were to see the young man still on campus a year later. We never learned the outcome of the student affairs office's actions because of student privacy concerns, but questions existed about how the process was handled.

KEEP IN MIND

It is critical that staff understand the institution's policy regarding calling the campus public safety department or police versus calling the community's police department. Sometimes it matters whether the problem is a student, staff, or public issue. This distinction is particularly critical if offenses are committed in the evening or on weekends when there are no library administrators, department heads, or perhaps any full-time personnel on duty, and the responsibility falls to a student employee. As an agent of the institution—whether a student employee or the director of the library—there is an obligation to report when a crime has been committed, and all library personnel should very clearly understand institutional procedures.

campus policies. Part of the college or university experience is learning about new viewpoints and expressing new ideas, and these things should be done in a way to not create a hostile or dangerous atmosphere. At the time we were writing this book, students at a number of U.S. institutions were expressing their political and social concerns through rallies and peaceful demonstrations, which is an important part of learning. On the most recent CIRP survey, 8.5 percent of respondents said they had "a pretty good chance" of participating in a student protest, the highest percentage since the 1967 survey (Eagan et al., 2015).

STUDENT GROUPS

Student affairs units oversee a variety of programs that relate to social integration and development of a sense of belonging. One such activity that exists at almost every academic institution is student government.

Student government and the institution's administration have a complex relationship. Just what is the role of student government in institutional affairs? At least in the United States, the role is modest; student government is to function as the voice of the student body, rather than being part of institutional governance. It provides a mechanism for collecting student views about institutional matters and conveying that information to the administration. Student views do matter, but ultimately the board of trustees (on which the student government president may serve as a student representative) governs the institution, something that few students understand and even some faculty forget from time to time. We will explore campus governance in chapter 6.

Being the voice of the student body is not a meaningless role. Beyond serving as a feedback mechanism, student government helps in formulating student behavior policies, with guidance from the student affairs office.

From a library point of view, student governments can be a useful ally or a vocal critic. Having a student government representative on the library advisory committee is a good idea. Short of being open 24/7/365, the library can count on having requests from the students to increase service hours from time to time. In general, student governments can be helpful in identifying new or modifying existing services.

The label "student organizations" incorporates a wide variety of groups that range from honor societies to intramural sports teams. Other groups include small publishing activities, political clubs, and cultural groups. They may be academic in character, such as an engineering society, or predominantly social in nature, such as Greek letter organizations. In large and often impersonal universities, such groups provide the anchor for student identification with the institution. Frequently the extracurricular activities are as important in influencing a student's values and attitudes as professors and courses taken, if not more so. These groups can be quite helpful in retaining students because part of retention involves building a sense of community, as we discussed earlier with the LLCs (living-learning communities).

One category of student organization that gains institutional and community attention, sometimes less than favorable, are Greek letter organizations. (Note that there are Greek letter organizations that are academic in character, such as Phi Beta Kappa and Beta Phi Mu, the librarians' honorary society. These are not the focus of this discussion.) Society, higher education, and fraternities and sororities themselves have debated the value of social Greek letter groups almost from the time when, in the nineteenth century, literary societies morphed into fraternities. Critics have a long list of reasons why such groups are detrimental to academic performance and why they are contrary to the goal of "open to all."

Supporters have equally long lists of ways the groups are beneficial, such as performing community service, developing lifelong friends and networks, and providing a much-needed source of peer support while in school. Some have argued that students who participate in Greek organizations perform better academically. Although surprisingly few studies focused specifically on academics have been conducted to date, DeBard and Sacks (2011)

👥 FROM THE AUTHORS

While developing an undergraduate-focused area in the library, Greenwell learned how important it is to build relationships with both student government and the student newspaper. She made a point of meeting with the new student government president at the beginning of each school year, and she and her colleagues would give a short presentation with a question-and-answer session to other members of the student government executive board as well as to the student senate. This degree of openness helped when the library needed to make changes that would affect students. It also helped in recruiting student advisory board members and generally getting feedback about library services and student needs.

When Greenwell needed greater campus support to change a long-standing printing issue beyond the library's control, she worked with student government leaders to show campus administrators how making a small change in that service would greatly simplify things for new students. It was only when she and student government leaders advocated for this change together that the multiple groups involved in the pay-for-print system came together and greatly improved the situation.

Greenwell also learned it was helpful to develop relationships with at least one student newspaper reporter so that library events and services might be more easily and frequently promoted. This connection was also helpful when the library needed to make a change that would be unpopular with students (such as cuts to hours) because having a relationship with the newspaper can facilitate getting out ahead of the story. Being proactive in contacting student leaders about unpopular changes (as well as exciting new services and events, of course) goes a long way in building a positive image with students.

KEEP IN MIND

The National Collegiate Athletic Association (NCAA) employs a three-division approach to its membership. Division I is the "big-time" level. To be a member, an institution must field at least fourteen sports—seven each for men and women. Division I schools must meet minimum financial aid awards for their athletics program and cannot exceed maximum financial aid awards for each sport. Division II institutions have to sponsor at least five sports for men and five for women (or four for men and six for women), with two team sports for each gender, each playing seasons represented by each gender, and have a limit on the number of scholarships the athletes may be awarded. Division II athletic program budgets are solely the institution's, like other academic departments on campus. Division III institutions also have to sponsor at least five sports for men and five for women, with two team sports for each gender, and each playing seasons represented by each gender. Division III athletics features student-athletes who receive no financial aid related to their athletic ability, and athletic departments are staffed and funded like any other department in the university.

examined academic success in an analysis of more than forty-five thousand student records from seventeen institutions. After controlling for high school GPA and ACT scores, they found that students who joined Greek letter organizations in their first year earned significantly higher grade point averages than students who did not.

More often than not, it is fraternities that draw the negative publicity. Students in these groups sometimes engage in behavior that many people regard as at least demeaning if not dangerous, or on some occasions even fatal. Perhaps the most common issue is the degree to which such groups encourage substance abuse and the attendant problems that can result from such behavior, such as sexual assault. Assault and alcohol use are much broader than fraternities and sororities, and they are issues that all academic institutions must address.

COLLEGIATE SPORTS

As we noted earlier, student affairs may be the unit responsible for sports activities, both intramural and intercollegiate, though in much larger intercollegiate programs, the unit is often separate. In chapter 2, we speculated that perhaps sports became an element in U.S. higher education as a means to burn off excess energy. Whatever the reasons were at the outset, one cannot deny that sports are now very important within higher education. Sometimes, especially if you watch television on a fall weekend, you come away with the impression that collegiate sports are the *only* reason schools exist. This impression may intensify upon learning that some of the schools receive millions of dollars each time their football teams appear on national television or that a collegiate coach has a multimillion-dollar employment contract. At the same time, student athletes can greatly benefit from these programs, as can the institution itself from the revenue and goodwill that sports teams can generate. We will only scratch the surface in this section because discussing the varied issues and concerns related to collegiate sports is beyond the scope of this book.

Students undertook organizing sports on campus in the mid-1800s, first among themselves (intramural) and soon after that with nearby schools (intercollegiate). There was no institutional involvement, no coaching, no special training or facilities—just a few young men in a vacant field competing for the right to say "our team is better than yours." Things began to change in the 1850s, when Rutgers played Princeton in football (today the game they played is called soccer in the United States), and there were coaches directing the game. From such a humble beginning, collegiate sports and their associated costs have mushroomed into multimillion-dollar enterprises.

Money is the primary reason for the state of U.S. collegiate sports today. Although most of the money is associated with two sports—football and men's basketball—many other sports are gaining ground. Women's basketball, men's and women's soccer, baseball, volleyball, men's ice hockey, and even lacrosse all have professional leagues that are partially dependent on "college farm teams" to develop professional skills. There is a high cost to fielding competitive teams; however, the revenue generated by successful teams is also large. Even schools that are less successful but are in leagues that are successful may realize substantial revenue from the league's success.

Another reason for participating is also money related. Having teams mentioned on television and online keeps the institution in the minds of alumni, especially after a successful season. Even if not all alumni are donors, many take pleasure from seeing their alma mater playing on television. Winning a national championship makes a significant difference in sports-related income and increases alumni donations.

The National Collegiate Athletic Association (NCAA) puts out occasional advertisements on television trying to make the case that "most NCAA athletes turn pro in something other than sports." The ad is factual—most athletes do go "pro" in something other than their chosen sport after they graduate or leave school, though a great many of those athletes had aspirations of a pro career. Some do go on to sign contracts for large sums of money.

Some professional athletes give back to their institution, as do some coaches. The athletics program might have a special arrangement to provide funding to the institution. Some arrangements may take the form of a long-term funding structure, typically through scholarships. Duke University's Department of Athletics is an interesting example because $1 of every home game ticket sold is given to the library (Free, 2011). Some athletics departments may provide large one-time payments, such as Ohio State's Department of Athletics, which gave $9 million to help renovate the main library (Turner, 2008).

Are college sports a problem for U.S. higher education? There are times when they seem to skew institutional funding priorities. Scholarship athletes, at least in the major sports, often have much higher expectations for going on to play professionally and may seem less committed to the academic side of the college experience. With tuition costs escalating faster than general inflation, having costly sports programs that don't support themselves as

---

▌▌▌▌ CHECK THIS OUT

Interested in learning more about college athletics? This classic text describes the history of intercollegiate athletics from 1910 to 1990. Although it has not been recently updated, it still provides a solid foundation for many issues facing athletics today.

Thelin, John R. 1996. *Games colleges play: Scandal and reform in intercollegiate athletics.* Baltimore: Johns Hopkins University Press.

part of the total cost mix seems inappropriate. However, college sports can certainly bring notoriety to the institution, and with that often comes generous donations from alumni. Sports can build a sense of unity among students and extend to the community as well to help strengthen town-and-gown relations. Like many issues in higher education, this is one that requires far more detail than we can cover here.

GRADUATION AND BEYOND

Although many institutions focus on metrics of "student success" related to keeping students enrolled and graduating, students and their families are ultimately interested in employment upon graduation. In a recent freshman attitudes report from Ruffalo Noel Levitz (2014) that focused on career decisions, 47 percent of incoming students wanted career counseling. Of these incoming freshmen, 21 percent indicated that they were "very confused" about which occupation to pursue. We do tend to expect a lot out of a young adult at age 18 to select an area of interest to study and ultimately a career path based in that area.

As we discussed earlier in this chapter, career success is very important to today's students. In the 2015 CIRP survey, 60 percent of respondents said that when choosing a college, they gave a rating of "very important" to "this college's graduates get good jobs" (Eagan et al., 2015). Clearly employment is on the minds of our students, and it will continue to be as the cost of higher education increases and the job market in some areas becomes even more competitive.

How do we define student success? Is it the campus graduation rate? Is it the rate of gainfully employed graduates or their average salary? Is it some measure of what students actually learned through their academic and social experiences? Perhaps it is a combination of all these things. If a student has gained a broad education, developed competence in his area of interest, and found a satisfying and well-matched career, that could be considered true student success. What do you think?

🔒 KEY POINTS TO REMEMBER

- Students are the lifeblood of higher education, both in terms of purpose and financially.
- Each passing year brings an increasingly diverse pool of potential applicants.
- With an increase in diversity comes a changing demographic makeup of the student body, such as an older, more independent, perhaps less academically prepared body, with some students being the first in their family to attend college.
- Changing demographics brings with it changes in the institution's programs and services.
- Although current students have different attitudes and priorities than those of the past, their basic reason for wanting a college degree has not changed: a better lifetime earning potential.
- Attracting and retaining students is critical for institutions, if for no other reason than financial stability.
- Learning communities, formal orientation programs, and student support services can help students succeed academically.
- Student discipline is a complex matter and often legalistic in character.
- Collegiate athletics play a role in higher education and its overall cost.
- The academic library can play a role throughout the recruitment and retention process.

REFERENCES

Alire, Camila. 2007. Word-of-mouth marketing: Abandoning the academic library ivory tower. *New Library World* 106, no. 11/12: 545–551.

Allen, David F. 2011. "SAIR and NCAIR best paper: Academic confidence and the impact of a living-learning community on persistence." Paper presented at the Annual Forum of the Association for Institutional Research, Toronto, Ontario, May 21–25. http://eric.ed.gov/?id=ED531717.

Association of College and Research Libraries. 2010. *The value of academic libraries: A comprehensive research review and report.* Researched by Megan Oakleaf. Chicago: Association of College and Research Libraries.

Association of College and Research Libraries. 2015. *Academic library contributions to student success: Documented practices from the field.* Prepared by Karen Brown. Contributions by Kara J. Malenfant. Chicago: Association of College and Research Libraries.

Biemiller, Lawrence. 2016. 3 small colleges close. Is that a trend? *Chronicle of Higher Education.* http://chronicle.com/article/3-Small-Colleges-Close-Is/236677.

Brower, Aaron M., and Karen Kurotsuchi Inkelas. 2010. Living-learning programs: One high-impact educational practice we now know a lot about. *Liberal Education* 96, no. 2: 36–43.

Carlson, Ronald H., and Christopher S. McChesney. 2015. Income sustainability through educational attainment. *Journal of Education and Training Studies* 3, no. 1: 108–115.

Dagher, Veronica. 2016. "College financial-aid offers: What families need to know." *Wall Street Journal,* online edition, April 9.

DeBard, Robert, and Casey Sacks. 2011. Greek membership: The relationship with first-year academic performance. *Journal of College Student Retention: Research, Theory and Practice* 13, no. 1: 109–126.

Eagan, K., E. B. Stolzenberg, A. K. Bates, M. C. Aragon, M. R. Suchard, and C. Rios-Aguilar. 2015. *The American freshman: National norms fall 2015.* Los Angeles: Higher Education Research Institute, University of California, Los Angeles. www.heri.ucla.edu/monographs/TheAmericanFreshman2015.pdf.

Engstrom, Cathy, and Vincent Tinto. 2008. Access without support is not opportunity. *Change* 40, no. 1: 46–50.

Free, David. 2011. Duke athletics to start library fund. *College and Research Libraries News* 72, no. 6: 318.

Gardner, Lee. 2016. What a university can learn from Wegmans. *Chronicle of Higher Education* 62, no. 42. www.chronicle.com/article/What-a-University-Can-Learn/237240.

Gasman, Marybeth, and Julie Vultaggio. 2008. Perspectives: A "legacy" of racial injustice in American higher education. *Diverse: Issues in Higher Education* 24, no. 25: 24.

Hoover, Eric. 2016. The enrollment manager as bogeyman. *Chronicle of Higher Education* 62, no. 42: A11.

Kena, Grace, Lauren Musu-Gillette, Jennifer Robinson, Xiaolei Wang, Amy Rathbun, Jijun Zhang, RTI International, et al. 2015. *The condition of education 2015.* National Center for Education Statistics.

Long, D. 2011. "Embedded right where the students live: A librarian in the university residence halls." In *Embedded librarians: Moving beyond one-shot instruction,* edited by C. Kvenild and K. Calkins, 99–211. Chicago: Association of College and Research Libraries.

Ngoc-Yen Tran. 2013. Making and shaping a library experience for students living in the residence halls: Designing a residence hall library and on-site librarian position at the University of Oregon libraries. *OLA Quarterly* 19, no. 2.

Rentz, Audrey L. 1996. "A history of student affairs." In *Student affairs practices in higher education,* 2d ed., edited by Audrey L. Rentz, 28–53. Springfield, IL: Charles C Thomas.

Rubin, Courtney. 2014. "Making a splash on campus." *New York Times,* September 21, 12–13.

Ruffalo Noel Levitz. 2014. *2014 national freshman motivation to complete college report.* Coralville, IA: Ruffalo Noel Levitz. www.noellevitz.com/FreshmanReport.

Spanierman, Lisa B., Jason R. Soble, Jennifer B. Mayfield, Helen A. Neville, Mark Aber, Lydia Khuri, and Belinda De La Rosa. 2013. Living learning communities and students' sense of community and belonging. *Journal of Student Affairs Research and Practice* 50, no. 3: 308–325.

Strothmann, M., and K. Antell. 2009. The live-in librarian: Developing library outreach to university residence halls. *Reference and User Services Quarterly* 50, no. 1: 48–58.

Svrluga, Susan. 2016. "A year after Sweet Briar was saved from closing, school leaders celebrate fundraising growth." *Washington Post,* July 12. https://www.washingtonpost.com/news/grade-point/wp/2016/07/12/a-year-after-sweet-briar-was-saved-from-closing-school-leaders-celebrate-fundraising-growth/.

Thelin, John R. 1996. *Games colleges play: Scandal and reform in intercollegiate athletics.* Baltimore: Johns Hopkins University Press.

Tinto, Vincent. 1993. *Leaving college: Rethinking the causes and cures for student attrition.* Chicago: University of Chicago Press.

Turner, Jamie. 2008. "Athletic department's gift helps OSU library renovation reach funding goal." www.cleveland.com/osu/index.ssf/2008/08/athletic_departments_gift_help.html.

Weston, Charles W. 2008. *Understanding the integrative role of an academic library for undergraduate student workers.* University of New Orleans Theses and Dissertations, Paper 700.

Wilensky, Rona. 2007. For some high-school students, going to college isn't the answer. *Chronicle of Higher Education* 23, no. 34: B18–B19.

Zemsky, Robert, Susan Shaman, and Daniel B. Shapiro. 2001. Revenue. *New Directions in Educational Research* no. 111: 9–20.

Zweifler, Seth, and Jonah Newman. 2013. Elite institutions: Far more diverse than they were 20 years ago. *Chronicle of Higher Education* 60, no. 9: B16–B19.

CHAPTER 5

Curriculum

U.S. higher education did not debate what the curriculum should be until the early nineteenth century. Until then, it was based on the liberal arts. Every graduate from every college was exposed to the same subjects taught mostly in the same manner. The only exception was in the area of theology, which was partly the reason various denominations established their own colleges—to ensure a steady stream of "properly" trained ministers for their faith. Graduates of different colleges generally had the same college experience. The commonality also meant that library collections were quite uniform in content from one college to another. That commonality began to fade in the early part of the nineteenth century as colleges expanded the topics and degrees they offered.

By the end of the nineteenth century, after adding a host of different practical degree programs and even more electives, institutional commonality was gone. Kenneth Boning (2007) noted that, at the height of elective course growth, student options "were so varied that students earning the same degree at the same institution may not have any of the same classes. . . . Overall, the emphasis on individualized education fragmented the academic community and brought dubiousness to the value of the baccalaureate degree" (p. 5).

As a result of the situation Boning described, there was pressure to bring back some of the old commonality. What that commonality should consist of and what its goals should be have been debated since the early twentieth century and continue to be debated today. This was also the period in which community colleges started, with the goal of educating students to transfer to four-year institutions. The influx of transfer students made it even more important that there be greater consistency in what was required to graduate from a four-year school. However, people inside and outside higher education continue to question the need for general education ("general ed" or "gen ed") courses, and, if there is a need, what those courses should be. Where the debate goes remains to be seen, and whatever the outcome, it will impact libraries. What is clear is that what courses exist will affect the library's collections and services.

WHAT IS GENERAL EDUCATION?

A very simple definition of *general education* might be this: a general education program is one in which students learn how to assess facts, make connections, and integrate information to gain new knowledge. From the library perspective, assessing information is a major contribution to a person's lifelong learning and ability to successfully handle changing circumstances. General education may be a reasonable goal, but it does not suggest how one would go about doing it, what the content of the courses would be, and how many general versus specialized courses should be part of a baccalaureate degree. These are the areas that generate heated debates. Another thing to consider is that general education courses will vary over time at a single institution because of periodic curricular reforms. Thus, there is no true commonality in the curriculum even within the institution, much less more widely.

Almost all U.S. institutions of higher education have some form of general education. The larger and more complex the institution, particularly with doctoral-granting institutions with a wide variety of majors, the more difficult it is to put together a meaningful core curriculum for all undergraduates. A very common approach is to employ a "distributive core." The size of the core varies but is generally between forty-six and fifty-two credit hours of required courses. In the distributive approach, a student has a list of broad areas and a list of "acceptable" courses under each topic. It is reminiscent of a restaurant menu from which a person selects two from column A, three from B, and so on until the meal/degree requirements are met. Is there articulation among the courses? Sometimes yes and sometimes no, depending on the institution's interest in the core. Even when the interest is high, linkages between core courses may be weak. Most of the courses are "lower division" or introductory in character and thus make it difficult to create a coherent whole.

Some institutions have attempted to move toward a curriculum modeled in integrative learning theory, which could help in making those linkages. The goal is to make the curriculum less a "menu-driven sprawl" and ultimately more practical and meaningful to the student (Berrett, 2016). The model's intention is to encourage interdisciplinary thinking by connecting ideas between classes as well as applying those ideas to real-world problems. Lowenstein (2015) describes an integrated learning approach to general education as learning basic facts and developing communication skills as well as achieving the following:

> A further accomplishment, which every institution would surely hope for, would be that students experience those discrete classes not as isolated and unrelated experiences but as integral parts of a coherent whole. . . . The integrated overview and enhanced intentionality, furthermore, create the best possible platform for a lifetime of learning since they provide a context for new experiences and ideas as they are encountered. (p. 121)

A major challenge, of course, is in the execution because such an approach would require a significant retooling of individual courses involving a substantial amount of faculty effort. As we discussed in chapter 3, although faculty may want to put more time into their teaching, at most large institutions the tenure ladder requires that a priority be put on research

---

▌▌▌ CHECK THIS OUT

Another relatively new approach to general education is the concept of meta-majors, in which programs are closely linked in content and the focus is on a student's interests with completion of the program being a key goal. Currently this approach is seen in community colleges (such as Lorain County Community College in Ohio) and several schools in the Florida College System (such as St. Petersburg College, Miami Dade College, North Florida Community College, and Pensacola State College). *Get with the Program,* a report by Davis Jenkins and Sung-Woo Cho at the Community College Research Center, provides more information and examples (http://ccrc.tc.columbia.edu/media/k2/attachments/accelerating-student-entry-completion.pdf).

and grants instead. We will come back to faculty issues related to curriculum reform later in this chapter.

The lack of commonality in the general education curriculum has generated federal government interest and concern over the years, particularly in the form of assessment. The Commission on the Future of Higher Education Report (more commonly known as the Spellings Report; U.S. Department of Education, 2006) explored the concept of general education at some length. Although the report did not specify a national core curriculum, it did recommend national testing of certain skills using a standardized test such as the Collegiate Learning Assessment (CLA), a commercial product developed by the Council for Aid to Education and the RAND Corporation. It is a written test intended to measure "college students' performance in analysis and problem solving, scientific and quantitative reasoning, critical reading and evaluation, and critiquing an argument, in addition to writing mechanics and effectiveness" (http://cae.org/flagship-assessments-cla-cwra/cla/). Accreditation requirements and an increasing public interest in accountability are driving more use of standardized general education outcome assessment measures. We will explore accreditation later in this chapter as well as in other chapters.

More recently, state governments have acted on an interest in a common general education curriculum with the creation of the Common Core State Standards Initiative for K–12 schools, adopted by most states at present though the status of implementation varies widely. Government interest in curriculum is a reflection of society-wide concerns about the cost and value of education as well as what, if anything, students have learned. Although the Common Core is focused on K–12 education, it does have implications for higher education (Nelson, 2013).

If the Common Core curriculum becomes fully realized nationwide, higher education institutions would have clearer expectations for the level of knowledge of incoming freshmen. Possibly higher education institutions could spend less time offering remediation and more time focusing on higher-level, major-specific courses. If the Common Core curriculum is successful, incoming freshmen could be more college-ready, or at least they would have experienced a more consistent level of high school education. Given the disconnect that often exists between K–12 and colleges and universities, not to mention the challenges that remain in implementing a consistent K–12 curriculum in most states, the possibility of this standard curriculum becoming a reality remains to be seen and will be interesting to watch over time.

Before we go further, we should note another phrase that some people employ by which they more or less mean general education: liberal education. Are the two terms synonymous? Only in the very broadest sense. Gary Miller (1988) in his book *The Meaning of General Education* drew a number of distinctions between the two concepts, which we summarize in table 5.1.

Some other differences distinguish the two curricula. It is generally accepted that general education has six broad approaches: heritage, counterpoint, instrumental, developmental or empowerment, social agenda, and valuing. As you would expect, *heritage* cores focus on enhancing a student's appreciation of cultural heritage. *Counterpoint* packages are efforts to expand a student's exposure to subjects outside the major that enrich the major at the same time. *Instrumental* is almost a synonym for liberal arts because such programs concentrate on writing, speaking, and analytical thinking skills. *Developmental* or *empowerment* packages emphasize skills that should lead a person to becoming a lifelong learner. *Social agenda*-purposed cores contain a set of courses that are topical and societal in nature, such as global warming, responsibilities of citizens in a democratic society, and worldwide health and hunger. *Valuing,* as the name suggests, centers on setting values, assessing what values exist in a situation, and, at some institutions, even inculcating a specific set of values in the students.

Virginia Smith (1993) noted that in reality a person ought not to refer to general education as a "program." She pointed out that, from an organizational point of view, general education is "accorded far less importance than the lowest discipline-based department . . . even the smallest discipline-based unit has someone designated as chair" (p. 248). By smallest and lowest discipline, she means the number of faculty and student majors, not the content of the discipline. Rather than a program, she suggests one should think of general ed as a "catalog construct—a listing of required courses/areas that the student must have on her or his transcript in order to graduate. It becomes the students' and advisors' responsibilities to make certain the requirements are met." Finally, Smith made a key point about general education at any institution: its shape "is determined by putting together pieces of a curriculum usually designed for some other purpose" (p. 248). Perhaps this makes a more integrated approach as we discussed earlier that much more important.

GENERAL EDUCATION	LIBERAL EDUCATION
Instrumentalist • Problem solving • Acquisition of skills	**Rationalist** • Life of the mind • Mental process
Psychological • Individual • Social change	**Logical/Essentialist** • Societal • Seeks universals

TABLE 5.1 Differences between general education and liberal education

DEBATING THE CURRICULUM

Curriculum reform has been likened to a "black hole" that swallows up enormous amounts of faculty time with very little coming out of the effort. As noted by Pittendrigh (2007), "The process of changing a general education curriculum has been compared to moving a graveyard" (p. 34). Along the same lines, Rhodes (2001) noted that "eyes glaze over; tempers shorten; people of generosity and goodwill become intolerant and those of sound judgment and thoughtful balance become rigid, hard line advocates" (p. B7). For some faculty, "general education can seem like an 'obstacle,' preventing advanced instruction in specialized field courses" (Fuess and Mitchell, 2011, p. 2).

Such are some thoughts regarding debating, much less changing, the core curriculum. From the library point of view, the difficulty of making such changes is a plus because it gives staff more time to plan for the adjustments that will be needed to meet new requirements.

Why is it so difficult to reach a consensus on what all students should be exposed to and, it is hoped, learn by the time they graduate, even within an institution, much less nationally? The answer is that multiple factors come into play, and their weight varies over time. Moreover, circumstances change within the institution.

Some people frame the debate as a battle between practicality (career) and theory (whole person). Opponents of broad general education programs claim, with a degree of truth behind their argument, that each passing year adds more and more complexity to a subject field, and students need more courses in that field to succeed. Thus, general education classes do not serve the long-term career interests of students because either they limit the number of specialized courses a student may take or they lengthen the overall degree program and increase students' costs. Supporters of general education argue that true long-term interests are better served by having a breadth of knowledge and knowing how to think effectively rather than by having a narrow subject focus. What do you think?

What constitutes the core curriculum, at most institutions, is typically a complex political process. Seven significant factors affect the final composition of the core—history, institutional issues, career versus whole person beliefs, accreditation bodies, societal issues and pressures, students' "voting" with their feet, and departmental power and strength.

👥 FROM THE AUTHORS

As an example later in this chapter will illustrate, delays in getting approval can allow the library staff time to begin the process of identifying potentially useful resources for a new program, discipline, or related initiative. In the example of the long period required for approval of an education doctorate program, the stretch of time provided invaluable lead time for the library as well as time to begin working with the department faculty on their priorities for materials acquisitions and development of subject-focused library instruction materials.

Of course, the library must be represented on curriculum committees or at least informed about new programs in order for this process to take place. Frequently the need for appropriate funding for library resources is glossed over until the issue becomes critical, as we will discuss later. We can't emphasize enough how important it is for the library to be involved or at least informed when new programs are in the works.

The last factor is often expressed in the form of departmental turf wars because often the departments with one or more core courses also get additional funding to handle the increased workload.

Obviously, history and institutional issues underlie the final decision. The traditional curricular approach often acts as a significant brake on radical reform efforts. Senior faculty and alumni tend to resist more than minor changes in the core curriculum. The institution's definition of its purpose also serves as a brake on reform and reformulation. It's uncommon for trustees to redefine an institution's mission unless they are facing a serious fiscal crisis.

Accreditation bodies can also influence curriculum decisions. There are two broad types of accreditation organizations. One type looks at the entire institution and is sometimes referred to as a regional agency—for example, the Middle States Commission on Higher Education, the Commission on Colleges of the Southern Association of Colleges and Schools, and the Western Association of Schools and Colleges. The second type, such as the National Association of Schools of Music and the American Library Association, addresses a specific subject-focused program at an institution. Both types can play a role in how big the core may be and how many specialized courses are required. Institutional and programmatic accreditations are important to parents and students as well as to the community at large, especially in

KEEP IN MIND

A fact of academic library life, at least in the more comprehensive institutions, is that accreditation activities seem to be never ending. It is a given that institution-wide accreditation visits will look into library operations. The same is almost always true for programmatic visits. No matter which type of visit is coming up, the library will be asked to provide information about its operations for the self-study document that is sent to the accrediting agency and its visiting team members.

In a medium or large college or university, there is likely to be at least one programmatic accreditation visit a year. Library staff members gather the requested self-study data and meet with visiting team members to address any concerns they may have that were not satisfactorily covered in the self-study. Consequently, the library subject specialist or liaison must know the collections in her specific subject assignment. This knowledge helps not only in the self-study but also in the external team's campus visit. The subject specialist or liaison role often solidifies a strong relationship with the program's or the department's faculty. We will cover this role in more depth in the chapters on library services and staffing.

the case of publicly funded schools. Accreditation matters to an institution if for no other reason than being fully accredited makes it easier to attract students. Essentially accreditation is a stamp of approval that the institution or program, based on an assessment by an outside agency, is in compliance with professional and community expectations.

Today both types of accreditation groups reflect a society-wide concern with assessment and accountability. The visiting team will ask pointed questions about the relationship between various courses and the institutional or programmatic mission and evidence of outcomes. The library's information literacy program staff can expect similar questions about their assessment activities, which we will cover in more depth in chapter 10.

Sometimes the accrediting agency's expectations can create major tension for those planning the curriculum when it comes to balancing core and specialized courses. Some programmatic agencies specify that a certain percentage of the total courses taken be in the program area. That requirement, of course, heightens the tensions between those focused on career interests and those who believe in lifelong skills. The argument of those in the latter group has been strengthened by data that show that people are now likely to change their career orientation several times during their working life as employers rapidly expand and contract their workforces because of changing economic circumstances.

We noted earlier that the process of determining curricula is complex, especially in publicly funded institutions. To the mix of institutional history, philosophical differences, and accrediting agencies you must add societal and political pressure. Starting in the 1980s (roughly from the elections of President Reagan and Prime Minister Margaret Thatcher in the United Kingdom), conservatives' interest in and influence on higher education and its curricula have grown. As Dan Smith (2005) wrote regarding conservative views and the push-pull between the core and discipline-oriented degrees, "This dichotomy between the more humanistic approach to university education and the desire to 'create functional skills' expresses a debate in the university that meshes well with the neoconservative agenda," which is one of "commodification and privatization" (p. 114). As a result, there is a widely held view that higher education does or should play a significant role in the "new economy" and that its focus ought to be on meeting that role.

More recently, governors in Florida ("Florida GOP vs. social science," 2011) and Kentucky ("Kentucky's governor vs. French literature," 2016) as well as former presidential candidates ("Marco Rubio vs. Aristotle," 2015; "Bush questions liberal arts," 2015) have questioned the value and practicality of certain majors. An editorial about accountability and postsecondary institutions in *Change* magazine noted that institutions should have "better performance on outcomes that the political process has deemed important and success in the labor market" ("When the customer is right," 2000, p. 6). The article went on to propose that this objective should be the focus of reforming the curriculum. Although none of this discussion directly suggests that liberal education is inappropriate, those wishing for more specialized or applied components in the baccalaureate degree use such arguments in their debate.

Bernard Shapiro (2003) disagreed with the strong shift to a "labor market oriented" curriculum for colleges and universities:

> Having responded—perhaps too quickly and all too well—to demands of the marketplace, these institutions are now filled with students more focused on the vocational and financial prospects of their graduation than with the larger, more civilizing mission of higher education. I believe this concern is legitimate. Indeed, I am convinced this is the case, not only for many students, but also for many faculty whose desire and apparent capacity to understand much about higher education outside their own particular specialties is very limited indeed. (p. 15)

Although Shapiro's interest was in the Canadian situation, his views resonate in the United States, and the debate is far from finished.

Certainly students and their parents vote with their feet and dollars when it comes to what type of curriculum they believe is most appropriate in today's environment. However, one wonders if they fully appreciate the value of a broad-based and lifelong learning-focused education when it comes to a lifetime of work. Balancing the needs to recover and pay

👥 FROM THE AUTHORS

Some of Greenwell's colleagues were actively involved in a general education curriculum reform effort that led to elements of information literacy being required in every gen ed course at the university. Although syllabi had to be approved by a faculty committee that typically included at least one librarian, how those information literacy skills were covered by the faculty and graduate assistants teaching those courses varied widely.

Some institutions require students to take an entire course focused on information literacy and research skills as part of the gen ed curriculum. Others may include an information literacy segment in another required gen ed course, such as a communication or composition course.

Either of these scenarios could be seen as a great opportunity for the academic library and quite a challenge at the same time, given the number of faculty and various disciplines involved, not to mention the sheer numbers of students who might need individualized attention. More sophisticated online delivery methods are making this instruction more scalable, though some would argue that such an approach is far from ideal. We will cover this technique in more detail when we discuss information literacy instruction in chapter 12.

for the cost of a degree and meet lifetime obligations is difficult even for those who have an appreciation of long-term factors.

The reality is that three undergraduate degree models are now in play: general or liberal education with no specialty (bachelor of arts), applied (e.g., bachelor of recreational studies), and mixed (e.g., bachelor of applied mathematics). The last model has been growing in favor over the past twenty or so years, in part because it helps avoid coming to grips with the fundamental issue: immediate application versus the ability to adjust effectively to changing life situations.

Our final element in the great curriculum debate relates to the political strength of the various departments and their discipline focus in the institution. Keep in mind that political strength is not always a function of faculty size and majors. Powerful departments are often able to drive final curriculum decisions. Some years ago the Carnegie Foundation for the Advancement of Teaching (1998) sponsored a study that commented on departmental power in postsecondary institutions and that is still relevant:

> We believe that research universities must be willing and able to break free of traditions. . . . Departments necessarily think in terms of protecting and advancing their own interests, defined in terms of number of faculty, courses, and majors. Initiatives for change coming from sources outside the department are viewed as threats rather than opportunities. (p. 14)

Although the report's focus was on research universities, the statement can and does apply to any academic institution. In our experience, departmental influence and power are significant factors in the direction of curricular change and development. Such power is even more of an issue in our next section, in which we discuss adding and dropping of courses and programs.

MODIFYING THE CURRICULUM

If an academic library is able to maintain a close relationship with only one faculty committee, that committee should be the one that reviews changes in courses and programs. This is why library liaison assignments to that committee are so important. The librarian assigned as the liaison needs to ensure that discussions and decisions by the committee are made known to the other librarians and library administrators. When the library liaison to the committee is weak, the duties should be reassigned to someone who is a more effective communicator.

Institutions employ a variety of labels for the body that decides curriculum, but the name almost always contains one or more of the following words: *courses, programs, studies, curriculum,* and *review.* The committee is the first level of institutional assessment of proposed curriculum changes. At the most basic level, the committee usually has the power to approve new courses. When it comes to expanding an existing program or starting a new one, the group normally only has recommendation authority, with the governing board retaining approval power.

An annual ritual for many librarians at the start of a new academic year is fielding at least one request from a newly hired faculty member for a meeting. Such meetings primarily involve requests for library materials in the person's research area as well as library support for the courses the person was hired to teach. Even when the person is to teach the same courses as the individual he replaced, the teaching approach will vary and often employ different library resources; likely the person's research area will have a different focus and require resources as well.

Depending on the institution, the amount of freedom the library has to meet such requests varies. In some instances, the vast majority of the materials budget is already allocated within the department, leaving almost no flexibility. When funds are thus allocated, all the librarian can do is suggest that the individual discuss the requests with departmental colleagues. If the person is scheduled to teach a course not previously offered at the institution, the department may be more likely to make some adjustment.

When the library has some flexibility in the materials budget, it is normally only in the area of books and media. Subscriptions to journals, databases, and other serials are generally both a fixed and an annually increasing expense in a library's budget. Just receiving funding adequate to cover the increased cost of existing subscriptions is a challenge, and rarely is any money available for new subscriptions. In such instances, even departmental colleagues may be unwilling to drop any subscriptions over which they may have some control.

The situation is even more challenging when more than just one or two new courses are being introduced. We have encountered new people who claimed to have been hired to develop a new specialty within an existing degree, a new certificate, or even a new degree and were just now informing the library of these developments. Any of these new elements in the curriculum can have a significant impact on a library's services as well as on collections.

The top library administrators also have a role to play in all this. Many of them sit on their respective provost's or dean's council, where major curricular changes and additions are shared. It is at that time that the library administrators should be working with their subject specialists to get an idea of the implications for the library's acquisitions budget and make those implications known to the council. This approach allows the possibility of the library having input in more than one venue.

A new certificate program is problematic, but not as much as a full degree. Usually a new certificate draws on existing programmatic strengths; thus, the library will already have some support resources in place. With existing resources in place, the library has some time to secure other desired materials and is likely not to have an unhappy faculty member, at least in terms of support for the new program.

 KEEP IN MIND

Even when all those involved have the best intentions and relations, a few newly approved courses will not be reported to the library in a timely manner. It is much rarer for a new certificate or degree program to slip between the cracks, but it does happen. There are a number of positive reasons for library staff to "show the colors" as it were by participating in activities such as open houses, receptions, and any other faculty and staff events that encourage networking. From such attendance, as long as librarians at the event do not stay together but, rather, talk with faculty about their research interests, courses, and departmental plans, the library can gain much-needed early warning about potential changes. Certainly this outreach helps in building all aspects of librarian-faculty relationships.

When blindsided by a new degree program, the library will face significant challenges. Almost certainly, no one will have thought to have library funding included in the startup budget. Another highly likely reality is that when a library "wish list" is finally developed, the list will be long and expensive. If one is lucky, there will be a year or two before students enroll in the program. With at least a year to prepare and with proper funding from some source other than existing library funds, the library can begin to build up some of the resources needed to support the new program. Lacking such lead time, it is inevitable that almost everyone involved in the program will be unhappy for as long as it takes to address the issues.

The ideal approach to the committee's review process from an academic library point of view is to have a checklist of points that each proposal addresses. One element in this list is a section asking about library resources and services that are required to support the proposed change. If new library materials are needed, the proposal should include an estimate of the cost of acquiring them. Such an approach ensures that the library is not blindsided by requests. It does not ensure that the funding will be available, but this approach does help maintain better relationships between new faculty and the library. It also makes clear what additional funding ought to be made available for the desired level of library support for the new course or program.

At universities lacking a doctoral program, one or two academic departments will usually have aspirations of offering a doctoral degree. A new doctoral program will not come as a surprise to the library because extensive campus-wide discussion of any such program will take place long before it ever reaches the governing board for final approval. One factor in the debate over starting such a program is the high cost. We discuss the costs of programs in more depth in a later chapter, but for now it's enough to say that undergraduate programs are the lowest cost per student, master's programs cost more, and doctoral programs are the most costly.

Up to this point we have discussed what the public typically thinks of as the curriculum of higher education. For many institutions, especially land-grant institutions, this is only a part of the total picture of course offerings. We turn now to two other big components in many institutions' total curriculum: continuing education and online learning programs.

CONTINUING EDUCATION

Continuing education is a broad concept. People apply the concept to a variety of educational experiences that range from participating in literacy programs to earning a degree through a distance education program. In between the two are other activities, such as enrolling in noncredit courses for self-enrichment, taking courses to earn a certificate or to update a degree or certificate, and engaging in self-directed learning. Such activities are a significant part of the total U.S. educational picture. They are significant enough that profit-oriented organizations offer courses. Professional groups and academic institutions (our sole focus here) are involved in offering workshops and programs. In the broadest sense we are looking at lifelong learning. Typically, students in such programs are older than the traditional baccalaureate student and may be returning to academia after a long break. These programs were once called "adult education," but given that many adults return to school for a variety of reasons, including for a first degree, the terms *continuing education* and *lifelong learning* are more widely used today.

In a sense, continuing education is about possibilities. Marsha Rossiter (2007) made this point in broad-brush terms:

👥 FROM THE AUTHORS

Evans has had five experiences working with departments that had hopes of implementing a doctoral program, PhD or applied. Only one of them succeeded in securing institutional approval for a degree. As a rule, securing approval is a long-term process requiring substantial amounts of time devoted to planning. In all five instances, the department chair or the proposal's lead faculty member came to the library to explore the idea long before preparing the first draft proposal. Having had some success in shepherding an applied doctoral proposal through the approval process at a research institution, Evans always recommended undertaking what he called a "dissertation feasibility" study early in the planning process.

A feasibility study draws on existing doctoral dissertations in the field(s) of the proposed degree. (Rarely does a doctoral program begin by offering work in the entire discipline but, rather, in just a few subfields based on existing faculty strengths and interest in directing a doctoral student's work.) Essentially the purpose of the study is to determine whether the dissertation could have been completed using the institution's resources, especially library resources. The most common assumptions surrounding doctoral degree proposals include the following:

- Only a few of the possible subfields in the discipline will be offered initially. Subfields offered reflect existing institutional resource strengths.
- Any meaningful dissertation will need to draw on some off-campus resources; however, many of the necessary resources will be locally available. A less than 50 percent level of accessibility of necessary resources in local library holdings indicates that substantial work will be required to build up appropriate resources.
- The number of specialties offered will expand over time.
- Enrollment will be low during the start-up period, which will reduce pressure on library services.
- Any such program will substantially increase institutional direct and indirect operating costs, including those of the library.

In one instance, a factor in moving the proposal forward was that the private university's dean of the school of education had been the academic vice president during the first five years of Evans's tenure as director of the library. The dean had had to struggle with finding funding to allow the library to acquire resources for new certificate and degree programs that had not factored those needs into their proposals. As a result, the dean fought for and secured special funding over a five-year period for library purchases of material to support the program once it was approved. In the final approved version, the program was a stand-alone degree at the private university.

A feasibility study provides the department and the library with realistic, useful data about existing collection strengths in the subfields. It also provides a basis for calculating some of the start-up costs in terms of library resources as well as a sense of how much time may be required to acquire the items. Of the five departments hoping to implement a doctoral program in this example, only one had succeeded as of 2016. Four of the PhD hopefuls had yet to demonstrate the need for a program or that adequate resources existed to support such a program should it be authorized. The successful program was

[CONTINUED ON FOLLOWING PAGE]

[CONTINUED]

an applied doctorate, an EdD (doctorate of education), and even this proposal went through a number of iterations. In its first form, it was to be a joint program with a nearby public university, with that university's library supplying all the resources for the students. (This approach was a result of a feasibility study involving sixteen dissertations in the subfields the schools of education wished to offer.)

The point we are making is that new degree programs require careful planning, with library involvement at the earliest developmental stages. Many faculty members and administrators do not fully appreciate the amount of time it takes for a library to identify, acquire, and process library collections in a new area of interest or how students may access information in the future. This is especially true for graduate-level programs.

We know that learning is a way of being in the world that describes our capacity to respond constructively to the constant change in our lives. It is the capacity to find the potential for learning in every new event and interaction with our environment. As we live, we learn our way into new possibilities for ourselves. (p. 5)

Expanding one's possibilities through learning, whether in terms of leisure or work, has become a significant source of income for many higher education institutions, regardless of type. At some institutions, it generates the second-largest revenue stream after on-campus degree candidates' tuition and fees. Expenses for such programs are somewhat higher than for traditional degree programs (not that those costs are low) because institutions must account for the increased levels of marketing required to compete with for-profit and professional organizations. All this means is greater marketing costs. Even with these added costs, such programs can generate large sums of cash for the institution.

Continuing education programs are relatively young in academia—only one hundred-plus years old. Perhaps the earliest continuing education programs date from the late 1860s in the United Kingdom, as a result of efforts at Cambridge and Oxford to assist some prospective students in London to qualify for admission (McLean, 2007, p. 4). U.S. origins lie in the land-grant program and the Wisconsin Idea that we discussed in chapter 2. The programs were then viewed as an "extension" of the campus, serving the nondegree needs of citizens of the state. Most academic institution–based programs started in the early twentieth century and continue growing today.

U.S. continuing education looks to three major markets for its students: individuals, communities (e.g., archives, libraries, and small businesses), and professional organizations (e.g., certified public accountants and educators). Community colleges are particularly active in continuing education. A rather typical breakdown of offerings at a community college are noncredit courses and workshops, business courses and workshops, and credit courses for nondegree candidates.

Spending some time looking over continuing education catalogs will quickly demonstrate how wide-ranging the topics being offered are and how they vary from term to term. All of this raises the question of how much support is necessary or should be available from the library. The answer depends on several variables. One major variable is the long-term versus short-term nature of the course or workshop. Often the offering is a one-time occurrence or the instructor varies from term to term, making it almost impossible to plan library services to meet course needs. The topic also matters; a course on making holiday gifts needs nominal support, at best, while one on world religions may require substantial

👥 FROM THE AUTHORS

Two examples of summer programs from Evans's experience were a six-week high school debate camp and an eight-week talented youth program. Greenwell also recalls working with high school debate camps at a different institution. These programs generated income for the institution and were thought to raise awareness in the students' minds of the possibilities of enrolling at the institution as an undergraduate. As these programs approached each summer, the library staff became more anxious. The label *talented youth* was most appropriate, especially when it came to thinking up pranks. Certainly the library was not the only facility on the receiving end of the mischief. However, for the library there was a constant battle to maintain the appropriate level of access to online resources for all users because one or two of the students attempted to hack into the library system or campus network—and sometimes succeeded.

Debaters presented a different challenge in their use of material required to prepare for debates and in general housekeeping in the photocopy areas. The library lost journal articles from bound journals because some of the young people cut or tore out material rather than spend money on photocopying. As the number of online databases increased, the mutilation rate dropped. Library staff and the program coordinators held annual meetings to discuss how to handle past and potential problems. Over time issues became less severe, but during the early years, the library staff felt under siege during these programs.

support. Support for academic offerings may present no special challenges if there are similar for-credit courses. Challenges do arise in long-standing certificate programs for which adequate library support is an important element in the success or failure of the program. Instructors tend to vary over time more often than in similar credit courses, which results in more variations in the course requirements and resources.

Another library challenge is to determine the privileges the adult learner should have. Will those privileges vary by type of course or workshop the individual enrolls in—noncredit, credit, or certificate? Does it matter if the student is on or off campus? How will the library gain this type of information? Especially challenging is the fact that the data vary from term to term. Many of the issues are not unlike those regarding part-time faculty, as we discussed in chapter 3.

Today's academic institutions must maximize the use of their campus and personnel. As a result, in addition to the academic year, most schools offer summer school and even intersession (between academic year terms) programs. Summer schools are often a mix of degree-related courses and typical continuing education offerings. Summer school may present some special library challenges when there are annual programs that operate for almost the entire summer break period and that are financially important but not degree oriented.

DISTANCE EDUCATION

Of special importance in adult and degree program education is the issue of distance education. As with summer school, distance education administration varies from institution to

---

 CHECK THIS OUT

A good overview of distance learning and academic libraries is Jon Ritterbush's "Assessing Academic Library Services to Distance Learners: A Literature Review of Perspectives from Librarians, Students, and Faculty" (*The Reference Librarian* 55, no. 1 [2014]: 26–36).

---

institution. Although not every academic institution offers distance education programs for earning degrees, the number of schools that do not shrinks year after year. In the not-too-distant future, such programs may have a greater number of students enrolled than will the on-campus programs.

As information and communication technologies continue to improve, the totally virtual degree becomes more acceptable both to students and to those who later employ the graduates. Schools not only are being forced to rethink their distance degree programs because of technological developments but also must evaluate or reevaluate how much the elements of the distance degree can or should vary from those of the on-campus degree.

An important element of an on-campus degree program that is missing in distance education is the "social" aspect of learning. Much learning occurs in the informal social interaction between students before class, over a cup of coffee, or in a study group. Patricia Sobrero (2008) discussed some of the ways to overcome the lack of social aspects of learning and ways to create effective e-learning communities. She identified five elements involved in creating such communities that are still relevant: leadership, negotiation, support, and maintaining and building trust. In many ways, the needs of an effective e-learning community are no different than those of any virtual group effort. Someone must be willing to lead the process without dominating the group. Building consensus and trust is even more significant than when working with a group physically located together because nonverbal communication is missing; for example, a comment that is clearly a joke in a face-to-face situation may fail in the virtual environment, even if the person has added a smiley emoji to the message.

In chapter 3 we noted that online teaching is significantly more time-consuming than face-to-face instruction. Instructors and their institutions discovered that they cannot just

---

SOMETHING TO PONDER

How do people learn? Jay Cross (2004) provided a short paragraph outlining some thoughts on the matter that remain relevant:

> One of the best ways to learn is social; we learn with and from other people. We learn by doing. Aristotle said, "What we have to learn to do, we learn by doing," and Einstein echoed, "The only source of knowledge is experience." Aristotle added, "We cannot learn without pain." Confucius said, "I hear and I forget. I see and I remember. I do and I understand." And I'll add that if I hear and see and do and then practice and teach, I understand even better. (p. 104)

👥 FROM THE AUTHORS

Evans experienced several distance education quality questions as a member of accreditation teams, as a consultant, and as a head of a library with a neighboring distance education program. As an accreditation team member, he found himself traveling on several occasions to a distance education site to interview students and investigate the quality of site support services. On one consulting assignment, undertaken at the request of the academic vice president because of on-campus student complaints at a school that had a major distance degree program, he found that the distance education program support needs from the library had completely distorted the balance between on- and off-campus student support. For example, the library had essentially allocated all the collection development funds to support distance education needs. A random sample of the online catalog database showed that no new books or media had been acquired in over eighteen years. Instead, the funds had gone toward databases and journals needed for the distance degree program.

Another distance education program was enlightening regarding the importance of maximizing distance learning revenue. Initially, the distance program was small, and only a few students came to the private university's library; in fact, there was no contact from the program's representative regarding access to library services. The library learned of the program's existence through the reference process with students from the program. As the distance program grew and more of its students arrived asking for not just reference assistance but essentially all the services available to the university's students, the library staff undertook a user study and found that just over 20 percent of all reference transactions were with distance learners. This figure represented the equivalent of one full-time reference staff member. This revelation led to a meeting between the university's head librarian, the university's academic vice president, and the person in charge of the local distance education site. The distance education representative refused even to put forward to her home institution the idea that some fee should be paid to the university for providing library services to its students—at the time numbering more than two hundred. In fact, she voiced the opinion that it was not her institution's responsibility to provide library services; such services would cost the program so much that it would have to close down. That situation, along with increased use by many other nonuniversity students and users, led the university to initiate a closed access policy limited to those having a fee-based user's card.

use technology to deliver a face-to-face course. To be effective, the course has to take on a new structure—it has to be redesigned. This process takes time and then the instructor must allow for more interaction time with students. Teaching online is quite a change from teaching in person, and being prepared is essential. Moving a course online is a time-consuming process with far more considerations than we can cover here.

Distance education should be an area of concern for any academic library. Libraries can not only support digital coursework but also offer their own online courses. The former has been a given; the latter is an area in which libraries must be more active. Although face-to-face information literacy instruction remains a common model, online instruction will become ever more critical, particularly as administrations seek more scalable delivery methods.

In the late 1970s and early 1980s, some institutions started moving into distance education. A few schools tried going nationwide with their courses but often were limited by the need for access to a physical facility and other support services such as libraries and testing centers. Not surprisingly, accreditation agencies began to question just how equal the on- and off-campus programs really were as well as the quality of the off-campus support services.

Today, technology can address most distance education library support issues (reference, e-reserves, database access, etc.). Nevertheless, the issues are of such importance to academic libraries that ACRL issued a set of standards for library support of distance education that have been updated several times, most recently in 2016. The standards include numerous expectations for financial support, technical infrastructure, access for users, assessment, personnel, management structure, and resources. The standards list the following essential services:

- research and consultation services
- online instructional and informational services in formats accessible to the greatest number of people, including those with disabilities
- reliable, rapid, secure access to online resources
- consultation services, including interaction as an embedded librarian
- a library user instruction program designed to instill independent and effective information and digital literacy skills, while specifically meeting the learner support needs of the distance learning community
- reciprocal or contractual borrowing, or interlibrary loan services in accordance with both Section 108, Reproductions by Libraries and Archives, of the Copyright Law and using a broad application of Section 107, Fair Use
- access to reserve and other instructional materials in accordance with Section 107, Fair Use, and Section 110, Exemptions for Certain Performances and Displays
- reliance upon copyright training and legal counsel
- institutional support for librarians providing clearance/compliance on copyright issues
- recognition of the importance of copyright for institutional administrators
- adequate service hours for optimum user access
- promotion of library services to the distance learning community, including documented and updated policies, management of information resources, and regulations and procedures for systematic development
- marketing of distance learning library services directly to distance learners
- prompt delivery to users of items obtained from the institution's collections, or through interlibrary loan agreement via courier or electronic delivery system
- point-of-use assistance with and instruction in the use of print and nonprint media and equipment
- provision of appropriate open access publications (ACRL, 2016)

With this level of detail, it's clear just how complex distance education support is for academic libraries. Many accrediting bodies give special attention to distance education support. As we mentioned earlier in this chapter, the library will be expected to prepare information for the self-study document and possibly participate in on-site interviews, so adhering to expectations for library support of distance learning is all the more important. We will come back to these services throughout the book.

🔒 KEY POINTS TO REMEMBER

- The debate regarding how much general and specialized education a graduate should experience is ongoing.
- The outcome of the debate will impact academic library services and collections.
- A variety of factors influence the final composition of the curriculum, such as institutional history and issues, beliefs about the value of educating the "whole person," societal concerns, accreditation agencies, student and parental interests, and departmental strength. All these factors vary over time; thus, library support must also vary.
- To most effectively support the institution's educational purposes, the library *must* maintain close ties with the faculty committee that reviews, approves, and recommends changes in courses and programs.
- Continuing education plays a significant role in many institutions in terms of curriculum issues as well as revenue. This area of the total curriculum sometimes does not receive much attention from libraries.
- Distance education is playing an ever greater role in higher education and in the not-too-distant future may be the major source of earned degrees from an institution. Library support of distance education programs is a complex issue and creates some challenges for balancing library services to students on and off campus.

REFERENCES

ACRL Association of College and Research Libraries. 2016. *Standards for distance learning library services.* www.ala.org/acrl/standards/guidelinesdistancelearning.

Berrett, Dan. 2016. General education gets an "integrative learning" makeover. *Chronicle of Higher Education.* www.chronicle.com/article/General-Education-Gets-an/237384.

Boning, Kenneth. 2007. Coherence in general education. *Journal of General Education* 56, no. 1: 1–16.

"Bush questions liberal arts; psych majors respond." 2015. *Inside Higher Ed.* https://www.insidehighered .com/quicktakes/2015/10/29/bush-questions-liberal-arts-psych-majors-respond.

Carnegie Foundation for the Advancement of Teaching. 1998. *Reinventing undergraduate education: A blueprint for America's research universities.* Modified 2001 by Melissa Bishop. Washington, DC: Carnegie Foundation for the Advancement of Teaching.

Cross, Jay. 2004. An informal history of e-learning. *On the Horizon* 12, no. 3: 103–110.

"Florida GOP vs. social science." 2011. *Inside Higher Ed.* https://www.insidehighered.com/ news/2011/10/12/florida_governor_challenges_idea_of_non_stem_degrees.

Fuess, Scott, and Nancy Mitchell. 2011. General education reform: Opportunities for institutional alignment. *Journal of General Education* 60, no. 1: 1–15.

"Kentucky's governor vs. French literature." 2016. *Inside Higher Ed.* https://www.insidehighered.com/ quicktakes/2016/02/01/kentuckys-governor-vs-french-literature.

Ko, Susan, and Daniel Rossen. 2010. *Teaching online: A practical guide.* New York: Routledge.

Lowenstein, M. 2015. General education, advising, and integrative learning. *Journal of General Education* 64, no 2: 117–130.

"Marco Rubio vs. Aristotle." 2015. *Inside Higher Ed.* https://www.insidehighered.com/quicktakes/2015/08/20/marco-rubio-vs-aristotle.

McLean, Scott. 2007. University extension and social change. *Adult Education Quarterly* 58, no. 1: 3–21.

Miller, Gary. 1988. *The meaning of general education.* New York: Teachers College Press.

Nelson, Libby. 2013. The common core on campus. *Inside Higher Ed.* https://www.insidehighered.com/news/2013/05/03/common-core-curriculum-k-12-could-have-far-reaching-effects-higher-education.

Pittendrigh, Adele. 2007. Reinventing the core: Community, dialogue and change. *Journal of General Education* 56, no. 1: 34 56.

Rhodes, Frank. 2001. A battle plan for professors to recapture the curriculum. *Chronicle of Higher Education* 48, no. 3: B7–B10.

Ritterbush, Jon. 2014. Assessing academic library services to distance learners: A literature review of perspectives from librarians, students, and faculty. *Reference Librarian* 55, no. 1: 26–36.

Rossiter, Marsha. 2007. Possible selves: Adult education perspective. *New Directions for Adult and Continuing Education* 114: 5–15.

Shapiro, Bernard. 2003. Canada's universities: Quantitative success, qualitative concerns. *Policy Options* 24, no. 8: 15–17.

Smith, Dan. 2005. Liberal arts vs. applied programming. *Canadian Journal of Higher Education* 35, no. 1: 111–132.

Smith, Virginia. 1993. "New dimension for general education." In *Higher learning in America, 1980–2000,* edited by Arthur Levine, 243–258. Baltimore: Johns Hopkins University Press.

Sobrero, Patricia. 2008. Essential components for successful virtual learning communities. *Journal of Extension* 46, no. 4: 1–11.

U.S. Department of Education. 2006. *A test of leadership: Charting the future of U.S. higher education.* Washington, DC: Department of Education.

"When the customer is right: Market-driven accountability in postsecondary education." 2000. *Change* 32, no. 3: 53–56.

CHAPTER 6

Governance

S ome of you may wonder why a chapter on governance is necessary; after all, every organization has a structure that provides the means for doing things, making decisions, and designating leadership roles. This is true. However, within higher education, unlike in other organizations, a very long tradition and belief exist about how governance should operate—sometimes the concept is labeled *shared governance* and at other times *collegial governance*. Whether this tradition has been fully operational in the recent past may be debatable. Nevertheless, the belief in the concept is widely held and has deep roots in today's colleges and universities.

What is shared or collegial governance? Does it really differ from other forms of organizational governance? Shared governance models have several common features. First and foremost is the idea that all participants in operational activities ought to have a voice in guiding those operations. Second, because of the need for broad input, the decision-making process tends to be slow in comparison to that of most other organizations. Third, decisions will likely reflect a consensus that builds up during discussions and that rarely fully reflects any one person's or group's position. Fourth, it is assumed that the process occurs within a community of peers. Finally, the process involves a great deal of interpersonal interaction. Combined, these elements make it difficult for a newcomer to quickly sort out how the process operates.

|||||| **CHECK THIS OUT**

The Association of American Universities (2013) defines shared governance as follows:

> The traditional concept of shared governance encompasses the joint efforts of the governing board, administration, and tenured faculty to govern a university internally. The composition of governing bodies varies among institutions; for example, some but not all governing boards include seats for student trustees. However, the division of responsibilities among the board, the administration, and the faculty remains broadly similar across institutions. Led by the president, the administration oversees the operation of the university, making the day-to-day decisions and implementing institutional policies. The faculty holds the primary responsibility for matters related to education and research such as setting the curriculum, while fiduciary responsibility and legal authority rest with the board.

We will explore each group and its responsibilities in detail in this chapter but found this description helpful for initially familiarizing you with the overall structure.

Most of these elements can be found in other organizational structure models such as participatory management. However, not all the elements are present in the other organizational models. Few organizational models have a tradition going back nearly eight hundred years. From the very beginnings of higher education, faculty and students have played an active role in making decisions about the process. The goal was a consensus that takes time, and although students and faculty were not full peers, the different voices were listened to respectfully. There is something to the idea that history does carry weight into the present.

Shared governance in U.S. higher education results in a complex and, at times, frustrating decision-making process and questions about who is in charge. A published organization chart may reflect the official version of how lines of communication and control operate. However, all organizations have an informal structure in addition to the formal lines of communication. In the case of higher education, the informal structure is much more important in terms of how things actually work. Learning how the institution really operates is important for any librarian joining an academic institution. Needless to say, you must start with the formal elements and then move on to the informal side in order to begin to understand what happens and how; the latter may take some time to sort through.

All higher education institutions, whether public or private, have seven broad groups that may have a voice in decision making: a governing board, a chief executive officer (usually called a president, but other titles also exist), the president's cabinet (usually vice presidents or vice chancellors), "middle level" administrators (deans, department chairs, and heads of other operating units such as information services or human resources), the faculty, the students, and the staff. For public institutions, another layer that adds to the complexity of governance is the state or other funding body.

ROLE OF THE STATE

The state also has a role, even if a minor one, in every academic institution within its borders. Its role in private institutions is primarily limited to issuing the charter that allows for the establishment of the school. As a source of funds for public institutions, the state has some say in the governance of those institutions. You may recall that in chapter 2 we mentioned that Harvard was the first school in the world to receive a charter from a legislative body. This pattern of legislative authority for U.S. higher education institutions is one of higher education's distinguishing features.

||||| CHECK THIS OUT

Does collegial or shared governance really matter in terms of academic library operations? Yes, and the influence goes beyond how the library structures its own governance. Here is a good article that shows how libraries can be involved:

Mix, Vickie Lynn. 2013. Library and university governance: Partners in student success. *Reference Services Review* 41, no. 2: 253–265.

We will come back to ways the library can contribute to student success many times throughout this book.

📠 AN INTERESTING FACT

New York had a statewide board of regents for all chartered academic institutions. Melvil Dewey, of Dewey Decimal fame, served as secretary of the state board of regents from 1888 through 1899. Under his stewardship the board required annual reports from the institutions, which Dewey then used to compile a list of institutions "in good standing" (*New York Times,* 1899).

During the nineteenth century, state legislatures were liberal in handing out charters with little regard for how sound the institution might be. They also took little interest in overseeing the institutions after granting the charter—there was no quality control beyond that exercised by the institution. Part of the reason for the lack of oversight of private schools was the *Dartmouth* decision by the U.S. Supreme Court indicating that the trustees should be in control (see the section "Post-War of Independence to 1865" in chapter 2). In some cases, state legislatures delegated the granting of charters to an ex officio agent who had no interest in higher education beyond collecting the appropriate fee for a charter. By the start of the twentieth century, states began to worry about the quality of higher education within institutions they had chartered, and the movement toward accreditation gained momentum.

Michael R. Mills (2007) summarized the role of states in public higher education: "States seem to stagger in different directions; some opt for more centralized organizations while others attempt to decentralize their systems" (p. 162). In broad terms, there are three state models:

- A statewide governing board responsible for all operations of public institutions
- A statewide coordinating board
- A statewide planning board, but lacking coordinating authority

A few institutions (University of Michigan, University of California, and University of Colorado, for example) exist as a state constitutional entity. That is, the university is established through the state constitution as are the legislative, judicial, and executive branches.

As for academic library operations, the state's role is generally minimal. That is not to say that state regulations do not intrude from time to time, especially when it comes to major purchases or statewide budget cuts. Required audits and inventories can be quite time-consuming. In the past, some states imposed rules on public academic library acquisitions practices that treated books and journals the same as office supplies or that required the library to put its journal subscriptions out for annual bids. Such practices disrupted subscriptions by creating delays in awarding a contract, even when the former vendor won the bid.

THOSE WHO ESTABLISH GUIDELINES

In any type of organization, all activities are being done by one of three categories of individuals—those who do the work, those who administer the work, and those who set guidelines for doing the work. Within academia, some of those roles are blurred, as we noted in the opening sections of this chapter. However, in theory, the institution's governing board is the body that establishes guidelines and policy. Although individuals debate where the responsibility for academic leadership ought to reside, how influential certain voices should be in determining institutional direction, or a host of other policy issues, no one argues that the governing board doesn't have the final legal authority when it comes to the institution.

Governing boards have several different titles depending on the history and nature of the school. Some institutions employ the term *trustees* and others use *regents.* Some of the oldest schools have labels such as *overseers, visitors,* and even *curators* for their board members.

Composition of the governing board has varied through time. At the start of the nineteenth century, schools were caught up in a struggle between sectarian and secular control of their boards. As you will recall, all the early colleges started as church-related institutions. As you might guess, the early boards consisted of clergy of the denomination that established the college, similar to the pattern in northern Europe. A few followed the English model of "collegial control" with occasional visitations by selected laypersons. Today, many such schools have only nominal connections with their founding denomination. Others, such as Catholic colleges and universities, have remained steadfast to their religious roots. However, even these institutions have changed their board compositions over time. A governing board made up of unpaid laypeople is a distinguishing feature of U.S. higher education.

Until the late nineteenth century, boards did in fact control the institutions, especially after the *Dartmouth* decision. However, many college presidents engaged in major struggles with their boards over the degree of control each had. By the late nineteenth century, presidents began to gain the ascendancy in terms of overall leadership. Several factors led to this outcome, including the growing complexity of programs and institutional size. Part-time lay board members simply lacked the detailed knowledge to do more than depend on the president for information and recommendations. Another factor was that, more and more, the presidents played the key role in selecting replacement board members.

👥 FROM THE AUTHORS

Evans once had the title "The Librarian" and worked with a subcommittee of the "Visitors Board" as part of his duties. At least once a year, several committee members made an appointment to meet with "The Librarian" to discuss library operations. All but one of those meetings were friendly and pleasant and revolved around what the committee might do to help move the library's activities forward. They were of enormous help in raising funds for special projects. However, Evans's decision to switch to the Library of Congress Classification system, after 120 years of using a homegrown system, triggered a "visit" from the entire committee and other interested institutional staff. The visit lasted a full day, but, with the assistance of the central library personnel, the library gained the approval of the committee to move ahead with the change. Certainly it is unusual to have even a subcommittee of the governing board take such an interest in library operational details, but it does happen.

Today, boards have an association to support their role as "overseers" of an institution, the Association of Governing Boards of Universities and Colleges (AGB). The association publishes a handbook for new board members, and this document is well worth a librarian's time to review in order to better understand the board's role in institutional governance. The book, along with seminars provided by the association, has led to much greater standardization and quality of board practices across the country. It has also helped explain higher education to new members who may not have in-depth knowledge of all that is involved in today's complex institutions, institutions that are far more complex than when those members attended college themselves. There is little doubt that governing boards are the keystone in governance structure and that they play a critical role in interpreting the institution to society, as well as in providing the mechanism for society's voice to be heard within higher education.

It is the governing board's power, authority, and responsibility to establish policies and serve as the last "court of appeal" for the institution. Our example relating to the changing of a library's classification system (see the sidebar "From the Authors") reveals both the final authority of the board as well as the tensions that can arise when the board becomes involved in institutional operational issues. Although the library system staff supported the move, several faculty members had objected to the change and voiced their concern to the overseers.

Some years ago, James L. Fisher (1991), a retired university president, outlined the following thirteen board responsibilities that still apply to today's boards:

- Appointing the president (perhaps the board's most important obligation)
- Evaluating the institution (this is in addition to any accreditation evaluations)
- Assessing board policies (this should occur every four to five years)
- Supporting the president (an important but delicate task because the board's duty is to the institution as a whole)
- Reviewing the president's performance (second only to the board's appointing powers)
- Reviewing the institutional mission (this should be done every four to five years)
- Reviewing and approving long-range plans (review, adjust, approve)
- Overseeing educational programs (guide but do not direct)
- Ensuring financial solvency (make final hard fiscal decisions, set tuition rates, monitor endowments)
- Preserving institutional independence (help resist undue outside influence)
- Representing both the institution and the public (a difficult balancing process at times)
- Serving as a court of appeal (the last stop before the civil legal system)
- Assessing the board's performance (hire an outside agent to assess the board's performance) (pp. 93–105)

Thinking about this list, you can imagine just how often boards are caught in the middle, sometimes between the school and society, sometimes between the president and the faculty, sometimes between students and their parents and the institution, and sometimes between any of these groups as well as other stakeholders. Boards of public institutions probably have the greatest difficulty in being the bridge between the institution and the state or society. Often board members are asked or expected to reflect the current "political will" rather than sound educational practice. Obviously, shifting political wills can cause serious challenges for degree programs.

One example of the complexity in a state system in terms of governing boards is California. Within the state are three separate multicampus institutions of higher education, each with its own governing structure. First are the regents of the University of California (UC), who oversee ten campuses. The board consists of the following members:

- Eighteen regents are appointed by the governor for twelve-year terms.
- One is a student appointed by the regents to a one-year term.
- Seven are ex officio members—the governor, lieutenant governor, speaker of the assembly, superintendent of public instruction, president and vice president of the alumni associations of UC, and the UC president.
- In addition, two faculty members—the chair and vice chair of the academic council—sit on the board as nonvoting members. (Regents of the University of California, 2016)

Second are the trustees of the California State University (CSU). They have twenty-three campuses under their purview. CSU's governing body has twenty-five members and meets seven times a year. "Board meetings allow for communication among the trustees, chancellor, campus presidents, executive committee members of the statewide Academic Senate, representatives of the California State Student Association, and officers of the statewide Alumni Council" (California State University, 2016).

Last is the board of governors of the California Community Colleges, which has seventy-two community college districts (each with a board of trustees) and 110 campuses. The following statement directly addresses governance:

> The 17-member Board is appointed by the governor and formally interacts with state and federal officials and other state organizations. The Board of Governors selects a chancellor for the system. The chancellor, through a formal process of consultation, brings recommendations to the board, which has the legislatively granted authority to develop and implement policy for the colleges.
>
> Additionally, each of the 72 community college districts in the state has a locally elected Board of Trustees, responsive to local community needs and charged with the operations of the local colleges. The governance system of the California Community Colleges is one which uses processes of shared governance. (California Community Colleges Chancellor's Office, 2016)

These examples illustrate just how complex governance is and how the "political will" might become a major factor for public higher education institutions. It probably is also a clear reason why decision-making times tend to be long, as the examples describe only the top level of the total process.

One of the ongoing criticisms or concerns about governing boards is their membership. As the emphasis on becoming a diverse institution has grown, so has the pressure to diversify board membership. Earlier we mentioned that the first U.S. boards were members of the clergy, then laypeople (alumni and other professionals), and now it is not uncommon for the majority of members to be businesspeople. Two significant advantages of having businesspeople on the board are that such people often, either personally or

> ▓▓▓ **CHECK THIS OUT**
>
> **King, C. Judson.** 2013. *Tailoring shared governance to the needs and opportunities of the times.* Research and Occasional Papers Series. Berkeley: University of California Center for Studies in Higher Education. www.cshe.berkeley.edu/publications/tailoring-shared-governance-needs -andopportunities-times.
>
> We used the University of California in our example because it is a rather complex and structured system of shared governance. King's paper provides a closer look at issues with shared governance and how it can be made most effective, using some examples from his fifty-plus years of experience in the University of California system.

through their contacts, provide financial support for the institution as well as much-needed political support.

The growth in the number of businesspeople on the boards has generated complaints, especially from faculty and staff, that these members try to impose a "corporate model" on the institution that is counter to shared governance. In keeping with that corporate model, some institutions are headed by former business executives or retired politicians. Finding the correct balance between being cost aware and being cost efficient is a challenge. Also business-dominated boards can fall into practicing micromanagement. Such micromanaging can arise in the following areas:

- Appointments and promotions (overriding faculty recommendations)
- Student recruiting strategies and tactics (second-guessing professionals)
- Course approval (rejecting a course approved by the faculty)
- Approval of public programs (rejecting a speaker or group because of disapproval of the presumed message or orientation)
- Apportionment (rejecting institutionally generated reallocation plans)
- Salary adjustments (overriding distribution plans made by the administration)

Most boards find the middle ground and provide the help, guidance, and voice that keep the institution moving forward without unduly influencing operations. Furthermore, most board members understand that effective governance and management of an institution represent a means to an end and are not ends in themselves. They know that the central purposes are scholarship and learning. Evidence of satisfactory progress and achievement is gratification enough for the vast majority of board members.

THOSE WHO ADMINISTER

The list of those who administer within the institution is long, complex, and sometimes muddled. There is, of course, the chief executive officer or president to whom several vice presidents—of academic affairs, student affairs, or business affairs, for example—may report to assist in the daily operations. Below this level on the academic side are deans, department chairs, and directors of centers or institutes, for example. Also located at this level are directors of various support services such as financial aid, admissions, and facilities.

The academic library can fall into various levels depending on the organizational structure of the institution and on whether the professional librarians are tenure-track. The head of the library may carry the title of director, dean, or university librarian. In some cases, the title may be associate vice provost or associate vice chancellor. Sometimes the campus information technology unit and the campus libraries are one entity, so the library leader might also hold the title of campus chief information officer (CIO). To whom the library reports varies as well. In some cases, the chief librarian might report to the provost or chancellor along with the other deans and be a regular member of the dean's council. In other cases, the library might report to academic affairs or some other administrative group. There are certainly many models, and when researching an institution with a job vacancy, it's important to do some research on the organizational structure, particularly before an interview.

Until the late nineteenth century, college presidents acted as the interpreters and justifiers of governing board actions to their faculties and students. That role reversed in the twentieth century and continued that way until just before the twenty-first century began. Today, most presidents are being asked to fill both roles as boards appear to be more activist, an outcome that institutional personnel may find counter to collegial governance.

During the first century or more of U.S. higher education, there was little concern about institutional governance. The reason, more often than not, was that only the governing board and the president, who was also an instructor, governed the school. In many ways the early college president was *the* college. His character became a reflection of the college. However, as the student body grew, so did the number of teachers, which in turn made administration and governance more complex. Students and teachers also began to assert their traditional roles in campus governance (more about this aspect later in this chapter).

After the U.S. Civil War, new administrators began to appear on campus, adding yet another layer of complexity. In the mid-1870s, Harvard's president Charles William Eliot appointed a faculty member "dean." This appointment opened a floodgate of new deans and department chairs—deans of faculty, deans of colleges, deans of student affairs, and deans of libraries, for example.

For much of the nineteenth and first half of the twentieth centuries, some institution presidents gained reputations of being "giants" in higher education, at least by their peers and society at large. Not many of those who had that reputation were popular with the faculty, staff, and students at their institutions because they tended to be highly autocratic and made little effort to even appear to consult on decisions or policy issues. Starting in the early 1900s, faculty began to reassert a little of their traditional role after the American

👥 FROM THE AUTHORS

As you might expect, increasing the number of administrators leads to increased personnel costs because many of these individuals no longer (or never did) teach and, in some cases, are not qualified to teach but can administer a campus program. The growth of this practice during the past century has not diminished; for example, when Evans started working at a university in 1988 there were forty-five full-time administrators, not counting department chairs. Upon his retirement in 2005, that number had grown to sixty-eight. Such growth is one of the factors that lead to the tuition increases that exceed the general inflation rate for the country.

Association of University Professors (AAUP) became active. Today, for many presidents, their primary role is to serve as a mediator between the many stakeholders in higher education. The major stakeholders are the following:

- Governing board members
- Faculty
- Students
- Staff
- Society at large (including the local community)
- Government bodies (local, state, and national)
- Accreditation agencies
- Business interests
- Parents of students
- Donors
- Alumni
- Other higher education institutions

Certainly these groups overlap somewhat, but you can imagine where a president might encounter very different views on the part of two or more of these groups on an important institutional issue.

As mediators, presidents seek to maintain peace between the factions and to foster progress. Of the two goals, progress is more essential, so eventually a side will be taken, at least in the view of those who do not like the decision, even when the president's position is actually some compromise between the various views. The faculty's ultimate option for expressing their unhappiness is to vote no confidence in the president. Other stakeholders have various modes for voicing their displeasure. What presidents need, and sometimes do not have, is ready access to each group; a fair opportunity to present their views in each forum; a chance to contrast reality with illusion(s); and, on occasion, a chance to argue for the position of reason as they see it. Ultimately they are responsible for the campus "family," as presidents increasingly choose to call it (Sandoval, 2016).

⦚⦚ CHECK THIS OUT

For a colorful and candid look at what it's like to be a university president, check out Steven Sample's story of his presidency at the University of Southern California. He describes what he learned throughout his career, which helped him become a better leader. Although the book has become popular with CEOs wanting a leadership formula ("work for those who work for you," "think free and gray," and so on), it remains a fascinating look at what the job of university president entails:

Sample, Steven B. 2003. *The contrarian's guide to leadership.* New York: Jossey-Bass.

Another president's story is William Chace's memoir from his time as an undergraduate to a faculty member to president at two universities. He provides a candid discussion of what it's like to be a university president:

Chace, William. 2006. *100 semesters: My adventures as student, professor, and university president, and what I learned along the way.* Princeton, NJ: Princeton University Press.

In light of these pressures, you probably would not be surprised to learn that presidential tenures have been decreasing in length. Until well into the twentieth century, presidents had almost lifetime tenures, assuming they wanted to stay. Certainly presidents were dismissed, but that was a rare and highly notable event. Today, the average tenure is seven years or less (American Council on Education, 2012). As the environment has become more complex, burnout is probably the major factor rather than board, faculty, or student displeasure with performance.

Earlier we noted that governments were one of the stakeholders in higher education. Although presidents are not the only individuals within the institution who must address governmental interests and concerns, as the primary administrators they are the lead persons as far as governmental agencies are concerned. We touched on the state role earlier, and the federal level also has a surprising amount of influence on institutional policy. For example, when an institution accepts federal funding (such as research grants or student aid), it must abide by federal regulations, including the employment regulations that come into play, or lose the funds.

If all the factors we mentioned are not enough to cause burnout, the list of skills, talents, and abilities that governing boards seek in their presidential candidates highlights the nearly impossible job today's college and university presidents face. The following list also reflects many of the interests or expectations that other stakeholders have for the president:

- Be a distinguished scholar with classroom and research credentials.
- Have solid local and national political connections while being politically savvy and able to work with all political points of view.
- Be highly visible on campus and accessible to everyone associated with the school.
- Attend all institutional functions from governing board meetings to student picnics and have a presence at any off-campus activity that may have an institutional implication or value.
- Be able to address all alumni expectations no matter how contradictory some might be.
- Support high academic standards and keep retention rates high.
- Be an advocate of premier athletic programs.
- Be an exceptional fund-raiser.
- Be the leader in collegial governance.
- Be an advocate for research excellence while maintaining tight fiscal reins on institutional expenditures.

The list could go on and on; however, it does outline many of the expectations placed on new presidents. Is it any wonder that presidents feel pulled in all directions and know that by setting priorities, which they must do, they will likely upset some people? Also, it is not surprising that people on campus wonder from time to time why the president has not been seen recently. It also suggests why presidential tenures keep getting shorter and shorter. Today's presidents find themselves being the fulcrum between various constituencies, internal and external, with differing values, interests, priorities, and perspectives.

Sometimes the campus library is fortunate to have a president who has an interest in the library and does all he can to support its activities. At other times, a president has no interest in the library. On rare occasions, there is a president who views the library as a major "black hole" that requires vast sums of money with no real return and blocks efforts to increase funding, perhaps even reducing funding. Each situation requires a different approach from the library as well as an understanding of campus politics and governance. The head of the library not only has to understand the politics of the institution at all levels but also has to delve into those politics as the primary advocate for the library in efforts to influence decision makers, their peers, and faculty and student governance.

On the other hand, frontline librarians can play an important advocacy role articulating the value of the campus library and their own value as well. These librarians have access to a multitude of campus faculty members and students (that the head of the library doesn't) through areas such as reference services, departmental liaisons, and information literacy instruction. Providing new library personnel with an orientation to the campus can help emphasize the fact that all library staff are an essential part of the library's marketing and advocacy activities. As we have mentioned previously, library personnel should try to serve on university committees and participate on faculty and staff senates as appropriate. The academic library supports the mission of the larger institution, so at every level, it's important for personnel to have basic knowledge of the institution and actively participate in institutional activities.

THOSE WHO DO

At the doing level there are three primary campus groups who expect or want a voice in institutional matters: faculty, students, and staff. How loud each voice is varies from institution to institution and according to the institution's philosophy regarding shared governance. The very origin of shared governance resides at this level. It goes back to the time when students and faculty made the decisions, and there were no administrators, much less governing boards. How well that system worked, at least in laying a solid foundation for higher education, is reflected in a little-known fact. If you go back to the sixteenth century in Western Europe and look at the institutions that existed then and that still exist in the twenty-first century, you would identify sixty-six organizations. Leading the list are the Catholic Church and the Lutheran Church, followed by the parliaments on the Isle of Man and Iceland and then sixty-two universities. This record is rather impressive for a governance model that many people believe is most ineffective.

Although the presidents, vice presidents, deans, and directors provide the institutional administrative structure, a variety of bodies (senates, councils, committees, and departments, for example) at the "doing" level also may play a role in decision making and institutional operations. Some suggest, as did William Bergquist (1992), that there is a dual culture at most institutions—managerial and collegial. Generally speaking, those at the doing level (collegial) have a louder voice on educational matters (courses, requirements, etc.) than they do on managerial issues such as finances. Gerald Kissler (1997) noted,

> At large campuses faculty have fewer interactions with administrators. Presidents seem distant; there are fewer opportunities to build trust and mutual respect. Also, faculty governance on large campuses operates through representative bodies rather than town meetings. Even if crisis conditions cause the president to call a campus meeting, many will not attend and the nature of a large gathering will lead to more of a presentation of information than an open discussion. (p. 457)

If "those who do" have little influence over budgets and allocations, in what areas do their voices matter? Some of the typical areas are courses, degree requirements, admission standards, distance education, and diversity issues.

The most common forum for voicing thoughts and communicating views to the administration is the senate or council (faculty, staff, and students will likely each have one). As the prior paragraph stated, most of such bodies are composed of elected representatives from the group(s) in question. This is the formal side of the process; the informal side also plays a role. Minor and Tierney (2005) wrote,

> From time to time one hears about a president who receives a vote of no confidence from the campus senate, or a senate that is dissolved by the president. Such cases exemplify campuses with troubled governance. However, dramatic examples of this kind are rare. The larger problem pertaining to shared governance rests with the ability to make decisions intended to improve the quality of the institution that have the substantial input and support of multiple groups of rather sporadically involved or disengaged contingencies. (p. 138)

One reasonably sound method for achieving such ongoing input and support is to have representative bodies that meet regularly with senior administrators. We should note that most of the literature on senates or councils focuses on the faculty; however, the process and issues apply to all such bodies, including any council(s) that exists in the library.

James Minor (2004) published a study that identified four models of faculty senates—functional, influential, ceremonial, and subverted. Although his research focused on faculty senates, his models apply to all such academic bodies. Functional senates, according to Minor, operate in a manner that reflects the interests of the disciplines to which their members belong. Although such groups do, at times, address campus-wide concerns, generally they tend to concentrate on self-interest topics. As in all of Minor's models, institutional bylaws govern the group's activities, and such groups tend to have a number of standing committees, such as a courses and programs committee. Often membership on such committees is a function of being a friend of a member of the senate's executive committee. Membership is tightly held to faculty only. Staff committees of this type tend to focus on salary, benefits, and working conditions, while faculty groups are particularly interested in faculty appointments, promotions and tenure, and curriculum issues. Needless to say,

👥 FROM THE AUTHORS

Academic libraries can be and are influenced by senates or councils. One obvious way is through a library advisory committee consisting of faculty and students. Such committees are often a standing committee of the faculty senate. We explore such bodies in more detail later in this book.

Evans had a library committee that required that all of its actions deemed "significant" (most matters the committee members voted on fell into that category) had to go to the faculty senate for ratification. (We mention student representation on this committee in chapter 3.) He also dealt with a request from the staff senate to have a seat on the committee. Not too surprisingly, this request took time to grant and required several appearances before the faculty senate to gain that body's approval. The faculty senate also granted the librarians a seat on that body, although librarians did not have faculty status. They also were allowed to run for "at large" seats. Often, the librarians held two seats. Sometimes excellent library service pays off in unexpected ways.

👥 FROM THE AUTHORS

Evans served on several Western Association visiting teams. He knows from two such experiences that the commission interprets the governance question to include staff, students, governing boards, and other interested parties. Also because of such experiences, he knows that the issue of governance, including library governance, can have a negative impact on the team's assessment of the institution.

student groups are primarily concerned with tuition rates and fees as well as housing and food services. Thus, you can see that groups falling into this model may reflect Minor's sporadic and disengaged category, which adds to the difficulty of having true collegial governance. Minor (2004) wrote that such groups "are not particularly assertive and usually do not set their own agendas. Instead, they respond to the initiatives and actions of the administration or issues that arise from the environment" (p. 349).

Influential bodies have and use real governance power. They come about through an institutional culture that legitimizes their authority. Generally, no one with administrative responsibilities may be a member of the body. With their greater power, such groups tend to have a broad-based campus focus and often are initiators of discussions and debates about issues. "These senates usually maintain collaborative rather than confrontational relationships with the administration" (Minor, 2004, p. 351).

Ceremonial senates, as the name suggests, carry little weight when it comes to campus decision making. Often these bodies come into existence where there are strong senior administrators who believe that actions must be taken swiftly. Such bodies are rarely created as ceremonial but evolve into this role over time, in part because of lack of interest on the part of faculty, staff, and students in governance. As a result, the administration takes on more of the authority and power to make decisions. Occasionally a very strong president or governing board that ignores input from others generates an atmosphere that leads to ceremonial bodies. Minor wrote that such groups are "a place where the faculty go to discuss what they think is going on or talk about decisions after they have been made" (Minor, 2004, p. 351).

You might wonder why an institution would bother trying to maintain a ceremonial governance body. There are probably a number of reasons for doing so. However, one major reason is accreditation. Regional accreditation agencies all address governance in their standards. For example, standard 7 of the Middle States Commission on Higher Education reads, in part, that an accredited institution must have

> a clearly articulated and transparent governance structure that outlines roles, responsibilities, and accountability for decision making by each constituency, including governing body, administration, faculty, staff and students. (Middle States Commission on Higher Education, 2015, p. 15)

As part of its accreditation process, the Western Association of Schools and Colleges employs a series of accountability questions that it expects the institution to answer with data or proof of how it addresses them. One of the association's questions is, "What process does the school use to evaluate its organization, governance structures, and decision-making procedures?" (Accrediting Commission for Schools, 2013, p. 30).

Minor's final model (subverted) is the least desirable, but you may well encounter one sometime during your career. A common circumstance that leads to such bodies is that informal networks dominate the decision-making process. Essentially the formal structure, which does exist, does not carry enough weight to overcome the views of a few influential people (senior faculty and staff) who are not members of the senate or council.

In one sense, shared governance and feedback exist, but they take place outside the formal structure and, often, do not reflect the majority view on the issue. As Minor (2004) noted, "Subverted senates usually suffer from negative cultural and communicative aspects that affect their role in campus decision making" (p. 353).

Regardless of where the senate or council falls on the continuum from functional to subverted, such bodies are an integral part of campus governance. The tradition of faculty and student voices being most important when it comes to educational decision making goes back to the very beginning of higher education.

CONCLUDING THOUGHTS ON CAMPUS GOVERNANCE

At the core of campus governance are three fundamental issues: decision making, resource acquisition, and resource allocation. The latter two might be subsets of decision making; however, these two can become volatile in a serious emergency, making shared governance almost a must. How to handle them in a timely and effective manner is the challenge.

"Those who do" often view administrators as generating an incredible amount of red tape, constraining creativity, being concerned only about keeping costs down. They also often think of administrators as a source of "outside" pressure(s) to alter the activities in undesirable ways. On the other hand, those who administer may from time to time view those who do as totally unconcerned about costs and where the money may come from, unwilling to respond to legitimate requests for accountability, willing to change only under the most dire of circumstances, and unable to grasp the fact that the supply of money is not limitless. Is it any wonder that campus governance is contentious from time to time? The Association of American Universities' (2013) statement on shared governance nicely sums up the importance of collaboration among the groups involved:

> While the ultimate legal authority of the university rests with the governing board, the success of shared governance lies in communication and cooperation among the different groups involved. The components of the institution are interdependent. By including multiple constituencies in decision-making processes, the university can ensure that different voices are heard and integrated into a cohesive vision. Shared governance thus provides the mechanisms to support the university's autonomy, enabling the institution to fulfill its educational, research, and service missions. (p. 3)

One interesting aspect of shared governance is authority. From an administrative perspective, authority is predicated on control and coordination by supervisors. Professional authority is predicated on autonomy and individual knowledge. These two types of campus authority also add to the challenges of campus governance. Thinking back to your basic management coursework, you will recall five types of power in society—coercive, reward, legitimate, referent, and expert (see Evans and Alire, 2013).

A quick review of the five types of power includes the following. For senior managers in higher education, including those in libraries, any use of coercive power—except in the worst of circumstances—is likely to lead to serious problems such as votes of no confidence. Even too much use of reward power can be detrimental over time. Most faculty and staff accept a modicum of legitimate power and authority use. For example, department heads have the power to set schedules, and library directors can commit their libraries to certain obligations in a consortium. (However, the wise holder of legitimate power will consult as much as possible before making a decision.) Referent power arises from others' acceptance of the power position because of who the holder is. Expert power resides in a person's special knowledge or skill. Referent and expert power are the stuff from which true collegial governance is made.

Another factor that confuses the governance picture is that most professionals have a dual orientation. Sometimes the orientation is described as a continuum with "cosmopolitan" at one end and "local" at the other. A professional with a strong cosmopolitan orientation is first and foremost discipline-committed, with the institution a distant second when it comes to issues that cut across both sides. You can easily tell a professional's orientation by the manner in which she describes her employment: "I teach [or work] at College X" is a local response. "I'm a professor of geology at University Y" is a typical response of a cosmopolitan. Orientation can matter a great deal, especially when it comes to trying to balance professional and institutional needs.

Other factors that muddle the picture are status, prestige, and rank. One example is the Nobel Prize–winning professor who has greater influence over other faculty within the institution than does the president or most members of the governing board. Thus, it is not always seniority or title that matters the most.

A closing thought on successful shared governance is from C. Judson King (2013) regarding what it takes for shared governance to be successful:

> Avenues for examining, assessing and improving shared governance include written delineation of roles and expectations in clear form, engendering and enabling changes in working methods to meet evolving needs and opportunities, seeking and implementing ways of moving the consultation process along more efficiently and rapidly, adherence to principles of subsidiarity of governance and correspondence of levels of consultation, continual reexamination of the ways in which the faculty senate and the university administration work together, making full information on issues available to both the administration and the faculty, reporting the spectrum of views within

 KEEP IN MIND

For the academic librarian, it is very helpful to understand campus governance and how the library plays a part in that structure. Greenwell learned how important it is for the academic librarian, particularly one in administration, to pay close attention to campus governing bodies and participate as relevant. She has worked for library deans and directors who never missed an opportunity to sit in on open board of trustees meetings and faculty senate meetings. This attendance is important for staying in touch with what's happening on campus and planning for library participation and support. There is an element of face time as well. Frequent library representation at such events shows a genuine interest but also keeps the library fresh in the minds of others around campus.

the Senate to the administration, assuring that participation in faculty senate work is attractive throughout the faculty, and finding ways to rectify the situation if that is not the case. (p. 7)

That's a tall order, but all those elements are important in keeping a cooperative, balanced, and successful governance structure.

🔒 KEY POINTS TO REMEMBER

- Academic governance is a complex process with many stakeholders who wish to have a voice in that process.
- Understanding this process is a key factor in how effective the librarians and academic library are in supporting the institution's mission.
- Some of the most significant stakeholders are trustees, administrators, faculty, students and parents, staff, and society.
- Governing boards are the final authority on institutional matters.
- Boards can and do take an interest in small operational matters from time to time but generally leave such matters to faculty and staff to handle.
- Boards have some obligation to provide society's voice to the institution, which can be a challenge at times because they must also take responsibility for maintaining the institution's mission.
- A board's foremost duty is to select and evaluate the performance of the institution's president.
- Presidents have the difficult role of explaining board actions to faculty, staff, and students as well as explaining the viewpoints, needs, and desires of those groups to the board. At times of high tension between the board and people within the institution, the challenge is especially great.
- Senates or councils for faculty, staff, and students can play a significant role in campus governance, if they make the effort.

REFERENCES

Accrediting Commission for Schools, Western Association of Schools and Colleges. 2013. *Postsecondary accreditation manual.* Burlingame, CA: Western Association of Schools and Colleges.

American Council on Education. 2012. *The American college president 2012.* Washington, DC: American Council on Education.

Association of American Universities. 2013. "Academic principles: A brief introduction." http://eric .ed.gov/?&id=ED555641.

Bergquist, William H. 1992. *Four cultures of the academy.* San Francisco, CA: Jossey-Bass.

California Community Colleges Chancellor's Office. 2016. "Board of governors." http://extranet.cccco .edu/SystemOperations/BoardofGovernors.aspx.

California State University. 2016. "About the board of trustees." https://www.calstate.edu/bot/overview .shtml.

Chace, William. 2006. *100 semesters: My adventures as student, professor, and university president, and what I learned along the way.* Princeton, NJ: Princeton University Press.

Evans, G. Edward, and Camila A. Alire. 2013. *Management basics for information professionals.* 3rd ed. New York: Neal-Schuman.

Fisher, James L. 1991. *The board and the president.* New York: American Council on Education/Macmillan.

King, C. Judson. 2013. *Tailoring shared governance to the needs and opportunities of the times.* Research and Occasional Papers Series. Berkeley: University of California Center for Studies in Higher Education. www.cshe.berkeley.edu/publications/tailoring-shared-governance-needs-andopportunities-times.

Kissler, Gerald. 1997. Who decides which budgets to cut? *Journal of Higher Education* 63, no. 5: 427–459.

Middle States Commission on Higher Education. 2015. *Standards for accreditation and requirements of affiliation.* Philadelphia: Middle States Commission on Higher Education.

Mills, Michael R. 2007. Stories of politics and policy. *Journal of Higher Education* 78, no. 2: 162–187.

Minor, James T. 2004. Understanding faculty senates. *Review of Higher Education* 27, no. 3: 343–363.

Minor, James T., and William Tierney. 2005. Dangers of deference: A case of polite governance. *Teachers College Record* 107, no. 1: 137–156.

Mix, Vickie Lynn. 2013. Library and university governance: Partners in student success. *Reference Services Review* 41, no. 2: 253–265.

New York Times. 1899. "Prof. Melvil Dewey resigns: Secretary of the state board of regents of the university gives up his office." December 23.

Regents of the University of California. 2016. "About the regents." www.universityofcalifornia.edu/regents/about.html.

Sample, Steven B. 2003. *The contrarian's guide to leadership.* New York: Jossey-Bass.

Sandoval, Gabriel. 2016. Why do so many college presidents call their campuses a "family"? *Chronicle of Higher Education.* www.chronicle.com/article/Why-Do-So-Many-College/237301.

CHAPTER 7

Funding

Money, or the lack thereof, has been a perennial issue for higher education institutions. In the following sections, we will look at expenditures and revenues in higher education. For the academic librarian, it is important to understand finances at the institutional level—where funds come from as well as how they are spent. We will also break down the academic library budgeting process.

Higher education's financial activities are complex. Part of that complexity arises from the multiplicity of revenue sources. Expenditures are equally varied, and there is only a modicum of connectivity between income streams and expenditures categories. The diversity of institutional types adds another layer of intricacy to sorting through where funds come from and how they are spent. Yet another issue is the presence of for-profit and nonprofit institutions essentially producing a similar "product."

Institutional finances address three major educational policy issues: quality, access, and efficiency. There is a rather widely held view within higher education, at the least on the nonprofit side, that a positive correlation exists between the level of funding and the quality of education provided. We are not certain that this view is actually proven to be the case. Certainly there is a relationship, but how strong it may be seems to be an open question. Clearly there is a connection between cost and who may gain access to higher education. Finding a balance between effectiveness and efficiency is always a challenge, and efficiency, at least in the past, was often ignored by many institutions.

The following questions underlie an institution's financial decisions:

- What is the best ratio of students to faculty?
- What is the best ratio of faculty to other staff?
- What is the best ratio of faculty and students to administrators?
- What level of student aid and tuition discount is best?

For public institutions, there is also the question of what, if any, difference there should be in tuition for in-state and out-of-state students. Ultimately, institutions must wrestle with the answer to the question of who pays or should pay. As Bruce Johnstone (2005) noted, should it be students and their parents? Taxpayers? Philanthropists? He also suggested two other thorny questions related to costs—how much education should society underwrite in some manner, and at what levels of efficiency should education be delivered (p. 370)? These questions are very much relevant today.

HIGHER EDUCATION FINANCES

As we have discussed several times, and as we realize you are likely to be all too familiar with, the cost of higher education is increasing at an astounding rate. After adjusting for inflation, between 2003–04 and 2013–14, the cost for undergraduate tuition, fees, room, and board at public institutions rose 34 percent, and the cost for the same at private, nonprofit institutions rose 25 percent. For the 2013–14 academic year, annual current dollar prices for undergraduate tuition, fees, room, and board were estimated to be $15,640 at public institutions, $40,614 at private nonprofit institutions, and $23,135 at private for-profit institutions (U.S. Department of Education, 2016). As you are reading this book, the cost of undergraduate tuition, fees, room, and board will likely have gone up substantially from those 2013–14 figures. This is not a new problem. Howard Bowen, the economist and former university president who closely studied higher education finances, noted in 1980 that "aggregate higher educational expenditures for all purposes grew prodigiously at the rate of 9.6 percent per annum over the nearly half century since 1929–30" (p. 256).

We are not going to provide numerous specific figures for you because it is fairly straightforward to find the most current figures using the *Digest of Education Statistics.* As part of the U.S. Institute of Education Sciences, the National Center for Education Statistics (NCES) collects U.S. statistical data from prekindergarten through graduate school. These data are freely available online. Topics include numbers of institutions, enrollments, faculty, graduates as well as graduation rates, persistence, institutional financial data, and a variety of other useful statistics. The NCES also provides data related to federal funding for education, educational characteristics of the workforce, attitudes toward education, and so forth. Of special interest to the academic librarian are the data available related to academic libraries.

Although different agencies interested in higher education employ a variety of categories when looking at expenditures and revenue, the NCES format has been around for many years, making it easier to compare results over time—thus our focus on its data. It is fairly straightforward to look at a single institution or single data set as well as create comparisons across two or many institutions using the report tool on the NCES website.

As for expenditures, the largest expense category within a higher education institution is salaries. Salaries and benefits account for well over half of all institutional costs. The same is true for academic libraries. Salaries and collection development funds generally account for about 80 percent of the library's total operating budget, which leaves very little for other activities. At some community colleges, salaries represent 85 percent or more of the total.

⟳ TRY THIS

In her library science classes, Greenwell likes to ask students to learn more about an institution of their choice, usually their own undergraduate institution or one in which they would like to be employed upon graduation. Learning more about the institution—its student body size, demographics, graduation rate, level of research activity, and so on—is helpful when applying for an academic library job at any level. When applying for an administrative position, such knowledge is pretty much essential. Certainly it's important to do some preinterview research about the academic library itself, but understanding the parent organization is so important. It is also important for you, the job seeker, to decide whether the institution is a good fit for you, and some basic facts about the institution are a good place to start. The NCES is a key resource for finding this kind of information, and it is freely available online. Take a look at some of the data for yourself at nces.ed.gov.

Student financial aid, as we noted earlier, is a constant concern for most institutions. How much income to devote to such aid is almost always a matter of long, if not heated, debates during the budget preparation cycle. The amount is generally a significant percentage of the remaining budget after salaries and benefits are subtracted.

Another significant cost category that has been growing is energy and utilities expenditures. Institutions are spending ever larger amounts on retrofitting facilities to be more energy efficient, installing solar panels to generate some electricity, and designing buildings that meet Leadership in Energy and Environmental Design (LEED) standards.

Two of the campus units that vie for much of the remaining funds are the library and information technology (IT). Both units seem to have a never-ending need for additional funds to enhance their services for the institution. We will talk more about information technology in chapter 9.

GRANTS AND RESEARCH

One area of institutional budgeting that may or may not help increase funding is research grants and projects. For institutions offering advanced degrees, this is a significant source of income as well as an expense. Why are grants important to the institution? First is the prestige factor. The number of faculty receiving grants as well as the dollar value of those grants play a role in how others view the institution. Grants also help attract top-quality faculty and students, which in turn adds to institutional status and reputation.

A second factor, which in many ways is more important, is the additional income grants provide for the institution. Many grants have two financial aspects. One is the money given to a researcher to carry out the desired work. The other aspect is the "overhead" money that goes to the institution for allowing the project to take place. Overhead is a charge for such things as rent on the space researchers use while engaged in the grant, the utilities consumed, support services such as the library, administrative costs, and so forth. Thus, when you hear that a researcher just received a $100,000 grant, usually the individual will not have the full amount. The researcher will likely have somewhat less based on the institution's overhead rate.

Overhead rates vary from institution to institution and by granting agency. The costs on which the rate is calculated also vary (e.g., salaries, total research cost, total cost less salaries). Faculty members and their departments that are extremely successful in securing grants often are able to have some of the overhead monies turned back to them for their use.

From the institutional perspective, grants and overhead are not just a source of operating funds; they also add much-needed equipment or facilities improvement that will last well beyond the life of the grant. Overhead and grant monies also frequently support staff salaries. Such monies may supplement the researcher's salary, and they may pay for graduate student assistants and other support staff. Individuals paid by such funds are often referred to as being on "soft" money, meaning the position lasts only for the length of the grant. Support staff positions may be partially funded by a number of grants rather than a single grant, which provides a slightly more stable position. Soft-funded positions do reduce some of the pressure on the host institution for allocating "hard" funds for support activities.

Earlier we stated that grants may or may not be cost-effective for an institution. A 2009 study reported by *Inside Higher Ed* suggested that, at least in some cases, getting a grant may cost the institution money (Stripling, 2009). According to the report,

Researchers at the University of Rochester School of Medicine & Dentistry found the cost of supporting newly recruited scientists costs an additional 40 cents over every dollar these new faculty generate from grants. While colleges may grow in prestige by expanding their research base, they're likely to dole out more money in start-up packages and other benefits for new faculty than they bring in through grants. (Stripling, 2009)

Senior faculty do indeed generate a positive cash flow from their research and grant activities; however, this may not be the case for junior faculty, even those in the hard science fields. Regardless of the overall costs involved, advanced-degree institutions will continue to require faculty members to engage in research and will expect their libraries to support those endeavors.

Research, especially in the sciences (both pure and applied), does raise some challenging issues with regard to intellectual property rights. Who "owns" the research results, in particular those that have commercial value? There is also the issue of sponsored research—research underwritten by a commercial enterprise or private individual. Is it appropriate for the institution to allow such work, and what rights does the public have to access the results? When the research was defense-related during the Cold War era, there were loud complaints against such work being conducted within higher education. Today, there are fewer comments about doing work for commercial entities.

When it comes to intellectual ownership of the content of a book written by a faculty or staff member, most institutions allow the author to retain full rights. Probably the reason for this arrangement is that the amount of money from royalties is too small to be of institutional interest, except perhaps in the case of a textbook such as Samuelson's *Economics*, now in its nineteenth edition. Even in such cases, the total amount involved is spread over a great number of years and is modest at best.

A commercially viable outcome of institutional research can mean hundreds of thousands or even millions of dollars in income in just a few years. In such cases, the institution becomes very interested. Because a book author and the inventor or discoverer of a commercially useful product or concept make use of institutional facilities and staff support, the results of which could not have been achieved by working at home, the institution takes the view that it should share in any income derived from the research.

Many of the large research universities have created a for-profit corporation (a foundation) to handle patents and other such research outcomes and realize a surprising amount of income from the foundation's activities. Usually the researcher receives a share of the income, but the institution retains ownership. New scientific discoveries may lead to profitable products, while advances in electronics, material sciences, and biotechnology can

---

 SOMETHING TO PONDER

Sponsored research raises some interesting questions regarding library support for such activities. There are questions about support for research activities that fall outside the core areas of institutional interest. Should there be special funding built into such projects to cover some of the support costs? Think about the bulleted questions in the text; how would you respond to each one?

spawn entire industries. Some academic libraries also have a foundation in addition to the campus-wide foundation.

Some university presidents have raised concerns about how far an institution should go in the area of potentially commercially valuable research. Some institutions, in particular those that are publicly funded, have tried to address the balancing of research needs of various types with institutional values by developing policies that address questions such as the following:

- How much right does the public have to know about institutional research when some or all of the funds to support the work are from public sources?
- How much public disclosure should be required of researchers who have a financial interest in a firm that may benefit directly or indirectly from that research and from institutional resources provided by public funds?
- Should researchers be disqualified from participating in research if they have a direct financial interest in the research sponsor?
- Should exclusive patents and licenses be granted to a corporation or private party if public or institutional funds underwrite some or all of the work?
- How much individual- or corporate-sponsored research should an institution allow? When such research is allowed, should the sponsor have exclusive rights to the results?

Achieving the best balance between making a profit and advancing human knowledge can be challenging.

ENDOWMENTS

Institutional endowments are a distinctive feature of U.S. higher education. At some schools, such as Harvard and Yale, large departments are devoted solely to managing the funds. Endowment income can be a significant component of an institution's annual revenue stream. During boom economic times, it can be wonderful to have the "extra" funds; during downtimes, there can be serious problems. The danger is that in good times the endowment income may become regarded as constant, with expenditures and plans built around that underlying assumption. When things go bad, major problems can arise—for example, the number of institutions that close may rise markedly following difficult economic times.

What is the size of U.S. higher education endowments? According to the National Association of College and University Business Officers' 2015 survey (NACUBO, 2016), endowment assets for the 812 reporting institutions totaled $529,000,000. In the first edition of this book, we reported on the 2008 survey, which revealed the value of 785 endowments as $523,834,000 (NACUBO, 2008). It is rather sobering to see that after eight years and with twenty-seven more institutions reporting, the total value of reported endowments increased by only a little more than $5 million. Certainly there has been an economic crisis since that time, clearly evidenced by the new report's statement that investment returns have fallen to 2.4 percent, further dropping the ten-year return to 6.3 percent (NACUBO, 2016). Despite this rather grim picture, endowments continue to play an important role in higher education funding, particularly in private institutions.

Overall management of the endowment is generally a governing board's responsibility, with the assistance of institutional staff. In most cases, this assistance is provided by the chief financial officer, if not full-time staff devoted to endowment management activities. From a fund management perspective, both the governing board and the institution take the position that the school will last forever and so should its endowment. As we suggested earlier, in bad times it is tempting to draw down the capital rather than just use the return on investments. Managing the endowment rests on three major factors: spending rate, investment policy, and fund-raising activities for the endowment. These factors are important to academic libraries because their endowments, in many cases, are incorporated into the overall institutional endowment; consequently, libraries have little or no control over their funds' management.

Endowment spending rate is most critical to the institution's overall annual revenue picture, and it is central to the endowment's long-term stability and growth. Two key questions need to be considered:

- How should the institution balance the need for income for annual expenses with the desire to increase the endowment for the future?
- How should the institution balance the needs of present faculty and students with those of future faculty and students?

THE BUDGET PROCESS

Fiscal management consists of three broad activities: identifying and securing funds, expending the funds, and accounting for and reporting on how you spent the funds. Being a good and effective steward of funds is complex regardless of the size of the academic library. Such stewardship begins by assessing what needs doing (especially user needs) and the cost of the requisite activities, establishing priorities with stakeholder input, creating a plan (the budget), reflecting the costs and priorities, and presenting the plan to the campus budget committee. We know of few, if any, cases in which the costs of desired activities are below the realistic amount of money you are likely to receive. Thus, setting priorities is a key element in fiscal planning and management and must be done with some understanding of the institutional circumstances.

Every library has a variety of needs, wants, and aspirations that exceed its financial means. The same is true of every other campus unit. This reality means that some choices must be made. Decisions about what will be possible to do now and what must wait are not easy at the best of times, but lacking a solid planning process that helps in setting

 SOMETHING TO PONDER

How would you go about setting priorities for the following? The library is requesting a 5 percent increase in funds for electronic resources. The law school dean wants a 10 percent increase in salary funds to help keep faculty from leaving to go into private practice. The vice president of facilities is requesting $2 million to install solar panels to help contain escalating energy costs. Enrollment management put forward a proposal to increase needs-based financial aid by 30 percent. Also on the table is a request from the dean of students for two additional FTEs to strengthen the student retention activities. You do not have funds to grant all the requests. What do you do?

priorities makes those decisions all the more difficult in trying financial times. Having a process for setting priorities is of great assistance when it comes to addressing conflicting "good" options and a lack of adequate funds to handle all of them. Often colleges and universities do not have a sound process for setting their priorities. The same can be said for some libraries, and setting priorities is essential to successfully using the funds you do have.

To be a truly effective fiscal manager, you should explore all possible sources of funding, not just campus resources. In the past, academic library directors faced only modest pressure to secure outside funding; when they did receive outside funding it was a nice plus but not expected. Today's library leaders are often required to engage in fund-raising not just for nice extras but for basic operating funds.

No matter where you seek funding, you must have a well-crafted request or proposal. Preparing such documents takes time and effort and a fair amount of creativity because you will be competing for the available funds with a great many other libraries as well as, in some cases, other types of nonprofit organizations.

The Budget as a Control Device

A budget is a plan that serves three interrelated purposes: planning, coordinating, and control. It represents choices made about alternative possible expenditures. Furthermore, it assists in coordinating work designed to achieve specific service goals. Funding authorities use budget requests and expenditures as means of comparing what the requested funds would accomplish and past outcomes. The budget request is one of the institution's most powerful tools for holding units accountable.

These purposes apply to all levels of a unit. The library senior staff use budgets to monitor overall performance. Frontline budget managers use the budget to track day-to-day performance as well as long-term activity—for example, the acquisitions unit develops plans for handling expenditures as evenly as possible to ensure a reasonable workflow throughout the fiscal year. Checking actual performance against the planned expenditure provides useful information for control and coordination purposes.

Higher education institutions start by projecting, or estimating, what their income will be from all income sources as well as the incoming class size. In point of fact, all budgeting is essentially forecasting—how much you will get and how much it will cost to operate over the budget cycle.

Overly optimistic predictions (such as misjudging the size of an incoming class) lead to budget problems. You rarely know before the start of the budgetary period exactly how much you will receive. Often, the actual allocation is unknown until after the start of the academic year and final enrollment numbers are in. Our experience has been that a conservative forecast is the safest and least disruptive to operations, and having a contingency plan makes managerial life somewhat easier. Being in a publicly funded institution is both a blessing and a curse. During stable economic and political times, the school can make reasonably accurate projections regarding upcoming appropriations. During other times, predictability disappears, making the early stages of the budget process very much a hopeful guess.

Because budgets are estimates, to be effective you must make expenditures adjustments as circumstances change. Budgets need to be flexible in order to meet rapid shifts in needs, but any major alteration requires careful thought and caution. Too many rapid changes can damage the integrity and stability of a budget as well as the organization. In most libraries, there is only a limited authority to make budget adjustments, and asking before doing is the best approach.

Financial planning and control consist of several basic steps:

1. Determine ongoing and desirable programs, and establish priorities.
2. Estimate the costs of plans for each subsidiary unit in monetary terms.
3. Combine all estimates into a well-balanced program. This will require investigation of each plan's financial feasibility and a comparison of the program with institutional goals.
4. Compare, for a given time, the estimates derived from step 3 with the actual results, making corrections for any significant differences.

A library's size does not materially affect the basic budgeting process, although in larger institutions each step is more complex and takes more time.

The third step of budgetary control—combining and coordinating subsidiary budgets—can be exceedingly complicated both for the library and the institution. It certainly involves more than just totaling the subsidiary requests. It must represent a total reflection of economic realities as well as institutional mission and goals. For this reason, large libraries often have a person whose sole job it is to coordinate the budget activities.

Finally, budget officers compare the actual performance (what has been accomplished, the volume of work, and so forth) with what was expected (the budget). At the same time, supervisors and top management need to look at the existing circumstances in order to decide whether a major or a minor shift in budget allotments is necessary or desirable. By doing this review every few months throughout the fiscal year, the library tries to address the unpredictability of the future.

Academic library budgets normally are of two types: operating and capital. *Operating budgets* identify amounts of money the service expects to expend on its activities (operating expense, or OE) over a specific time frame, usually a twelve-month fiscal year. Different institutions use different fiscal years (some examples are January 1 to December 31, June 1 to May 31, July 1 to June 30, and October 1 to September 30), so budget preparation cycles

👥 FROM THE AUTHORS

In addition to the institutional level, the library will likely have a budget or business officer responsible for providing day-to-day budget oversight, managing purchases, and making sure the library is in line with institutional business procedures. Greenwell learned that at any level, it is helpful to get to know those staff, particularly if your position requires frequent purchases or contract negotiations. Certainly the dean or director of the library would have a close relationship with the business or budget officer, but even as an associate dean or associate university librarian, director, department head, or any librarian with purchasing responsibilities, it is important to build that relationship. Better understanding of campus practices and required procedures makes conducting any sort of purchasing business much more straightforward. The same can be said for working closely with the personnel handling the library's human resources, marketing, IT, and other administrative functions, and we will explore those in later chapters.

can cause surprising problems for information service consortiums attempting to fund co-operative projects. Operating budgets include items such as salaries, office supplies, and professional development expenses.

Capital budgets address planned expenditures on equipment. Expenditures for technology (hardware and infrastructure, for example) usually fall into the capital expense category. One example of this category is desktop and laptop computers for the library, which might be purchased on a three- to five-year cycle. Preparation of capital budget requests may, or may not, follow the operating budget sequence. In some cases, the time period for the capital budget may be longer or shorter than for the operating budget.

Another expense category is recurring or nonrecurring costs. Examples of *recurring* costs include salaries and database and journal subscriptions because those expenses are ongoing. Examples of *nonrecurring* costs are individual items purchased one time, such as furnishings or office supplies. Although purchasing office supplies is an ongoing process, there is no recurring cost for a single office supply item as there is for a staff member's salary or a journal subscription.

The Budget Cycle

The budget cycle, regardless of time frame, plays a role in the control aspect of budgeting. Good budget managers are normally dealing with at least four fiscal years at any time. Those fiscal years are the past year, this year, next year, and the year after that.

For the current year, the library manager must monitor expenditures, compare what has occurred against expectations, and make appropriate adjustments. A common practice requires senior managers to provide additional justifications to the funding body for the requested budget for the coming fiscal year. As part of that process, the manager is likely to have to answer questions about the expenditures in the past fiscal year. Because budgets are estimates, funding bodies usually look at how well the requesting unit actually used its appropriated funds in prior years. Senior management must be ready to defend past expenditures, explain how the library is doing with current funding, and justify why extra funds are necessary for the coming fiscal year. Assuming, for example, that the library's fiscal year is July 1 to June 30, this process would most often occur sometime between July and December.

During the latter part of the fiscal year (April or May in our preceding example), many organizations ask for the initial request for the future fiscal year. To develop a realistic request, the library must think about how well it handled questions about past budgets, review the status of the current budget, make an educated guess about what will be available in the coming year's budget, and make strategic choices about initiatives when requesting new monies. Keep in mind that an important part of making the budget request is to emphasize how much the library appreciates the current funding support before starting to defend expenditures and ask for more funding.

Budget Preparation

A natural question arises of who is responsible for the budget. From a legal point of view, the library's director is responsible, just as he is for everything that takes place within the library. From an operational perspective, there are a variety of possibilities. Only in the smallest library is the director solely responsible for handling the operational budget. Almost every medium-sized and large library, with several units or departments, usually has delegated some discretionary spending power to some units. Very large libraries usually have one or more full-time people handling budget activities.

The initial budget preparation should begin with library supervisors providing their estimates of their funding needs to their immediate supervisors and ultimately to senior management. Each successive management level combines and coordinates all subunit budgets and then passes its total on up. Finally, top management assesses all this information and formulates the overall budget.

Every library hopes to have a stable or, at best, a predictable fiscal environment. To some extent, the planning cycle assists in creating such an environment. By setting up a budget or financial planning committee, senior management accomplishes several things. First, it involves more people in the monitoring activities. Second, it involves others in thinking about future needs. Third, it provides lower-level managers with solid budgetary planning and development experience. Finally, it can build a commitment to the library and its institution by generating some understanding of the restraints on budgetary freedom that both have.

Having a contingency plan for possible library budget shortfalls is part of a stable environment. Such a plan will help avoid making hasty decisions that may be as harmful as the loss of funding. In cutting back, the people most affected, at least initially, are staff. Several studies have shown that cutting back adversely affects morale, job satisfaction, and staff retention; these in turn impact productivity at the time when it is most needed (Shaughnessy, 1989).

Some of the short-term tactics for dealing with fiscal distress include hiring freezes, staff reductions through attrition, furloughs, across-the-board cuts, and deferred maintenance and equipment replacement. Unfortunately, fiscal distress for a library is not always a short-term problem. In the long term, Band-Aid solutions will not work, and their use often severely damages support from both staff and users.

An example of short-term tactics is cutting funds for database access services. Users are hurt in the long term, and they may turn to other resources if cutbacks are too severe. Hiring freezes are less damaging, at least initially, to users, but certainly create challenges for personnel. Using a combination of cuts takes more time and effort, but, in the long run, is more likely to result in retained users, more effective services, and stronger morale among personnel. This is an example of how a thoughtfully developed contingency plan demonstrates its value.

Glen Holt (2005) wrote an article about "getting beyond the pain" in which he reviewed the depressing list of budgetary woes at the state or provincial and national levels in Canada, the United Kingdom, and the United States during the early years of the twenty-first century, which are as bad or worse today. Although his focus was on the public library

---

||||| CHECK THIS OUT

One book that may help in setting priorities for library budget cuts is David Stern's *How Libraries Make Tough Choices in Difficult Times: Purposeful Abandonment* (Chandos Information Professional Series; Oxford: Chandos Publishing, 2013). This practical guide offers a framework to help a manager potentially Do, Delegate, Delay, or Drop existing services and resources.

IIIII CHECK THIS OUT

Although it has broadened its focus in the past several years, *The Bottom Line* remains a good journal focused on research related to the financial aspects of information organizations. Academic libraries remain a large part of the discussion, at least in recent issues. This journal is worth looking at if you want to dig deeper into the financial side of things.

Another journal that we refer to frequently is the *Journal of Academic Librarianship.* This journal looks broadly at a variety of issues related to academic libraries, including, of course, financial matters.

---

environment, his comments are well worth considering by academic librarians. He noted that the American Library Association estimated there had been $111 million in cuts in public library funding between 2004 and the time he wrote the article. Holt provides some ideas for addressing the situation: demonstrate the critical nature of the service (at least some of its elements), demonstrate the service benefits, think broadly about possible funding sources, place greater emphasis on user- and client-focused service, and recognize that globalization does have an impact on the international marketplace for information and spend some time pondering the implications of those impacts. He concludes, "At the same time however, we must recognize the drastic changes that we will have to make to keep up with new ways of working and funding" (p. 189).

Every academic library, regardless of the service community's size, faces four ongoing financial issues. The first involves trying to develop and maintain appropriate facilities and responsive user services while remaining within budget. Unfortunately, few library budgets take the volume of work into account—or, rather, few funding authorities do so. It simply is a matter of trying to respond to changing needs while knowing there is little prospect of additional funding until the next fiscal period.

The second financial issue relates to the requirement of continually building and maintaining collections. Collection growth requires space (both physical and virtual require money) and time and staff effort (which requires money). Securing funding for collection resources, particularly one-time funds, is somewhat easier, at least in comparison to getting additional space or personnel.

The third financial issue relates to the second and revolves around the need for more access to electronic resources. Database vendors are not shy about increasing their prices each year at rates far above general inflation.

Finally, there are staffing concerns. Like subscriptions, staffing is an ongoing commitment that escalates in cost each year if staff members receive annual salary increases. Even when there are no salary increases, there will be an increase in benefits costs, such as health insurance, or in staff training and development costs to meet the challenges of continuous change.

Presenting and Defending the Budget Request

If you are in the early part of your career, you may not have the opportunity to make budget requests right away. You may need to request a budget for a particular project or initiative, however, and, as you move up in the ranks, the kinds of budget requests you make will be-come more substantial. We feel that this section will help you understand this process, no matter where you are in your career. Understanding all that is involved in the process can better explain why a particular request was or was not funded.

Preparing a budget request is often easier than presenting and defending it. This reality stems from the fact that all the campus units compete for the finite pool of funds, and each seeks to prove that its needs are the most urgent. Thus, the more care that you put into the preparation of a budget request and the reasons for requested increases, the more likely you are to secure the amount sought. Those units that do win the "battle of the budget" are usually the ones that recognize and act on the fact that budgeting is a very political process.

We drew the following material from Wildavsky (2006), but it is not a substitute for reading his entire book, which contains many good ideas. Some readers have difficulty translating his emphasis on the U.S. federal government into a library context. We suggest simply substituting the title of the library's campus chief executive officer for the word *president* and the title of the campus budget committee for the word *Congress*. Doing so usually makes clear why Wildavsky's ideas are relevant to library budgeting.

Despite all the press given to such concepts as program and planning budgeting sys-tems (PPBSs) and zero-based budgeting (ZBB), most organizational budgets are basically line budgets. Responsibility center management (RCM) is another budget type that some large universities have adopted; although their article is older, James G. Neal and Lynn Smith (1995) do an excellent job of explaining RCM and how such a structure potentially affects the academic library. Organizations often find that when they do move to one of the "newer" budgeting modes, the result is much the same—an incremental budget—because after an initial start-up, people use the past year as their starting point. An incremental bud-get usually increases in size each passing year, if by nothing more than an inflation figure.

The incremental approach is present in most academic library budgets because of the long-term commitments (e.g., salaries, benefits, and collection development funds for books, media, databases, and journal subscriptions). If the user base increases, there will be pressure to hire additional staff. Annual salary merit and cost-of-living increases are diffi-cult to control because withholding such increases is only temporary—staff pressure will mount to make up for the losses they suffered. Lobbying is, or should be, part of the library's budget preparation and presentation. Perhaps a label that carries a less negative connota-tion, at least in the United States, is *advocacy*. Both terms relate to the process of influencing people about the importance or value of an issue, cause, or service.

Gloria Meraz (2002) describes three areas on which librarians can focus in terms of lobbying: positioning oneself to be an effective advocate, achieving the most from advocacy

---

|||||| CHECK THIS OUT

All academic librarians ought to read the classic book by Aaron Wildavsky, *The New Politics of the Budgetary Process*, 5th edition (Boston: Little, Brown, 2006). Some information professionals, especially students, have difficulty accepting Wildavsky's ideas because the text deals with the U.S. government and, to a lesser extent, state governments. They see information services as cultural havens somehow removed from the "ugliness" of politics. Most graduates who read some or all of Wildavsky as students quickly see the connection when they take their first position.

> ||||| **CHECK THIS OUT**
>
> The National Association of College and University Business Officers (NACUBO) has published a more in-depth look at responsibility center management (RCM)–style budgets. If your institution adopts this model, it is well worth your time to read this book:
>
> **Curry, John R., Andrew L. Laws, and Jon C. Strauss.** 2013. *Responsibility center management: A guide to balancing academic entrepreneurship with fiscal responsibility.* 2d ed. Washington, DC: NACUBO.

sessions, and understanding the advocacy arena. One of her telling points is that "decision makers tend to allocate funding to departments or agencies that are in trouble (crisis). . . . [W]ithout showing some sort of crisis, libraries are not likely to receive large allocations of resources" (p. 68). She notes that most libraries do not have to make up the crisis; all they need to do is show the crisis.

One element that the advocacy effort should draw on is the user base, which will be as vocal or as silent as the library leads users to believe they should be. A large user base is fine, but if users are silent during budget crunches, they are not politically useful. A little extra help extended to users—especially to politically influential groups—can go a long way at budget request time. There is nothing wrong with saying, "Look, we know we are doing a good job for you, but with a little help and a little more money, here is how we can better serve you!" People who are willing to speak for the library at budget hearings can have a positive effect on funding agencies. The letter to a college dean from a happy faculty member can be very useful, especially if it occurs year-round, and can create a strong, positive attitude in an influential person's mind before she begins thinking about budgets and the library as a competitor.

Some years ago, Jennifer Cargill (1987) wrote a short but to-the-point article about "getting the budget message out." At that time, as it is today, one of the most difficult messages to convey to funding authorities as well as to users was the high rate of inflation of subscription prices. Finding a simple, accurate, and short way of explaining to noninformation professionals why such price increase percentages are so large year after year is a challenge. As much as you might like one, there is no magic formula explaining the situation.

Because the business office personnel do the digging, provide the reports, and make assessments and recommendations, their influence is significant. As we mentioned earlier, good relationships are important within the library and with campus business office personnel as well. Developing a good working relationship with budget or business office (the label varies from institution to institution) staff members is an excellent idea, especially with the staff of the person who heads the committee that first hears the library's budget request. If your relationship is a year-round one, it will be easier to maintain, and your chances of success will improve further. Keeping in touch, finding out what will be needed for the hearings well in advance, identifying possible areas of concern, and offering assistance within reasonable limits are all methods of developing a good working relationship.

Study the mood of the institution with an eye on adjusting your approach as moods shift. During "hold the line on spending" periods, let your request demonstrate how well you are cooperating. Do not try to paint too rosy a picture—play it straight, and do not try to put one over on funding officers. You may be successful in this subterfuge once or twice because of all the other matters they have to consider, but eventually they will catch up to you. And when they do, you will lose the goodwill you developed over time, and the library will probably suffer for a long time to come.

When presenting plans for new programs, be cautious in what you promise. Do not promise more than you know you can deliver, even when you think you can do much better. It is better to under-promise and over-deliver. As tempting as it may be to make promises in order to get money, resist! Funding officers' memories are long and detailed when necessary, and failure to deliver on past promises raises serious doubts about current promises.

Does all this sound too political for a library? It should not, because it reflects the unwritten rules by which governments and other funding bodies play the budget-politics game.

INCOME GENERATION

Today, few academic libraries expect to receive all the funds they need from their institutions, or at least not enough to operate the way they would like. We include in new sources the traditional private individual donor, grants and gifts from foundations, grants from various government agencies both outright and for services provided to the agency, a Friends group, income generation from service activities, and partnerships with various organizations including profit-oriented ones. At best, we can only briefly touch on these topics.

Developing and maintaining a special and positive image is important for all libraries—it becomes essential for fund-raising. There will be no opportunity for securing extra funds if the service's image is anything but positive. Having a positive image is not enough. You must communicate this image to users, to the public, and to prospective sources of new funding. Granting agencies are just as interested in the image of their grantees as are individual donors and private foundations. This is an area in which having a marketing plan linked to an active public relations program is essential in identifying special funding niches and opportunities. From an income generation point of view, this niche may need modification or amplification to fully explain what your library does exceptionally well. We indicated earlier that finding sources of funding other than the institution for "lightbulbs and toilet paper" is a challenge. Foundations, donors, and other grant-giving organizations are interested in funding only special projects that have a very high probability of success and that are sustainable after the funding is gone. Securing funding for such an activity may free up general operating funds for important or special activities that are underfunded, if at all. Part of the niche aspect is using in-house expertise or doing something no other library in the area does or can do as well. There will be competition from other organizations seeking extra funding, and it will require an investment of time to be successful.

||||| CHECK THIS OUT

Two recent articles from *The Bottom Line* provide some practical recommendations for getting more staff involved in fund-raising efforts. The entire issue is worth a look if you are interested in learning more about library fund-raising.

Crumpton, Michael A. 2016. Cultivating an organizational effort for development. *Bottom Line* 29, no. 2: 97–113.
Whitchurch, Jesse, and Alberta Comer. 2016. Creating a culture of philanthropy. *Bottom Line* 29, no. 2: 114–122.

👥 FROM THE AUTHORS

When thinking about fund-raising, Greenwell remembers something a very successful development officer once told her. She had seen another library's newsletter that listed some items that library would like a donor to purchase. The wish list included things like back files of journal collections, a high-end scanner, a golf cart for library deliveries, and so forth. This is a fairly common approach to fund-raising, and she thought it was a great idea. The development officer told her it wasn't the way their library should go, saying, "Success breeds more success." What he meant was that donors and potential donors want to hear stories about how the library (its personnel, spaces, collections) changes the life of students, researchers, community members. A laundry list of things that couldn't be included in the library budget inspires no one, but stories about real people achieving their goals because of the library inspire everyone.

Fund-raising (also called development, philanthropy, or advancement) requires planning and leadership. It will not be effective if your approach is "I'll do it when I have time." An increasing number of academic libraries, particularly large ones, have a full-time development officer who may be employed by the library or by the central development office with time devoted to the library. Whether the library employs a full-time professional or not, many organizations depend on the efforts of several people who devote some of their time to fund-raising as a team approach. As with any team, one person must be in charge to call meetings, set agendas, propose ideas, implement plans, push the initiative forward, and monitor outcomes—in essence, to provide the leadership.

Fund-raising is increasingly becoming an important part of any academic library administrator's job, though many librarians may be involved in fund-raising at some level. After all, fund-raising is largely about relationship building, so who better to help in building those relationships than librarians on the ground. The engineering librarian might be the best person to start a conversation with a successful alum who is interested in preparing future engineers. A librarian in special collections might be a good person to show unique materials to a philanthropist with an interest in the humanities. Further, that special collections librarian can demonstrate how undergraduates are increasingly using those materials to better understand history and learn how to conduct original research.

Regardless of source, income generation is a matter of the right person asking the right source for the right amount for the right project at the right time and in the right way. As you might imagine, getting all those "rights" right takes planning, practice, preparation, and practical experience. Workshops help, but only real-world experience and a few disappointments along the way will translate theory and ideas into "money in the bank."

Additional funding may be available from a variety of sources. One source is internally generated, assuming that campus policy allows the library to keep income it generates. Some institutions don't allow any, others allow some, and a few allow full retention. One long-standing internal revenue source for libraries is the sale of duplicate or otherwise unwanted gifts and donations. "Gifts in kind" to libraries are very common; how the unneeded items are disposed of varies. Publicly supported libraries need to be aware of any regulations regarding the disposal of public property and the point at which an item gains such status—in some instances it becomes public property upon acceptance whereas in other cases it becomes public property only when added to the collection. There may be tax implications for both the donor and recipient. Donors may receive tax deductions for donations to not-for-profit organizations.

Many academic libraries impose fines for rule infractions, lost or damaged items, and the like, all of which generate income. More recently, academic libraries have been dropping fines for late materials given the increasing number of studies showing that library fines have little effect on when materials are returned (Reed, Blackburn, and Sifton 2014; Rupp, Sweetman, and Perry, 2010; Mosley, 2004; Mitchell, 2000). Other sources of income might include locker rentals, photocopy fees, or, a rarity, some proceeds from a coffeehouse or restaurant located in the library.

For libraries with fine income, how the campus treats that income can have an impact on the budget. Many public institutions require that all fines go into the general operating fund, not credited to the agency collecting the fine. As you might guess, not getting monies paid for a lost or damaged item can become a drain on your budget if you repair or replace the item. This situation, in turn, puts more pressure on you to raise monies from somewhere else. A similar situation may exist for fees charged for services, although it is much more common for the service to be able to retain all or most of that income.

Another quasi-internal source is activities undertaken by a support group on behalf of the library—Friends of the Library, Library Associates, Supporters of Library A, or some other title. Such groups may be no more formal than some volunteers handling an ongoing book sale, or they may be a formal legal entity (foundation). There may be special types of internal funds such as endowments, wills, trusts, living trusts, and so forth.

As libraries generate an ever greater amount of their total budget from non-campus sources, they may create a foundation to handle outside funds. In the United States, such foundations are legal entities and generally have a 501(c)(3) status with the Internal Revenue Service (IRS). Such status means that they must not engage in any type of political activity. A major reason for having a foundation is to raise funds that are generally not taken into consideration when establishing the library's share of campus funds. Another plus is that the foundation may invest the funds raised to generate additional income. Without a doubt, such bodies can be very effective fund-raisers because they are almost always composed of individuals who strongly support the service and its programs. Never underestimate the power of user voices when it comes to fund-raising.

Creating a strong, positive relationship with the support group is essential. In many cases members pay an annual fee and expect to be approached for donations to special

---

⦚⦚⦚ CHECK THIS OUT

Since 1995, academic and research librarians and development officers have gathered annually to discuss fund-raising issues at the Academic Library Advancement and Development Network (ALADN) conference. ALADN is a community open to anyone interested, so no membership is required to attend the conference, which moves annually to institutions interested in hosting. The ALADN discussion list, LIBDEV, is a great source of information and is open for participation as well. The University of Florida hosts the ALADN website, which includes links to past conferences and job postings for development positions. Those postings would be helpful for a librarian seeking to create a new development officer position in the library. Check it out at www.uflib.ufl.edu/aladn/.

projects, perhaps for the acquisition of an important archive or piece of equipment. In return, the library organizes special events for the members such as an annual dinner, a lecture, or a series of lectures, or it offers special behind-the-scenes tours. All such events become relationship-building opportunities as well as fund-raising opportunities.

There are also some rare, and in the past overlooked, opportunities to raise some substantial amounts of money locally: wills and trusts, or planned giving. Clearly, bequests in a will become a source of funds only at death. However, today many nonprofit groups actively work with people to be included in their will. Living trusts, on the other hand, come in many shapes and sizes. Some may generate income for the library only during the donor's lifetime, others may generate income for both the donor and the library during the donor's lifetime, and still others become effective only on the donor's death. Planned giving is likely to increase in importance for libraries over the coming years.

Partnerships with businesses are one of the newer fund-raising approaches for libraries, at least in the United States. Many libraries prefer to use the term *collaboration,* as it seems less profit-oriented. Glen Holt (2005) listed several reasons for seeking "corporate partnerships." His last reason, in our opinion, is the most telling: "Co-funding through sponsorships can be a great way to build and share current and potential audiences between the public and private sector" (p. 35). Think broadly and imaginatively to find sponsorship

👥 FROM THE AUTHORS

There are times in higher education when it seems as if, no matter what the official budgetary system is, there is an unofficial system in reality. One such system we experienced has sometimes been labeled "The King's Decree." Probably a better label today would be "The King's Counselor's Decree." This may happen when there is an institution-wide budget committee with a membership that reflects various campus components and that changes each year. The committee may spend months listening to unit heads pitch their budget requests and several weeks trying to sort out priorities in terms of available funds, only to have institution leaders thank the group and indicate that its members will be informed about what the budget will be. At best the process informs a growing number of staff, over time, about institutional income and expenses. At worst it leads to a cynicism about the value of the presumed participatory process.

Another informal system is what has been called "Every Tub on Its Own Bottom." Harvard University uses a form of this method in that every unit is expected to draw much of its funding from its own sources. In the case of libraries, this approach generally means that any new activity has to find outside funding. Also, a majority of a library's collection development funds often come from endowment funds rather than from the institution. Needless to say, such an approach can lead to serious imbalances in services and collections.

A third notion, widely held, is that "The Squeaky Wheel Gets the Grease." Evans always started a new directorship by meeting with each staff person one on one. In one such meeting, a department head said, "You should know I'm a firm believer in the idea that the squeaky wheel gets the grease." Evans allowed as how that was sometimes the case, but it was also true that a wheel that squeaked too much could be taken off. Years later, at her retirement party, the department head said that she always remembered that conversation whenever she came to request special funding for something.

possibilities. Partnerships with businesses can be extended to acquiring expertise that is not available within the service. Local radio and television stations may provide airtime, local newspaper reporters can brief staff on how to write good copy, and public relations companies may well be prepared to offer their help to not-for-profit services.

Grants and gifts from foundations and government agencies are our final "other funding" source category. The art of grantsmanship is something you can develop—like any art it takes practice and then more practice before you have a degree of consistent success. Seeking grants is usually library project-focused, such as seed money for a new program, partial support of a facilities project, funds for new or replacement equipment, and the like. As a result, grant-seeking requires carefully thought-out plans; in the case of facilities, for example, it may require the existence of working drawings for the project.

An important step, in fact a key step, is to be certain you know what a foundation's or agency's current funding priorities are. Although an organization's broad interest seldom changes over time, its annual funding priorities within that broad area may in fact vary from year to year. Do your research before making a call or sending a letter of inquiry. Most granting agencies have websites where you can do a substantial amount of research about mission, priorities of the current funding cycle, what the funding cycle is, proposal guidelines, deadlines, and much more. Most grant-giving agencies are willing to talk by phone to explore projects. This contact can save the time of the agency and the library, if the nature of the proposed project can be outlined to determine whether it is within the scope of the agency. If it is, a valuable contact has been made.

If you have no prior experience in grant or proposal preparation, taking a workshop or two is well worth the time and possible expense. Some grant-giving agencies organize workshops to outline their requirements. Also, when possible, seek the assistance of an experienced grant writer. Be prepared to fail to get a grant on your first few efforts; keep trying and you will succeed. The good news is that, with many foundations, once you are successful, your chances of receiving later grants go up, assuming you have delivered on the first grant.

Even if the fund-raising is a part-time activity, there is an institutional cost. Time spent on fund-raising is time not spent on library activities. The library's position as part of the campus whole usually means that it must get approval before undertaking fund-raising activities. Campus development officers usually have the final say on such efforts. They do not want several campus units approaching the same source with different proposals—it makes the institution look bad. There also may be an existing relationship between the funding source and another campus unit that ought not to be jeopardized. Other reasons are to coordinate fund-raising activities and to share campus fund-raising expertise. Finally, there is an institutional need to ensure that the amount requested reflects actual costs as well as institutional priorities.

As we've emphasized, cultivating relationships is a key to successful fund-raising. Major donations or modest ongoing gifts usually arise from long-term relationships based on respect and trust. For individual donors, this often means social contacts in a variety of settings, few of which relate directly to fund-raising. For foundations and granting agencies, it means successful projects that delivered the promised outcomes.

Part of developing and cultivating prospects involves making sure the work is completed as planned and on time. Sending a funding agency a final report on the project, especially if this is not a requirement, reminds the agency of your service and what good value the agency's funds generate. Even more effective are the less formal contacts and communication; even just sending holiday greetings can help you keep in touch. The same idea applies to individual donors. Sending lists of items purchased for the collection using a donor's money or endowment income is a common library practice. Although donors for a new building or space in the service receive invitations to attend the grand opening, they are often forgotten until the next fund-raising effort takes place. Letting such donors know about favorable reactions of customers and the public to the new space is a great way to keep in touch.

PLANNING AND BUDGETING

Linkages between planning and budgeting in higher education tend to be rather weak. Strategic, long-range, rolling plans are common, but when you look at how, or if, those plans link to annual budget cycles, it is often difficult to find even indirect linkages. You will recall from your Management 101 course that a budget is a plan (an estimate of what it will cost to operate over a period of time); consequently there should not be a problem with establishing linkages to other plans.

Long-term plans almost always reflect an institution's quest for more prestige, higher quality, and enrollment gains. This is where there should be clear links between aspirations and financial reality. Without that connection, financial and political problems are almost certain to arise. We suggest that the following five factors are essential to creating a sound system that links planning and budgeting for all campus units, not just the library:

- Have realistic estimates of what the cost would be for each action item in long- term and strategic plans.
- Estimate changes in revenues and prices for the action items over time in order to gain a sense of what the costs will be in one year, two years, or longer. Keep in mind that, in most cases, the longer the wait, the greater the cost.
- Allow for disproportionate budget shifts (unexpected gains or losses in revenues), and do not allow budget drift to occur unchecked.
- Monitor and reflect changes in institutional priorities as part of the annual budget process. This approach usually calls for some weighting system for the various budgetary components—will the library's first priority carry as much weight as the law school dean's first priority, or, within the library, will the reference department's first priority be equal to special collections' first priority, and so forth?
- Manage the conflicting pressures. You must understand that contenders for resources always attempt to exert as much influence as possible over decisions on how to allocate scarce resources.

No matter what method an institution employs, costs will increase over time for existing activities and at some point in time exceed available funding. When that occurs, the institution must either find additional money or cut expenses. This is when having an established system for assessing priorities proves its worth. It is also when Howard Bowen's (1980) five natural laws of higher education become most apparent:

- The dominant goals of an institution are educational excellence, prestige, and influence.

- In the quest for excellence, prestige, and influence, there is virtually no limit to the amount of money an institution could spend on seemingly fruitful educational ends.
- Each institution raises all the money it can.
- Each institution spends all the money it raises.
- The cumulative effect of the preceding four laws is toward ever-increasing expenditures. (pp. 19–20)

Creating sound linkages between plans (aspirations) and fiscal reality is essential for the library and its parent institution. Without those linkages, the challenges of where to get adequate funds to maintain existing services or what to cut will become an annual painful process. Ultimately, as we have noted several times in this book, the result will be closure.

🔒 KEY POINTS TO REMEMBER

- Expenditures on higher education in the United States are a significant element of the gross national product. Library expenditures are an important part of that total.
- Private institutions do in fact receive some funding from governments, usually in the form of research and student aid funding. Although not large amounts compared to those of public schools, the funds are important, but they rarely impact library finances.
- Although overall budgets have been increasing, the percentage spent on direct instruction has been declining recently. Library funding nationwide has maintained a surprisingly constant percentage of the total spent over the better part of eighty years.
- Personnel costs normally represent the major expense for academic institutions, including libraries. Only collection development funding comes close to matching library personnel costs.
- Benefits expenses are often overlooked by most academic employees, although those benefits may represent as much as 30 percent of their total compensation.
- Research funding and grants can be important revenue streams for institutions offering advanced degrees.
- Grants can also raise some challenging issues related to balancing core institutional values and income generation as well as how much institutional support, such as libraries, is appropriate for noncore activities.
- Endowment building and management are increasingly important for higher education institutions and their libraries.
- Linkages between planning and budgeting need to be as strong as possible.
- Libraries should spend time and effort creating the strongest possible links between planning and budgeting.
- Fiscal management is about securing, expending, and accounting for the essential monies to operate the best possible library service.
- Budgeting is more than managing this year's allocation; it includes thinking about what you will need in the future as well as how well you managed previous allocations.
- Budgeting is a political process and requires careful monitoring of the library's environment if you hope to secure adequate funding.
- Securing funds from sources other than campus sources will become an increasingly important part of the library's fiscal management activities.

REFERENCES

Bowen, Howard R. 1980. *The cost of higher education: How much do colleges and universities spend per student and how much should they spend?* San Francisco, CA: Jossey-Bass.

Cargill, Jennifer. 1987. Waiting for the auditor: Some interim advice. *Wilson Library Bulletin* 67, no. 9: 45–47.

Crumpton, Michael A. 2016. Cultivating an organizational effort for development. *Bottom Line* 29, no. 2: 97–113.

Holt, Glen. 2005. Getting beyond the pain: Understanding and dealing with declining library funding. *Bottom Line* 18, no. 4: 185–190.

Johnstone, D. Bruce. 2005. "Financing higher education: Who should pay?" In *American higher education in the twenty-first century,* 2d ed., edited by Philip Altbach, Robert Berdahl, and Patricia Gumport, 369–392. Baltimore: Johns Hopkins University Press.

Meraz, Gloria. 2002. The essentials of financial strength through sound lobbying fundamentals. *Bottom Line* 15, no. 2: 64–69.

Mitchell, Gregory A. 2000. Fineless circulation at EKU Libraries: An evaluation. *Kentucky Libraries* 64, no. 1: 17–19.

Mosley, P. A. 2004. Moving away from overdue fines: One academic library's new direction. *Journal of Access Services* 2, no. 1: 11–21.

NACUBO National Association of College and University Business Officers. 2008. *NACUBO endowment study—2007.* Washington, DC: NACUBO.

NACUBO National Association of College and University Business Officers. 2016. *NACUBO-Commonfund study of endowments—2015.* www.nacubo.org/Research/NACUBO-Commonfund_Study_of _Endowments.html.

Neal, James G., and Lynn Smith. 1995. Responsibility center management and the university library. *Bottom Line: Managing Library Finances* 8, no. 4: 17–20.

Reed, Kathleen, Jean Blackburn, and Daniel Sifton. 2014. Putting a sacred cow out to pasture: Assessing the removal of fines and reduction of barriers at a small academic library. *Journal of Academic Librarianship* 40, nos. 3/4: 275–280.

Rupp, E., K. Sweetman, and D. Perry. 2010. Updating circulation policy for the 21st century. *Journal of Access Services* 7, no. 3: 159–175.

Shaughnessy, Thomas. 1989. Management strategies for financial crisis. *Journal of Library Administration* 11, no. 1: 67.

Stern, David. 2013. *How libraries make tough choices in difficult times: Purposeful abandonment.* Chandos Information Professional Series. Oxford: Chandos Publishing.

Stripling, Jack. 2009. (Hidden) cost of doing business. *Inside Higher Ed.* https://www.insidehighered .com/news/2009/01/07/hidden-cost-doing-business.

U.S. Department of Education. 2016. *Digest of education statistics.* Washington, DC: Government Printing Office. nces.ed.gov.

Whitchurch, Jesse, and Alberta Comer. 2016. Creating a culture of philanthropy. *Bottom Line* 29, no. 2: 114–122.

Wildavsky, Aaron. 2006. *The new politics of the budgetary process.* 5th ed. Boston: Little, Brown.

CHAPTER 8

Facilities

U ntil relatively recently, a student's higher education experience included the physical campus, and an important institutional goal was to make college life a memorable experience—imagine the stereotypical image of large brick or stone buildings covered with ivy, with at least one sporting some type of tower, and, depending on the school's proclivity for athletics, a large stadium. Phrases such as *ivory tower* are still often the public's shorthand for higher education. As we've mentioned several times, though an increasing number of institutions offer more courses and even entire programs online, top-notch campus facilities remain important in the recruitment process, particularly for new undergraduates.

When we were students in library science programs, we did not realize how important it is to have a broad understanding of facilities issues—building planning and design, maintenance, not to mention safety and security—and we will cover these practical but essential matters in this chapter. Trust us—at some point in your career, knowing about carpeting

---

‖‖‖ CHECK THIS OUT

Although we will cover library space design at the end of the chapter, you might be interested now in some background on recent trends. If so, check out this very brief, two-page overview that describes changing student needs and how the library is addressing those needs through learning spaces. This report is one of many from EDUCAUSE's 7 Things You Should Know series. These open access reports address seven basic questions about a new initiative, technology, or practice.

Lippincott, Joan, and Stacey Greenwell. 2011. *7 things you should know about the modern learning commons.* Louisville, CO: EDUCAUSE Learning Initiative. https://library.educause.edu/~/media/files/library/2011/4/eli7071-pdf.pdf.

For a much more in-depth look, check out the SPEC Kit focused on next-generation learning spaces. At their beginning in 1973, SPEC Kits were intended for Association of Research Libraries (ARL) members but have since grown in audience and popularity. Their focus is on current research library practices and policies in a variety of areas, and these publications combine survey results and various forms of example documentation from ARL libraries, such as organizational charts and sample job descriptions. Note that SPEC Kits from 2006 to the present are freely available, so these are great resources for many research library topics you may need to explore.

Brown, Sherri, Charlie Bennett, Bruce Henson, and Alison Valk. 2014. *SPEC Kit 342: Next-gen learning spaces.* Washington, DC: Association of Research Libraries. http://publications.arl.org/Next-Gen-Learning-Spaces-SPEC-Kit-342/.

may be important. New trends in library spaces have been fueled by the evolving needs of students through curricular changes, technology requirements, and study habits. Many libraries are increasingly moving physical collections off-site as well as combining service points if not libraries themselves, and we will conclude the chapter with a discussion of several of these trends in library space design.

At any large higher education institution, there are a variety of building types—for example, offices, classrooms, libraries, laboratories, research facilities, athletic facilities, maintenance facilities, and parking structures. Each type of facility will have special management challenges, and, of course, there are costs to build and maintain these facilities. Some campuses are as large and complex as a small town, and managing any of them includes three broad functional areas: planning and acquisition; maintenance, operations, and security; and assignment and utilization.

Who is responsible for each of these three functional areas depends on the size and organization of the campus, though typically there is a centralized staff with overall responsibility for campus facilities. Planning and acquisition functions generally involve the central facilities personnel and one or all of the expected tenants of the building. This area also typically involves outside expertise, such as architects and infrastructure specialists. As for management and operation, some campuses take a semi-decentralized approach, and the occupants are expected to take on these responsibilities. Buildings that are solely occupied by one activity or administrative unit are likely to fall into this category. On many campuses, libraries are considered stand-alone facilities, and library management tends to have some responsibility for how the building is used and maintained. For libraries housed inside a larger building, such as a classroom or research building, it is less likely that library personnel will have direct involvement with facility issues beyond the library space itself.

Assignment and reutilization are generally two of the more centralized aspects of campus facilities management. Libraries become part of this activity at various times. For example, physical collection growth over time means that some libraries eventually exceed their storage capacity. There are several options for handling such growth, with one of the more common ones, particularly for large research libraries, being moving more physical collections off-site or online, or, in the case of smaller libraries, downsizing the collection and perhaps sharing more extensively through cooperative agreements. We will discuss collections issues more specifically in chapter 11, and in this chapter we will address various options for collection growth as they pertain to physical space in library facilities.

A given on almost every campus is that there is never enough space to address all needs, including those for classrooms, office space, lab space, parking, and so on. Who gets how much space, where, and for how long and who is first in line can bring out the worst in campus politics. Libraries are often involved in such priority struggles because many exhaust some of their collection space each year, while seeking to create new learning spaces and services within the allotted facility. At the same time, campus administrators in need of space are looking to libraries, or at least their collection spaces, as possible candidates

 KEEP IN MIND

Throughout this chapter, we use the campus library as the higher education facilities example. Library buildings are among the most complex buildings on campus in terms of operations and maintenance.

👥 FROM THE AUTHORS

Greenwell, like Evans, is quite familiar with floor covering issues. It seems that as soon as one area of the library has been re-carpeted, it's time to work on the next one. If choosing carpet, carpet tiles can be a good option for easy spot replacement in case of spills and other inevitable mishaps. When carpeting small parts of the library at a time, it is important to consider dye lots to make sure the new carpet matches the slightly older carpet. Another consideration is whether it is possible to recycle the old carpet.

Though potentially more expensive up front, hard floorings can be more durable and are easier to keep clean, though noise should be considered. Another consideration is how slippery those floors can become in locations with frequent rainfall or melting snow. Although, perhaps surprisingly, you will find several articles and a good bit of commentary related to floor coverings in the library literature, Greenwell advises working with interior designers and campus facilities personnel to learn about the best options because those individuals will be the most knowledgeable and have the most current information about the best choices for high-traffic spaces like libraries.

for other uses. Holder and Lannon (2015) provided examples of library spaces that have been downsized and consolidated, particularly in subject-specialized small libraries. As we will discuss later in this chapter, these consolidated libraries, the growth of the learning commons model, and the combining of library services with other campus partners further increase the challenge of space allocation in the library.

HOW ACADEMIC LIBRARIES DIFFER FROM OTHER CAMPUS BUILDINGS

Academic libraries are complex and atypical of most campus buildings. First, physical collections typically tend to grow, particularly in research libraries, and those collections require more space. Although space needs around campus grow over time, libraries can accurately project, more or less, when they will exhaust space for growing collections. A challenge in designing new library space is getting the entire planning group to fully comprehend the notion of ongoing growth. Even though more libraries are moving part or all of their physical collections off-site or online, what remains tends to grow or must be heavily maintained to fit within the allotted space. At one time, new library buildings were ideally designed with twenty years of growth space in mind. It was difficult for many administrators and donors to understand opening a grand, new library with so many empty shelves, but that was the ideal scenario to handle collection growth. Today physical collections do not grow nearly at that rate, or in some cases they do not grow at all as we will discuss later, though growth certainly needs to be considered in a new library or renovation project.

Another factor that contributes to the library's atypical role is its hours of operation. It's common for the library to be open for service more than nearly any other building on campus. In a space that is open overnight, on weekends, and on many holidays when the rest of campus is closed, staff often have to take on more building responsibility or at least be aware of campus procedures for obtaining maintenance or security assistance.

As a result of long service hours, a third factor is greater wear and tear on the building and its furniture and equipment. The only campus buildings that probably receive as much use and abuse are residence halls, though residence halls have breaks in service between terms and are periodically taken out of service during the summer so they may be refurbished. This freshening up rarely occurs for a campus library. Even when such work is planned, library staff normally still provide service, likely having to work around the repair and remodeling activities.

One example of a wear-and-tear issue is floor coverings. Floors are usually carpeted to reduce unwanted noise, though more recently the trend has somewhat moved back to hard floorings for libraries because of durability and easier cleaning. Carpeting has to be replaced regularly, especially in entryways and other high-traffic areas. Replacing floor coverings in high-traffic areas while maintaining some level of service can be a challenge, not to mention the challenge of finding funding every few years to replace part or all of the library carpeting.

Whether it is floor coverings or other maintenance needs, deferring library building maintenance is a poor option because the cost of doing the work will only escalate over time. Be aware of the term *deferred building maintenance* because many central facilities personnel and other campus administrators will use it to keep yearly maintenance costs down. This approach is discussed later in the chapter.

PLANNING FOR RENOVATIONS

Planning any new or extensive renovation is a team effort between campus facilities personnel and those who will occupy the new space. Only a few academic librarians have the experience of planning a brand new library. However, almost everyone in the field will have to deal with major additions, remodeling, or working on plans for a remote storage facility at some time during a career. Team planning is essential. None of these projects should reside solely in the hands of senior administrators; those who have to make the space work as well as those who will use the space must be involved to achieve a successful outcome.

Perceived needs generally exceed the funds available by far, so some serious thinking must be done when it comes to space priorities. One sad fact is that the planning process takes time; for a new building, this will likely be several years. As the time line extends, the cost of construction escalates, which often means that at the very end of the planning process something called *value engineering* has to take place. Value engineering is a nice way of saying, "You have to reduce the cost of the project by x dollars."

In an ideal situation, a new or remodeled facility should be the following:

· Flexible	· User-focused	· Economical to operate and maintain
· Adaptable	· Energy efficient	· Comfortable
· Expandable	· Secure	· Inspiring
· Accessible	· Scalable	· Attractive

↻ TRY THIS

As a current or future librarian, do you see anything missing from the list of facility attributes? As a current library user, what is most important to you and why?

KEEP IN MIND

Soliciting input by bringing users and staff together in focus groups provides helpful advice and gives them a sense of ownership in the project. This is a good practice for any change in services, but it is especially important when planning new or renovated facilities. We will continue to emphasize the importance of user input in any sort of planning you do, facilities-related or otherwise.

Flexibility is essential because the use of the space changes over time. A classic example is the facility changes that have been necessary as computing needs have changed. Older buildings required installation of additional electricity and network cabling to create computer labs, service points, and office areas. As technology became more sophisticated, it was more important to add wireless Internet access points, not to mention more electrical outlets to power the myriad electronic devices carried by library users. Greenwell has spent much of her career working in a state-of-the-art library that was constructed in 1998, but even a building that new and impressive has required updates to accommodate new technologies and workflows.

When major renovations are necessary, such as the need to create a new classroom or add more group study rooms, a modular building with few, if any, internal weight-bearing walls is desirable. Internal weight-bearing walls cannot be moved as needed without causing structural damage or requiring very expensive structural work. The same can be said for accessible ceilings and floors, which allow for somewhat easier modifications in lighting, wiring, and HVAC (heating, ventilation, and air conditioning).

Given the need for library growth, having a facility that can be expanded is highly desirable. Funds for an addition or for remodeling may be easier to raise than funds for an entirely new building because such work rarely costs as much as new construction. Many campuses have little expansion room for new buildings, and, as we mentioned earlier, competition on campus for new construction is fierce; new classroom buildings, research buildings, residence halls, and athletic facilities, not to mention parking structures, are often higher priorities compared to a new library building. When designing a building for expansion, the designer needs to consider how future expansion will relate to the existing structure. Sometimes libraries discover that the area originally designated for future expansion turns out to be unsuitable or no longer available when the time comes to expand. This outcome can be true whether the expansion was identified within the building or as a future addition to the building.

The design must take into account the needs of users and staff with disabilities. Retrofitting space to meet standards such as the Americans with Disabilities Act (ADA) can be very expensive because such retrofits cover just about every aspect of the building from entry doors to aisle width to a host of other issues. Compliance with the law is essential, of course, and examining related issues beyond the requirements is important for the comfort and safety of all users. How easy is it for a library user to acquire a book from the stacks for checkout? How clear are library navigation plans, and do they support all users? Are there ways to find help easily on non-staffed floors of the library? These considerations are so important when remodeling or designing a new facility, and consultation with experts is essential.

Ideally, the primary planning team for a new library or a major renovation consists of six or more persons: an architect, a library representative, a specialist or space planning consultant, a designer, a representative of the parent institution (most likely from the campus facilities unit), and a library user. Larger teams are possible, but the larger the group, the longer the process takes. Clearly many people will need to have input to the project at different stages, but every additional person involved in every aspect of the project slows the planning activities.

The need for an architect is apparent. The library representative will be one or more of the senior management team, if not *the* senior manager, because decisions need to be made reasonably quickly, especially in later stages of the project. Campus representation is necessary to monitor project costs and to ensure that the design will fit into the campus master plan.

A library building consultant provides expertise that is helpful in achieving a successful outcome because few of the other planning team members are likely to have much, if any, prior experience with such planning (Boone, 2003). Few librarians, or architects for that matter, have had experience with such a project, and even fewer have had that experience more than once. Planning any new building is a complex task, and libraries are among the most complex buildings to design effectively. Like any construction project, it requires highly detailed data. Final working drawings specify everything down to nail and screw sizes. The consultant is usually the only person on the planning team with multiple experiences in developing effective designs for library service operations. A consultant's role will be to ensure that at least the interior design will be functional and as cost-effective to operate as possible.

A key document in the planning process is a building program. It is the outcome of a joint effort between library personnel and the consultant outlining the functions that take place, the space requirements for those functions, the relationship between functions, and other key issues such as projected growth. The architect uses the information to develop some alternative layouts and creates some schematic designs for the team to review. Often these designs are used to raise funds for the project. To that end, the building program normally includes information about the existing services, collections, staff, and service population along with data about the campus. At the heart of the building program, and essential for the architect, are data sheets for all the activities and units built into the new facility. Data sheets cover not only the equipment and people that will occupy the space but also the relationship of that space to other spaces within the facility.

The design phase of the project has several stages—the conceptual drawings, the schematic drawings, and final working drawings. Each stage brings the project closer to reality.

 KEEP IN MIND

Professional journals such as *American Libraries* and *Library Journal* publish annual reviews of new and renovated library premises that are helpful in planning or even just dreaming. These are excellent sources of information about trends in architectural practices, design, and furnishings. These reviews also provide cost data.

Greenwell has long made a habit of visiting academic libraries in the area while attending a library conference or even vacationing. Visiting other libraries is helpful when thinking about renovations, and these visits also spur ideas about new signage or even service point configuration, as we will discuss later in the book. The annual journal reviews are a great source for libraries that should be on your "must visit" list.

▌▌▌▌ **CHECK THIS OUT**

The ALA divisions ACRL (Association of College and Research Libraries) and LLAMA (Library Leadership and Management Association) have worked together to assemble a collection of resources useful for academic library design and planning, including user studies, standards and guidelines, green building resources, furniture, and much more. The purpose of the site is to help not only librarians but also architects and building consultants, particularly through use of examples of new and renovated academic libraries:

Academic Library Building Design: Resources for Planning, http://acrl.libguides.com/c.php?g=459032&p=3138018.

The initial stage is very important for achieving a functional building because it is in this stage that various concepts may be laid out, with minimal cost, in order to gain a sense of the relationships and gross square footages for various activities. This is also the point at which input from staff, students, faculty, and other stakeholders is most valuable. By the second stage, aspects of the building are more fixed. The final design elements are put into place in the last stage. After this point, changes become more problematic and costly to implement.

The first stage yields conceptual drawings reflecting several different exterior designs and some blocks of interior space indicating personnel work areas, collection space, and the like, and their relationships to one another. Selection of the exterior design and shape of the facility occurs at this point, and the choice can have major implications for the project. A plain square or rectangular building is the least costly. As the exterior walls become more complex (L-shaped, curved, or irregular in some way), the cost of the exterior rises, possibly leaving less money for the interior.

Concerns about being green (see, for example, the LEED rating system) can present some significant cost considerations. Many of the new designs and features of LEED projects are more costly to install but over the life of the building save money. The challenge is to balance currently available funds and long-term operational costs. Some institutions may forgo LEED standardization because of the cost but still try to follow sustainability principles as much as possible. Examples of this approach are state-funded capital projects in Maryland (www .slslaw.com/blog/general-blog/marylands-move-away-leed-certified-construction).

Some academic libraries become campus symbols or monuments. This stature generally translates into a dramatic architectural statement. Such statements are usually costly and do little to help the library provide effective, quality service. A simple cube or shoebox design does not usually make much of a statement. Conflicts over exterior statements versus the requirement for adequate functional interior space frequently emerge during this stage. Such struggles can be particularly trying when there is a donor involved whose name will go on the building and who expects to have a "memorial" on campus.

The second stage yields the schematic drawings showing the architect's interpretation of the building program. These drawings start to reflect building and safety codes. Staff and user input is critical at this stage because both groups will have to work in and use the space. The planning team should listen carefully to their comments and, whenever possible, incorporate those observations into the final design. It is at this stage that major adjustments in the location of a particular activity are the easiest to make because most of the detailed drafting comes later. An important consideration at this stage is the estimate of the operational costs for the facility and how they may be minimized.

Final working drawings are the last design stage. Here the drawings are complete to the last detail—which way a door opens, how wide it is, what it is made of, what color it is, and so forth. Working drawings reflect all aspects of the building, and, along with the specifications documents, become the basis on which contractors bid on the construction. There is a final review and approval process by the institution that in essence states, "Yes, this is actually what we want built in all its detail." This stage is so critical because anything forgotten in the design or inaccurately placed in the final drawings, although it may be correctable or added, costs additional money. In the United States, such corrections are known as change orders; the more change orders, the less money will be available for furniture and equipment. So a thorough review of the construction documents is critical to the level of funding available to finish the project as planned.

With a possible trend toward the development of joint-use services, such as at the San Jose State University library which shares a single facility with the city library, the planning of facilities raises new possibilities for collaboration beyond just the physical facility aspect. The needs of all users and staff must be taken into account, and there can be conflicting interests. But good communication, a positive approach to planning, and goodwill can overcome difficulties and produce a cost-effective solution.

MANAGING THE FACILITY

Among the challenging tasks for managers in all types of organizations is that of managing a facility. Changes in the operating environment increase responsibility and accountability, which necessitates the following:

- Addressing the health and safety issues of staff, users, and collections
- Giving more attention to environmental factors such as energy efficiency
- Maintaining up-to-date technology while restraining technology expenses
- Keeping overall operating costs down

Many librarians at some point in their careers will manage a facility, and there are a number of considerations that we will discuss in the following sections. Keep in mind that service hours are generally longer than any single staff member's workday, often covering seven days a week and sometimes even 24/7. Inevitably problems will arise when few, if any, seasoned

 KEEP IN MIND

Assigning a staff member to do at least a daily walkabout is one way to help spot housekeeping problems. Working together with housekeeping staff is essential, and it is important to maintain good relationships between the library and housekeeping staff. Why not invite housekeeping staff to library parties? Custodians are often the lowest paid employees on campus, and it's important to make them feel valued and part of the team serving library users. Their role is so important in making the library a safe and comfortable place for all to enjoy.

👥 FROM THE AUTHORS

One small example from our experience of the need to oversee housekeeping matters was an ongoing discussion with a custodial staff supervisor regarding the vacuuming of carpets on stairways. Although there was an agreement that custodians should vacuum floor carpets every day, the contract said nothing about the carpeted stairs *between floors.* The supervisor would vacuum the stairs but for an extra fee. Although it was a minor matter, it took time and generated occasional negative comments from users and staff. Who would have thought that becoming an academic librarian might entail spending time determining who cleans the stairways?

staff members are on duty and a critical decision must be made. As we've mentioned, it's important that all personnel receive appropriate, ongoing training and information.

Housekeeping Matters

Housekeeping is a critical issue because poorly performed work can affect the health and safety of staff and users. Good housekeeping starts at ground level with questions such as, Who picks up litter and empties wastebaskets? How often? How often are the public and staff restrooms cleaned and provisioned?

Other housekeeping issues include lights that burn out, temperature fluctuations, sun control, and plumbing. What happens when a user reports late on a Saturday afternoon that a water faucet in the restroom will not shut off and water is spilling over on the floor? Is there someone to call? Will someone fix it before the start of the next shift? What does the staff do until the problem is resolved? Having plans and procedures in place assists in handling such issues. The library should have an emergency response plan in place that guides staff in determining what to do in such a case, albeit not a major disaster. At small and medium-sized libraries in which staff may not have formal responsibility delegated to them for housekeeping matters, all staff from the most senior professional to student employees play a role in ensuring that the premises are maintained to the highest possible standard. At larger libraries it may be possible to assign a full-time person to oversee facility issues and coordinate with campus personnel assigned to those responsibilities, but even then, all staff should monitor library spaces and report any problems.

Managing Risk and the Unexpected

Academic libraries, like any other facility on campus, must assess risks to people and library resources and develop plans for handling potential problems. It is fine to have a library disaster plan for events such as water leaks or earthquakes, but if that plan is not integrated into a campus-wide plan, much of its value will be lost.

Risk management is a campus-wide issue because the school's equivalent of homeowners insurance is campus-wide rather than by building. As with any insurance, the fewer claims filed, the less costly the policy will be. Most institutional insurance firms have risk managers who are generally willing to assist in assessing the risk factors in a building.

||||| **CHECK THIS OUT**

Although Project Information Literacy (PIL) is known primarily for its information literacy–focused reports about how students find, evaluate, and use information, the organization has launched a Practitioner Series. The first report in the series covers planning academic library spaces, based on interviews with architects, librarians, and consultants:

Head, Alison J. (2016). *Planning and Designing Academic Library Learning Spaces.* www.projectinfolit.org/uploads/2/7/5/4/27541717/pil_libspace_report_12_6_16.pdf.

Two challenging areas are how to place a value on the library's general collections for insurance purposes and what to do about items in rare books or special collections and archives. If a Shakespeare First Folio is stolen or burned, you are not too likely to find a replacement copy. So what is the point in having funds for replacement? This view is often expressed by insurers and senior campus managers. Insurers talk of making the insured "whole" after a claim and see little point in paying out for something that cannot be replaced. On the institutional side, having coverage for multimillion-dollar items that cannot be replaced only drives up the cost of the insurance. A risk management program will identify risks and analyze the situation, the potential costs involved, and how those costs can be effectively and efficiently managed.

HEALTH, SAFETY, AND SECURITY

Health, safety, and security are critical issues for staff and users. Many hazards can emerge in managing facilities open to the public, and employers have a duty to care for staff and users. Laws enacted at either the national or local levels govern some points (for example, the number and placement of emergency exits). However, some health, safety, and security issues are not addressed in building codes, national legislation (ADA, for example), or insurance policies. It is up to the staff to address these potential problems. Having a team of staff members (such as a disaster preparedness committee) who not only draw up plans for emergencies but also look for potential hazards is one method for handling these areas.

For years, the issue of controlling temperature and humidity levels in libraries has been challenging. In addition to individual preferences for temperature, over time systems break down, need to be taken out of service for maintenance, and simply wear out. As with other custodial work, the people responsible for servicing the HVAC systems are rarely part of the library staff. This means that response times and levels of service become matters of discussion and complaints. Many institutions have a staff member in charge of managing institutional energy costs. There can be some heated debates with such individuals when it comes to temperature and humidity levels that are necessary for libraries.

Another challenge is to balance concerns for people and concerns for collections. Generally people need a warmer environment than is desirable for collections; thus, compromises become necessary. Both staff and customers generally prefer a working temperature at or near 72 degrees Fahrenheit with 50 to 60 percent humidity. Ideal storage conditions for collections, however, are 60 degrees Fahrenheit and 50 percent or less humidity. Intermixing people, equipment, and collections—a long-standing library planning concept—usually results in setting the desired levels in terms of people and technology. Separation of collections and other elements, such as the human element, may not be feasible or affordable, though in larger libraries that approach is more likely.

Academic libraries, regardless of type, have some long-term preservation responsibilities. Research university libraries have the greatest responsibility, but even community colleges have at least a modest amount of concern in this area. Institutions commit substantial amounts of money to acquire materials for collections as well as equipment that must, or should, last a great many years. The greater the preservation time frame, the greater the likelihood that preservation conditions will outweigh considerations for human comfort. The comfort of people tends to prevail in public access areas whereas the preservation of collections takes precedence in restricted areas.

Safety concerns fall into three major areas: safety from physical harm, safety of belongings, and psychological safety. Senior librarians must address all these areas and balance the needs of people, collections, and technology.

To gain an overview of safety issues, it is necessary to conduct a security audit as part of the risk management program. One way is to create a security checklist drawing on the expert advice from campus facilities management and then carry out the survey. If this expertise is not available from within the organization, then the local police or fire department, or both, and the insurance company will usually be able to provide professional advice, for they have an interest in seeing that safe conditions exist and generally welcome inquiries. These external bodies need to be aware of potential hazards before a crisis occurs.

A security audit covers all the safety areas noted previously. Basics about existing fire protection equipment and emergency exits should be part of a survey. Unfortunately, people and "thing" safety can again come into conflict. In any academic library, there will be one or more emergency exits located in areas not visible to staff from their workstations. Although emergency exits provide for people's safety, they also provide a means by which people may leave at any time, taking materials and equipment with them without following borrowing procedures.

One method to control the problem of material loss is to design service points within sight of all such exits. However, even in modest-sized buildings, this is almost impossible to accomplish. Another method is to install door alarms. Usually the best that happens in such cases is that the staff knows an unauthorized use of an exit occurred, though by the time a staff member gets to the offending door, the exiting person is no longer in sight. Higher levels of security, such as video cameras or designated security staff, may be necessary, with the benefits of these measures weighed against the installation and ongoing costs.

Collection items sometimes have a way of leaving the building without benefit of being checked out. Many libraries, not just academic, install a security system similar to those employed in retail stores to help control loss rates. These systems use electronic strips, radio frequency identification (RFID) chips, or both placed in collection items and an exit control unit that sounds an alarm if the item has not been properly discharged. These systems are expensive to purchase, and the annual costs can be substantial. In making a decision about investing in a security system, managers should collect data on the following:

- Thefts, including:
  - User complaints about mutilated materials
  - Number of items listed as lost
  - Random sample of collection inventory

- Users "forgetting" to check out items
- The amount of money spent annually on replacements
- The cost of installing and maintaining a security system and an estimate of annual cost

With these data in hand, a decision can be made about the cost-benefit of installing a collection security system.

Crime

In the workplace, as well as anywhere the public gathers, there are security issues. In our experience, students have mixed faith about the honesty of their peers. They often come to the library to study with their backpacks and laptops and work for a while before deciding to go to the restroom or out for something to eat or drink, leaving behind their belongings and returning later to find something or everything missing. They leave their things unattended even when there are signs present warning against such behavior.

Academic libraries have had their share of criminal activities over the years, from minor vandalism to murder and terroristic acts. No setting is immune to such activity. It is usually low-level problems that keep staff busy, such as items going missing from a workspace, confrontations over who should get to use a study space, and theft of collection items. However, anyone who stays in the profession long-term will likely witness or experience serious antisocial behavior, including but not limited to physical violence or worse. One key to providing a secure atmosphere is to work with campus security to develop guidelines for handling various behaviors ranging from the upset user to the worst type of behavior. These guidelines should cover how much or how little the staff should do to handle the situation, when to call campus security, when to call local police, and to whom within the library the staff member should report the incident.

A security audit will assist in identifying areas with greater or lesser potential for trouble. User spaces in isolated or remote parts of the building are higher risk than large, open areas that have many user spaces. Poorly lit and remote staircases are also high-risk areas. Academic library managers have a range of options:

- Do nothing (let the individual assume all risk)
- Devote some staff time to patrolling the building (which reduces time for productive work)
- Hire security staff or a firm to patrol the building (a costly but effective option)
- Install a variety of electronic surveillance equipment (costly and could carry unexpected legal consequences, such as questions of privacy)

Often at closing time only two or three staff members are on duty to close down the facility. Depending on the size of the library, the person on duty could be a staff member from another unit, a student employee, or even a security officer. Some academic libraries are in areas where crime is frequent, or they may be geographically isolated, making the staff vulnerable, particularly during night shifts. Many campuses provide escort services for students and staff during night service hours.

Few people, if any, decide to work in a library because they want to be police officers. They are often surprised to find that they may have to monitor behaviors and perhaps become involved in some unpleasant encounters. Having guidelines as well as providing training will help reduce the stress that may arise from this aspect of working in any type of library.

Disaster Management

During the course of your academic library career, you are likely to have to deal with one or more facility disasters: major vandalism, leaking water pipes, wind damage and other natural disasters, fire, and possibly even terroristic acts.

An outcome of a security audit should be a comprehensive security plan. One element of a good plan addresses day-to-day problems. Another element is a disaster preparedness plan. Developing such a plan requires time and effort but is essential if the library is to successfully deal with a disaster. Every department must participate in the plan's development because the plan affects everyone. A steering committee with a representative from each unit is most effective when it comes to developing a plan as well as regularly reviewing and updating the plan. Keys to developing a successful disaster preparedness plan include the following:

- A realistic assessment of potential disasters
- Consideration of handling the differences between a service disaster and one that is part of a larger local or regional disaster
- Determination of collection salvage priorities
- Determination of insurance coverage and authority to commit funds for recovery
- Procedures to activate when a disaster or incident occurs
- Staff training to ensure that the procedures work and that staff are aware of them
- A telephone tree for emergency telephone calls, starting with the person who will direct the recovery efforts
- A list with telephone numbers of recovery resource vendors and service providers
- A schedule for regular reviews of the plan and updates of information
- Development of a partnership with local libraries to which users can be directed when a disaster strikes

The most common disaster is water damage, and not just from major storms or firefighting efforts. Water pipes break. Even an unremarkable rain can cause damage if building maintenance has been deferred for too long; we will come back to deferred maintenance later in

---

↻ TRY THIS

Create a list of the types of disasters that might occur in an academic library with which you are familiar. List all the points that should be included in a disaster management program, taking into account the disasters you have identified.

ᴸᴸ FROM THE AUTHORS

Greenwell has outfitted several library spaces with furnishings and has greatly enjoyed the process of working with students and staff to select the most comfortable, most durable furniture possible. As we mentioned earlier about carpeting, it is important to consult with interior designers and other experts. One thing to keep in mind, though, is the length of warranty coverage on furnishings—what is covered and for how long. It's amazing how quickly seemingly sturdy chairs can fall to pieces in a very busy library. Large, rolling whiteboards—a very popular amenity with many students—need to hold up to having thousands of markings and being pushed all over the library.

Although furnishings are an expensive investment that the library should take reasonable measures to protect, at the same time it's important for library users to enjoy and maximize their use of furnishings. You might have heard the phrase "better broken than dusty," and Greenwell feels that adage applies here.

A final tip—for years Greenwell has found that students want furnishings on wheels. Students are going to move furnishings no matter what, so wheels simply facilitate that process. When asked by a colleague for furnishing advice, Greenwell simply said, "Everything on wheels!"

this chapter. Having some of the necessary recovery supplies on hand and having some practice with salvaging water-soaked materials provide the best chance of saving the highest possible percentage of damaged items.

Recovery plans for various natural disasters—earthquakes, hurricanes, tornadoes, and typhoons—vary with the disaster type, expected frequency, and damage expected. Other factors to consider in writing a plan are the age of the facility and the disaster recovery plans that exist campus-wide.

Thought must go into developing a plan for handling information technology equipment in the event of a disaster. Although you can replace equipment, data recovery may be critical to returning to service. Without a plan, the recovery process can take a substantial amount of time, or the data may be totally lost. Hence, it is important that you have a regular backup schedule and recovery plan, though given the cloud-based systems in use today, backup and recovery may be less of an issue. We will discuss this aspect further in chapter 9.

One thing is certain about a major disaster: not everything will be salvageable. Some documents will be destroyed while most will have some damage, but there will not be time or money to save everything. Thus, it is essential to set collection priorities *before* the disaster strikes. What is irreplaceable (first priority), what is expensive and perhaps difficult to replace but is replaceable (second priority), and what is easy to replace (last priority) are typical academic library priorities. Setting these priorities will prove more difficult than you might imagine because staff members will have differing views depending on their primary area of responsibility.

A recovery plan must also address the financial aspects of the situation. Time is of the essence in the recovery of documents, and the time can translate into dollars. Waiting seventy-two hours or more to process wet paper materials means that there is little point in trying to recover them. Waiting to get approval to commit funds to handle recovery efforts after disaster strikes will probably mean missing the window of opportunity to save paper-based materials. Senior library management will not have unlimited emergency spending authority, but having reasonable upper-limit spending power is essential. This is why it is necessary to know the level of insurance coverage, the average salvage costs for high-priority materials, and where to go for advice and assistance. All are important keys to managing the recovery efforts.

The presence or absence of a trained recovery team is a key factor in saving as much as possible. Often the person responsible for library preservation activities is head of the team, assuming that the individual works well under high pressure and stress. Having a regular practice of fire drills, building evacuation, and handling of firefighting equipment creates awareness of procedures to be followed in an emergency and ensures that the premises can be speedily and safely evacuated. A fire drill can identify any problems that may have been overlooked, such as hazards that temporarily block stairs or aisles.

Another aspect of disaster management is dealing with the emotional impact that the staff and users will experience (Klasson, 2002). The feelings that are generated need understanding, and it is important to have a plan in place to address those feelings. Knowing about counseling services that can be contacted if required is important because the full impact of the incident may not be immediately evident.

DEFERRED MAINTENANCE

Before leaving our discussion of facility management and maintenance issues, we need to look at the issue of deferred maintenance—that is, not carrying out repairs or retrofits on existing buildings as soon as called for by the building's condition. During periods of budget shortfalls, one of the easy places to cut expenses is in facility maintenance. Decisions to defer are relatively easy to make. Sometimes the work is not done until after a significant problem occurs and then the cost is substantially higher than it would have been had the

👥 FROM THE AUTHORS

One example from our experience of deferring maintenance until too late took place in California (Loyola Marymount University, LMU). However, a similar issue could occur anywhere. In California, with its history of relatively frequent earthquakes, the state and cities have developed building and structural codes to improve safety during seismic "events." However, it has been a slow process of learning what does and does not work after each significant earthquake, which in turn leads to code modifications. Since the early 1980s, the codes have included the requirement that newly installed or modified library shelving be "seismically" braced. The codes do not usually require retrofitting to meet the new standards unless the library rearranges its existing, unbraced stacks.

The LMU library identified that a major section of the periodical stacks was without such bracing and that installing the bracing would cost $32,000. For several years the library requested funds to retrofit the old shelving, but the project was deferred to the bottom of the priority list. In 1994, the Northridge earthquake took care of the priorities. All the unbraced shelving came down, destroying the shelves as well as the journals they housed. The cost of repairs just for the stacks came to $114,000, and the journal replacement costs added another $201,000.

problem been corrected in the first place. This happens because repair costs escalate due to costs associated with damage done to the building's contents—damage to floor coverings, furniture, and equipment in addition to the contents.

Deferring building repairs may be a standard method for reducing overall institutional expenses in tough economic times; however, the costs of eventually taking care of the issues can be very high. Campus facilities managers usually have three types of projects: preventive, scheduled, and deferred maintenance. Most managers probably even have a list of projects that require attention *if* funds are available. The "if" looms very large on most campuses. What happens is that other institutional priorities push aside the ready-to-go projects, and each passing year escalates the final cost of doing even one of the projects.

TRENDS IN LIBRARY SPACES

As we've mentioned, there never seems to be enough space on campus to meet everyone's desires. Although libraries often require more space for growing collections and services, many are moving selected materials off-site to gain needed space. Materials moved off-site tend to be those that are seldom used, particularly in subject areas that are less likely to be browsed. Some subjects lend themselves to partial or completely online collections; engineering is a good example given the discipline's long and heavy focus on electronic collections, and the trend in the past several years has been to consider moving those physical collections to off-site storage. Stanford, Cornell, and the University of Texas at San Antonio are a few of many examples of campuses that have moved engineering collections partly or fully to off-site storage, relying primarily on online access and retrieval of physical collections from storage as needed.

Off-site storage facilities are often warehouse-like spaces located off campus to keep costs low. These are typically configured in a high-density fashion, with books stacked high and shelving as close as code will allow. Some libraries, however, keep their high-density storage on-site, perhaps even making retrieval a bit of a spectacle through the use of visible robotic retrieval. North Carolina State, California State University-Northridge, and the University of Louisville are a few of several examples of libraries with an on-site robotic retrieval system. In our discussion of collections in chapter 11, we will talk more about storage facilities and why certain things might be located in storage, whether off-campus or on campus.

⟳ TRY THIS

As a library user and current or future librarian, think about the kinds of spaces that you find comfortable for working. What is the lighting like? What kinds of furniture do you gravitate toward? How important is it for you to be near a window? Thinking about these things from your own perspective can remind you of the importance of seeking user input when designing new spaces. Of course you can't design something to satisfy all users, but conducting surveys and focus groups can help you understand the user population on campus so the library can better address users' needs and desires. When conducting user studies, Greenwell found a frequent request to be free coffee, which is something many of us would enjoy!

Before we close out our discussion of facilities, we would like to talk a bit about the concept of "library as place" and how that idea continues to keep campus libraries packed with students, even in an age of smartphones. Ray Oldenburg (1999) described how important "third places" are to us—essentially these are community spaces that are not the home or workplace. Coffeehouses, bookstores, and, of course, libraries are all examples of third places. What's so powerful about the library is that it typically offers a wide variety of amenities for work or entertainment, and it still serves as that "third place" to get away. Even for students and faculty who use physical collections less frequently, the library remains an intellectual, inspiring, and comfortable place to complete academic work or to relax.

Many librarians have embraced the idea of the library as place and have sought ways to make the academic library as inviting as possible and to encourage as much "one-stop shopping" as feasible. Donald Beagle (1999) coined the phrase "information commons" to describe library spaces that combine library and technology services in a comfortable space. Specifically, this concept includes such elements as library resources and research assistance; technology equipment and support; and comfortable, flexible, and inviting spaces.

Since 1999, the concept has changed names multiple times, from information commons to knowledge commons to learning commons, though the intent is ultimately the same—a space with the appropriate resources and assistance to facilitate learning and creativity. In some libraries and commons spaces, the products of that learning and creation might be put on display (videos, artwork, scientific posters, etc.) to inspire other students. The co-location of other services is an increasingly popular move, going back to that concept we mentioned of "one-stop shopping." Why not have tutoring services, the writing center, and a multimedia lab adjacent to the library research and IT assistance desk? Think how much it would benefit students to have everything they need to complete a project all conveniently located in the library. If you add to that comfortable furnishings as well as food and drink, you have likely created a very popular "third place."

🛈 KEY POINTS TO REMEMBER

- Academic facilities management rests on three pillars: planning and acquisition, maintenance and operations, and assignment and utilization.
- Academic libraries are among the most complex buildings on a campus from a design and operational point of view.
- Libraries tend to receive more use and abuse than other buildings, with the exception of residence halls.
- Libraries' annual growth in physical collection size means that staff members are likely to be involved in some type of facility planning activities from time to time.
- When planning a new library, having an experienced library planning consultant on the planning team is a key factor in creating a functional building.
- Managing a library facility is a surprisingly complex and constant activity, if service is to be of high quality and staff and users are to have a space that is safe and healthy.
- Having a plan for handling problems such as water leaks as well as having practiced recovery activities are the best strategies for keeping losses to a minimum.
- Deferring maintenance of a facility for too long often invites losses that are greater than the cost of correcting the problem earlier.
- Reassigning facility space on a campus is an ongoing issue, and libraries add to the challenge of assigning or reassigning existing areas as well as creating new spaces.

REFERENCES

Beagle, Donald. 1999. Conceptualizing an information commons. *Journal of Academic Librarianship* 25, no. 2: 82–89.

Boone, Michael. 2003. Library facility planning—The consultant's view: A chat with Andrea Michaels. *Library Hi Tech* 21, no. 2: 246–252.

Brown, Sherri, Charlie Bennett, Bruce Henson, and Alison Valk. 2014. *SPEC Kit 342: Next-gen learning spaces*. Washington, DC: Association of Research Libraries. http://publications.arl.org/Next-Gen-Learning-Spaces-SPEC-Kit-342/.

Head, Alison J. (2016). *Planning and designing academic library learning spaces: Expert perspectives of architects, librarians, and library consultants.* www.projectinfolit.org/uploads/2/7/5/4/27541717/pil_libspace_report_12_6_16.pdf.

Holder, Sara, and Amber Lannon. 2015. *Difficult decisions: Closing and merging academic libraries*. Chicago: Association of College and Research Libraries.

Klasson, Maj. 2002. Rhetoric and realism: Young user reactions on the Linkoping fire and its consequences for education and democracy. *Library Review* 51, nos. 3/4: 171–180.

Lippincott, Joan, and Stacey Greenwell. 2011. *7 things you should know about the modern learning commons*. EDUCAUSE Learning Initiative. https://library.educause.edu/~/media/files/library/2011/4/eli7071-pdf.pdf.

Oldenburg, Ray. 1999. *The great good place: Cafés, coffee shops, bookstores, bars, hair salons, and other hangouts at the heart of a community*. New York: Marlowe.

CHAPTER 9

Technology

The role of higher education institutions revolves around the discovery, interpretation, transfer, and application of knowledge. Information and communication technology (or ICT, which is a more encompassing term than *information technology*) continues to re-shape how those functions and actions are performed. To understand higher education to-day, consider ICT's impact on all aspects of an institution from research to public service, from student recruitment to financial management, and everything in between. Blurton (2002) defines ICT as

> a diverse set of technological tools and resources used to communicate, and to create, disseminate, store, and manage information. Communication and information are at the very heart of the educational process, consequently ICT-use in education has a long history. ICT has played an educational role in formal and non-formal settings, in pro-grams provided by governmental agencies, public and private educational institutions, for-profit corporations and non-profit groups, and secular and religious communities.

One concern is that some in the public, including those who make policy, believe ICT creates knowledge, and it does not. What ICT does change is how researchers, scholars, teachers, and students gain access to existing knowledge, data, and information. ICT also provides more mechanisms for people to collaborate in the process of developing new knowledge and understanding. Ultimately, ICT is a tool for helping researchers, scholars, teachers, and students do their work.

When the public thinks about information technology and higher education, their thoughts may turn to how technology has changed instruction. In chapter 4, we discussed how today's students are different from those of the past, primarily in their understanding and use of ICT. Student preferences regarding technology have had some impact on instruc-tional styles. Distance education has had an impact on how instructors structure and pre-sent their courses. However, there is a fairly large number of faculty who are still learning to use ICT tools and who have only modest interest in thinking about how to incorporate such tools into their courses.

Although the lecture format is still a common teaching style, some students prefer learning in a more nonlinear fashion, developing peer study groups, creating their own con-tent, and using ICT tools to facilitate their learning. Essentially, students build their own environment that allows for interactive, collaborative learning. In chapter 8, we mentioned the concept of the learning commons and how such spaces provide flexibility for learning in this fashion. Many colleges and universities have recognized these preferences, at least to some degree, by modifying existing classrooms or creating new, "smart" ones. The idea is to provide the most technologically savvy faculty with a high level of ICT capability while encouraging the less technologically oriented to begin to use more of these tools.

ICT has been used to facilitate research longer than it has been used for teaching. The Internet, for example, was originally created to speed up and enhance scientists' collaborative activities. This potential of ICT continues to grow, especially because specialized collaborative software is now used in many disciplines, not just the hard sciences.

ICT opens up more possibilities for interdisciplinary, collaborative research. Faculty can use these tools to collaborate more frequently and more widely. Multiple roles such as team leader, team member, consultant for a team, or simply observer in another research group are very feasible using ICT tools.

ICT will continue to transform scholarly communication. As with learning, the online world allows the creation of spontaneous communities of people worldwide with common research interests and the ability to quickly share information without the long delays so common in scholarly publishing. A researcher can maintain daily contacts with others specializing in his areas of interest. Certainly technology raises the potential to greatly reduce the cost of disseminating research findings. For technology to realize its scholarly communication potential there must be open, online, free repositories of high-quality material

👥 FROM THE AUTHORS

One of the last major assignments that Evans had before retiring was to chair a committee to design and oversee the installation and operation of smart classrooms for Loyola Marymount University. A factor in undertaking the assignment was that the library had the responsibility of supplying media to the classrooms and had been lobbying for upgrading the rooms. Sometimes one should be cautious about what one lobbies for.

The first smart classrooms were new (thirty-six classrooms) and contained a variety of ICT equipment—an instructor's station that controlled all the equipment, computers, a video projector, a document camera, media players, Internet and cable television connections, and a telephone connected to what became known as classroom management. Each room cost $54,000 just for the equipment. There were additional costs for creation of the necessary integrating software to make the technology as easy as possible to use and, of course, for installation. The new rooms were very popular with the younger faculty and students. As a result, the registrar, who handled class scheduling, lobbied for having all the old classrooms upgraded. By 2003, there were 132 such classrooms, and, as you might guess, the cost per room was much higher, approximately $85,000 per room, in part because of the challenges of converting rooms designed for the 1960s.

Not surprisingly, there were several operational challenges as well. All faculty members using a smart classroom for the first time required varying degrees of orientation to using the technology. Some faculty members never did seem able to master the control panel, and a student worker frequently had to be dispatched to assist them. Maintaining the technology was an ongoing issue, and by the time the last classroom was converted, it was time to upgrade the first rooms.

As we emphasize throughout this chapter, it is essential that technology be purchased and used not just for the sake of having the technology but because it solves a problem, simplifies a situation, or improves the learning environment. When adopting new technology, it is essential that a support, training, and replacement plan be in place.

👥 FROM THE AUTHORS

Here's an example of interactive, collaborative learning. One of Greenwell's colleagues told her about an entire class collaborating on a shared document (using Google Docs) to create classroom notes. The faculty member was unaware that the class was using the same document to take notes at the same time while asking each other questions and annotating and responding to those questions. The faculty member learned of the process after the semester ended, loved it, and encouraged future classes to do the same.

that are stable in the long term. We have mentioned this requirement previously and will address it further in the chapter focused on collections. A Council on Library and Information Resources (2008) report summed up the changing nature of scholarly communication:

> Researchers are asking new questions and are developing new methodological approaches and intellectual strategies. These methods may entail new methods of scholarly communication—for example, a greater reliance on data sets and multimedia presentations. This, in turn, has profound consequences for academic publications: it is difficult to imagine traditional printed books and journals adequately capturing these novel approaches. With the predicted rise in new forms of scholarship, the promotion-and-tenure process, which favors print publications, especially in the humanities, will need to be rethought. (p. 2)

Certainly it is true that ICT has had a significant impact on scholarly communication, and this continues to be the case, affecting not only the library but other campus units as well.

One of the more interesting relationships between campus units is the one between the library and centralized technology services because they often have differing views about

▥ CHECK THIS OUT

Does the use of media and technology tools influence learning? That's the core of the Clark-Kozma debate that began in the early 1980s with Clark taking the stance that these tools are simply delivery tools, and Kozma arguing that some tools are well suited to facilitate learning. Clark and Kozma have continued to write about this issue, and the debate is ongoing among educational technology professionals.

We talk throughout this chapter about how higher education institutions plan for, purchase, and use ICT tools, and it's interesting to consider the evidence and theory behind whether these tools influence learning (or do not). The following articles provide an overview of the debate and summarize the thoughts of other educational technology faculty, particularly as the debate pertains to current technologies such as gaming platforms:

Becker, Katrin. 2010. "The Clark-Kozma debate in the 21st century." CNIE Conference 2010, Heritage Matters: Inspiring Tomorrow, Saint John, New Brunswick, May 16–19, 2010. http://hdl.handle.net/11205/143.
Hastings, Nancy B., and Monica W. Tracey. 2005. Does media affect learning: Where are we now? *TechTrends: Linking Research and Practice to Improve Learning* 49, no. 2: 28–30.

what the goal of technology should be in an academic setting. One focus of technology services is on keeping tight security. Libraries, on the other hand, typically want the broadest possible access. An example of this division is the differing approaches to accessing online library resources as well as wireless connectivity for campus guests, particularly at public institutions with a mandate to provide services to the community. Technology services may require a registration process and somewhat complicated procedures for guest user access. The library may tend to see campus guest access to online library resources as no different than accessing physical collections; therefore, the process should be as simple (and private) as possible. Whatever their differences may be, technology services and the library must work together if the institution is to be successful.

Just as was the case with facilities in the previous chapter, we will use the library as the focal point of this chapter. Again, the library is likely the campus unit—other than computing services and online education—that most heavily uses technology to carry out its daily activities.

Managing campus ICT, whether from the library perspective or that of any other campus unit, presents managers with some interesting challenges. Just maintaining current technology seems to require large amounts of time. There is the challenge of maintaining currency while considering what is happening on the changing horizon. Finding funding to stay current is a problem at most institutions. For example, when the library buys computers for student labs, service points, internal staffing, and so forth, a plan needs to be in place to refresh that hardware in three to five years. This is the case for any campus unit, but given all the computing-heavy service activities in a library (catalog and database computers; lab computers; instruction room computers; computers for staff needs including, perhaps,

---

⚙ ILS DEFINED

An integrated library system (ILS), also known as a library management system (LMS) or library services platform (LSP) is an enterprise resource planning system for a library, used to track items owned, orders made, bills paid, and patrons who have borrowed.

An ILS usually comprises a relational database, software to interact with that database, and two graphical user interfaces (one for patrons, one for staff). Most ILSes separate software functions into discrete programs called modules, each of them integrated with a unified interface. Examples of modules might include:

- acquisitions (ordering, receiving, and invoicing materials)
- cataloging (classifying and indexing materials)
- circulation (lending materials to patrons and receiving them back)
- serials (tracking magazine, journals, and newspaper holdings)
- the OPAC (Online Public Access Catalog, the public interface for users)

Each patron and item has a unique ID in the database that allows the ILS to track its activity.

Larger libraries use an ILS to order and acquire, receive and invoice, catalog, circulate, track and shelve materials. Smaller libraries, such as those in private homes or nonprofit organizations (like churches or synagogues, for instance), often forgo the expense and maintenance required to run an ILS. (https://en.wikipedia.org/w/index .php?title=Integrated_library_system&oldid=732993655)

high-end digitization work; etc.), planning is essential. Academic libraries are generally not technologically self-sufficient except for the largest libraries, and their needs form part of the overall provision of information and communication technology within a campus.

ACADEMIC LIBRARIES AND INFORMATION AND COMMUNICATION TECHNOLOGY

Libraries have a long history of using computer technology. The Library of Congress developed work applications for the first-generation systems (approximately 1951-1958), which moved into other large libraries in the early 1960s. Libraries of all types are an example of an organizational environment that shifted quite rapidly from dependence on manual systems to an almost total dependence on technology.

Libraries have employed most of the major computer systems, starting in the 1960s with mainframes, shifting to minicomputers in the late 1970s, adopting the client/server model in the 1980s, moving to web-based technology in the 1990s, and, in the 2010s, changing to a virtualized or cloud-based model reminiscent of the client/server model of the 1980s. Librarians demanded ever-growing functionality in the systems they acquired, and by the mid-1980s the term *integrated library system* was filling the professional literature, and more holdings were acquired in a digital format. What started in the back room of technical services is now center stage in all aspects of academic library daily operations.

ICT impacts every library staff member and user. Library resource acquisitions and cataloging activities have been computer-based for years, long before many other campus units began automating paper-based systems. Users remotely access services ranging from reference to document delivery along with access to databases, and for some years now this access has been the expected norm at many higher education institutions. Having access to technology and using it effectively and efficiently allows libraries to anticipate and quickly adjust to changing circumstances to meet the emerging needs of their stakeholders.

||||| CHECK THIS OUT

We have previously mentioned the ECAR/EDUCAUSE 7 Things You Should Know series. This report discusses the concept of virtualizing applications so that students and faculty can access software not installed on their own devices. In some cases, libraries may use the virtual environment as the operating system for computer lab and instruction room computers. This 7 Things report provides a concise overview:

EDUCAUSE Learning Initiative. 2014. *7 things you should know about cloud storage and collaboration.* https://library.educause.edu/~/media/files/library/2014/5/eli7108-pdf.pdf.

The 7 Things You Should Know series also includes a report on cloud-based collaboration and storage. Simply put, cloud-based systems utilize centralized sharing of computing storage and processing. The idea is that this method achieves greatest efficiency and is, therefore, more cost-effective. Read more about it in this report:

EDUCAUSE Learning Initiative. 2016. *7 things you should know about virtualized desktops.* https://library.educause.edu/resources/2016/11/7-things-you-should-know-about-virtualized-desktops.

LONG-TERM TECHNOLOGY PLANNING

A key factor in maintaining a successful ICT program is careful long-range planning. Accurately predicting future changes in technology direction and the timing of those changes are difficult beyond eighteen to twenty-four months. Nevertheless, the best insurance for handling technology as cost-effectively as possible is to develop at least a five-year plan.

By treating the process as a rolling plan, the benefits of long-term planning can be gained while maintaining the flexibility to adjust the plan to address a changing environment. The planning and management strategies discussed in chapter 8 apply in this context. What makes long-term technology planning somewhat different from other planning is the almost certain knowledge that the plan will probably never be carried out exactly the way it is presented and that each year will result in modifications as needs and technologies change.

👥 FROM THE AUTHORS

One of Greenwell's first jobs in an academic library was the management of the library's desktop computers around campus. Every four years, those computers were scheduled to be replaced with new ones. The cost of the computers was spread out over four years so that the cost was a recurring item in the library's budget rather than a large, one-time cost that needed to be funded every four years. This approach made it more likely that funds would be available to replace the computers on schedule, and they needed to be replaced regularly because they had important functions as lab computers, instruction room computers, service desk computers, staff computers, and so on.

When managed well, computers can generally last a few years, and a four-year replacement cycle worked well for that library. Some libraries may opt to refresh computer equipment more frequently if they can afford to do so; others may not be in the position to refresh computer equipment very often, to the point that service issues may arise. As we emphasize in this chapter, having a plan for technology purchases is so important.

One way to spread the cost of new computers over four years is to work with a leasing company for financing. The library will receive new computers to the library's specifications and will pay the leasing company annually for four years. Terms vary, of course, but often the cost is the purchase price of the computers plus an interest fee split over four years (or three or five years, depending on the terms). Some companies might require the old computers to be returned, but a more common agreement is that the library can keep the four-year-old computers at the end of the lease agreement. The computers aren't valuable at that point and become more of a headache for shipping and storing from the perspective of the leasing company.

The plan for funding was just one part of the replacement equation because the department had to carefully plan the logistics for trading out a few hundred computers on a holiday when the campus libraries were closed. This operation required frequent communication among departments and collaboration with campus technology services, not to mention the development of considerable documentation. This was a short-term project, but it took months to plan prior to each rollout of new computers every four years. As we discuss long-term technology planning, consider all the factors that would be involved in a project of this magnitude.

||||| **CHECK THIS OUT**

A report that can help you in speculating about what's on the horizon for technology in higher education is the annual *Horizon Report.* The New Media Consortium conducts research annually to examine emerging technologies that will be of significance to teaching and learning over the near term (one year or less), mid-term (two to three years), and far term (four to five years). The *Horizon Report* is a summary of the consortium's research findings. Note that there is a separate academic library–focused edition of the report that is also worth reviewing annually.

Adams Becker, S., M. Cummins, A. Davis, A. Freeman, C. Hall Giesinger, and V. Ananthanarayanan. 2017. *NMC horizon report: 2017 higher education edition.* Austin, TX: The New Media Consortium.
NMC Horizon Report, https://www.nmc.org/nmc-horizon/.

Library and IT managers must think about and plan for ICT from several viewpoints, and most important are the following strategic considerations:

- Factors such as competitive differentiation
- Overall improvement in decision making
- Improved operational processes

Thinking about technology both offensively and defensively is also a useful exercise. From an offensive perspective, considering how to achieve or realize maximum benefit from the use of ICT is vital. Defensively, think in terms of controlled growth and what is happening in similar libraries.

Critical success factors (CSFs) are the five or six areas in which "things *have* to go right" or "failure will hurt performance the most." CSFs are very useful in technology planning, and in many ways they are easier to identify than organization-wide CSFs. From an academic library point of view, one of the technology CSFs is network reliability. Another CSF

👥 **FROM THE AUTHORS**

Greenwell can't emphasize enough how important it is to acquire and use technology to solve a problem, rather than purchase technology and then try to find some use for it. For example, when tablet computers first came on the market, many libraries felt they needed to acquire them, but not all had a plan in place for who would use them, how they would be used, or how such personal devices could be configured to work properly in a shared environment. Some libraries did the same with 3-D printers, not considering the skill level required to use modeling software or the ongoing cost of supplies and maintenance.

The desire to have shiny new toys can be great, but without any sort of plan, they can be an incredible waste of funds and time. That's not to say that you shouldn't be looking at new technologies and how they could benefit library users and staff (really, all librarians should be doing this to some extent), but having a plan in place is important before making an investment.

is the reliability of the integrated library system (ILS). These factors become useful in planning the architecture and long-term needs of information services technology in a library setting.

There are a number of models for technology planning; we favor Emberton's (1987) holistic approach. The following presents the holistic planning mode for information technology. The first step is to gain agreement, or verify, that the current statement of the library's mission and goals reflects the actual desires of management and any other approving body. If this agreement exists and if the library has been conscientious about its planning activities relating to function and to specific goals and objectives, the next step is to review those functions and activities in terms of which ones might benefit from some technology application.

One obvious advantage of starting with mission and goals is that they are both general in character, which means the uncertainty about future directions of specific technologies is less of an issue. Using objectives that are more specific and that reflect the purposes of current functions and activities allows the manager to plan this and next year's technology requirements in a realistic manner.

Another step is to examine each goal, objective, function, and activity and ask the question, could ICT assist in its performance or achievement? Related questions are the following: What type and how much technology would, or could, be appropriate? What problem does the technology address? One example of a goal would be to allow students to directly self-book group study rooms online. By using such a general statement and assuming that the library decides technology is a factor in achieving or maintaining such a goal, managers can develop a long-range plan with a long-term direction without too much concern about unexpected technological change. This approach does not necessarily lock the library into a particular technology solution for the long term. It also makes it easier for the decision makers to look at what is available today and consider expert opinions about future trends when deciding what to do during the next twelve to eighteen months.

Basic technical issues also play a key role in a successful planning process. It becomes important to have answers to questions such as the following:

- Do any organizational policies influence decision making?
- What types of data are required to reach an informed decision?
- Which technology offers the greatest payoff in relation to service goals and objectives?
- What are the functional advantages, if any, of the new technology?
- What are the technical prerequisites for using a specific technology?
- If different objectives require different technologies, what are the compatibility issues?
- Does the library have the infrastructure to support the new technology?
- Is the technology an open system or proprietary? If proprietary, how difficult would it be to migrate to another system in the future?
- Which technical strategy will be most effective?
- How will staff and users be affected?
- What are the staffing and training requirements?
- What are the user education requirements?
- What are the short- and long-term implications of the use of this technology?

↻ TRY THIS

List six areas of expenditure on information and communication technology. Which do you expect to increase in the next five years, and which may decrease?

Beyond technical considerations, there are political and end user issues associated with technology planning that take many forms. The following are some of the more typical questions to ask:

- What is the campus-wide attitude toward expenditures on technology? Is it a long-term or short-term view?
- Does organizational policy centralize ICT services, or are they decentralized?
- Will the expenditure for and implementation of the technology create relationship problems with other units in the parent institution or with collaborating libraries?
- What is the library's track record with funding authorities when it comes to implementing technology?
- Will all end users be able to access or benefit from the proposed technology?
- Is there an issue regarding differing end user platforms or average users' systems capability?
- Does the proposed technology relate to and meet the immediate and long-term needs of end users?
- Does the proposed technology restrict or constrain end user creativity in using technology?
- Is the system flexible enough to meet all end user needs?
- Are there any training implications for end users?

The planning must involve functional, institutional, use, risk, and staffing analysis as well as take into account implementation and hardware assessment. Library managers must remember that technology planning is more than developing hardware and software systems; it requires understanding of the organization, its purpose(s), and its customers. Library managers' goal should be to create an information environment appropriate for the library while meeting the parent organization's needs, not to add technology for technology's sake or to "prove" the library is up-to-date. In essence, technology development follows the process of problem definition and data collecting, conceptual design, detailed design, and implementation. Table 9.1 summarizes some of the key ICT planning issues.

CONTROLLING TECHNOLOGY COSTS

Controlling technology costs is a continual challenge. Libraries, for example, traditionally have two categories of expense that are ongoing and always increasing: salaries and subscription costs. Both present challenges for the library and its institution. Some techniques for controlling salary expenses include not granting or creating additional staff positions, limiting annual salary increases, imposing hiring freezes, and, occasionally, furloughing employees or, at worst, cutting existing positions. Options for controlling subscription price increases are generally fewer: drop some subscriptions or curtail other expenditures in order to cover journal and database costs.

When it comes to the cost of migrating from one generation of equipment to another, there is no option other than not doing so. Unlike with some other capital expenditures, the useful life span of technology is dropping, so managers must view the financial investments in this area as being short term. The payoff comes from the more efficient use of staff time and enhanced service to users. Although managers at all levels understand that the useful life of equipment is getting shorter, funding officials in some organizations may not yet accept this fact. Dugan (2002) identified three types of costs in the introduction of ICT: one-time or extraordinary costs, initial costs, and recurring costs. He then described a model designed to identify and anticipate costs.

In order to minimize the risk of making a wrong purchasing decision, Marshall University introduced a decision-making governance model by merging the Office of Computing with the University Libraries both administratively and financially (Prisk and Brooks, 2005). The new entity's strategy took account of expectations, the sales pitch, why the product was chosen, what went wrong, and what was learned. The concept of merging campus libraries with campus technology services is not a new one and is still seen in the higher education community. In 2012 the *Journal of Library Administration* published an entire issue devoted to the intersection of libraries and campus technology services, including the merger of campus computing and libraries at Bryn Mawr (Shore, 2012), the merger of academic computing and libraries at Columbia (Renfro and Neal, 2012), and the dissolution of a merged organization at the University of Southern California (Quinlan and McHarg, 2012).

Funding concerns underlie all aspects of managing a library, particularly when it comes to ICT purchases. ICT can, if not properly controlled, use all the available equipment funding and still require more. System migrations are particularly costly, and without a good plan, it can be easy to underestimate the overall cost of the project. In addition to the obvious hardware and software costs, there are often reprogramming or reformatting expenses, or both, and always staff and user training expenses. At some point in your career, you will likely be involved in the migration of the ILS. Even if you are not in the IT department, the migration will have some impact on your work. As we mentioned earlier, the ILS serves essentially as the inventory control system for the library's holdings. There will be downtime as well as possible changes in procedures and workflow. There will be new interfaces for you to learn and to teach to users.

- Long- and short-range plans are essential.
- In-depth needs assessment is a key to success.
- Establishing and implementing a maintenance schedule maximizes return on investment in technology.
- Developing a regular upgrading plan assists in determining long-term costs.
- Building a replacement fund over time is essential to reduce sticker shock over price increases.
- Investing in training and developing a knowledgeable staff is essential.

TABLE 9.1 Key information and communication technology planning issues

Earlier in this section, we mentioned two categories of expense that are ever-increasing: salaries and subscription costs. Technology costs are the third component in the ongoing, ever-increasing cost category for many libraries. Such costs are generally beyond the control of library managers. Unlike with journals, managers are not as able to decide to "cancel" technology, but, as with journals, it is sometimes possible to join consortia to gain better deals from vendors.

Because libraries are dependent on technology to carry out their daily activities, though they may be able to delay an expenditure for a time, eventually an upgrade must occur. When a vendor no longer supports older technology, either a new version has to be acquired or the cost and frustration of attempting to maintain the existing technology on one's own has to take place. The ILS is a good example of this because eventually the system must be upgraded or replaced or otherwise the vendor will no longer provide support. Libraries that opt to use an open source ILS will not have the same pressures from a vendor, though upgrades and maintenance are important in that situation as well.

One factor that makes ICT increasingly expensive is the demand for even greater functionality. Functionality requires development by the vendor, the cost of which is incorporated into the price of new software. Academic librarians who have been involved in several acquisitions of an ILS liken the process to buying a new automobile. It seems as if everything is an "option at an additional cost."

Establishing a set of system requirements prior to starting a search is very useful in controlling costs. It likely may be required as part of a request for proposal (RFP) process. The RFP is a document that describes the system requirements and is open to potential suppliers to submit bids (price quotations) that meet those requirements. Many universities require an RFP and at least three bids for a major purchase, and an ILS is often considered a major purchase.

Owning a personal computer, smartphone, or tablet demonstrates the problem of the constant need to upgrade. Just when you think you are up to the standard, you find a new application that exceeds your device's capability. In the institutional setting this scenario repeats itself over and over again as employees will likely have multiple devices and changing needs over time. End users request additional features and functionality, software

⚙ OPEN SOURCE DEFINED

Open source software is computer source code that is made available for users to change and distribute for any purpose. Of particular interest for libraries are the various open source ILS systems as well as other add-on applications available (study room booking, course reserves, event calendars, etc.). Library consultant Eric Lease Morgan (2004) points out that open source software is "only as free as a free kitten." When acquiring a free kitten, the new owner needs to consider the time and funding required to properly care for the kitten. The same can be said for "free" software because ongoing maintenance and upgrades are required, not to mention in-depth knowledge of how the particular system is coded. When making a major system purchase, it is wise to consider the pros and cons of using open source versus other vendor options. For some academic libraries, the heavy investment in human resources to manage an open source system might be more beneficial than paying a vendor, though this outcome varies according to local needs and circumstances.

producers create a new product meeting those desires, and system requirements escalate along with costs. Working with staff to keep technology expectations at a reasonable level is essential in managing technology.

A trend in some colleges and universities is to outsource specific services to control costs (maintenance services, custodial services, dining services, and technology services are some examples). Providers of these specialist services are able to employ a wide range of expertise and amortize costs over a number of customers, which *may* reduce overall ICT costs for an institution. Outsourcing requires a very clear understanding of expectations on the part of the customer and supplier, a consideration of what would happen if the supplier fails, a careful examination of internal costs, a legal contract, and close monitoring of the quality of service provided.

STAFF TRAINING

One aspect of managing technology involves making certain staff at every level have the necessary background and training to handle the technology in place as well as the technology the institution plans to acquire. Funding for staff development opportunities is usually limited. In the case of technology, such opportunities are essential. The challenge is to decide how to allocate the available funding.

Managers must plan for three types of training: (a) of the entire staff for a new system, (b) for new staff, and (c) for end users. With this range in mind, it is evident why training costs must be a line item in the annual budget. One aspect of training is the need to demonstrate, not just tell, how something is done. Sometimes it is possible to use a mentor approach. One advantage is that the mentor is better able to relate to the special needs of her coworker than is a general trainer. Training in groups is more cost-effective than the one-on-one approach, and this is true for both staff and end users.

FUTURE DIRECTIONS

In 2004, Bell and Shank described the need for a "blended librarian" skill set. Essentially this librarian has traditional research skills, technology troubleshooting skills, and instructional

👥 FROM THE AUTHORS

Evans worked at an institution that struggled with controlling institutional ICT costs. At one point, the university president made a surprise announcement on a Friday that all the ICT services were to be outsourced the following Monday. ICT staff had the weekend to decide if they would accept a position with the outsourcing firm. In any event, they would cease being university employees at 5:00 p.m. that day. The president also announced that he had signed a seven-year contract with the company.

The turmoil that followed did not end the following Monday. After four years, and with much higher ICT costs, the contract was cancelled. Many of the former staff members once again became university employees. The notion of achieving cost saving through outsourcing any activity needs long and careful thought.

design skills. This skill set is particularly relevant today as academic libraries increasingly blur the lines between library services and technology services. For example, in the learning commons model that we discussed in the previous chapter, an important part of successful commons spaces is technology tools and services. User support is the most important thing—having staff with the technical expertise and appropriate training and consultation skills to help users be successful.

A second important element of the future library is having the necessary tools, such as multimedia software, equipment checkout, and, increasingly, makerspaces that include a wide variety of tools and equipment. All types of printing and scanning are included in this category, along with other kinds of specialized tools that would be too expensive or unfeasible for a student to have in a residence hall room (certainly a 3-D printer would fall into this category, but a tripod, a sewing machine, a DVD player, or perhaps even a desktop printer-scanner would also be an expensive thing taking up unnecessary space).

As we've discussed previously, the successful academic library of the future listens to user needs and addresses those needs as efficiently and effectively as possible. This approach is certainly important when researching, purchasing, implementing, and maintaining ICT tools. Careful planning is a key part of this process, as is having an ongoing cycle of user training and equipment maintenance and support. Continuing to develop your "blended librarian" skills will help you navigate the ever-changing world of ICT and academic libraries.

🔒 KEY POINTS TO REMEMBER

- Technology provides access to information for users and generates management information to aid decision making.
- Technology improves productivity and assists in data collection, analysis, and use.
- Staff time is freed up through the implementation of some technologies, which also can make a library operate more cost-effectively.
- The proportion of the budget spent on the initial investment and associated recurrent costs will continue to increase and dominate annual expenditures.
- A major investment is needed to train staff to work effectively and efficiently with new or updated technologies.
- Rapid technological change will continue.
- Technology requires careful planning and control.

REFERENCES

Adams Becker, S., M. Cummins, A. Davis, A. Freeman, C. Hall Giesinger, and V. Ananthanarayanan. 2017. *NMC horizon report: 2017 higher education edition.* Austin, TX: The New Media Consortium.

Becker, Katrin. 2010. "The Clark-Kozma debate in the 21st century." CNIE Conference 2010, Heritage Matters: Inspiring Tomorrow, Saint John, New Brunswick, May 16–19, 2010. http://hdl.handle.net/11205/143.

Bell, Steven J., and John Shank. 2004. The blended librarian: A blueprint for redefining the teaching and learning role of academic librarians. *College and Research Libraries News* 65, no. 7: 372–375.

Blurton, C. 2002. *New directions of ICT-use in education.* www.unesco.org/education/lwf/dl/edict.pdf.

Council on Library and Information Resources. 2008. *No brief candle: Reconceiving research libraries for the 21st century.* Washington, DC: Council on Library and Information Resources.

Dugan, Robert E. 2002. Information technology budget and costs: Do you know what your information technology costs each year? *Journal of Academic Librarianship* 28, no. 4: 238-243.

EDUCAUSE Learning Initiative. 2014. *7 things you should know about cloud storage and collaboration.* https://library.educause.edu/~/media/files/library/2014/5/eli7108-pdf.pdf.

EDUCAUSE Learning Initiative. 2016. *7 things you should know about virtualized desktops.* https://library.educause.edu/resources/2016/11/7-things-you-should-know-about-virtualized-desktops.

Emberton, John. 1987. Effective information system planning and implementation. *Information Age* 9, no. 3: 159-162.

Hastings, Nancy B., and Monica W. Tracey. 2005. Does media affect learning: Where are we now? *TechTrends: Linking Research and Practice to Improve Learning* 49, no. 2: 28-30.

Morgan, Eric Lease. 2004. *Open source software in libraries.* Updated 2012. http://infomotions.com/musings/biblioacid/.

Prisk, Dennis P., and Monica G. Brooks. 2005. Hip high-tech purchases don't always turn out as planned. *Computers in Libraries* 25, no. 10: 10-12, 14, 16.

Quinlan, Catherine, and Hugh McHarg. 2012. The emerging library: Structure, culture, and lessons learned from the dissolution of a combined libraries-IT organization. *Journal of Library Administration* 52, no. 2: 147-161.

Renfro, Patricia, and James G. Neal. 2012. The integration of libraries and academic computing at Columbia: New opportunities for internal and external collaboration. *Journal of Library Administration* 52, no. 2: 162-171.

Shore, Elliott. 2012. Embracing hybridity: The merged organization, Alt/Ac and higher education. *Journal of Library Administration* 52, no. 2: 189.

Wikipedia, the Free Encyclopedia. 2016. S.v. "Integrated library system." https://en.wikipedia.org/w/index.php?title=Integrated_library_system&oldid=732993655.

CHAPTER 10

The Academy, Accreditation, and Accountability

Society's interest in higher education has varied over time; from a long-term perspective, it is only in the past one hundred years or so that there has been widespread interest. At best, during the first seven hundred years, only students, teachers, and some townspeople cared much about higher education and its activities. What interest there was focused on student behavior and payment of debts. During U.S. colonial times, interest broadened slightly, and some people started questioning the value of a liberal arts education when the country needed economic development. As nineteenth-century colleges and universities expanded their course offerings with a practical focus, more and more people outside academia took an interest in what was being taught and, to some degree, how it was taught. In an earlier chapter, we noted Melvil Dewey's role in producing an annual list of New York State colleges and universities "in good standing." Throughout the last two centuries, U.S. society has taken an ever-growing interest in higher education—what it does, how it does it, and how much it costs.

Six aspects of higher education that today's society, or at least a segment of society, takes an active interest in are what is taught, how it's taught, whether a degree is worth the time to secure it, the quality of what is taught, the value for money spent (tuition, tax payments, or donations), and whether the public actually gains anything of lasting value. *Accountability* and *assessment,* at least in terms of higher education, are sometimes used interchangeably, although they do have different meanings. One way to think of higher education assessment and accountability is this: When we, in higher education, look at our performance to measure success and outcomes, it is assessment; when outsiders look at our performance, it is accountability.

Three of the most important "A"s for addressing performance questions are accountability, assessment, and accreditation. For the vast majority of the public, the last "A"—accreditation—is what they have heard about, and they may have some notion of what being accredited means. Accreditation activities involve both assessment and accountability, and, in reality, the three concepts are tightly intertwined in higher education.

ACCREDITATION

We have mentioned accreditation in several chapters; here we take a more in-depth look at the process. All the topics we covered in the preceding chapters are also the areas of primary concern for accrediting agencies. Academic libraries and accreditation are intertwined; almost every campus accreditation process involves the library. The reason is that all the institution's educational programs draw on library resources and services to some extent.

Therefore, it is not surprising that accreditation teams take an interest in the library's activities and programs.

There has been an evolution in the U.S. accreditation process over the past 130-plus years since the process started. During most of the first two-thirds of the twentieth century, accreditation standards tended to focus on inputs (e.g., dollars spent, student GPAs, journal subscriptions held) with little or no concern about what the outcomes were for the inputs. Starting in the late 1970s, the focus began to shift toward what was accomplished as a result of the inputs. By the early 1990s, the shift toward outcome assessment was well in place. The expectation for more and better outcome data from the accredited institutions has increased with each passing year.

For the public, accredited status serves as an indication of a college's or university's quality and good standing. Accreditation has become the means for defining and ensuring higher education quality. Accreditation agencies (they are nongovernmental bodies) also serve as "gatekeepers." Being accredited is a key to having access to billions of dollars in federal and state funds.

Many people are unaware that accreditation began in the United States as a method by which colleges attempted to ensure that high school graduates would be capable of doing undergraduate-level work. Today's regional accreditation agencies still accredit secondary education programs within their region. By the early 1990s, higher education institutions were under increasing pressure to ensure their quality. Our present system of accreditation is a large complex of public and private interests. Although, officially speaking, undergoing the process is voluntary, the fact that having accredited status is required for receiving public funds makes accreditation close to mandatory.

As of early 2017, there were more than one hundred accrediting agencies in the United States. These agencies are divided into three broad categories—regional, national, and specialized. The U.S. Department of Education (USDE) accredits approximately seventy-five of these agencies, and the Council for Higher Education Accreditation (CHEA) accredits approximately sixty. Regional agencies (see table 10.1 for the coverage of the six regional groups) accredit more than three thousand institutions of the type most people think of as being higher educational. National agencies accredit both degree and nondegree institutions; many of these institutions are single-focus, for-profit operations.

The "approved" accreditors on the USDE and CHEA lists are not identical. The primary difference between the two lists lies in the specialized category. Specialized agencies cover programs in specific fields such as education, music, and library and information studies. An example of the difference is that ALA appears only on the CHEA list. This circumstance does not mean that ALA-accredited programs are unable to access federal funds; there is no problem because these programs are part of an institution accredited by a regional association that is on the USDE list.

USDE and CHEA have slightly different accreditation standards. USDE looks at multiple criteria when deciding whether to add an agency to its approved list. In its review, USDE (U.S. Department of Education, 2017) looks at how the agency handles assessment of these areas:

- Student achievement in relation to the institutional mission
- Curriculum
- Faculty
- Facilities, equipment, and supplies
- Fiscal and administrative capacity

U.S. ACCREDITATION ASSOCIATION	REGIONS COVERED		
1 New England Association of Schools and Colleges	Connecticut Maine	Massachusetts New Hampshire	Rhode Island Vermont
2 Middle States Commission on Higher Education	Delaware District of Columbia Maryland	New Jersey New York Pennsylvania	Puerto Rico U.S. Virgin Islands
3 Southern Association of Colleges and Schools Commission on Colleges	Alabama Florida Georgia Kentucky	Louisiana Mississippi North Carolina South Carolina	Tennessee Texas Virginia Latin America
4 Higher Learning Commission	Arkansas Arizona Colorado Iowa Illinois Indiana Kansas	Michigan Minnesota Missouri North Dakota Nebraska New Mexico	Ohio Oklahoma South Dakota West Virginia Wisconsin Wyoming
5 Northwest Association of Accredited Schools	Alaska Idaho Montana	Nevada Oregon	Utah Washington

6 Western Association of Schools and Colleges Senior College and University Commission	American Samoa
	California
	Commonwealth of
	  Northern Marianas
		East Asia
		Federated States
		  of Micronesia
		Fiji
			Guam
			Hawaii
			Republic of
			  Marshall Islands

TABLE 10.1 U.S. regional accreditation associations

- Student support services (the library often lies here within regional standards)
- Recruitment and admission policies
- Program length and objectives
- Student complaints

CHEA employs a broader and a shorter list of standards for its approval process of accrediting agencies. The following are areas the agency reviews:

- Advancement of academic quality
- Demonstration of accountability
- Encouragement of purposeful change and innovation
- Employment of appropriate and fair decision making
- Ongoing reassessment of the accrediting agency's accreditation process
- Possession of sufficient resources for accreditation activities (Eaton, 2015, pp. 6–7)

In addition to having access to federal and state funding, having ongoing accredited status (being accredited is not a one-time event) offers several potential benefits:

- It encourages institutional improvement through continuous self-study and evaluation.
- It provides some assurance to the public that the institution has appropriate educational objectives.
- It provides some assurance that the institution appears to be substantially accomplishing its goals.
- It provides assurance that the institution meets minimum accreditation standards.
- It provides some degree of consumer protection in terms of institutional quality.

Three additional benefits of accreditation, as outlined by USDE (U.S. Department of Education, 2017), are the following:

- It protects an institution against harmful internal and external pressure.
- It creates goals for self-improvement of weaker programs and for stimulating a general raising of standards among educational institutions.
- It involves the faculty and staff comprehensively in institutional evaluation and planning.

Almost all accredited institutions view the process as time-consuming but resulting in positive institutional changes and outcomes. Few institutions believe the process impacts their mission because few agencies raise questions about the mission beyond those asking about how the mission is reflected in the various accreditation standards. Essentially, accrediting agencies believe that the governing board has the right to set the mission without interference; if the board says its mission is to educate students to go to Mars, then the visiting team's purpose is to see how that mission is implemented and how well accomplishment of that mission meets the agency's standards.

Given that there are so many agencies, is it any wonder that academic libraries always seem to be involved in one or more accreditation activities every year? There are data to be collected long before any site visit, meetings with visiting teams, and often follow-up activities after the visiting team's final report arrives.

Looking at regional agencies, which are the only bodies to fully assess the entire institution, you will see that their standards vary from one another while covering all the aspects of USDE and CHEA requirements. Also, most of them have two or more commissions that handle secondary education, community colleges, and colleges and universities.

Accredited institutions pay an annual membership fee that provides the necessary operating funds for the agencies. The institutions also pay a fee for and the expenses associated with site visits.

Being accredited is an ongoing process. The longest full accreditation term, from a regional agency, is ten years. However, shorter periods are fairly common because any substantive change at an institution may require a team visit that focuses on the change(s). You can review some of the variations and actions of the Southern Association of Colleges and Schools Commission on Colleges by going to www.sacscoc.org/membershipInfo.asp to see, institution by institution, the most recent action and the next scheduled visit.

A typical process starts with the institution developing a self-study. This process can last from twelve to eighteen months as all campus units write up their responses to the standards and guidelines that apply to their respective areas. Usually the library has its own sections to write while also being asked to assist teaching departments in gathering data that relate to their areas (such as library use by majors or materials expenditures since the last accreditation visit). The institution's accreditation officer takes all the unit material and prepares a draft self-study that will eventually go to the agency office to be distributed to visiting team members. Because the final self-study cannot begin to include all the material submitted by campus units, there is often an extended period of discussion about what should be included in the study and what material is to be made available to the on-campus site visitors.

The site visit may last two or three days for a special visit to a week for a comprehensive review. In Evans's experience, both as a team member and as the senior librarian at an institution being reviewed, issues not covered in the self-study or the supplemental materials may arise that will require additional information. Sometimes this information can be library-related. On the last day of the visit, the team usually presents an oral report to interested parties on campus. Typically the oral report does not include recommendations that the team will make to the accrediting agency.

Visiting teams submit their written reports and recommendation(s) to the accrediting agency. The labels vary among institutions, though the following are typically the possible

---

||||| CHECK THIS OUT

We mentioned ARL SPEC Kits initially in chapter 8, describing how they can be a valuable snapshot of current research, practices, and policies in a variety of areas. We recommend the one focused on library involvement in the accreditation process:

Mercer, Holly, and Michael Maciel. 2012. *SPEC Kit 330: Library contribution to accreditation.* Washington, DC: Association of Research Libraries. http://publications.arl.org/Library -Contribution-to-Accreditation-SPEC-Kit-330/.

||||| **CHECK THIS OUT**

- New England Association of Schools and Colleges: www.neasc.org
- Middle States Commission on Higher Education: www.msche.org
- Southern Association of Colleges and Schools Commission on Colleges: www.sacscoc.org/
- Higher Learning Commission: https://www.hlcommission.org/
- Northwest Commission on Colleges and Universities: www.nwccu.org
- Western Association of Schools and Colleges Senior College and University Commission: www.wascsenior.org

---

outcomes depending on the type of visit and what the team found:

- Grant candidacy or initial accreditation
- Deny candidacy or initial accreditation
- Defer action
- Continue accreditation between capacity and educational effectiveness reviews
- Reaffirm accreditation
- Issue a formal notice of concern
- Issue a warning
- Impose probation
- Issue an order to show cause
- Terminate accreditation

On occasion, library support, especially for distance learning activities, comes up when the visiting team recommends a shorter reaccreditation term with specific areas of concern. Rarely, though, is it just a library-related concern. Before the agency makes its final decision regarding the recommendations, the institution has an opportunity to correct any errors of fact. Here again, the library is often called upon to supply data.

INFORMATION LITERACY AND ACCREDITATION

Academic libraries have two challenges when their institutions undergo an accreditation review. They must address the campus-wide support of educational programs and research as well as demonstrate the outcomes of their own instructional activities, such as teaching information literacy courses. In chapter 12, we'll discuss information literacy instruction as a library service in more detail; our focus here is on how the assessment of that instruction is important to the accreditation process. Kenneth Smith (2000), in a presentation to the Association of Research Libraries, made the following point that is very much relevant today:

> How does the focus on learning outcomes affect the mission of the library? Like other communities at the University, the library must move from a content view (books, subject knowledge) to a competency view (what students will be able to do). Within the new environment, we need to measure the ways in which the library is contributing to

the learning that the university values. . . . What is important is how the library's capabilities can provide solutions that measurably impact the quality of learning. It will require a significant period of learning new ways to participate and new roles for the library professionals. (pp. 32, 36)

Smith presented some sample outcomes that could be library relevant, such as students becoming self-reliant in the search for information, being able to assess bias and credibility of information in its various forms, and having a grasp of intellectual property in terms of social, ethical, political, and economic issues and concerns.

The challenge is how to develop meaningful measures to assess the factors that Smith (2000) outlined and become more actively involved in the overall educational process. Laura Saunders (2007), in an article examining regional accreditation agencies' approach to assessing information literacy, concluded by saying,

> By getting involved in curriculum development and assessment, the library can raise its profile on campus and increase its perceived value to the institution, which will be invaluable at a time when libraries nationwide are facing increased competition and tight budgets in the face of continued questions about the importance of a physical library to campus life. . . . In order to accomplish these important tasks, librarians must first be aware of accreditation standards, and how the library can partner with faculty and administrators in support of the goal of its parent institution. (p. 325)

Megan Oakleaf and Neal Kaske (2009) suggested that, if the librarians teaching information literacy courses think of assessing course work as a continuous cycle, then they have the means of breaking down a large challenge into small, manageable pieces. Oakleaf and Kaske's assessment cycle consists of the following seven elements:

- Identifying desired learning outcomes
- Creating appropriate learning activities
- Implementing the learning activities
- Gathering data to gauge learning outcomes
- Interpreting data and identifying the issues that require addressing

👥 FROM THE AUTHORS

An example from Evans's experience of issues not covered in the supplemental information occurred during a specialty review (electrical engineering). A member of the visiting team who was assigned to the library came from an institution that employed the same integrated library system (ILS) as did the host institution. The person had done some homework prior to his visit regarding the report capability of the ILS. Upon his arrival at the host library, he requested that the library produce a report of library use not just by major but also by the student's year (freshman, sophomore, etc.). He knew that the system could produce the information and that the engineering department had not included this information in its self-study. Librarians must be ready to field such surprise requests during a site visit.

- Taking action and making decisions to address the issues
- Reviewing learning goals (p. 283)

Perhaps there is an eighth element that fits between creating and implementing learning activities: designing methods to collect appropriate data regarding the outcomes. Oakleaf and Kaske conclude their article with the following:

> When selecting an assessment approach, librarians should strive to follow best practices whenever possible. Using multiple methods and practicing continuous assessments are among the best practices to consider. . . . By using multiple methods, librarians gain a variety of assessment feedback. . . . Practicing continuous assessment allows librarians to "get started" with assessment rather than waiting to "get it perfect." (p. 283)

When formulating learning activities and collecting data, it is wise to keep in mind some of the types of questions accreditation visiting teams like to ask, such as these:

- Are your learning outcomes linked to the library and institutional missions? How well?
- What evidence do you have of student learning?
- What method(s) do you employ to assess the learning outcomes? Why do you use those methods? (This is particularly important because for so long libraries have relied on output measures—number of classes taught, total number of students reached, and the like—rather than outcome measures that indicate whether objectives were achieved.)
- Do you assess your assessment process?
- How do you communicate the outcome results to the various interested stakeholders?

What are some of the options commonly employed to gather assessment data? There are the long-standing pre- and post-tests as well as in-class performance tests. Self-reporting techniques include surveys, focus groups, and interviews. Some other options are portfolios and concept mapping. More recently, a popular assessment approach has been to evaluate student artifacts (papers, bibliographies, speeches, etc.) using a rubric-based method.

We've mentioned previously some standards documents developed by the Association of College and Research Libraries (ACRL). In 2000, ACRL created the Information Literacy

---

▌▌▌ CHECK THIS OUT

The following are a few good articles that discuss various considerations when implementing the Framework for Information Literacy:

Jacobson, Trudi E., and Craig Gibson. 2015. First thoughts on implementing the Framework for Information Literacy. *Communications in Information Literacy* 9, no. 2: 102–110.

Kuglitsch, Rebecca Z. 2015. Teaching for transfer: Reconciling the Framework with disciplinary information literacy. *portal: Libraries and the Academy* 15, no. 3: 457–470.

Oakleaf, Megan. 2014. A roadmap for assessing student learning using the new Framework for Information Literacy for Higher Education. *Journal of Academic Librarianship* 40, no. 5: 510–514.

ⅢⅢⅢ CHECK THIS OUT

The Library Assessment Conference is a biennial conference cosponsored by ARL. The conference's goal is "to build and further a vibrant library assessment community by bringing together interested practitioners and researchers who have responsibility or interest in the broad field of library assessment." The conference website includes proceedings from past conferences: http://libraryassessment.org/archive/index.shtml.

Standards for Higher Education. These standards were widely used by many academic libraries to develop local assessment methods. A big shift in national standards occurred when, in 2016, ACRL approved a new Framework for Information Literacy for Higher Education with the intent to sunset the original standards in 2017. The new standards are called a "framework" because they form a group of core concepts. The Framework is based on threshold concept theory, which suggests that ideas serve as levels to higher understanding. The following are the six concepts, or frames:

- Authority Is Constructed and Contextual
- Information Creation as a Process
- Information Has Value
- Research as Inquiry
- Scholarship as Conversation
- Searching as Strategic Exploration

Some critics of the Framework question the theory behind it, and others feel that it is too theory-based and would be challenging to translate into practice. Supporters point out that the Framework provides support for integrating information literacy skills into the curriculum because it supports deeper faculty-librarian collaborations than does the "one shot" model (a single class session of instruction), which we will revisit in the "Services" chapter.

BEYOND ACCREDITATION

Accountability goes well beyond accreditation because there are stakeholders who have an interest in holding higher education institutions accountable for actions taken or not taken. One obvious stakeholder is the funding body of the institution. Taxpayers and state legislatures are vitally concerned about use of funds allocated to higher education. In the case of private institutions, parents and students expect that the money paid for an education will be properly and effectively expended. From a management point of view, each managerial level is accountable for what it does all the way up to the governing board. As we noted in the opening section of this chapter, society, in the broadest sense, has an interest in what takes place in higher education. There are some individuals with no direct connection to an academic institution who may be highly interested in the curriculum—for example, how institutions teach evolution (this topic also comes up in high schools). Another common concern is the degree to which personal political or social views influence how a course is presented. Still others may be concerned about the amount of indirect support given schools, such as tax exemptions, for example.

It is not only accountability issues that drive or ought to drive efforts to assess library programs and services. Providing the highest-quality service is a key component in demonstrating value for money and of gaining user support. Some years ago, Brian Quinn (1997) wrote,

> The concept of service quality is somewhat elusive and resists easy definition, but essentially it emphasizes gap reduction—reducing any gap that may exist between a customer's expectations and the customer's perception of the quality of service provided. More traditional measures of academic library quality such as collection size are considered to be of secondary importance. (p. 359)

Today ever-growing competition with other information providers impacts the user's perception. Ease of access and speed of responses, for example, create challenges for the user to continue to view traditional library services as quality services.

Perceptions of quality will vary from person to person and even by geographic region. Having some national means of addressing library user perceptions of service quality has led to such efforts as LibQUAL+, which is a set of tools for soliciting, tracking, understanding, and acting upon user opinions of service quality (www.libqual.org). The survey is an outgrowth of a joint effort by the Association of Research Libraries and Texas A&M University and is based on work done by Zeithaml, Parasuraman, and Berry (1990) on measuring for-profit organization service quality (SERVQUAL). Although some people (e.g., Edgar, 2006; Dennis, Greenwood, and Watson, 2013) have raised questions about the adequacy of LibQUAL+ as a sole assessment method, it can be a useful tool. Some institutions outside the United States have even chosen to modify it for their needs (e.g., Dahan et al., 2016; Xi et al., 2016; Rehman, Kyrillidou, and Hameed, 2014). Conducting such a study can provide data that are both local and comparative with other libraries. It is, in essence, a gap measurement process of the type Quinn (1997) mentioned. Individuals complete a survey form that asks them to indicate, using a nine-point scale, three responses to each question: the person's minimal expectation for a service, the person's desired expectation, and, last, the perceived level of service. A "gap" is present when there are differences between expectations and perceptions.

▌▌▌▌ CHECK THIS OUT

Here are five examples of the use of LibQUAL+ in a variety of academic library settings:

Halling, T. Derek, and Esthere Carrigan. 2012. Navigating user feedback channels to chart an evidence-based course for library redesign. *Evidence-Based Library and Information Practice* 7, no. 1: 70–81.

Harvey, Eugene J., and Maureen Lindstrom. 2013. LibQUAL+® and the information commons initiative at Buffalo State College: 2003 to 2009. *Evidence-Based Library and Information Practice* 8, no. 2: 68–84.

McCaffrey, Ciara, and Michelle Breen. 2016. Quiet in the library: An evidence-based approach to improving the student experience. *portal: Libraries and the Academy* 16, no. 4: 775–791.

Roy, Abhik, Adwait Khare, Ben S. C. Liu, Linda M. Hawkes, and Janice Swiatek-Kelley. 2012. An investigation of affect of service using a LibQUAL+™ survey and an experimental study. *Journal of Academic Librarianship* 38, no. 3: 153–160.

Voorbij, Henk. 2012. The use of LibQUAL+ by European research libraries. *Performance Measurement and Metrics* 13, no. 3: 154–168.

Few, if any, libraries participate in the survey every year. In 2015, 123 institutions participated; 172 participated in 2012. See the LibQUAL+ website (www.libqual.org) for annual participation rates and institutional names. The survey is also used internationally. The service is not inexpensive; in 2017, it cost $3,200 to participate in the survey with additional costs for extra analysis. Each year ARL creates norm tables based on that year's responses so a library can compare its data with a broader base. The participating libraries, of course, receive both a summary of their data and the raw data so they can engage in further analysis. Thus, a library gains insights into its service quality both locally and nationally, which is a form of benchmarking. As an incentive to collect more frequent data for benchmarking purposes, ARL offers discounts to institutions that regularly participate in the survey. ARL also offers a shorter version of LibQUAL+ called LibQUAL+ Lite. The LibQUAL+ Lite version takes approximately ten to thirteen minutes to complete. According to the LibQUAL+ website,

> The LibQUAL+ Lite protocol is being implemented in such a manner that individual libraries will determine what percentage of their users will RANDOMLY be assigned the traditional LibQUAL+ protocol, and what percentage will RANDOMLY be assigned the LibQUAL+ Lite protocol. (https://www.libqual.org/about/about_lq/LQ_lite)

Some libraries employ another service similar to LibQUAL+, called Counting Opinions, for assessment purposes. The organization's statement of purpose and service is "comprehensive, cost-effective, real-time solutions designed for libraries, in support of customer insight, operational improvements and advocacy efforts" (www.countingopinions.com). The organization's list of customers includes both academic and public libraries. Two of the company's products are LibSat (a continuous customer satisfaction survey) and LibPAS (library performance assessment). The Measuring Information Service Outcomes (MISO) survey is another product that focuses on IT and library services, addressing questions such as these:

- What services and resources are important to our constituents, and how successfully do our organizations deliver them?
- How effectively do we communicate with our campus communities about our services and resources?
- How skilled are our constituents in the use of software and library databases? What additional skills do they wish to learn, and how do they wish to learn?
- Which software and hardware tools do our constituents use, and which of these tools do they own?
- What roles do our constituents play on campus? What demographic factors identify them?
- What benchmarks can be established for excellent delivery of library and computing services? (www.misosurvey.org)

In addition to products available for purchase, some libraries choose to develop their own in-house surveys, though external benchmarking would be unlikely given a local survey's uniqueness.

Benchmarking

To some degree, LibQUAL+ offers a limited form of benchmarking capability; however, the technique is generally a stand-alone process. Benchmarking, at least in U.S. libraries, is a relatively recent phenomenon as jurisdictions and organizations have become increasingly concerned about operating costs. Benchmarking is basically a tool for either internal or external comparisons. The National Association of College and University Business Officers (NACUBO) has been conducting a number of benchmarking studies of various areas in academic institutions since the mid-1990s. These are large-scale efforts involving various member institutions in the United States and Canada. There have been several such projects relating to libraries over the years; the data have not been published because they are viewed as confidential. Since 2007, NACUBO has provided a tool to assist member organizations with their benchmarking processes (www.nacubo.org/Research/NACUBO_Benchmarking_Tool.html).

The goal of benchmarking is to provide data that can help managers answer the following questions:

- How well are we doing compared to others?
- How good do we want to be?
- Who is doing the best?
- How do they do it?
- How can we adapt what they do to our organization?

There are four basic types of benchmarking—internal, competitive, industry, and best in class. As the label suggests, *internal benchmarking* looks at internal practices within an organization. An example is what it costs to create a purchase order in various departments across a campus. A *competitive benchmarking* project might collect data on the cost of creating purchase orders in various departments in a number of institutions. *Industry benchmarking* would collect data from all or a representative sample of all organizations within an "industry." The NACUBO benchmarks are essentially an industry effort. *Best-in-class benchmarking* collects information across industries, essentially seeking the most effective practices.

Internal benchmarking may also vary between vertical and horizontal projects. A *vertical project* seeks to quantify the costs, workloads, and productivity of a defined functional area—for example, handling accounts payable. A *horizontal study* analyzes the cost and productivity of a single process that crosses two or more functional areas; an example is database searching in acquisitions, cataloging, and document delivery. The NACUBO studies have several objectives:

- To assist participating institutions to identify best practices
- To provide data that may allow participants to identify areas for improvement
- To provide data to assess relationships between inputs (primarily resource costs) and outputs (generally the quantity and quality of products and services)
- To introduce the concepts of "process improvement" and awareness of the value of benchmarking

When developing a benchmarking project, a key issue is establishing for each benchmark a clear understanding by all participants of what it will measure and what to include in the data collected for that benchmark. Understanding what will and will not be included—time, staff salaries, equipment costs, staff benefits—is essential if the data are to be useful. A common problem in first-time projects is not making clear what to include in staff costs: just salary, salary and directed benefits such as health insurance, or all of those plus vacation and sick leave costs. If several approaches are used, the data will be essentially useless for comparative purposes.

One of the problems for the first NACUBO library project was the failure to establish clear guidelines for handling multiple campuses and libraries in which the entities have separate operating budgets. For the Loyola Marymount University (LMU) library, there were two problems. The first was the fact that Loyola Law School has a separate campus as well as name but shares the same governing board as LMU. Rarely does the institution issue data combining the LMU library with the law school library; however, at many other institutions, such combined reporting is common. The second issue was the fact that the LMU library also functions as the university's official archives and records management unit. Although the holdings are not included in the library's statistics, the staffing costs and other operating costs are part of the overall operating budget. Issues such as these should be thoughtfully addressed at the outset.

Quality Management

Defining quality in a library setting is more difficult when the outcome is not a physical product. How can "quality service" be defined? Can it be just user satisfaction? But doing so leaves one with a conundrum because someone may be satisfied with information provided by a librarian but not know that information is incomplete or even inaccurate or out-of-date. Should the user discover such "errors," he is likely to judge the information or service as less than satisfactory. Such issues give rise to the questions of when and how often to measure customer satisfaction.

Parasuraman, Zeithaml, and Berry (1985) identified the following ten dimensions that, to a greater or lesser degree, determine the quality of a service:

1. Reliability or consistency
2. Responsiveness or timeliness
3. Competence
4. Access or approachability
5. Courtesy
6. Communication
7. Credibility
8. Security (including confidentiality)
9. Understanding the customer's needs
10. Tangibles (such as physical facilities, appearance of personnel, and tools or equipment) (p. 47)

All these elements apply to the academic library environment and can form a starting point for defining quality in a given environment. The following sections address the issues of quality, efficiency, and effectiveness.

Six Sigma–Lean Six Sigma

Six Sigma was created from statistical and quality management modeling tools developed by Joseph Juran (1964). The goal of the Six Sigma process is to improve quality by eliminating manufacturing operations. Likewise Lean, another concept, originally was a quality control process developed for the automotive industry. Since their inception, the two tools have been modified to work in any situation in which quality is a primary interest. Essentially Lean Six Sigma tries to achieve a balance between doing just quality or just speed of operations.

One example of an academic library employing the Lean Six Sigma method is in Sarah Murphy's (2009) article. She discussed the applicability of the concept to one service element at the Ohio State University (OSU) libraries. Library service is a fleeting event and presents challenges regarding when and how often to assess such transactions. As Murphy stated, "Services are both intangible and heterogeneous, inviting variability in processes as customers and providers contribute to the inputs and outputs of the service product" (p. 216). The focus of her project was OSU library's process for managing and answering users' e-mail questions. She concluded her article with this statement:

> Libraries can customize and borrow a number of quality management systems and tools from the business community to both assess their service process and continuously improve their operations. By adopting an approach like Lean Six Sigma, a library can respond better to changing customer needs and desires by creating an infrastructure that supports, nurtures, and sustains a culture of assessment and change. (p. 224)

Balanced Scorecard

Yet another technique for improving performance began in the early 1990s with Robert Kaplan and David Norton's (1992) article in the *Harvard Business Review*. Their technique—balanced scorecard—is a way to organize and present large quantities of complex interrelated data in a manner that fosters better managerial decision making. The approach views the service from four perspectives for which metrics are developed and data are collected and analyzed (www.balancedscorecard.org):

- Learning and growth perspective
- Business process perspective
- Customer perspective
- Financial perspective

Alfred Willis (2004) published an article based on interviews with two key University of Virginia library administrators who were lead figures in using the balanced scorecard at the library. Jim Self, in responding to a question regarding the value of the technique, said, "It can focus the library. It makes the library as an organization decide what is important. It can be used to improve organizational performance. It broadens our perspective in a structured way, and gives us a more balanced view of our work" (p. 66). Lynda White's response to the question was, "Our balanced scorecard is so user-oriented, it fits really well with what we value. Many of our metrics focus on the results for our users whether or not they are technically in the user perspective" (p. 66). Given the librarian interest in the balanced scorecard approach, ARL has partnered with Ascendant Strategy Management Group to provide training to help librarians use the balanced scorecard approach to work in a research library (www.arl.org/focus-areas/statistics-assessment/balanced-scorecard).

Cost Analysis

Another factor that drives assessment is the economic conditions for higher education. As funding shrinks, libraries must become more efficient as well as effective. Operations research can play a role in demonstrating a library's focus on effectiveness, efficiency, quality, and accountability.

Conducting internal cost studies provides useful data and occasionally reveals unexpected insights. Three of the most common reasons for engaging in such projects are to identify possible cost reduction areas and tasks, to provide data for cost recovery programs, and to evaluate alternatives for carrying out a task or activity. Such studies can, and in most cases should, take a pragmatic approach to data collecting. That is, one should not worry too much about using complex models or statistical analysis because basic statistics are often sufficient for local projects. A balanced discussion touching on the pros and cons of cost studies (although it is essentially pro) is Joseph Hewitt's (1989) "Using Cost Data Judiciously." Hewitt makes a point with which we strongly agree:

> Cost studies are a useful, at times necessary, tool of management in libraries. They tend to be used selectively for specific purposes. In decision making, they are used with sensitivity as data illuminating a single (albeit important) factor involved in complex decisions. . . . On the whole, librarians using cost studies are aware of their limitations and dangers and are attempting to make use of cost studies as tools of rational, humane management. (pp. 50–51)

Work Analysis

Work analysis, also sometimes called operations research, can have a place in demonstrating library accountability, cost containment, and assessment. As is true of the preceding assessment methods, this book can provide only a little background and suggest some sources for gaining in-depth information.

Work analysis assessment normally begins with asking some standard questions. The questions are easy to ask but sometimes painful for staff to answer. The following are the basic questions:

| What is done? | Where is it done? | Who does it? |
| Why is it done? | When is it done? | How is it done? |

Richard Dougherty (2008) made a concise case for engaging in work analysis:

> Library administrators have been faced with many difficult and painful choices in recent years as budgets have remained persistently tight, and society and governments demand greater accountability among social institutions such as libraries. . . . One way

to free up staff time and dollar resources is to streamline processes and procedures, or better yet, get rid of existing operations that are redundant or unnecessary. I was particularly taken by a recent comment attributed to a Hewlett-Packard official who observed: "If a thing is not worth doing, it is not worth doing well." (p. ix)

The first sentence in this quotation also provides an excellent summary of why this chapter is essential in a book about academic librarianship.

LIBRARY VALUE AND USER STUDIES

We described several traditional assessment methods and wanted to close out the chapter by touching on some other models that contribute to overall assessment and accountability efforts. Although time-consuming and labor intensive, ethnographic studies such as the one undertaken at the University of Rochester (Foster and Gibbons, 2007) provide a detailed look at the needs of students based on their daily activities and preferences. The study provided students with opportunities to make some creative suggestions about how the library might provide and market services. When services are user-focused and user-designed to some extent, ultimately they will be more valuable to the user. We have mentioned ARL SPEC Kits elsewhere in the book, and Fox and Doshi (2011) provide an excellent one focused on the library user experience.

▐▐▐▐ CHECK THIS OUT

A follow-up to the studies done at the University of Rochester is a CLIR report based on a seminar conducted on participatory design in academic libraries. The report includes numerous examples of studies and processes undertaken at several academic institutions, such as encouraging students to draw ideal study spaces or share elements of their ideal library in a photo booth activity.

Council on Library Information Resources, Nancy Fried Foster, and Peter Tobia. 2014. *Participatory design in academic libraries: New reports and findings.* Washington, DC: Council on Library and Information Resources.

In the 2010s, more academic libraries began considering ways to attempt to quantify library value and demonstrate the impact of library collections and services on the retention of students and their overall academic success. Many of these studies are correlational, so they don't confirm causation—that library use yields better grades or an inclination to stay enrolled. Even controlling for multiple variables, it is challenging to quantify the full benefits of library use and overall library value. Several studies have been successful in making small claims about library value (Cox and Jantti, 2012; Soria, Fransen, and Nackerud, 2013; Stone and Ramsden, 2013). In addition, ARL and ACRL have developed programs to support academic librarians in learning how to conduct research projects that can better demonstrate the value of their libraries (ACRL, 2010; ARL, 2012). It will be interesting to see how these projects develop in the next few years because it's likely accountability will become increasingly more important.

👥 FROM THE AUTHORS

We've emphasized many times how important it is to promote the library and its services to your users. The first principle of marketing is finding out what users need. This can be done through focus groups, surveys, interviews, usability studies, observations, and so forth. Once an academic library learns what the student, faculty, and staff needs are, then the library needs to deliver. Strategic planning plays a key role here. When the resource is provided by the library, the library needs to let its users know what it has to offer through promotion. In other words, "We asked you what you want. You told us. We've got it; here it is!"

An excellent resource for learning more about marketing library services is Brian Mathews's *Marketing Today's Academic Library: A Bold New Approach to Communicating with Students* (ALA Editions, 2009).

🔖 KEY POINTS TO REMEMBER

- Today's society has a vested interest in higher education regarding such matters as what is taught, how it is taught, whether a degree is worth the time to secure it, the quality of what is taught, whether there is value for money spent, and whether the public actually gains anything of lasting value.
- Assessment and accountability are intertwined concepts. Assessment is examining our own performance, and accountability is having outsiders examine our performance.
- For higher education, the accreditation process is a means of engaging in assessment (self-study) and demonstrating accountability to stakeholders.
- Accreditation is one of the key elements in higher education's efforts to demonstrate quality and accountability.
- Although going through the accreditation process is voluntary because being accredited is a requirement for receiving federal and state funds, reputable institutions invest in the work and costs associated with gaining and keeping accredited status.
- Academic libraries in medium-sized and large institutions can expect to have some accreditation activities each year, from supplying self-study data to addressing concerns raised by a visiting team.
- Academic libraries often face dual responsibilities during a comprehensive accreditation visit, such as providing general data regarding curriculum and research support and demonstrating the learning outcomes of their information literacy programs.
- Accountability goes far beyond the accreditation process. The number of stakeholders expecting to have a say in what takes place within the academy is large and diverse. Academic institutions and their libraries employ a variety of techniques to demonstrate their accountability.
- LibQUAL+ is one process that assists in demonstrating accountability.
- A wide variety of assessment techniques are available to academic libraries that will assist them in demonstrating their commitment to ongoing assessment, accountability, and cost containment.

REFERENCES

ACRL Association of College and Research Libraries. 2010. *The value of academic libraries: A comprehensive research review and report.* Chicago: Association of College and Research Libraries.

ARL Association of Research Libraries. 2012. *LibValue: Value, outcomes, and return on investment.* www.libvalue.org.

Council on Library and Information Resources, Nancy Fried Foster, and Peter Tobia. 2014. *Participatory design in academic libraries: New reports and findings.* Washington, DC: Council on Library and Information Resources.

Cox, B., and M. Jantti. 2012. Discovering the impact of library use and student performance. *EDUCAUSE Review.*

Dahan, Suziyana Mat, Mohd Yusof Taib, Nurhaizan Mohd Zainudin, and Fadzida Ismail. 2016. Surveying users' perception of academic library services quality: A case study in Universiti Malaysia Pahang (UMP) Library. *Journal of Academic Librarianship* 42, no. 1: 38–43.

Dennis, Melissa, Judy Greenwood, and Alex Watson. 2013. LibQUAL+ revisited: Further analysis of qualitative and quantitative survey results at the University of Mississippi. *Journal of Academic Librarianship* 39, no. 6: 512–516.

Dougherty, Richard. 2008. *Streamlining library services: What we do, how much time it takes, what it costs, and how we can do it better.* Lanham, MD: Scarecrow Press.

Eaton, Judith S. 2015. *An overview of U.S. accreditation.* Washington, DC: Council for Higher Education Accreditation. https://www.chea.org/userfiles/uploads/Overview%20of%20US%20Accreditation%20 2015.pdf.

Edgar, William B. 2006. Questioning LibQUAL+: Expanding its assessment of academic library effectiveness. *portal: Libraries and the Academy* 6, no. 4: 445–465.

Foster, Nancy, and Susan Gibbons. 2007. *Studying students: The Undergraduate Research Project at the University of Rochester.* Chicago: Association of College and Research Libraries.

Fox, Robert, and Ameet Doshi. 2011. *SPEC Kit 322: Library user experience.* Washington, DC: Association of Research Libraries.

Halling, T. Derek, and Esthere Carrigan. 2012. Navigating user feedback channels to chart an evidence-based course for library redesign. *Evidence-Based Library and Information Practice* 7, no. 1: 70–81.

Harvey, Eugene J., and Maureen Lindstrom. 2013. LibQUAL+® and the information commons initiative at Buffalo State College: 2003 to 2009. *Evidence-Based Library and Information Practice* 8, no. 2: 68–84.

Hewitt, Joseph. 1989. "Using cost data judiciously." In *Cost-effective technical services: How to track, manage, and justify internal operations,* edited by Gary Pitkin, 50–55. New York: Neal-Schuman.

Jacobson, Trudi E., and Craig Gibson. 2015. First thoughts on implementing the Framework for Information Literacy. *Communications in Information Literacy* 9, no. 2: 102–110.

Juran, Joseph M. 1964. *Managerial breakthrough.* New York: McGraw-Hill.

Kaplan, Robert S., and David P. Norton. 1992. The balanced scorecard: Measures that drive performance. *Harvard Business Review* 70, no. 1: 71–79.

Kuglitsch, Rebecca Z. 2015. Teaching for transfer: Reconciling the Framework with disciplinary information literacy. *portal: Libraries and the Academy* 15, no. 3: 457–470.

Mathews, Brian. 2009. *Marketing today's academic library: A bold new approach to communicating with students.* Chicago: ALA Editions.

McCaffrey, Ciara, and Michelle Breen. 2016. Quiet in the library: An evidence-based approach to improving the student experience. *portal: Libraries and the Academy* 16, no. 4: 775–791.

Mercer, Holly, and Michael Maciel. 2012. *SPEC Kit 330: Library contribution to accreditation.* Washington, DC: Association of Research Libraries. http://publications.arl.org/Library-Contribution-to -Accreditation-SPEC-Kit-330/.

Murphy, Sarah Anne. 2009. Leveraging Lean Six Sigma to culture, nurture, and sustain assessment and change in the academic library environment. *College and Research Libraries* 70, no. 3: 215–225.

Oakleaf, Megan. 2014. A roadmap for assessing student learning using the new Framework for Information Literacy for Higher Education. *Journal of Academic Librarianship* 40, no. 5: 510-514.

Oakleaf, Megan, and Neal Kaske. 2009. Guiding questions for assessing information literacy in higher education. *portal: Libraries and the Academy* 9, no. 2: 273-286.

Parasuraman, A., Valarie A. Zeithaml, and Leonard L. Berry. 1985. A conceptual model of service quality and its implications for future research. *Journal of Marketing* 49, no. 4: 41-50.

Quinn, Brian. 1997. Adapting service quality concepts to academic libraries. *Journal of Academic Librarianship* 23, no. 5: 359-369.

Rehman, Shafiq, Martha Kyrillidou, and Imran Hameed. 2014. Reliability and validity of a modified LibQUAL+® survey in Pakistan: An Urdu language experience. *Malaysian Journal of Library and Information Science* 19, no. 2: 83-102.

Roy, Abhik, Adwait Khare, Ben S. C. Liu, Linda M. Hawkes, and Janice Swiatek-Kelley. 2012. An investigation of affect of service using a LibQUAL+™ survey and an experimental study. *Journal of Academic Librarianship* 38, no. 3: 153-160.

Saunders, Laura. 2007. Regional accreditation organizations' treatment of information literacy: Definitions, collaboration, and assessment. *Journal of Academic Librarianship* 33, no. 3: 317-326.

Smith, Kenneth R. 2000. "New roles and responsibilities for the university library: Advancing student learning through outcome assessment." Paper presented to the Association of Research Libraries, University of Arizona, May 4. Reprinted in the *Journal of Library Administration* 35, no. 4 (2001): 29-36.

Soria, K. M., J. Fransen, and S. Nackerud. 2013. Library use and undergraduate student outcomes: New evidence for students' retention and academic success. *portal: Libraries and the Academy* 13, no. 2: 147-164.

Stone, G., and B. Ramsden. 2013. Library impact data project: Looking for the link between library usage and student attainment. *College and Research Libraries* 74, no. 6: 546-559.

U.S. Department of Education. 2017. *Financial aid for postsecondary students: Overview of accreditation in the United States.* www.ed.gov/admins/finaid/accred/index.html.

Voorbij, Henk. 2012. The use of LibQUAL+ by European research libraries. *Performance Measurement and Metrics* 13, no. 3: 154-168.

Willis, Alfred. 2004. Using the balanced scorecard at the University of Virginia Library. *Library Administration and Management* 18, no. 2: 64-67.

Xi, Qingkui, Xinquan Li, Heng Zhao, Qun He, and Zizheng Cai. 2016. Service quality assessment at the Nanjing Agricultural University based on LibQUAL+. *Science and Technology Libraries* 35, no. 4: 338-349.

Zeithaml, Valarie A., A. Parasuraman, and Leonard L. Berry. 1990. *Delivering quality service: Balancing customer perceptions and expectations.* New York: Free Press.

CHAPTER 11

Collections

Although good public services are essential, collections are the foundation of academic library services. We refer to collections broadly to include not only physical materials, such as books, journals, government publications, and audiovisual and unique special collections materials, but also the myriad types of online collections libraries organize and disseminate, such as journals, databases, digitized special collections, and data repositories. In a real sense, higher education is built on the knowledge of humankind contained within these collections, and almost all academics acknowledge the importance of the intellectual content of library collections. As Karen Schmidt (2004) wrote, "It is important to reflect that the organization of knowledge and the ways in which libraries cull and prioritize it for its users are a premium asset regardless of the format of the material" (p. 370). Formats will continue to change, but access to the content within those formats remains most important. Quite some time ago, Gordon Williams (1964) wrote:

> Written records are usually desirable because of the meanings the words can communicate to anyone who can read them; what is wanted is what we may call, for lack of a better term, the intellectual content of words. Fundamentally, the written record itself is merely a carrier, a vehicle; and it is what is carried, not the carrier, that is usually of primary importance. (p. 374)

Those carriers of information are quite different today than they were in 1964 or even just a few years ago. Today we're seeing a revolution in scholarly publishing for a variety of reasons, some of which we covered in chapter 3 in our discussion of peer review, university presses, and the open access (OA) movement. The cost of scholarly content has continued to rise to unsustainable levels, particularly with annual subscription costs to scientific journals. The growth of open access repositories and publishing venues has created opportunities to make more scholarly content freely available. The open movement has extended to educational resources such as textbooks and other open education resources (OERs). Large-scale digitization projects are making unique special collections materials once hidden away in archives now freely available for the world to learn from and enjoy.

Increasingly there is a movement to refer to collections more broadly as scholarly communications. Some libraries, such as at MIT, have shifted focus from collections to the broader scholarly communications by renaming the department and moving the collections budget under the umbrella of scholarly communications (Finnie, 2016). One definition of scholarly communication that we like comes from Stephanie Davis-Kahl and Merinda Kaye Hensley (2013), who described scholarly communication as "the systems by which results of scholarship are created, registered, evaluated, disseminated, preserved, and reshaped into new scholarship with an emphasis on sharing." Libraries have long placed a priority on sharing through borrowing policies and cooperative agreements, and scholarly communication's emphasis on sharing is a good fit within the academic library.

One of the more theoretical writers on academic library collection issues was the late Ross Atkinson. In one of his last publications, Atkinson (2006) suggested that academic library collections serve three basic purposes, and his analysis is still relevant. The first purpose is to provide institutional capital: "Collections attract scholars, graduate students, government support, and donor funding—and add prestige to the institution" (p. 245). A second purpose for having library collections is to provide long-term preservation of the items: "The collection of material, in order to ensure their long-term access, remains the primary challenge and responsibility of research libraries, regardless of changes in technology or ideology" (p. 245). Atkinson's final suggestion has been a matter of debate within the profession and academy for many years: "to privilege [select] particular objects as more useful or reliable than others" (p. 245). In essence, who has, or should have, the power to determine what is good and not so good for long-term preservation and access?

In the following sections, we will consider the history of academic library collections and discuss basic collection management practices. These practices are relevant no matter the format of the material, and we feel it is essential that the new academic librarian in particular have a foundation in collection management.

PAST AND PRESENT PRACTICE

Collection development and management is a relatively new concept for librarianship, at least as far as using a single term to describe a group of activities relating to both the collections and a role of librarians. Although many use the two terms interchangeably, they actually have different meanings—collection *development* relates to the building of collections, while collection *management* covers everything from building to preservation. We cover the full spectrum of activities in this chapter. It was not until the 1970s and early 1980s that the term *collection development* appeared in the literature and in job announcements as a position responsibility. Until then, the focus had been on acquiring items for the collection and trying to secure the maximum number of items that were likely to be of interest to the faculty and students with the available funds.

▌▌▌ CHECK THIS OUT

We've mentioned several times that *portal: Libraries and the Academy* is an excellent journal worth following. The July 2014 issue (volume 14, number 3) is focused on the future of academic libraries, and the entire issue is worth examining. Topics covered include the future of teaching and learning in libraries, measuring the value of libraries in undergraduate education, designing better library experiences, working with IT, the role of libraries in social justice, and more. Of particular interest related to collections are two articles:

Dempsey, Lorcan, Constance Malpas, and Brian Lavoie. 2014. Collection directions: The evolution of library collections and collecting. *portal: Libraries and the Academy* 14, no. 3: 393–423.

Levine-Clark, Michael. 2014. Access to everything: Building the future academic library collection. *portal: Libraries and the Academy* 14, no. 3: 425–437.

⚏ FROM THE AUTHORS

Evans experienced the shift from faculty to librarian selection of collection materials in the 1990s. When he took over the directorship of a medium-sized academic library (1988), the faculty had total control over expenditures for library materials, and the budget for collections was $450,000. As the institution's fiscal health became stronger, so did funding for acquisitions. Also during this time, the institution increased its emphasis on the notion that all faculty members should be "productive scholars" as well as exemplary teachers. Through a slow process, library staff were able to demonstrate their collection development skills, and by the mid-1990s, the faculty library committee and faculty senate agreed to drop the faculty handbook statement that the faculty had sole responsibility for selection. Certainly the fact that by then collection funds were over $2 million also assisted in the shift in responsibility.

You may recall from chapter 2 that until well into the nineteenth century, U.S. academic library collections grew slowly, primarily from donations rather than purchases. Collections were small because the institutional mission and curriculum did not require significant library support—the focus was on mastering a limited number of approved texts that fit the liberal arts concept and any religious beliefs of the denomination that supported the college.

During the nineteenth century, collections grew substantially as the curriculum expanded and teaching methods changed. From the earliest times until today, at least in smaller institutions with limited funding, the power to select books resided with the faculty. To some extent, the view expressed by Pierce Butler (1945) would still be supported by some teaching faculty: "The Librarian may be a technical specialist—in the technologies of book preservation and use—but he is never a subject specialist" (p. 10). The notion of subject specialists and bibliographers as library personnel would not come about for many years after Butler wrote his book. Even when it did come to pass, it was initially a practice among Association of Research Libraries (ARL) institutions before becoming more widespread.

The shift to allowing academic librarians to make most of the selection decisions was partially a function of time and money. After World War II, teaching faculties saw their class sizes increase because of the G.I. Bill (P.L. 78–348). Teaching larger classes coupled with having to engage in some scholarly activity resulted in faculty having less time for book selection activities except in those institutions where there was no pressure to engage in research. At this point, librarians stepped in to handle the selection process. The trend toward librarian selection got a significant boost not only from post–World War II demands on university faculty but also through several national cooperative acquisitions projects undertaken by ARL institutions and through which institutional selection responsibilities became national in scope and thus greatly increased.

As collections grew and an increasing emphasis was placed on evaluating existing collections, librarians began to note some of the drawbacks of faculty selection. Perhaps John Ryland (1982) put the case against faculty selection most concisely: "Faculty selection leads to major problems: the wrong books selected because of lack of time, unbalanced collections, and a tendency to overbuy in periodicals" (p. 14). Today, when a departmental faculty member is assigned to work with the librarian(s) selecting in a subject area, that person may often be an untenured faculty member. This extra time commitment can be challenging to individuals who will be under pressure to prove their worth as a teacher and researcher in order to gain tenure.

IMPACT OF WORLD WAR II AND ASSOCIATION OF RESEARCH LIBRARIES COOPERATIVE PROJECTS

Academic libraries in the early twentieth century had modest amounts of money for acquiring items for their collections. The stock market crash in 1929 and the ensuing Great Depression caused serious reductions in acquisitions funds. The result was a sharp decline in purchases of materials from other countries, which were generally modest in the best of times and rather minimal for non-Western European countries. When World War II military and government officials turned to research libraries for information about areas of actual and potential conflict, the results were disappointing. There was a recognition well before the United States entered the war that perhaps a reasonable goal for research libraries would be to have one copy of everything of research interest published anywhere in the world in at least one U.S. library. The expectation was that all such material would be cataloged within thirty days and reported to the National Union Catalog. That monumental goal was agreed to at a meeting held in Farmington, Connecticut, in late 1942 and became known as the Farmington Plan. Obviously not too much could be accomplished during the war; however, after the war, the plan served as a base for research library collection development. The plan broadened in collecting scope during the Korean War by adding the word *intelligence*—one copy of everything of research and intelligence interest.

A large percentage of today's research library collections is a direct result of the Farmington Plan, as are other post-World War II cooperative acquisitions programs. How did the Farmington Plan address the ambitious goal of having at least one copy of research or intelligence interest in a U.S. research library? The basic structure was developed using the model that the Library of Congress (LC) and research libraries created to distribute the books gathered in postwar Germany. If there was only one copy available, LC retained it; additional copies were allocated on the basis of having a widespread regional distribution and existing collection strengths. Essentially, long term, the plan distributed collection and subject responsibility among libraries based on their institutional research interests and collection strength. The plan operated until 1972, when it became too complex, costly, and operationally difficult for libraries to manage.

The demise of the Farmington Plan was a slow process. ARL collection development personnel had growing doubts about the quality and value of the material their overseas agents were shipping. Shifting institutional interests also played a role, and libraries dropped some of their subject responsibilities. An ongoing problem was the expectation for quick cataloging of the material. Not every library was able to find a qualified cataloger

---

||||| CHECK THIS OUT

Anyone interested in learning more about the role of academic libraries in World War II should read Luther H. Evans's "Research Libraries in the War Period, 1939–45" (*Library Quarterly* 17, no. 4 [1947]: 241–262).

> ||||| **CHECK THIS OUT**
>
> If you are interested in better understanding the true legacy of the Farmington Plan and later cooperative efforts, see Ralph Wagner's detailed monograph *A History of the Farmington Plan* (Lanham, MD: Scarecrow Press, 2002).

to process materials in all the languages in which it was collecting. It is also likely that new cooperative projects played a role in ending the plan.

One such cooperative program was the Latin American Cooperative Acquisitions Program (LACAP) that began in 1959. This project was somewhat unusual in that it was initially a combination of a few research libraries and a commercial vendor (Stechert-Hafner). The vendor agreed to send a representative to Latin American countries to gather items that would be covered by blanket orders from participating libraries. The notion was that someone well versed in the book trade would be able to make better judgments about what was appropriate for libraries than would local agents with only minimal understanding of the libraries' needs. In fact, the first representative was a librarian. Eventually the program grew from the original seven libraries to between thirty and forty during the 1970s.

Another program during the same time frame as the Farmington Plan was LC's PL-480 (Public Law 480) effort. This program started in 1960 with LC acquiring books and newspapers from Egypt, India, and Pakistan using "excess currencies." (Excess currencies arose from the sale of surplus agricultural products in countries in which payment was made in the local currency and could not be converted into U.S. dollars.) Unlike some of the other cooperative acquisitions projects, this one was not limited to research libraries; many academic libraries benefited from a growing inflow of English-language materials from overseas. The ARL libraries also received indigenous-language materials that were viewed as supplementing the Farmington Plan responsibilities. Needless to say, there were challenges in finding catalogers who could handle all the languages of materials that arrived as part of the project. Later the program expanded its coverage to include Israel (1965), Nepal (1966), Ceylon (1967), Yugoslavia (1968), and Poland (1972).

A variant program that continues today as the Center for Research Libraries (CRL, www.crl.edu) started out as the Midwest Inter-Library Corporation (MILC). MILC began in 1949 as a regional cooperative remote storage facility. (As we mentioned in chapter 8, research libraries have been remotely storing collections for many years and have discussed the concept for even longer.) From the outset, MILC-CRL acquired some low-use materials (e.g., college catalogs and state government publications) on behalf of its membership. Rather quickly, CRL became a national library asset that continues to acquire and lend a variety of low-use materials. It often picked up Farmington Plan subject responsibilities when a library wished to drop the subject. Today, membership is open to any library willing to pay the annual membership fee.

Our final example is the National Program for Acquisitions and Cataloging (NPAC). The project focused on the Library of Congress and was not really cooperative except that research libraries were encouraged to report their foreign acquisitions and note any items for which no cataloging was available in LC's depository card sets. From the outset of the Farmington Plan, a major stumbling block had been in knowing who actually had what. The various overseas acquisition programs led to a flood of materials in languages that were beyond the capability of the local cataloging staff to handle. One outcome was that more and more material was put into the processing backlog with very minimal local records. NPAC was designed to help address this shortcoming. Looking back, it seems clear that less thought was given to handling the material than to its acquisition.

As a result of these initiatives, what some in the field call "just in case" collecting—as opposed to "just in time"—became firmly embedded in research library collecting programs. Many of the collections in today's research libraries are a direct result of the Farmington Plan and other cooperative acquisitions programs and constitute a significant portion of today's legacy collections. Many of today's commentators about academic librarianship deride "just in case" collecting given the amount of information available electronically, the speed of on-demand acquisitions programs, and the swift delivery of interlibrary loan materials, though there is seldom consideration of why "just in case" collecting was initially undertaken.

In today's world, how would "just in time" function in a world conflict? As Luther Evans (1947) noted, "War investigation has demonstrated that while much in a library may belong in the 'little used' category, librarians as a group can ignore nothing which may conceivably be needed for present or future research" (p. 243). Certainly how research libraries might address such a concept in a digital environment is a different question, as is whether they should even be concerned. Ralph Wagner (2002) perhaps made the best case for recalling the reason behind the Farmington Plan and other large-scale cooperative efforts post–World War II on the part of research libraries:

> The Farmington Plan was conceived in the information crisis of World War II and extended outside the Western world in the information crisis of the Korean War. The question posed at the time of crisis remains: who will acquire the publications that are of little or no current research value, but may prove to be essential in the future. . . . Yet the Farmington Plan's failure was almost certainly dictated by the nature of its central concern. Marginal library materials are and will remain politically marginal. They are the concern of scholars working in obscure fields, who are unlikely to unite in support of the concept of collecting the marginal. They are also today's legacy to tomorrow's scholars . . . but who have no voice in today's decisions. (pp. 402–403)

DEVELOPING ACADEMIC LIBRARY COLLECTIONS

For many new academic librarians, one daunting early task is gaining an understanding of how collection development actually works in a particular library. Although some new academic librarians may have taken a course in collection development or management during their professional degree program, such courses usually cover all types of libraries as well as the basics; thus, there is no significant emphasis on the academic library environment. New academic librarians also often find in their first professional position that collection development is only one of numerous job responsibilities assigned to them. Thinking broadly, academic library collection development consists of learning and working on the following areas:

- Differentiation of the responsibilities of librarians and faculty in the collection development process
- Assessment of campus users' needs
- Collection development fiscal issues

- The local collection development policy
- Selection sources (reviews, publishers, and any consortial arrangements)
- How the library balances collections among formats
- Local acquisitions systems, approval plans, and standing or blanket order plans
- Local standards for assessing collections
- Issues of storage and deselection
- Preservation issues

Gaining an understanding of all these areas while trying to master all the aspects of a new position is a challenge for anyone, not just the recent graduate. Thus, it is no wonder that collection development is often viewed by new academic librarians with a certain amount of apprehension.

Learning the nature of collection development duties is often an early task for the new academic librarian. For a liaison librarian, it is likely that collection development was mentioned in the position advertisement and during the job interview. However, unless the position is solely devoted to collection development, it is unlikely that the responsibilities and local collection development practices were given more time and attention in the interview than were the other duties of the position.

Assessing Needs

Part of the challenge for those involved in collection development and management lies in understanding the needs of users as well as in learning what already exists within the collection. Understanding campus users' needs is a never-ending learning process for effective librarian selectors. They are always on the alert for news of changes in the subject areas for which they are responsible. Each year they may look for changes in course descriptions, degree requirements, and any departmental faculty in their areas. They may serve on campus curriculum committees and make it a practice to join any faculty from their area of responsibility at events such as new faculty orientations, departmental meetings, symposia, and the like. This is an excellent way to develop solid working relationships with the faculty as well as learn about any changes being discussed in the department. Certainly it is an opportunity to learn about faculty research interests. In addition, effective selectors make one-on-one appointments with interested faculty every year or two to discuss library resources and gain feedback. These activities were the antecedent to what is today's more complex liaison concept, which we will cover in chapter 12. If the librarian has only one or two subject areas to cover, finding time regularly to read one or two of the more general journals in those subjects provides potential conversation openers at social functions as well as early warning of potential shifts in research interests.

Collection Policy

One of the first collection development documents a new selector should spend time studying is the library's collection policy. The reality is that in most libraries, not just academic, such policies are not living documents in the sense that they are consulted and revised regularly. However, such policies will provide a broad overview of the relationship between collection development and the library mission as well as a general sense of the depth of collecting across disciplines. They generally spell out responsibilities—faculty and student roles in selection, who handles gifts and gift policies, how complaints are handled, and similar matters. The policy usually describes the fund allocation model the library uses. What the selector gains from spending a few hours perusing the policy is a sense of the library's approach to collection development. The remaining learning tasks are about how the collection development program actually operates. It is not unusual to find that there are some marked differences between the policy and practice.

Selection Resources

The new academic librarian will need to learn about selection resources for the assigned subject(s). If the position was vacant for some time (a likely situation—see chapter 14 for a discussion of search committees and the time it can take for a position to be filled), one or more other selectors probably filled in to some degree. These individuals will be able to provide valuable information about selection resources and perhaps some insights about the departments. Often such individuals are pleased to serve as mentors, at least for a while, and provide helpful information regarding the campus and the library.

For the new academic librarian, learning who are the reliable publishers and editors takes time, and making some errors along the way is to be expected. Keep in mind the old saying that "no library of a million volumes can be all bad." In today's environment of "just in time" collecting, many items will be judged a mistake if immediate use is the measure of good and bad. With time, the number of mistakes will drop, and some of the early mistakes will prove worthwhile after all. Although the goal should be to make as few poor selections as possible, all selectors do this from time to time.

Many large libraries have long-standing cooperative agreements whose antecedents somewhat reflect the ideas embedded in the Farmington Plan. Although existing plans may not be as extensive as the earlier ARL efforts, they are often designed to reduce duplication while expanding the total resources available to students and scholars. Many selectors, when their library is part of a consortium, may check to determine what library already holds the item before making the final purchase decision. It is not uncommon for nearby academic libraries to formally agree to share areas of collection building when they are part of a larger consortium.

Many ARL libraries have multiple branches across the campus. Learning who collects what in a multiple library environment takes time and effort. Few books today are truly single-topic works. When there is an economics library, a botany library, and an anthropology library on campus, which library should purchase a book about the economic impact of coffee growing by indigenous people? Even with a shared database, knowing which selector may be considering such a purchase may not forestall unintended duplications. It's important to discuss and develop some basic working principles regarding cross-disciplinary acquisitions, particularly given the cross-disciplinary nature of so much research today.

Collection Balance

The previous paragraph relates to another learning task—the overall balance that the library strives to achieve among formats as well as among subjects. Often this outcome is straightforward in terms of broad categories, but when it comes to what the balance should be within various subject areas, the task is more complex. Often there are differences of opinion among library personnel, between the library and the faculty, and even between faculty members in the same subject area. Sorting out these differences and reaching an acceptable compromise takes time and patience. It can be challenging for the new academic librarian just learning the organizational culture and power structure.

Many collection development units, especially in larger libraries, have generated a "conspectus" that lists by subject at least three aspects of the collection—existing collection strength, current collecting level, and desired level of collection strength. If nothing else, engaging in the creation of a conspectus helps selectors focus on long-term goals. It is easy to get caught up in the details of daily activities and forget long-term goals. Building a conspectus, when thoughtfully done, also encourages selectors to review current holdings.

Collection Funding

Learning how collection development funding is handled takes time, especially regarding how funds are allocated, because the process can vary from year to year. The broad issues are straightforward, but learning when and how funds may be transferred from one category to another is more involved. What was possible to do in one year may not be the case later as overall budget conditions change. In tight budget situations, senior library administrators may limit transfers and even freeze purchases altogether because of the possibility of having funds taken back by the institution. It's not uncommon for the academic library to have to return a percentage of its operating budget during a challenging fiscal year. Given that the vast majority of a library's operating budget consists of salary and collection development funds, it is not surprising that the funds needed to meet the recall amount usually come from the collection funds rather than any other category.

At some small institutions, faculty members may retain the sole responsibility for collection development. A small amount of funding may be set aside for library personnel selections, but remaining funds are allocated to teaching departments, a practice that can generate some heated interdepartmental debates. Even where librarians have full

👥 FROM THE AUTHORS

Evans faced a challenge regarding the appropriate materials to collect soon after becoming the director of a subject library at a large university. In the course of assessing library needs in one-on-one meetings with the entire departmental faculty, it became clear there was an almost universal desire for the library to build a video collection. The collection would be for class reserves to supplement in-class material as well as for student projects. Upon requesting funds for such purchases, Evans was informed that the library system did not collect nonprint materials. After several somewhat testy sessions with the campus-wide library collection development committee, his library was reluctantly given permission to add such material—if he could raise all the necessary funds for equipment, videos, and processing costs. A brief meeting with several key faculty members led to a donation of $100,000 to start building the video collection and covering the attendant costs.

responsibility for collection development, allocation arguments can arise. In general, scientists depend on journal titles (often costing tens of thousands of dollars per title annually) and use few books. On the other hand, humanists tend to be more dependent on books and less so on journals. Achieving some balance between costly scientific journal needs and less-expensive-per-title costs for the humanists' books can be a contentious process. Add in class sizes and numbers of majors and minors in a subject area and you have the ingredients for much debate over how to fairly allocate the funds.

If the debate involved only this perception of fairness, the allocation process would be complex; however, the argument does not end there. There are other funding needs to consider such as document delivery (per item charges, for example), replacement items, retrospective materials, and interdisciplinary materials in any format. It takes time to learn how the final allocation decisions are made and who makes them. As mentioned previously, perhaps the least pleasant collection development task is handling the all too common need to address budget shortfalls, unexpected funding recalls, and inadequate budget increases for collections. Questions such as the following are all too common: Do we make an across-the-board cut in all acquisitions funds? Do we cut the book budget in the hope that there will be enough left to cover our journal subscriptions?

Every answer will have some intended and unintended consequences. For example, the decision to maintain journals will not impact the science faculty but will have an impact on the humanists who are book dependent. An across-the-board cut may mean many subscriptions will need to lapse; how does one decide which titles to drop, and will all departments have to lose titles? Dropping one chemistry title will usually save a substantial amount but may have more serious consequences for the department than cutting ten titles that faculty in the English department consult. An interesting article addressing the issue of journal cancellation is Carey, Elfstrand, and Hijleh's (2005) "An Evidenced-Based Approach for Gaining Faculty Acceptance in a Serials Cancellation Project."

Acquisition Procedures

Local acquisition procedures are usually reasonably easy to grasp. One area that does take some experience to understand is how vendors are chosen. The larger the library, the greater the number of vendors the library is likely to use. No single vendor, regardless of what a sales representative may say, is able to supply all the items a library will acquire, subscribe to, or lease. Even modest-sized libraries use a number of vendors. The usual practice is for the acquisitions department to select the vendor of choice for an order; however, the person selecting the item should pass on any special information about a request, such as a rush order for a class reserve, for example. Such information may impact which vendor gets the order.

There are several categories of acquisitions that new selectors must master. Learning what standing orders and blanket orders, if any, are in place for the selector's subject areas will save time and trouble. The two orders are similar in character. The term *standing order* usually applies to serial titles such as transactions, conference proceedings, and other series that appear irregularly and often in very small press runs. Having a standing order with the publisher to automatically ship a copy upon publication saves library staff time and ensures that the library secures a copy. A *blanket order* usually applies to books and again calls for the automatic shipment of a class of publication as items appear. Both systems also ensure payment to the publisher without having to process individual orders. Essentially each process saves the library and the vendor time and effort.

Approval plans are a variation of these approaches and are widely employed in many academic libraries. As with the blanket order, approved books (or electronic approval shelves) arrive automatically and regularly. Unlike the other automatic plans, the library is generally not committed to purchasing the items in the shipment (or electronic delivery). Selectors can examine the items and decide whether they should be acquired. Selectors have a limited amount of time in which to review each shipment (or electronic delivery); generally unwanted items must be returned within a certain time frame, and all non-returned items will be billed to the library. The decision to keep or not must be made in a timely manner because none of the approval materials have any ownership indication on them (they could not be returned if they did) and, thus, what retail outlets refer to as "shrinkage" (items missing for no known reason) can occur. The risk of loss increases the longer the items remain on the approval shelves. Approval plans may be negotiated with the vendor so that items come precataloged for the collection. In such cases, returns are typically not permitted. First and foremost with any approval plan is to maintain a detailed profile for the vendor to use, and such profiles must be reviewed regularly.

Assessment

Assessment of collections is a part of the library's ongoing obligation to demonstrate accountability and efforts to improve its operational activities and services. Libraries often engage in major collection assessment projects; however, good selectors engage in ongoing assessments of their areas of responsibility on their own. Major assessment projects are frequently the result of the need to send items to a storage facility or as a preliminary step for a cooperative project.

As mentioned previously, good collection development personnel usually engage in ongoing small-scale assessment projects. For example, a selector might every year or two compare the reviews found in a publication such as *Choice: Current Reviews for Academic Libraries* for her subject area(s) responsibilities. *Choice* also publishes an annual list of the "best of the best." Checking the major journals in the subject responsibility areas may also identify similar lists of core titles. Meetings with faculty can provide excellent opportunities to learn about their individual views regarding collection quality and needs.

When it comes to assessing the collection for storage or withdrawal purposes, integrated library system (ILS) reports are major time savers. Probably the best predictor of future use is past use, and the goal of most remote storage or withdrawal and weeding efforts is to pull items from the shelves that will have the lowest possible use. Clearly use

---

▌▌▌▌ CHECK THIS OUT

We mentioned ARL SPEC Kits initially in chapter 8, describing how they can be a valuable snapshot of current research, practices, and policies in a variety of areas. We recommend this one considering various methods and measures of collection assessment:

Harker, Karen R., and Janette Klein. 2015. *SPEC Kit 352: Collection assessment.* Washington, DC: Association of Research Libraries. http://publications.arl.org/Collection-Assessment-SPEC-Kit-352/.

will be a factor in deciding what to withdraw or weed from the collection. ILS systems can produce circulation use data for items in the collection. At one time, selecting items for storage meant spending hours and hours in the stacks looking at the date due slip in each book and pulling those that met the storage parameters. The items still must be pulled from the shelves, but today the judgment calls are made from reports. Many systems have the capability of including data about in-house use as well, if the library has elected to commit staff to inputting data. One common faculty complaint about storage efforts is that faculty members use items at the library, and, thus, circulated use data fail to reflect the actual use of "important" titles. Some faculty members even suggest that they not only use items at the library but also return them to the shelf, so their use is not reflected in any database.

Other criteria for selecting items for storage are age and availability online. Age can be a useful criterion in the hard sciences in which new information often supersedes older data—for example, a book on cancer treatments published in the 1980s is a good candidate for remote storage or perhaps even withdrawal. Paper-based journals occupy a very large amount of shelf space in most academic libraries. With so many journal titles available online, remote storage of such titles is a good option. Furthermore, today's users tend to want only online access. However, there are some reasons to store the paper issues that are in the collection. One reason is that in the early days of full-text online, there was no color, and often complex charts that originally appeared in color were lost as they appeared only in black, white, and shades of gray. Another reason is that many journals and magazines carry (or once carried) advertisements that were and in some cases still are not part of the e-databases. For marketing courses as well as graphic design courses, such material is important.

When it comes to cooperative resource-sharing efforts, the likely assessment process will be based on a random sample of the collection areas under consideration for sharing as well as on looking at general use of the items in the sample. Even in statewide efforts, such as OhioLINK, individual libraries can decide to have some classes of material (e.g., audiovisual materials, special collection items, or a classification number) not represented in the sharing aspect.

Remote Storage

Academic libraries have faced collection storage challenges for more than one hundred years. As we noted in chapter 2, Harvard president Charles Eliot suggested in 1901 that rather than build additional library space on campus, the university should store "dead books" away from campus (Carpenter, 1986, p. 122). Scott Seaman (2005) opened his essay on remote storage with the following: "The Association of Research Libraries (ARL) estimates that member libraries added 9,480,045 volumes to their collections in 2001–2002. Given a conservative estimate, one would expect such magnitude of materials to occupy 1,185,000 linear feet of shelving space or 225 miles of shelves annually" (p. 20). We may be in the digital age, but most academic libraries are still (2017) acquiring volumes that require storage space.

Planners of new academic library facilities may occasionally include space collection growth and remain within budget. Such a feat is rare today because the issue goes beyond dollars needed. Senior campus administrators may likely be concerned about additional space for physical collections, particularly empty shelves.

👥 FROM THE AUTHORS

A mention of the library's compact shelving system remains a part of the official campus tour where Greenwell works. Although compact shelving is not a new concept, and at that library the shelving system has been in place for twenty years, potential students have likely never seen such a system in their high school or local public libraries. Greenwell finds it amusing that compact shelving remains somewhat of a novelty with potential students. Library users still ask questions about the safety features of compact shelving systems, and some may be initially reluctant to go into a compact shelving aisle.

Even in the best of times there is likely to be a substantial lapse in time between when the library staff raises the issue of needing growth space and when such space becomes available. Some years ago, Evans was involved in a nationwide study of academic library building projects. The study team found that on average the time between a library first making the case for additional space and the space becoming available was 8.9 years.

Librarians have had to be creative in order to manage collection growth and not negatively impact service too much. Even when staff are aware that it will take time to get space and begin to raise the issue early on, users will begin to notice changes. Easy steps, such as withdrawing superseded items or low-use duplicate copies, only buy a small amount of growth space. At times the library may be able to reduce stack aisle width to the minimum allowed and gain some space. Another possibility is to reduce user space in order to add stacks, which is not a popular option for anyone.

In some cases, where the floor loading will allow it, a library can install compact shelving units. Compact shelving units are mounted on rails so a person can open an aisle where needed. In an area where the library may have had ten open access aisles, compact shelving would reduce that to one aisle and add one or two extra stack ranges. Such shelving is not cheap, but it is less costly than acquiring additional square footage and increases stack capacity by between 25 and 30 percent. One advantage of such shelving is that it can be redeployed in a new facility, thus adding collection storage space without adding to the square footage. A number of libraries have successfully employed compact shelving, with several safety features added, and have maintained the open stack concept.

For many libraries, a remote storage facility for low-use items some distance from the campus has become a norm. Such facilities are usually located in areas where the cost of land is low—normally any vacant land existing on campus is far too valuable to use for a storage unit. There are several models for such units, such as an institutionally owned and operated system and several variations of joint use or shared facilities. Earlier in the chapter we mentioned the Center for Research Libraries, which began as a shared storage facility and now has a storage operation and, more important, an organization that acquires a variety of low-use materials that might otherwise occupy valuable shelf space in a number of academic libraries around the country. Another example of cooperative storage is from the University of California system, which built two "regional storage" units, one in northern and the other in southern California. These units accept items from public and private academic libraries and employ high-density storage techniques, such as compact shelving, shelving by size, and double or triple shelving of items.

Some libraries have engaged third-party vendors for low-use storage. There are commercial firms that specialize in storing records for companies and allow the organization to add as well as retrieve material. Some of these facilities have better temperature and humidity control than the library. Needless to say, these facilities charge more for their services. They may store standard 1.2-cubic-foot records boxes for a monthly fee, and there are charges per box for intake and retrieval. Although rather expensive, this approach does work for relatively short-term storage.

Some institutions have included high-density storage capability in a new building plan (University of Nevada, Las Vegas, and Santa Clara University, for example). The systems arc a modified version of automated warehousing retrieval systems. They are costly, but they maximize the storage capacity of the building's footprint. J. P. McCarty (2005) raised a significant question about the storage of low-use materials: "Why invest in housing and servicing an activity which information systems will probably make either totally or partially redundant in the not too distant future?" (p. 90). Many outside academic librarianship may indeed wonder what the answer ought to be. One response might well draw on the issues raised earlier in this chapter regarding "just in case" collecting. The following section on preservation also holds part of a meaningful response.

Preservation Issues

Even in large research libraries with a conservation or preservation department, everyone on the library staff should take an interest in protecting the well-being of collections, especially staff with responsibility for purchasing items for the collection in the first place. Academic libraries have spent billions of dollars on the selection, acquisition, processing, and storage of their collections over the years. Allowing such investments to deteriorate because of neglect, poor housekeeping, and various other hazards is unacceptable.

At its most basic level, preservation begins with everyone on the staff knowing accepted housekeeping procedures, such as how to remove and reshelve materials. What may at first appear to be stereotypical picky library practices can over the years save a library much-needed funds by reducing the number of items that require some type of preservation treatment, such as rebinding or special boxing, for example.

Some housekeeping issues that relate to both preservation and health are insects and mold. Knowing what to look for when working in the stacks can keep down insect problems such as book lice, silverfish, and cockroaches. If such insects are actually seen, there is probably a serious infestation occurring because they tend to be active in the dark. The notion of the musty-smelling bookshop or library being a sign of scholarship is really a sign of possible mold problems. Mold has on occasion become so widespread and significant that libraries have had to close while the mold is cleaned up at significant expense. With both issues, the more quickly the library addresses the problem, the less costly it will be for people, the collection, and the library.

IIIIII **CHECK THIS OUT**

This is a good guide to learning about the basic principles and standards for preservation of many different formats:

Harvey, D. R., and Martha R. Mahard. 2014. *The preservation management handbook: A 21st-century guide for libraries, archives, and museums.* Lanham, MD: Rowman and Littlefield.

When working in the stacks, collection development personnel should be looking also for items in need of attention. One major problem is acidic or brittle paper that, over time, can turn a book into "cornflakes" when handled. Preserving such material is a challenge. If the title is of less interest to the library and if a copy can be identified in a de-acidified collection, perhaps withdrawing the local copy is the best option. Other options are to encase the item in a protective container (also called a phase box) or send it to a storage facility, which reduces the handling risks, or to do both. Another possibility is to purchase a replacement copy; however, the replacement is not likely to be in much better condition because the cause of the brittleness started at the time the paper was manufactured. The most costly option is to have the item de-acidified (this treatment only stops the chemical process causing the brittleness) and perhaps have the pages strengthened. This option is undertaken only for very important items.

Many academic libraries house a special collections department and perhaps the institutional archives. Special collections tend to include rare books and perhaps institutional documents, depending on how the university is organized. For public institutions, there are often guidelines relating to how long the institution must keep important documentation. In addition to these materials, special collections and archives units typically contain unique materials, which include myriad items from letters and journals to photographs and films to ephemera such as a subject's personal mementos or even a lock of hair. These items can be treasures for researchers; in fact, some have said that research libraries today are largely defined by their unique materials. Along with preserving these materials, making those unique collections more accessible through providing better finding aids and digitizing material where permissible has become an essential part of today's special collections and archives. In addition to making more of these unique materials available online, an increasing number of institutions are encouraging more classes to visit and work directly with these primary source materials. Although security and preservation issues must be considered, providing students the opportunity to work closely with these historic items can be a memorable and valuable learning experience.

Although acid-free paper can last for hundreds of years, even a thousand years, we have little solid information about the life span of digital formats. We do know that, at present,

---

║║║ CHECK THIS OUT

For a detailed look at making special collections and archival materials more available as well as using them in a composition classroom setting, check out two articles in this Research Libraries Issues (RLI) Report 283:

Carter, Lisa R. 2013. *Special at the core: Aligning, integrating, and mainstreaming special collections in the research library.* http://publications.arl.org/rli283/1.
Vetter, Matthew, and Sara Harrington. 2013. *Integrating special collections into the composition classroom: A case study of collaborative digital curriculum.* http://publications.arl.org/rli283/16.

We recommend reviewing other RLI reports. Published cooperatively through the Association of Research Libraries (ARL), the Coalition for Networked Information (CNI), and the Scholarly Publishing and Academic Resources Coalition (SPARC), these freely available reports cover topics such as library impact on undergraduate student learning, data visualization in research libraries, the transformation of scholarly communications, diversity, copyright, and much more.

the digital records are not stable over time. Kevin Bradley (2007) made the point regarding the need to preserve all cultural heritage items and how the field has addressed that need:

> Digital preservation has, at the least, a lexical link to preservation, and, at best, a philosophical and conceptual base embedded in the aspirations of traditional conservators. The profession of preservation and conservation matured both technically and philosophically in response to the 1966 disaster that saw the River Arno in Florence break its banks and wreak disaster upon a store of priceless cultural heritage objects. Practitioners and thinkers in the conservation field rallied in the salvage effort, and, in the aftermath of the flood, participated in a long reevaluation of traditional practices. (p. 151)

Bradley's article went on to explore the complex issues related to digital preservation.

Scholars today can read the Dead Sea Scrolls written thousands of years ago as well as provide interpretations of their meaning. On the other hand, it may be difficult—perhaps impossible—to read digital data we stored only a decade ago. Regarding long-term access, libraries and society face two broad challenges when it comes to the data people create and store digitally. First is the issue of how that information and data are stored and just how long those particular media will last and remain error-free. Second are the issues related to hardware, operating systems, and software capable of retrieving the information or data.

In addition to these concerns, libraries have to wonder about the long-term commitment of commercial vendors of databases after the older materials cease to provide an adequate income stream. Who will indefinitely archive such material and at what cost? As more academic libraries create institutional repositories, thoughtful consideration needs to be given to long-term preservation and how to maintain document integrity. Yaniv Levi (2008) stated,

> While many libraries and information centers have digital asset management systems or digital repositories for managing and storing digital objects, these systems are not designed with the preservation of the digital knowledge in mind. Rather they focus on access management, or facilitating the day-to-day use of digital content by users. On the other hand, digital preservation is about guaranteeing the future usability of accessibility to digital content. (p. 22)

The following are a few examples of the types of problems libraries and others face in terms of digital longevity. Daniel Cohen (2005) noted that "the Library of Congress, which holds roughly 150,000 audio CDs in conditions almost certainly far better than those of personal collections, estimates that between 1 and 10 percent of the discs in their collection already contain serious data errors" (p. 14). Another example of lost data was reported in an article (Tangley, 1998) that described NASA's frustration when, in 1996, scientists tried to read magnetic tape data from the 1976 Viking Mars mission. They found that 10 to 20 percent of the data were missing—this despite the fact that the laboratory had tried to maintain the tapes according to "standard guidelines." Danny Bradbury (2007) related the story of how the BBC in the early 2000s decided to reissue a 1950s television series for which the company had discarded the original tapes. The BBC eventually recovered all the episodes primarily from private individuals who had taped the show off the air. A major challenge was that most of the tapes came from the United States, which employs a different television standard than the United Kingdom. As Bradbury noted, "the BBC did a lot of work building hardware that would intelligently convert NTSC [National Television Standards

Committee, the U.S. broadcast system] recording back into PAL [Phase Alternating Line system, used in Europe]" (p. 42).

LICENSING CONSIDERATIONS

Electronic resources, which include databases, journals, e-books, data sets, images, videos, and more, have become a large part of an academic library's collections. Selection of these resources builds on the criteria that have been used when selecting paper-based titles. One difference is that there are both technical and content issues to think about as well as the fact that often the product under consideration contains multiple titles that frequently cut across disciplines. Brian Quinn (2008) made this point:

> Decisions regarding titles that represent a substantial investment, such as databases, or that involve an ongoing investment, such as subscriptions to journals, are commonly made in a group context. Important collection development decisions are made by groups whose members often consist of various stakeholders . . . all of whom are involved in developing the collection. (p. 10)

Having an understanding of the library and campus cultures is important for a new academic librarian who is considering whether to advocate for a particular product or title.

What are some of the most significant differences between electronic and paper-based selection decisions? Unlike paper-based acquisitions, most electronic products are available only through a license. The standard license for a product often contains some limitations regarding access to and use of the material that may be problematic for the library. Some of the issues that may arise in the license are restrictions that may limit or forbid the use of the content for interlibrary lending; caps on the number of individuals who may access the material at the same time (simultaneous users); limits on use of the material by nonstudents, faculty, and staff (outside users); conditions relating to remote access (proxy server issues as well as in-library use); and holding the library liable for how an individual makes use of the information gathered.

Depending on the content of the license, the library may wish to negotiate with the vendor regarding limitations. The license is a legal document, and institutional attorneys may likely become involved in the negotiations. Mark Watson (2008) explored the question of whether a library needs a legal consultant to address licensing issues:

> It is simply a fact of licensing life that where librarians care about the content, interface, or ability to perform interlibrary loan, the lawyers are looking for assurance that the university will not be subject to unlimited indemnification provisions, or that obligations for attorney fees will be subject to the limitations and conditions of the state constitution. . . . To sum up, I think the forces shaping our libraries today make employing a library lawyer a good, forward thinking idea. (p. 13)

Another factor to consider is that, when a library cancels a paper-based subscription, it still has the paper copies it paid for and may retain those items indefinitely. When a library cancels a subscription to an electronic resource, however, there is a question regarding what, if any, rights the library has to long-term access to the content published during the time it paid for access. Ease of use is another consideration regarding electronic resources. Will the new product or service require staff training? How easy will it be for the users to navigate? Is the item accessible for users with visual and other disabilities? In terms of websites, there is also an issue of selecting and maintaining links and how to handle that ongoing task.

When it comes to large database products, often they are available through one or more consortia to which the library belongs. Generally, a library will have a free trial period during which to assess the product or service and then decide whether to acquire the package. The question then becomes what will the package cost? It is not uncommon for the cost of the product or service to vary among consortia because the consortium's price is often based on how many of its members take part in the deal. Many vendors base their academic pricing on the institutional student full-time equivalent (FTE). The rate is x cents per student FTE, and as the total number of FTEs at institutions in the consortium increases, the rate drops. Thus, determining the final cost for each library can take some time.

Considering all the factors we have described in this chapter, academic library collection management may be a challenge for the new academic librarian. However, it can be one of the most satisfying and rewarding work activities. The keys to successfully mastering collection development duties are to learn as much as possible about existing policies as well as institutional knowledge and to focus on the changing needs of library users.

🔒 KEY POINTS TO REMEMBER

- Collection development decisions should focus primarily on the content rather than the medium.
- A large proportion of today's legacy collections arose from a national security need and not some misguided desire to build the biggest academic library.
- Effective academic library collection development is a shared effort between library staff, faculty, students, and other academic libraries.
- Collection development duties, though challenging, can also be enjoyable, satisfying, and rewarding.
- New academic librarians with collection development responsibilities should focus on learning the following:

  - Responsibilities of librarians and faculty in the collection development process
  - Methods for assessing campus users' needs
  - Local collection development policy
  - Selection sources employed by the library
  - Manner in which the library handles collection development fiscal issues and allocations
  - Local acquisitions system(s) and existing approval plans, standing order plans, and blanket order plans
  - Local standards for assessing the collections
  - Manner in which the library handles issues of storage and deselection
  - Local issues related to preservation and access

REFERENCES

Atkinson, Ross. 2006. Six key challenges for the future of collection development. *Library Resources and Technical Services* 50, no. 4: 244–251.

Bradbury, Danny. 2007. See you in 2050. *Engineering and Technology* 2, no. 11: 42–44.

Bradley, Kevin. 2007. Defining digital sustainability. *Library Trends* 56, no. 1: 148–163.

Butler, Pierce. 1945. *Books and libraries in wartime.* Chicago: University of Chicago Press.

Carey, Ronadin, Stephen Elfstrand, and Renee Hijleh. 2005. An evidenced-based approach for gaining faculty acceptance in a serials cancellation project. *Collection Management* 30, no. 2: 59–72.

Carpenter, Kenneth E. 1986. *The first 350 years of the Harvard University Library.* Cambridge, MA: Harvard University Library.

Carter, Lisa R. 2013. *Special at the core: Aligning, integrating, and mainstreaming special collections in the research library.* http://publications.arl.org/rli283/1.

Cohen, Daniel J. 2005. The future of preserving the past. *CRM Journal* 2, no. 2: 6–19.

Davis-Kahl, Stephanie, and Merinda Kaye Hensley, eds. 2013. *Common ground at the nexus of information literacy and scholarly communication.* Chicago: Association of College and Research Libraries.

Dempsey, Lorcan, Constance Malpas, and Brian Lavoie. 2014. Collection directions: The evolution of library collections and collecting. *portal: Libraries and the Academy* 14, no. 3: 393–423.

Evans, Luther H. 1947. Research libraries in the war period, 1939–45. *Library Quarterly* 17, no. 4: 241–262.

Finnie, Ellen. 2016. Being earnest with collections—voting with our dollars: Making a new home for the collections budget in the MIT Libraries. *Against the Grain* 28, no. 4: 90–92.

Harker, Karen R., and Janette Klein. 2015. *SPEC Kit 352: Collection assessment.* Washington, DC: Association of Research Libraries. http://publications.arl.org/Collection-Assessment-SPEC-Kit-352/.

Harvey, D. R., and Martha R. Mahard. 2014. *The preservation management handbook: A 21st-century guide for libraries, archives, and museums.* Lanham, MD: Rowman and Littlefield.

Levi, Yaniv. 2008. Digital preservation: An ever-growing challenge. *Information Today* 25, no. 8: 22.

Levine-Clark, Michael. 2014. Access to everything: Building the future academic library collection. *portal: Libraries and the Academy* 14, no. 3: 425–437.

McCarty, J. P. 2005. The print block and the digital cylinder. *Library Management* 26, nos. 1/2: 89–96.

Quinn, Brian. 2008. The psychology of group decision making in collection development. *Library Collections, Acquisitions, and Technical Services* 32, no. 1: 10–18.

Ryland, John. 1982. Collection development and selection: Who should do it? *Library Acquisitions: Practice and Theory* 6, no. 1: 13–17.

Schmidt, Karen. 2004. Past perfect, future tense: A survey of issues in collection development. *Library Collections, Acquisitions, and Technical Services* 28, no. 4: 360–372.

Seaman, Scott. 2005. Collaborative collection management in a high-density storage facility. *College and Research Libraries* 66, no. 1: 20–27.

Tangley, Laura. 1998. "Whoops, there goes another CD-ROM." *U.S. News and World Report,* February 16, 67–68.

Vetter, Matthew, and Sara Harrington. 2013. Integrating special collections into the composition classroom: A case study of collaborative digital curriculum. http://publications.arl.org/rli283/16.

Wagner, Ralph. 2002. *A history of the Farmington Plan.* Lanham, MD: Scarecrow Press.

Watson, Mark. 2008. Licensing electronic resources: Is a lawyer in your future? *Technicalities* 28, no. 4: 1, 11–13.

Williams, Gordon. 1964. The librarian's role in the development of library book collections. *Library Quarterly* 34, no. 4: 374–386.

CHAPTER 12

Services

Services and collections are the cornerstones of academic library operations. Although some library services are similar in any type of library (basic circulation services, for example), others, such as liaison activities, are unique to academic libraries. We'll discuss those services in this chapter. Library school will help prepare you for working in library services, but those services will continue to evolve. As with collection management, there is much to learn on the job, and continuing education will remain important throughout your career.

Students, faculty, and staff have a variety of choices in where to go to secure information for coursework, research, and other needs. Thus, the library needs to generate a loyal user base, one that is satisfied with service and collection quality. If services and collections do not measure up to expectations or keep pace with changing user needs, repeat use cannot be ensured (Hernon, Nitecki, and Altman, 1999). Without those repeat users, it's hard to build a loyal user base that will advocate for the library's budgetary, personnel, and space needs.

The issue of attracting and keeping campus users was central to a 2001 article with the words "Deserted Library" in the title (Carlson, 2001). The article generated debate within and outside the profession about the need for academic libraries. The debate even led a few senior campus administrators to consider canceling library building projects.

The notion of a deserted library had not yet fully dissipated by 2010. Charles Martell (2008) wrote about the decline in circulation and reference transactions using data from Association of Research Libraries (ARL) statistical reports from 1995 to 2006. Martell concluded his article by stating,

> In mystery stories and political thrillers the advice is often "follow the money." In the library setting one might do better to "follow the user." Clearly today's users have substituted virtual use for in-person use. While they may be absent, they are not inactive. Networked electronic resources via library portals and the Internet have provided users with benefits that go far beyond anything available when physical use was the only alternative. (p. 406)

Rachel Applegate (2008) looked at reference transactions, employing a broader data set than just ARL reports. She found that from 2002 to 2004 there were differences in transactions based on the Carnegie Classification (see chapter 1 for a review of the Carnegie classes). Although ARL institutions showed a decline in reference transactions, master's institutions showed an increase. Applegate concluded her article with the following:

> A fruitful approach to understanding the future of reference in academic libraries can include the following: studying a wider range of in-library and out-of-library informa-

tion-seeking activities; broadening and deepening—and in some cases abandoning—the definition of "transaction"; and incorporating a sensitivity to the differing missions, cultures, and activities of the variety of academic institutions for which the American system of higher education is justifiably famous. (p. 187)

Perhaps the librarian's view of declining transaction numbers is still somewhat tied to the profession's long-standing method of collecting input data as measures of worth. As we discussed in chapter 10, we need to rethink that approach and develop other measures of worth. New or renovated library facilities can actually increase gate counts substantially, and various service transactions have an impact well beyond their former levels (Demas, 2005; Dotson and Garris, 2008; Freeman, 2005; Gayton, 2008; Shill and Tonner, 2004). Although many have bemoaned decreasing library visits, the gate count for a typical week in U.S. academic libraries in fall 2012 actually increased by over two million compared to fall 2008 (Phan, et al., 2009; Phan, Hardesty, and Hug, 2014). Even Carlson (2013), when revisiting the idea of the "deserted library," pointed out that much of his writing is done in a college library. He described "deserted libraries" as "outdated, unimaginative, and sterile places," and the libraries that remain valuable are "ones that found ways to appeal to people's sensibilities and needs."

👥 FROM THE AUTHORS

A debate about Carlson's (2001) article took place in mid-2002 at the institution where Evans was the associate academic vice president for learning resources. The library and the university had been working on plans for a new library for over ten years. There had even been a design with working drawings, a request for construction bids issued, and a groundbreaking ceremony in 1998. Unfortunately the major donor encountered serious financial problems, and the project was put on hold. Throughout that process, the vice president for business and finance fought the concept of a new library. His position was that everything a student needed was available online; thus, there was no need for a new facility.

The vice president for business and finance distributed copies of Carlson's article to all senior campus administrators along with a memo stating that this material "proved" his case that the university did not need to invest in a new library. Although it took the better part of a year to counteract the effort, the support of students, faculty, alumni, and several of the vice presidents put the planning process back on track. In 2009, a new library was opened at the university. The success is attributable to great service by the library staff, some careful marketing, and strong advocacy by library staff and their supporters.

CUSTOMER SERVICE

Besides the overall service ethic of academic libraries, economics is a motivator for improving customer service. Some librarians prefer the term *patron* or *user* (which we use frequently in this book), but for this discussion, we will refer to the process as *customer service.* Academic funding authorities are facing tighter financial situations, and evidence of good customer service helps libraries argue more effectively for support when funding is prioritized. As Debbie Schachter (2006) noted, "Excellence in customer service leads to greater use of library services, better coordination with other departments, and a greater chance of ensuring the security of library funding" (pp. 8-9). Another driving force, also influenced by economics, is the increased pressure for accountability on the part of funding authorities. Libraries may address accountability by documenting outcomes of service programs—pointing out how they contribute to the mission of their parent institutions—and by showing evidence of good customer service based on users' level of satisfaction.

Wehmeyer, Auchter, and Hirshon (1996) distilled from library literature the following items of consensus about customer service plans that are still relevant:

> *Frontline staff are vital to the plan's success.* Public service personnel generally are the only library staff users will encounter. Thus, their attitudes and actions during their interactions with users become a key, if not *the* key, factor in public perceptions regarding the library and its services.
> *Service is a product.* Service quality is a significant element in the library's value-added process in relationship with competitor information services.
> *Understand your customer.* Assessing users' information wants and needs is essential to developing excellent service programs.
> *There is no quick fix.* Quality service requires ongoing review and adjustments as users' interests are constantly changing. (p. 174)

It is possible to view customer service interactions as either transaction-based or relationship-based. Transaction-based service occurs at the point of need, such as when a student checks out a book. This is the type of service on which most organizations, including libraries, have typically focused in the past. However, the realization that building loyalty is the best way to retain customers has caused many organizations to focus on relationship-based service. This focus is most clearly reflected in the relationship that public services staff develop with their users. Academic librarians often develop collegial relationships with faculty and are able to offer specialized assistance with their research and teaching, as we'll discuss later in this chapter in the section on liaison services. Offering personalized library services can make those services more useful and attractive to users, enhancing their perception of the value of library services.

The idea that libraries have a business function is anathema to some library personnel as well as to some users. It implies a paradigm shift. Businesses exist for the bottom line, to make a profit, and libraries, at least in the past, were not in the income-generating business. There are increasing pressures on libraries to recover some of the costs of their services, and some libraries may even have target income levels for the fiscal year. People who dislike the notion of "libraries in business" believe that libraries provide intellectual value to their users. This intellectual value, they argue, is a public good that enriches their communities beyond dollars and cents. Equating (or reducing) libraries to the level of a capitalist enterprise transforms libraries from cultural icons to something like transitory storefronts. However, it is also true that libraries are under enormous pressure today to demonstrate evidence of accountability. As Weingand (1997) stated,

> Librarians who flinch at the word *customer* are operating out of an outmoded paradigm. This older paradigm portrays the library as a "public good," with as high a ranking on

the "goodness" scale as the national flag, parenthood, and apple pie. As a public good, the library "should" receive public support. However, today's library is in increasingly tight competition for declining resources, and unless it adopts and masters the language and techniques of its competitors, it faces a future of declining support and significance. (p. 3)

Whether or not you agree with Weingand's perspective, there is an ever-growing challenge from competitors such as Google and Amazon. Borrowing and adapting the principles of customer satisfaction from the corporate world can be a pragmatic way to improve library services and better serve our customers. It is also a way to demonstrate the value of the library to its organization and community.

The remainder of this chapter covers the basic public services one encounters in most academic libraries: reference and instruction, circulation, interlibrary loan and document delivery, and reserve services. We'll conclude with a discussion about the role of the library liaison.

REFERENCE SERVICES

Reference service in academic libraries is a relatively recent activity, as you may recall from chapter 2. Today reference is no longer entirely the face-to-face activity it once was because there are now a variety of options for online services as well as more options for 24/7 service. Most colleges and universities have sizable distance education programs and student populations who depend on the library's online services. Online services are increasingly popular, and a challenge for the reference desk staffer is to juggle in-person requests and requests that come in by phone, e-mail, chat, and text message. In most libraries, the users who are physically present have first priority, though online users need to be acknowledged and advised of the time frame when assistance can be offered. This recognition will be particularly important as the number of online requests for help increases.

It is true that reference transactions on average are declining, and it's likely that trend will continue. Users can often satisfy their basic information needs through their own online searches. For higher-level research requests, users tend to make consultation appointments or attend a class with a librarian rather than visit a physical desk. Partly as a result of this decline, combined service points are becoming more popular. Instead of separate reference and circulation desks (and perhaps even technology, tutoring, and other support), those services combine to work from one central service desk. On the positive side, the combined desk generally minimizes user confusion about how to find help. The personnel present at the desk, however, must be trained in handling a variety of service needs and have a thorough understanding of how to address referrals. Leuzinger (2013) described the experience at the University of North Texas of merging six service desks into one and, after receiving formal feedback from staff, concluded,

> We have experienced a boost in staff morale, camaraderie, and trust . . . because staff have a greater understanding and appreciation for the skills their co-workers bring to the table. . . . We are now providing a better service for our patrons overall, given their verbal feedback at our service desk as well as through anonymous surveys. Our patrons are appreciative of and responsive to our new service model and our single service point desk. (p. 533)

Combining service desks also has financial implications because it can save in staffing costs.

Another financial consideration is whether to staff the reference desk with librarians. At one time, at most institutions, the reference desk was staffed solely by librarians. Some libraries have adopted a model of triage service with librarians being on call but not on the front line. Others train staff or graduate assistants to handle reference requests. Practices vary among institutions. In a national survey regarding reference services (Coleman, Mallon and Lo, 2016), 41.2 percent of the 606 respondents reported a decrease over the past two years in the number of hours employees with an MLS provided reference services at in-person service points. Dennis B. Miles (2013) in a study of 119 libraries at master's granting institutions found that 77 percent of respondents used a reference librarian at the desk at least some of the time.

When librarians staff the desk, they can provide high-level service and can observe patterns in student and faculty needs. However, given the number of "real" reference inquiries at the desk, it's not very cost-effective to staff the desk with librarians. Susan Ryan (2008) concluded her article on reference staffing cost-effectiveness with this statement: "The following findings should lead library administrators to reconsider staffing a traditional reference desk with librarians" (p. 398). Her findings were that only 11 percent of the reference transactions in her study fell into the "research" category, 89 percent of the questions could be addressed by "trained students and staff members," and 59 percent of the interactions were handled using the librarian's knowledge of the building. Her article was reviewed by Merkley (2009), who concluded, among other things, that "Ryan rightly emphasizes that individual libraries should assess their current reference models to see if new staffing complements or even new methods of service would provide more value for their user communities" (p. 147).

At any service point, the breadth of questions that can arise remains a challenge. For the novice staff member, a person heading toward the desk can create some anxiety; will it be an easy transaction, or will it be so difficult that the novice has no clue about where to start? There are some questions for which library resources simply cannot provide an answer. Some novices have difficulty telling a user, after a diligent search, "I'm sorry, but I cannot find what you need. I need to refer you to my colleague, _____." Learning when to pass a request on or asking a colleague for assistance is not a sign of incompetence. Rather, it is recognition of the library's goal of providing the best possible service to its users. This concept is so important for all service personnel to understand.

The organization of reference services and collections can take several forms. The three most common forms in academic libraries are *central* or general reference, *divisional*

👥 FROM THE AUTHORS

While working in library administration, Greenwell felt strongly about continuing to do library work and interact with users, so she worked a regular reference desk shift. Although the level of expertise needed at the desk was frequently minimal, she felt it was valuable for better understanding library users as well as how library equipment was used, how signage was interpreted, and generally what users needed to make their library experience the best possible.

reference, and *departmental* reference. The organization of reference service depends on many factors, the more important ones being philosophy of the library, physical layout of the building, size of the library's collection, abilities of the staff, type of libraries and type(s) of user, and financial resources.

A central or general reference department organization brings together all reference materials in one physical location. Some arguments for this form of organization are the following:

- Reference materials are easier to locate because they are shelved together.
- Because knowledge is interrelated and interdisciplinary, it is easier to do reference work if all the material is kept together.
- It is not necessary to purchase duplicate materials or to duplicate services.
- It is possible to make more economical use of staff at one service point rather than staffing several service points.

Today, nearly all libraries that have a reference collection have a generalized one, though some large research libraries still have divisional collections within a single library.

Divisional collections bring together reference materials for a group of related subjects within a section or floor of the library. A rather common divisional approach is to categorize the collection by social sciences, humanities, and natural sciences. Whatever the divisional arrangement, it should be suited for the building floor plan and institutional focus. Some of the arguments in favor of divisional reference organization are the following:

- A smaller reference collection is easier to use.
- The reference materials and the general collection on a particular subject

---

IIIII CHECK THIS OUT

An excellent introduction to the basics of pedagogy and instructional design is Char Booth's book on the topic. Her four-part framework provides readers with a step-by-step approach for designing instruction confidently. If you are interested in instruction, this is a must-read.

Booth, Char. 2011. *Reflective teaching, effective learning: Instructional literacy for library educators.* Chicago: American Library Association.

We mentioned Steven Bell and John Shank's "blended librarian" approach in chapter 9, and this guide provides a detailed look at that concept as well as a framework for designing instruction.

Bell, Steven J., and John D. Shank. 2007. *Academic librarianship by design: A blended librarian's guide to the tools and techniques.* Chicago: American Library Association.

Finally, Dani Cook and Kevin Klipfel provide a strong overview of educational theory and research behind learning. Their five principles for structuring information literacy instruction are grounded in theory and are easily applicable.

Cook, Dani Brecher, and Kevin Michael Klipfel. 2015. How do students learn? An outline of a cognitive psychological model for information literacy instruction. *Reference and User Services Quarterly* 55, no. 1: 34–41.

are often closer together in a divisional arrangement, allowing easier access to both types of materials.

- Reference staff members who are subject specialists can use their talents and provide better service for specialized reference inquiries when they work in their area of expertise.

Collections in branch libraries, as one would expect, are usually restricted to a single subject (e.g., geology) or a broader discipline or profession (e.g., engineering or medicine). Having a dual arrangement allows the library and users to reap the benefits of both the centralized and divisional reference formats. This arrangement, in the past, did cause confusion for newcomers about where to go for assistance. Today, many libraries have consolidated service points and no longer maintain multiple service desks, and the ability to get online assistance has helped reduce confusion and frustration.

INSTRUCTIONAL SERVICES

An important service that may be part of the reference department or may be organized within a stand-alone department is library instruction. We discussed information literacy instruction, particularly as assessment of student learning outcomes relates to accreditation, in chapter 10, but it is worth mentioning again. Although traditional, in-person reference requests may be declining on average, most libraries still see numerous requests from instructors for classroom instruction or instructional materials. Classroom instruction typically consists of a single class period session (often called a "one shot"). This method is still a popular means of instruction, yet it has been shown to provide limited benefits.

Other forms of instruction may complement or even replace one-shot instruction, particularly given the rise in distance education. Course guides, websites, videos, and other online tools can help students build their information literacy skills and learn how to better find, evaluate, and use information. Some librarians are experimenting with working directly with online courses by serving as an "embedded librarian," which allows them to provide instruction and research assistance at the point of need. Those providing one-shot instruction may choose to "flip" their classroom and ask students to complete assignments online ahead of the class session. This technique provides more time in person to practice developing search strategies, finding articles, and so forth while the librarian is present and ready to assist.

CIRCULATION SERVICES

John Moorman (2006) defined library circulation as "the process by which items in a collection are taken out of the library by a user and returned to the library" (p. 263). This relatively straightforward definition, though accurate, belies the complexity of the activities encompassed by the term *circulation activities*. For example, some things circulation staff must know include the rules for what users may borrow, who may borrow those materials, how to maintain the collection, and, most important, how to handle upset or angry people. Julie Todaro and Mark Smith (2006) noted that "beyond basic skills, directional reference, and specialized training in customer interactions dealing with money, circulation staff need training in handling difficult customers as well as advanced conflict resolution" (p. 23). Todaro and Smith also mentioned that when staff members must collect money, especially fines or special fees, public relations becomes critical. For example, some institutions have rules regarding how much money a borrower may owe and still be allowed to borrow additional materials. A user who is over the fine limit and thus blocked from further borrowing may become very upset by the blockage and take that frustration out on the circulation staff member.

Circulation department staff members are the true front line of the library because they are the staff members most likely to be contacted by users regarding services. Indeed, they are often the only staff members with whom the public interacts. The circulation desk is also the point at which service quality must start, if for no other reason than the unit's physical location—close to the entrance, which means the circulation staff are the first staff members a user sees on entering the library. This is usually where users' first and most important impressions of the library are formed.

It is not uncommon for circulation personnel to believe that they are the least appreciated and most misunderstood by both the public and their colleagues. Part of this sense can arise from circulation staff not being fully aware of the importance of their work in terms of quality service. In difficult budget times, circulation staff may see vacant positions in their department remaining unfilled or some positions even being cut. Feelings of inferiority can also arise from insufficient support and praise from library managers. Managers who understand and communicate the value of the circulation staff's activities can make all the difference between quality and lackluster service as well as between poor and good morale.

Circulation units are often supervised by a support staff member rather than a librarian. Whoever has the supervisory responsibilities, if the operation is to be successful, must train unit personnel (the largest number of whom will likely be students) in proper stacks (collection) maintenance activities and diplomatic relationships with users in what are occasionally somewhat confrontational situations. We addressed some of the most significant stacks maintenance issues in chapter 11.

Handling Confrontational Situations

A circulation unit is not the only public service point at which difficult user behavior occurs, but it is a frequent point of trouble. Training for the inevitable problem situation consists of three key components: reducing tensions, maintaining control, and defusing the situation. Why the *inevitable* in the preceding sentence? Enforcing rules, imposing limits, and collecting fines carry a high risk of having to face someone who is upset, annoyed, frustrated, or angry. The emotional response can range from mildly sarcastic comments to physical violence. Needless to say, the goal of training is to provide staff with techniques and knowledge to deal with these situations.

Reducing tensions begins by lessening your own tension. Anyone with even modest experience in public service activities will have likely developed a sense for when trouble may arise. "Taking a deep breath" may seem like a trite statement, but doing so when the possibility of trouble arises actually helps reduce your stress level so you can better deal with a demanding situation. When a problem occurs, being ready is the first step in overall tension reduction. Although it may be difficult, try not to take complainers' comments or criticism personally. Remember, working in public service requires you to tolerate some rudeness;

however, it does not mean accepting abusive behavior. Having the ability to differentiate between rudeness and abuse and what to do when the behavior becomes the latter is a valuable skill. Essentially, the first principle of handling a problem patron or difficult situation is to know that we can control ourselves and how to respond, that we may be able to influence the situation, but that we cannot control others' behavior.

Step two is to try to keep the situation as low key as possible. One of the most important aspects of controlling the situation is to use your active listening skills. Proper listening helps in better understanding the actual issue that is causing the frustration, and it conveys respect for the speaker. The better one understands the issue, the better the chance of guiding the situation to a positive outcome. Making it clear that you recognize the person's point of view without suggesting that those views are justified can assist in keeping the situation from escalating. Understanding nonverbal body language is also part of maintaining control of the situation; for example, a speaker with a clenched fist may well be signaling increasing difficulty in controlling emotions. Keeping the focus on the library issue is essential to keeping as much control as possible.

Defusing the situation depends on understanding the issue of concern. With such an understanding, you will know if you have the authority to address the issue or not. If not, calling the supervisor will do several things; most important, it will indicate to the person that the concern is being taken seriously and actively looked into. It also brings another person into the situation. Given academic libraries' long service hours, there may not be anyone on duty who has the authority to handle the complaint. In such cases, having the person write out the concern will also help defuse tensions. Indicating that the purpose for having the person do the writing is to ensure that the person's position is accurately conveyed to those who can resolve the issue can make the individual feel empowered. Occasionally, just the act of writing reduces the person's emotions.

Confidentiality

One issue of major importance is user confidentiality. To be consistent with ALA's Library Bill of Rights (www.ala.org/advocacy/intfreedom/librarybill), circulation personnel are ethically bound to not reveal the reading habits of borrowers under the principle of intellectual freedom, which is the right to read whatever one wishes. The ALA Code of Ethics (www.ala.org/advocacy/proethics/codeofethics/codeethics) states, "We protect each library user's right to privacy and confidentiality with respect to information sought or received and resources consulted, borrowed, acquired or transmitted." Only the user and the circulation staff, in the legitimate performance of their duties, have a right to know what information sources the user consulted or checked out, and circulation staff have an obligation to prevent others from obtaining this information.

Probably as long as libraries have existed, police, government officials, ministers, parents, spouses, and others have asked library staff about the reading habits of borrowers. Only during the past eighty-plus years, however, has the library profession expressed a desire to keep circulation records confidential. In 1938, the American Library Association's Code of Ethics specified the confidentiality of library records, the first formal acknowledgment of this issue in the United States. The profession's stand on confidentiality has remained strong in the face of legislation such as the USA PATRIOT (Uniting and Strengthening America by Providing Appropriate Tools Required to Intercept and Obstruct Terrorism) Act of 2001 that threatens user confidentiality.

Interlibrary Loan and Document Delivery

Despite the tremendous increase in the amount of information available online and in licensed databases available to users, you may be surprised to learn that there is still a significant demand for interlibrary loans (ILLs). We include in this category all items borrowed from other libraries to satisfy the needs of library users. In the context of interlibrary loan, document delivery has several different variations. One aspect involves purchasing information from commercial document suppliers when access from other libraries is either unavailable or too slow. Another version of document delivery is conveying library-owned materials, by mail or online, directly to library clientele. Staff members frequently do this to assist users who live at a distance or are otherwise unable to come to the library. It may also be offered as a service enhancement—for example, by academic libraries for faculty. An active interlibrary loan program is a significant commitment of library resources. Numerous studies of average ILL costs have been done over time, and the cost of loans is going down slightly, though most of that cost is staff time. A 2012 study revealed average borrowing costs of $12.11 for loans and $7.93 for nonreturnable items (Leon and Kress, 2012).

Reserve Services

Reserve services are characteristic of colleges and universities. Instructors sometimes wish to supplement the library collection in order to support their teaching. Instructors assign various types of material—for example, copies of journal articles, their own personal copies of books or other instructional materials, videos, copies of quizzes and answers, and so on. Libraries support this instructional endeavor by establishing policies and procedures to make those reserved materials available to students. The concept goes back to the late nineteenth century and, until relatively recently, was a means of limiting borrowing periods for print materials so that all the students in a class would have fair access to the material. Rather than a borrowing period of a month or even an academic term, reserve items could be limited to a few hours or days per circulation. Traditional reserve service guaranteed that assigned course materials were available on a first come, first served basis.

Today, reserve service is primarily electronic in nature, although it may include a small number of paper-based materials, such as a faculty member's personal items, print material not suitable for scanning, sample term papers, and research reports. As the volume of digitized material on reserve has grown, the nature of the work has changed. In the past, the reserve desk was probably the service point with the highest rate of unhappy people. Students complained that material was not put on reserve fast enough, that service was poor and waiting times too long. Faculty sometimes complained about the time it took to process assigned material, about the amount of work they had to do before material went on reserve, and about copyright limitations. Library staff complained that the amount of time it took to process materials was too great and that faculty did not provide sufficient time to process reserve items before assigning them, did not appreciate or adhere to copyright restrictions, placed excessive quantities of material on reserve that students never looked at, and were slow to remove items when they were no longer assigned.

Online reserve systems have changed most of those complaints; perhaps the major issue now is between copyright holders and academic libraries and their home institutions. Because of copyright concerns, some academic libraries have ceased to offer online course reserve services. Syracuse University, the University of Arizona, and the University of

Wisconsin-Madison are three such examples, and others continue to assess whether the library should still provide this service. San Diego State University, one of the first to provide online course reserves in the early 1990s, ended its program in 2010 (Goodson and Frederiksen, 2011).

In addition, there are questions regarding the value of reserve services. Writers have commented on the low use of some reserve items as well as on the high cost of administration (for example, Bradley, 2007, and De Jager, 2001). In addition, there are pedagogic arguments against reserve services. There is evidence that using assigned reserve materials has no significant influence on academic performance. A study at the University of Virginia measured the correlation between more than eight thousand students' use of reserve materials and the grades they received in their courses. The study revealed only a weak connection between reserve use and grades. The study also revealed that depending on reserve readings may even obstruct the educational process. Relying on reserve services to provide library materials may discourage students from using the rest of the library and learning necessary library use skills. It also prevents the serendipitous discovery of information that occurs through normal library use (Self, 1987).

The principle guaranteeing the confidentiality of circulation records is the same in reserve and circulation units. Although the reading is required and assigned by a faculty member, no one has a right to know what anyone else reads without that person's permission. Faculty wishing to find out which students have done the required reading for their class may find it difficult to understand this principle. Revealing circulation records, however, violates the library's responsibility to guard the intellectual freedom of the students. The question may arise whether faculty have the right to see the circulation records for personally owned items placed on reserve: the answer is that they do not. While the materials are in the custody of the library, the principle of confidentiality applies to all materials issued and controlled by the library, even if only temporarily held. What a library may furnish that does not violate borrower confidentiality are data about the number of times an item circulated. Information can also be furnished about the number of individual students who checked out reserve material. Essentially, any information that does not identify an individual will not violate confidentiality.

The most vexing legal consideration in reserve operations is adherence to copyright law. Copyright law grants the copyright holder exclusive rights to reproduce, distribute, adapt, perform, and display his creations. However, federal law recognizes that the public should also have some access to copyrighted information without having to ask permission or pay royalties. The law's "fair use" exemption is the most applicable provision for libraries:

> Fair use of a copyrighted work, including such use by reproduction in copies . . . for purposes such as criticism, comment, news reporting, teaching (including multiple copies for classroom use), scholarship, or research, is not an infringement of copyright. (17 USC § 107)

The criteria libraries use to determine whether use or reproduction of a copyrighted work qualifies as fair use include four factors:

The purpose and character of the use. Is the use for a commercial or educational purpose?

The nature of the work. Is the copyrighted item a work of fiction (more restrictions) or nonfiction (fewer limitations)?

> *The amount and substantiality of the portion copied.* Copying a limited portion
> points more toward fair use.
> *The effect on the market value.* Will use affect the publisher's sales?

However difficult and confusing copyright is in terms of print-based materials, it is even more so for digital items. Digitizing copyrighted works involves copying and distribution, so those items must conform to copyright law. Libraries are in the difficult position of trying to provide access to digital resources while remaining in copyright compliance. Although copyright law offers no clear and direct answers about the scope of fair use for electronic reserves, a number of different interpretations of the law may be found in the literature.

Higher education and its libraries face some serious challenges regarding fair use. There have always been issues between educators and copyright holders over the concept of fair use and just how much material can be used under the concept. The digital age and its associated technologies that allow for easy file-sharing and the relatively easy generation of digital copies that are indistinguishable from the original has raised the stakes in the minds of copyright holders. Melanie Schlosser (2006) noted that "copyright law is famously difficult to understand and apply with precision" (p. 12).

Recently, universities and their libraries have learned that the answer to the question "is this fair use?" is all too often "it depends." Lawyers representing the Association of American Publishers (AAP) have approached a number of universities (for example, the University of California, Cornell, Hofstra, Marquette, and Syracuse) regarding "alleged infringement" activities of their e-reserve services. Andrew R. Albanese (2007) discussed the differing opinions about how friendly the dialogue was between AAP and institutional attorneys. Starting from the position of alleged infringements, the prospect of a lawsuit was never off the table. An interesting sidelight is that most of the discussions were with private institutions that, unlike public institutions which have sovereign immunity, would be liable for any damages awarded to AAP. More recent has been the case of Cambridge Press versus Georgia State University. As Albanese noted, "For now, in today's world, managing e-reserves is about managing risk" (p. 38). A library's policy on copying will generally reflect the institution's risk tolerance for litigation, and libraries should seek legal counsel before adopting an electronic reserve policy.

LIBRARY LIAISON SERVICES

Liaison duties are common in academic libraries, not just in ARL institutions. In 2008, ACRL data showed that the concept was already in place or under serious consideration in all types of academic libraries (Dempsey, 2008). Just what constitutes a liaison's responsibilities is evolving and varies from institution to institution. To some degree the liaison model has its roots in several other concepts because the work often involves reference, instruction, collection development, and other key library services.

Perhaps the most comprehensive list of possible liaison roles appeared in Karen Williams's (2009) article in which she outlined ten areas of work:

- Campus engagement
- Content/collection development and management
- Teaching and learning

- Scholarly communication
- E-scholarship and digital tools
- Reference/help services
- Outreach (to the local community)
- Fund-raising
- Exhibit and event planning
- Leadership (pp. 4–5)

In the same issue as the Williams article, Elizabeth A. Dupuis (2009) noted,

> Responding strategically to economic pressures, many libraries are taking a fresh look at the changing needs of faculty and students and realigning the library's priorities. . . . [T]he librarian's role as an educational partner is recognized as one area of strategic importance for the long-term vitality of research libraries and the effectiveness of campus teaching and learning initiatives. (p. 9)

In order for librarians to take on liaison roles, a number of skills need to be learned or developed, and LIS schools might consider adding some coursework to support the development of these skills. Some of the skill sets that the liaison positions require are a high level of communication and presentation ability, flexibility and comfort with ambiguity, project management, and promotion and marketing. In a small library where everyone may be called upon to serve as a liaison, these skills are even more essential. John Rodwell and Linden Fairburn (2008) discussed these and many other skills needed for an effective liaison program. Some of the specific duties might be providing integrated instruction throughout the term of the course, developing appropriate alerting services for faculty and graduate students, and developing and offering stand-alone courses that link information service and a subject area.

A related, or perhaps another, variation of the liaison concept is the "embedded" librarian. David Shumaker (2009) identified four distinguishing aspects of embedded librarian positions: office location (outside the library), who funds the salary (solely from the library or shared with another department), who handles the individual's performance review (conducted solely or jointly by a nonlibrarian), and participation in both library and customer group meetings. Certainly the concept has gained wide acceptance in the special library environment. In the case of academic libraries, it appears as if some liaison positions would fit the special library definition of an embedded librarian (Shumaker, 2009), although most would not.

||||| CHECK THIS OUT

We mentioned ARL SPEC Kits initially in chapter 8, describing how they can be a valuable snapshot of current research, practices, and policies in a variety of areas. We recommend this one focused on recent changes in the liaison role:

Miller, Rebecca K., and Lauren Pressley. 2015. *SPEC Kit 349: Evolution of library liaisons.* Washington, DC: Association of Research Libraries. http://publications.arl.org/Evolution -Library-Liaisons-SPEC-Kit-349/.

❗ KEY POINTS TO REMEMBER

- Quality services are essential to ongoing institutional support.
- Quality services arise out of a team effort on the part of the entire staff, including student employees.
- Customer service models from the commercial world have proven useful in academic library environments.
- Circulation is important to quality library service and is more complex than many people realize.
- Circulation units are a key element in maintaining user confidentiality regarding library use.
- Reserve services have recently changed markedly. E-reserves have increased the need to have some library staff who are conversant with copyright laws, especially the definition of fair use in terms of the most recent court decisions.
- Liaison work to academic departments is one of the special aspects of academic library service that does not exist in other types of libraries. What being a library liaison means varies from library to library.

REFERENCES

Albanese, Andrew R. 2007. Down with e-reserve. *Library Journal* 132, no.16: 36–38.

Applegate, Rachel. 2008. Whose decline? Which academic libraries are "deserted" in terms of reference transactions? *Reference and User Services Quarterly* 48, no. 2: 176–189.

Bell, Steven J., and John D. Shank. 2007. *Academic librarianship by design: A blended librarian's guide to the tools and techniques.* Chicago: American Library Association.

Booth, Char. 2011. *Reflective teaching, effective learning: Instructional literacy for library educators.* Chicago: American Library Association.

Bradley, Karen. 2007. Reading noncompliance: A case study and reflection. *Mountainrise: The International Journal of the Scholarship of Teaching and Learning* 4, no. 1: 1–16.

Carlson, Scott. 2001. The deserted library: As students work online reading rooms empty—Leading some campuses to add Starbucks. *Chronicle of Higher Education* (November 16): A1, A35.

Carlson, Scott. 2013. For making the most of college, it's still location, location, location. *Chronicle of Higher Education* (February 4). www.chronicle.com/article/For-Making-the-Most-of/136985/.

Coleman, Jason, Melissa N. Mallon, and Leo Lo. 2016. Recent changes to reference services in academic libraries and their relationship to perceived quality: Results of a national survey. *Journal of Library Administration* 56, no. 6: 673–696.

Cook, Dani Brecher, and Kevin Michael Klipfel. 2015. How do students learn? An outline of a cognitive psychological model for information literacy instruction. *Reference and User Services Quarterly* 55, no. 1: 34–41.

De Jager, Karin. 2001. "Impacts and outcomes: Searching for the most elusive indicators of academic library performance." In *Meaningful measures for emerging realities. Proceedings of the 4th Northumbria International Conference on Performance Measurement in Libraries and Information Services*, 291–297. Washington, DC: Association of Research Libraries.

Demas, S. 2005. "From the ashes of Alexandria: What's happening in the college library?" In *Library as place: Rethinking roles, rethinking space.* Washington, DC: Council on Library and Information Resources.

Dempsey, Lorcan. 2008. Reconfiguring the library systems environment. *portal: Library and the Academy* 8, no. 8: 111-120.

Dotson, Daniel S., and Joshua B. Garris. 2008. Counting more than the gate: Developing building use statistics to create better facilities for today's academic library users. *Library Philosophy and Practice* (September): 1-13.

Dupuis, Elizabeth A. 2009. Amplifying the educational role of librarians. *Research Library Issues* 265 (August): 9-14. http://publications.arl.org/rli265/10.

Freeman, Geoffrey T. 2005. *Library as place: Rethinking roles, rethinking space.* CLIR Pub. 129. Washington, DC: Council on Library and Information Resources.

Gayton, Jeffrey. 2008. Academic libraries: "Social" or "communal"? The nature and future of academic libraries. *Journal of Academic Librarianship* 34, no. 1: 60-66.

Goodson, Kymberly Anne, and Linda Frederiksen. 2011. E-reserves in transition: Exploring new possibilities in e-reserves service delivery. *Journal of Interlibrary Loan, Document Delivery and Electronic Reserves* 21, nos. 1/2: 33-56.

Hernon, Peter, Danuta A. Nitecki, and Ellen Altman. 1999. Service quality and customer satisfaction: An assessment and future directions. *Journal of Academic Librarianship* 25, no. 1: 9-17.

Leon, Lars, and Nancy Kress. 2012. Looking at resource sharing costs. *Interlending and Document Supply* 40, no. 2: 81-87.

Leuzinger, Julie. 2013. Reducing service points in the academic library. *College and Research Libraries News* 74, no. 10: 530-533.

Martell, Charles. 2008. The absent user: Physical use of the academic library collections and services continues to decline, 1995-2006. *Journal of Academic Librarianship* 34, no. 5: 400-407.

Merkley, Cari. 2009. Staffing an academic reference desk with librarians is not cost-effective. *Evidence-Based Library and Information Practice* 4, no. 2: 143-147.

Miles, Dennis B. 2013. Shall we get rid of the reference desk? *Reference and User Services Quarterly* 52, no. 4: 320-333.

Miller, Rebecca K., and Lauren Pressley. 2015. *SPEC Kit 349: Evolution of library liaisons.* Washington, DC: Association of Research Libraries. http://publications.arl.org/Evolution-Library-Liaisons-SPEC-Kit-349/

Moorman, John A. 2006. *Running a small library.* New York: Neal-Schuman.

Phan, T., L. Hardesty, C. Sheckells, and D. Davis. 2009. *Academic libraries: 2008* (NCES 2010-348). Washington, DC: National Center for Education Statistics, Institute of Education Sciences, U.S. Department of Education.

Phan, T., L. Hardesty, and J. Hug. 2014. *Academic libraries: 2012* (NCES 2014-038). Washington, DC: U.S. Department of Education, National Center for Education Statistics.

Rodwell, John, and Linden Fairburn. 2008. Dangerous liaisons? Defining the faculty liaison librarian service model, its effectiveness and sustainability. *Library Management* 29, nos. 1/2: 116-124.

Ryan, Susan. 2008. Reference transactions analysis: The cost-effectiveness of staffing a traditional academic reference desk. *Journal of Academic Librarianship* 34, no. 5: 389-399.

Schachter, Debbie. 2006. The true value of customer service. *Information Outlook* 10, no. 8: 8-9.

Schlosser, Melanie. 2006. Fair use in the digital environment: A research guide. *Reference and User Services Quarterly* 46, no. 1: 11-17.

Self, James. 1987. Reserve readings and student grades: Analysis of a case study. *Library and Information Science Reports* 9, no. 1: 29-40.

Shill, Harold B., and Shawn Tonner. 2004. Does the building still matter? Usage patterns in new, expanded, and renovated libraries. *College and Research Libraries* 65, no. 2: 123-150.

Shumaker, David 2009. *Models of embedded librarianship: Final report.* Washington, DC: School of Library and Information Science, Catholic University of America. https://www.sla.org/wp-content/uploads/2017/05/EmbeddedLibrarianshipFinalRptRev.pdf.

Todaro, Julie, and Mark Smith. 2006. *Training library staff and volunteers to provide extraordinary customer service*. New York: Neal-Schuman.

Wehmeyer, Susan, Dorothy Auchter, and Arnold Hirshon. 1996. Saying what we will do, and doing what we say: Implementing a customer service plan. *Journal of Academic Librarianship* 22, no. 3: 173–180.

Weingand, Darlene E. 1997. *Customer service excellence: A concise guide for librarians*. Chicago: American Library Association.

Williams, Karen. 2009. A framework for articulating new library roles. *Research Library Issues* 265 (August): 3–8. http://old.arl.org/bm~doc/rli-265-williams.pdf.

CHAPTER 13

Staffing

S taff are the key to service success, not technology, not collections, and not the library's physical facilities. Certainly all those factors are important, but it is how well staff members perform their duties that make users think highly of the library. Gaining the services of the best and brightest people requires thoughtful planning and ongoing attention. Almost every full-time staff member has some supervisory responsibilities. If nothing more, a staff member may help supervise part-time student assistants. Although some may not think this task requires knowledge of human resources (HR), even working with an intern or a volunteer has HR implications.

Academic libraries have several categories of employees. The category labels vary from library to library; however, there essentially are four basic groups, each with an expected minimum level of education:

- Full-time individuals who have a master's degree in library and information science or a subject graduate degree or both (librarians and professionals)
- Full-time individuals with degrees ranging from bachelor's to postgraduate in an area of specialty outside library and information science (information technologists and other specialists in areas such as human resources, development, or public relations)
- Full-time individuals with an academic degree or high school diploma (paraprofessionals, support staff, library assistants, or clerical staff)
- Part-time individuals with or without a degree (student assistants, interns, volunteers)

Given the competitive job market, there may be individuals with the MLS serving in paraprofessional positions, individuals with bachelor's degrees serving as interns, and so forth. The preceding list is simply the typical breakdown of positions. As the size of an academic library increases, so does the variety of staff categories it employs and the complexity of its HR functions.

In the remainder of this section, we outline several key trends impacting full-time library employees. Budget reductions, downsizing, and changing staffing patterns create an environment of uncertainty, tension, and often fear. These worries arise as organizations make changes to their structure in order to do more without having additional resources. It seems likely this situation will continue for the foreseeable future.

Some years ago, Paula T. Kaufman (1992) noted that the categories used to classify library employees "can create problems, tensions, and conflicts between library non-professional and professional staffs" (p. 214). Some of these tensions arise from understanding the types of library work and who does what. Individuals lacking a library degree may now do what was once thought of as a librarian's job. Liz Lane and Barbara Stewart (1998) wisely noted that "many staff members are being assigned higher-level work which then requires an upward reclassification of jobs. . . . Work previously done at lower levels has either become automated, outsourced to a library vendor, or is not done anymore" (p. 156). This still happens.

One area in which tension can arise is the status of librarians on campus. Librarian and support staff tensions can be pronounced when librarians are seeking to move from nonfaculty to faculty status. In such a situation, some support staff may harbor doubts about why librarians should gain special treatment when everyone on staff is important to providing quality service. Some staff do not understand the responsibilities of faculty positions and look only at face time. That is, they do not see the evening and weekend time that librarians must put in to do their jobs. This is particularly true for librarians who have significant teaching responsibilities or research requirements. John Buschman (2016) has pointed out that the amount of evening and weekend work time is increasing for all faculty.

Workloads continue to increase and generally do not generate additional staffing, even in the form of extra student employee assistance. Existing staff find themselves called on to undertake more tasks and learn new skill sets. New librarian position announcements increasingly include new skill sets as well. In a study that compared academic librarian job advertisements in 2011 to those from 1996 and 1988, Therese F. Triumph and Penny M. Beile (2015) found numerous new position titles, many of which are specialized. The researchers noted,

> Among the job titles that first appear in the 2011 study are digital, electronic resources, emerging technologies, metadata, scholarly communication, and web services librarians. These titles likewise indicate that the primary drivers are emerging technologies and digital materials. (p. 735)

Triumph and Beile found more unique jobs in 2011 compared to 1996. This outcome could lead one to think that the job market is improving, though likely it is more a case of a wider diversity in job titles and increasing specialization. The position of liaison librarian, for example, as we discussed in chapter 12, now often includes responsibilities such as scholarly communication, data management, publishing, marketing, and other areas of growth, particularly within research libraries.

The final, and perhaps most important, trend is that of the librarian job market. Much has been written about the predicted librarian shortage, which has yet to fully materialize, and likely you may already be familiar with numerous blog posts and articles discussing this issue and its impact on new professionals as well as our profession as a whole. At many institutions, librarians of retirement age remain, whether for the enjoyment of library work

👥 FROM THE AUTHORS

A library director colleague whom Greenwell admires pointed out that not only do some staff not understand the responsibilities of faculty positions but also some faculty don't appreciate staff. Greenwell's colleague is a firm believer that everyone's job, from librarian to student worker, is important and essential to the good running of the library. Her philosophy is that no job is beneath her (whether checking out books, closing the library, etc.), and that's a great quality to have, especially as a library director.

▏▏▏▏▏ **CHECK THIS OUT**

A comprehensive title on diversity in the workplace is Barbara I. Dewey and Loretta Parham's *Achieving Diversity: A How-to-Do-It Manual for Librarians* (New York: Neal-Schuman, 2006).

---

or, perhaps more likely, for financial reasons. The Annoyed Librarian (2016), an anonymous blogger for *Library Journal,* has written about this issue for at least ten years, citing numerous sources and conducting some analysis. Others, such as Brett Bonfield (2011), have conducted in-depth analysis that is quite concerning for new librarians seeking to enter the profession full time if those patterns continue. The *Occupational Outlook Handbook* projects a 2 percent growth rate in all types of librarian positions through 2024, which is slower than the average growth rate of 7 percent for other occupations (Bureau of Labor Statistics, 2016a). We certainly hope to see an increase in academic librarian position vacancies, particularly for new professionals.

In this chapter, we explore many major issues related to HR in an academic library setting. Having a basic knowledge of HR activities and their potential impact on service quality is beneficial for all staff members, the library, and its parent institution.

LIBRARIANS

In today's world, the difference between a librarian and other staff categories is probably most apparent in the HR department and least apparent in terms of users' perceptions. HR can differentiate between the categories because it maintains the job descriptions and salary classifications. None of these attributes are apparent on a daily basis in the library. It is almost impossible for users to know who holds what job title.

Individuals holding positions designated as "librarian" generally have a master's degree in library science (MLS) or library and information science (MLIS). Some large libraries have subject librarians who may hold a graduate degree in their assigned subject area rather than an MLS or MLIS. In some cases, a subject degree may be required. James G. Neal (2005) discussed the potential new perspectives these librarians bring in his reflections about "feral professionals," which he describes as those professionals who are without the MLS or MLIS and, as a result, "have been 'raised' in other environments and bring to the academic library a 'feral' set of values, outlooks, styles, and expectations" (p. 302). Some librarians may be hired without an MLS or MLIS because they satisfy a frequent phrase in position advertisements: "MLS/MLIS or equivalent required," though what is equivalent varies among individual institutional needs. However, the vast majority of academic librarians do in fact have an MLS or MLIS degree.

Some time ago, Catherine Murray-Rust (2005) wrote,

> For over a century librarians and others in academe have debated the issue of faculty status for librarians. Do librarians play the same role as teaching or research faculty members? Is academic freedom a problem for librarians? Do librarians have real faculty status if they do not earn tenure the way other faculty members do? Although some librarians now have faculty status, the pros and cons continue to be argued passionately. (p. B10)

In spite of the passion about this issue, it is still a matter very much in the air at many institutions. The Association of College and Research Libraries (ACRL) has taken a strong interest in the topic for the better part of fifty years and produced a number of documents on the subject. ACRL (2011) put forward new guidelines regarding faculty status. The guidelines cover ten topics: professional responsibilities, library governance, college and university governance, compensation, tenure, promotion, leaves and research funds, academic freedom, grievance, and dismissal.

In terms of college and university governance, the guidelines state, "Librarians should be eligible for membership in the faculty senate or equivalent governing body. They should have the same degree of representation as other academic units on all college or university governing bodies." The typical way in which academic librarians, regardless of status, generally get to participate in such activities is through committee assignments. At some institutions where librarians do not have faculty status, librarians still serve on the campus faculty senate. As we noted in chapter 5, having a library presence on the committee that handles new courses and programs is of great benefit in terms of library planning.

ACRL (2010) also has developed a set of guidelines for appointment, promotion, and tenure of academic librarians. One of the provisions that relates to the requirements for promotion in academic rank as well as tenure is relatively brief, but it is significant in terms of implications for librarians:

> All activities shall be judged by professional colleagues on and/or off the campus on the basis of their contribution to scholarship, the profession of librarianship, and library service. The basic criterion for promotion in academic rank is to perform professional level tasks that contribute to the educational and research mission of the institution.

Evidence of this level of performance may be judged by colleagues on the library faculty, members of the academic community outside the library, and professional colleagues outside the academic institution.

One of the challenges for librarians gaining tenure is the impact of having performance judged by "members of the academic community outside of the library." In a recently established program, candidates may not have developed a wide academic community outside the library. Some teaching faculty, and even some librarians at other institutions, may doubt that librarians should have faculty status. Those who feel strongly about this can complicate the review process.

Like other faculty members, tenure-track librarians face the challenge of convincing their peers that they are worthy of tenure or promotion or both. The seven-year window for achieving that goal—a rather firm standard at most academic institutions—seems to fly by quickly. Being able to meet requirements of one's primary librarian assignment, research,

---

||||| CHECK THIS OUT

A highly readable essay about the process of preparing the material that goes forward to the group that will make the tenure decision is "Our Excellent Adventure: A Somewhat Irreverent Look at How Three Tenure Track Librarians Prepared Their Dossiers and Lived to Tell About It," by Kathleen A. Hanna, Ann O'Bryan, and Kevin F. Petsche (*College and Research Libraries News* 69, no. 9 [2008]: 554–556).

▥▥ **CHECK THIS OUT**

John D. Shank's article, "The Blended Librarian: A Job Announcement Analysis of the Newly Emerging Position of Instructional Design Librarian" (*College and Research Libraries* 67, no. 6 [2006]: 515–524), describes some of the factors that are changing all the roles librarians play with the increasing need for instructional design and information technology skills as well as research skills.

Lindsay O'Neill does an excellent job of describing what it's like to be an instructional design librarian in a newly created position: http://acrlog.org/2015/01/20/the-making-of-an-instructional-design-librarian/.

and service can seem daunting to a new librarian. It may seem like teaching faculty have a slightly easier time because they are better able to control their working time and are generally on a shorter contract (nine or ten months). Librarians, on the other hand, have a host of job responsibilities that are generally not flexible, and there is an expectation that a standard forty-plus-hour workweek will be put in all year. Even when the library makes some provision for research time, there are staffing challenges. We have noted in several chapters how difficult it is to secure additional staff positions. Although libraries with faculty status may build research time into their librarian positions, it can be challenging to succeed. Research time may result in more work for other staff members who must take up the slack, and when it comes to sabbaticals, staffing challenges can be even more significant.

Another challenge for many new graduates is that they often do not have a strong research background from either their undergraduate or graduate education, unlike the teaching faculty. Identifying a reasonable research topic can be a daunting task, as is developing a sound research methodology. Their library school may not have had a required research methods course. Even if the person had such a course, she can likely benefit from some serious mentoring (we cover mentoring in chapter 14). Nikhat Ghouse and Jennifer Church-Duran (2008) succinctly stated the issue when they wrote about a newcomer's transition to higher education:

> These challenges are heightened for academic librarians, who often do not have the same transitional experiences as teaching faculty. The developmental challenges specific to academic librarianship are diverse and include navigating the transition into the profession, comprehending the complexity of the academic library culture, and appreciating the demands of research and scholarship. In exploring ways to successfully address these challenges, mentoring relationships are a consistently popular option for library faculty and staff. (p. 373)

How many institutions have faculty status programs for librarians? William H. Walters (2016) looked at faculty status in Association of Research Libraries (ARL) libraries and determined that 52 percent of those institutions grant nominal faculty status to librarians. This percentage is pretty close to what Mary K. Bolin found in 2008. It will be interesting to see how that number changes over time. Does faculty status make sense for librarians? Jacalyn Bryan (2007) makes an excellent point when concluding her article about faculty status: "Academic librarians in each college and university should seek the model that works best for them in their individual situation" (p. 785).

SUPPORT STAFF

Support staff members are the backbone of library services. Without them, few libraries could offer the variety and quality of services that they do. Deciding on a label and required background of those holding support staff positions in academic libraries is not easy. Years ago, Elin Christianson (1973) reported on the various labels used to designate library personnel who did not hold an MLS as well as on the attitudes about those labels. The list included library aide, library associate, library assistant, library clerk, library technician, nonprofessional, paraprofessional, support staff, and subprofessional. The only label that did not elicit at least a few negative responses from those holding such positions at the time was *library technician*. *Paraprofessional* received only a few negative comments, and today there would likely be even less because of the rise of such groups as paralegals, paramedics, and so forth. In fact, the term *paralibrarian* is seen more frequently, notably in the *Library Journal* Paralibrarian of the Year Award. Ultimately there is still no consensus about what the label should be, probably because of a lack of agreement about what education or training is required to hold such positions.

One reason for the confusion about labels and the use of the phrase *library degree* is that there are community college programs that offer courses and certificates in librarianship. One example is the Library Information Technology program (www.bluegrass.kctcs.edu/en/BCIS/LIT.aspx) at Bluegrass Community and Technical College (BCTC) in Kentucky. BCTC offers undergraduate library science courses that can lead to an Academic Certificate in Library Information Technology or an Associate of Applied Science in Information Management and Design with the Library Information Technology Option. There are many such courses and certificate programs across the country.

The *Occupational Outlook Handbook* (*OOH*) describes the duties of a library technician in an academic library:

> Academic library technicians and assistants help students, faculties, and staff in colleges and universities access resources and information related to coursework or research projects. Some help teach students how to access and use library resources. They may work at service desks for reserve materials, special collections, or computer labs. (Bureau of Labor Statistics, 2016b)

As for education requirements, the *OOH* indicates that many libraries prefer to hire candidates for these positions who have a degree or postsecondary certificate. The *OOH* describes the course work in a certificate program as including work in "acquisitions, cataloguing, circulation, reference, and automated library systems." Given the skill requirements, is it any wonder there is some confusion regarding the qualifications necessary to be a "librarian" versus a "library technician"?

It is our opinion that career-oriented individuals form the core of academic library support staff. Career-oriented people tend to have a strong interest in the organization as well as the field in general. They are quick to volunteer to take on new tasks, especially those that offer opportunities to learn new skills or gain new knowledge. We must note that career-oriented individuals, when overworked and undervalued, can quickly become job-oriented. This is an outcome that all good supervisors should work to avoid. Providing support for excellent support staff is essential. This support obviously includes that of a financial nature, but also important is the opportunity for promotion and development of new skills. Later in this chapter, we will discuss training and staff development.

OTHER FULL-TIME STAFF

A variety of full-time employees work in academic libraries, especially in ARL libraries, and do not fall into the previous categories we have discussed. The most obvious are clerical staff such as administrative assistants. These positions typically require general office skills, and one does not need any prior background in library operations to carry out job responsibilities. Other clerical positions might include processing notices to users (overdue notices or document delivery notices, for example) or monitoring the security of library exits.

Beyond clerical staff, there are several job categories of nonlibrarian professionals. We will briefly discuss five of the most common categories you are likely to encounter in ARL and, increasingly, other academic libraries. Furthermore, we touch on some of the issues that may arise from the presence of such categories. The most common category is ICT (information and communication technology) personnel. We discussed a number of ICT functions in academic libraries in chapter 9. Almost all academic libraries have one or more staff members, some with an MLS and many without, who have technology-related job responsibilities. When large research libraries first began to computerize their activities in the 1960s, many developed in-house systems that were the forerunners of today's ILS packages, and this work required personnel with computer expertise. As late as the early 1990s, when an academic library purchased an ILS, a computer specialist was part of the expected project cost package. By the mid-1990s, most vendor-supplied ILSs did not require more than the type of support that existing library staff could provide. Existing ICT staff shifted their focus from the ILS to many other technologies of growing interest to academic libraries, such as in-house systems and large digitization projects. The vast majority of people holding these positions have a degree or extensive experience in computer science rather than an MLS.

A rather recent nonlibrarian staffing category is the development officer. The need for such officers has been growing as libraries must seek more noninstitutional funding to support programs and services. Individuals holding a development officer position support library administrators in their fund-raising activities. In our experience, people in this category usually have fund-raising experience and education, though some may also have the MLS. The campus development office may assign one of its staff to assist the library in fund-raising. We have found that the library is only one of several campus units this person is responsible for and, initially, the person will likely have little real understanding of library operations. One of the first challenges the development officer faces is that "no one graduates from the library," so growing relationships with loyal supporters can be far more challenging than in traditional departments and programs. We encourage library development officers to become involved in the Academic Library Advancement and Development Network (ALADN), an academic fund-raising community of peers that holds an annual conference.

Another staff category, which goes well beyond large research libraries, is the business officer. Job responsibilities for such individuals, as the job title suggests, are to assist senior administrators in the myriad business activities of the library. This position is often the chief financial officer for the library. Few people in this category have an MLS. They will likely have an undergraduate or graduate degree in business, public administration, or a related field.

Personnel work is complicated, and in large research libraries the variety of job categories makes the process more complex. For this reason, some ARL libraries have in-house human resources (HR) officers or even a department. As is the case with development officers, some may have an MLS, though most have a degree in an HR-related field. Also, like the development officer, the library HR officer must work closely and cooperatively with his campus counterpart.

Our last category—public relations (PR) officer—is found primarily in ARL libraries, though more libraries are hiring staff for this function. This position helps the library market the academic library or "tell the library's story." Many academic libraries are involved in systematic marketing of their services and resources. This officer works closely with academic library administrators, librarians, and the development officer to market the library to the rest of the college or university. Also important is marketing the library to prospective donors. Academic libraries that employ PR people tend to have official marketing plans in place. The PR person is the point person at times of academic library disaster or crisis. Some people in these positions may have an MLS, though many do not.

As one might expect, such a wide variety of job categories with differing educational and skill requirements can lead to several staffing concerns and issues. One such issue that may create staff tensions is faculty status for librarians. How to handle other professional categories in this case can be challenging, especially when there are individuals with similar backgrounds and job titles in other campus units that do not offer such opportunities.

Perhaps the most common concern is salary differentials. Libraries, like their campuses, are not exempt from the need to match the local market rates for nonlibrarian positions. A high local rate for some job categories may require paying a similar high rate in order to attract and retain people with those skill sets. This requirement, in turn, can upset efforts to maintain salary equity, both on campus and in the library. In addition to the local rate, there are often campus issues of salary equity.

One significant challenge related to the preceding job categories is how much, if any, familiarity people holding such a position have with academic libraries and their activities. If beginning academic librarians need time to gain a level of comfort in their first full-time position (see chapter 14 for a discussion of adjusting to the first position), how much more challenging must it be for those without the background of MLS course work? On occasion, there are individuals holding nonlibrarian positions who initially do not see the need to understand the library environment because of the belief that an organization is an organization in terms of their job responsibilities. Two positions for which this type of situation may arise are development and business. Success comes when librarians and nonlibrarians recognize the need for both groups to make an effort to understand the values and commitment of everyone in order to achieve the library's missions and goals.

Our last factor relates to the concept of customer service. All professions discuss and value this concept. However, there are differences in what customer service means. The beginning point for librarianship's service concept is gaining an understanding of end user demands, needs, wants, and desires. Once there is some understanding of these factors,

---

IIIII CHECK THIS OUT

We highly recommend that you spend time reviewing Kimberly B. Sweetman's *Managing Student Assistants* (New York: Neal-Schuman, 2007). It will pay dividends in the long run regardless of how new or seasoned a librarian you are. The exercises she has at the end of each chapter are particularly useful.

libraries attempt to create services to effectively address those factors within available resources. This is not always the case for some professional groups. For example, medical doctors base their service on their professional judgment of what is wrong and how to best address it, not on what the patient thinks she needs or wants. Often it takes some time for nonlibrarian professionals to fully grasp what library customer service is and what factors are key to providing such service.

STUDENT EMPLOYEES

The literature of our field pays little attention to part-time library staff. We think this is unfortunate because the work of part-timers is critical to quality public service. Just think about the many part-time employees who reshelve materials or handle physical processing of materials for the collection. This work has major implications for customer service.

Although one is likely to encounter part-time employees in almost any job category, one common and important part-time group in academic libraries is student employees. Student employees are a significant portion of the library staff in most academic libraries. For many libraries, quality service would be impossible without the aid of student employees. The work such individuals perform should receive the same attention and thought as is given to the work of full-time employees.

Employment in the library can help pay for the high cost of getting a degree, and few students view such work as a test of a possible career in librarianship. Classes and social activities are high priorities; thus, student employee motivation and supervision can be larger challenges than for full- or part-time staff. Looking at the early literature about student employees, you probably would come away with the view that student employees are too much trouble and not worth the effort. The focus then was on the problems of employing students. We believe part of the problem was not spending enough time on developing true job descriptions for what students will do, not to mention providing appropriate training and mentoring. What is clear today is that academic libraries are utterly dependent on such labor. Student employment benefits students as well. Providing student employees with income to support college costs is important, of course. Students also get the opportunity to learn new skills in a somewhat flexible, supportive work environment, and the skills they

---

‖‖‖‖ CHECK THIS OUT

Student employees are increasingly being asked to do more in the library, particularly as budgets are cut and the workload becomes greater for full-time employees. Some institutions have experimented with training undergraduate student employees to offer reference and instruction assistance. These articles describe and evaluate some of these programs:

Bodemer, B. B. 2014. They CAN and they SHOULD: Undergraduates providing peer reference and instruction. *College and Research Libraries* 75, no. 2: 162–178.

Mestre, Lori S., and Jessica M. LeCrone. 2015. Elevating the student assistant: An integrated development program for student library assistants. *College and Undergraduate Libraries* 22, no. 1: 1–20.

Murphy, Jo Ann. 2016. Enhancing the student experience: A case study of a library peer mentor program. *College and Undergraduate Libraries* 23, no. 2: 151–167.

gain from this workplace experience can help them be successful in whatever future career they choose.

Beyond the obvious benefit of having valuable work accomplished at a modest cost, not to mention the role that campus employment can play in student retention, students bring several benefits to the library. One benefit, in our view, is that as peers they are often viewed as more approachable than full-time staff. Student employees are more likely to have a sound idea of what technologies students use as well as how best to approach other students with marketing messages. Such information can be of great value when planning or modifying services. Yet another benefit is that students can assist full-time staff in better understanding today's students from a social and cultural perspective. Finally, student employees are a pool from which to recruit individuals to our field.

Just as you want to retain full-time staff, you want to retain student employees for as long as possible. There is an obvious built-in student turnover; nevertheless, keeping the best employees for as long as possible lowers training costs as well as supervision costs. One step to take, even if it is not well implemented with full-time staff, is to create student work teams. Consider building teams around a set of duties rather than scheduled work times. Teams need leaders, and this arrangement provides opportunities for promotion and rewards. With multiple work schedules, there may be opportunities for assistant leaders. Such a structure may also allow for the creation of a student career ladder with appropriate pay differentials. Regardless of the work structure, students should be held just as accountable for the quality of their work as are full-time staff.

THE STAFFING PROCESS

Selecting appropriate staff, regardless of category—full-time, part-time, and even volunteers—requires significant time, planning, and effort. Library staff do become involved in the HR process on an operational level, whether the library has its own HR department or not. Because of this, we have included a short discussion of major HR issues. During your career, you are likely to be involved from time to time in all the issues we cover, from selection to retirement. Understanding some of the key points of the recruitment and selection process is useful when you are looking for a job as well as when you are asked to serve on a search committee. When you become a supervisor, you will need to develop a sense of what goes into a job description, how to orient and train new people, and how to handle the inevitable performance appraisal process.

HR departments expect library staff involvement in a number of key steps in the staffing process. Those steps are some variation of the following:

- Determining needs and succession planning
- Job description
- Recruitment
- Selection
- Orientation and training
- Evaluation
- Coaching and discipline
- Resignation, termination, and retirement

Determining staffing needs is usually the responsibility of senior managers and consists of two lists. One is a wish list of positions that would be wonderful to have, if only funding were available; it is often a long list, and it is a special occasion when a new FTE is finally funded. The second list covers expected vacancies as a result of retirements, promotions, and resignations.

Recruitment and Selection

The job description is the foundation for getting the best and brightest people. The U.S. Department of Labor suggests a process for developing job descriptions and deciding on the proper selection of instruments. The suggested process starts with the library's organizational goals that a particular job is to assist in fulfilling. Designing a job requires answering questions such as "What activities are necessary to accomplish organizational goals?" Answering this apparently simple question is usually more complex than a person might expect. It requires detailed information in order to be useful. The goal is to be as comprehensive as possible in listing the tasks. Being too brief or broad only creates more work later in the process. For example, a response for a circulation employee should be more than "check out materials." It should cover all aspects of the work, such as checking the user's borrowing status, providing answers to questions about item availability or items the person could not locate, and deactivating security tags. Such detail is essential for developing sound job descriptions because it helps you identify the necessary skills and knowledge to successfully perform the work.

Another step is establishing job success criteria—the keys to selecting the right person for the right position. This step is also the most difficult and subjective in the model. The goal of the process is to determine what distinguishes successful from unsuccessful performance in the position. What constitutes success will vary as the work changes. For example, being courteous to users is always important, but what if a person is courteous while providing incorrect information? What about a person who is great with users but is unwilling or unable to work well with other staff members? Thinking through the success criteria for a job makes it much easier to select the right person for the position and allows you to develop questions to ask candidates that most accurately reflect the skills, knowledge, and service attitude needed for success. Job specifications are the skills, traits, knowledge, and experience that, when combined, result in successful performance. The job specifications are what you see in job descriptions and advertisements, such as educational background or degree required, years of experience, and a list of the specific skills sought.

Orientation

Creating a sound orientation program is critical for a new employee as well as the library. The first few days on the job are important for fitting in, encouraging retention, and forming the person's views about the library. A well-planned orientation, including training required for the position, will make it more likely that the new employee will succeed in the position and want to stay.

Generally, the first week should be equally divided between position training and learning about the library and its parent organization. For most people, the first days on a new job can be stressful and confusing. The common practice of taking new people around to meet everyone, assuming there are more than a dozen people to meet, leaves them with a blur of faces, a few names (rarely connected to the right faces), and a vague sense of what others do. Breaking up the process over several days gives the new employee a better chance to absorb information and make meaningful connections. Starting with the home unit and working outward allows the new employee to gain a sense of where the position fits in the scheme of things and how it is important to library operations. After this, you might move on to other units to allow the new employee to gain an overall picture of operations. Linking a new employee to someone at his level in the work group provides a personal connection and can lead to a possible mentoring relationship.

Retention

A major concern for today's organizations is retaining their best people. Loyalty to employees is important. Otherwise employees can easily have the mind-set, "Why should I have any loyalty to the organization if it has none for me?" Staffing changes—real or imagined—or some perceived threat that isn't communicated can encourage good employees to seek other employment.

About 25 percent of newly hired employees experience "new-job regrets" (Gardner, 2007). These regrets can arise from the employer overselling the nature of the position or some other aspect of the environment. If you properly follow the steps we outlined previously regarding job descriptions, there should be few problems related to the nature of the work. An employer may unknowingly oversell when there is a critical need to fill the position, and the recruiter falls into the trap of making the institution, opportunities, benefits, and so forth appear better than they actually are. In the long run, overselling or misrepresenting the position makes for very unhappy people—both the new hire and yourself. When the remorse is strong, the probability that the person will quit is extremely high.

Maria Bagshaw (2006) suggested some ways to help with the retention of student workers in particular:

> Of course, more money would be nice. But we are not permitted to give our student workers raises—they receive the minimum wage. So, we use little things to let them know they are important to us: a candy bowl for finals week, or a pizza party at the end of the year. Above all, treat your student workers like the adults they are. Take their education as seriously as they do. In return, they will offer great service with minimal professional staff input and financial resources. (p. 44)

Retention of student workers is just as important as retaining any other category of library employee. A supervisor may have a number of applicants at the beginning of the academic year, but finding students becomes more difficult as the year progresses. Finding the right mix of Bagshaw's "little things" throughout the year, not just during finals or end-of-year celebrations, is one element in long-term student retention.

Training and Staff Development

One key method for gaining and retaining staff loyalty is to have programs in place that provide ample opportunities for staff to grow and develop. Without a doubt, this strategy will help with the long-term retention of the best and brightest people. There are two basic training and development areas to consider—specific job-related skills and career development competencies and opportunities.

‖‖ CHECK THIS OUT

A book that will help any manager or supervisor become a more effective leader is *Academic Librarians as Emotionally Intelligent Leaders* by Peter Hernon, Joan Giesecke, and Camila A. Alire (Westport, CT: Libraries Unlimited, 2008).

We all continue to face a rapidly changing technological environment. Keeping staff current with changes related to their activities can be a challenge, especially when budgets are static. Failing to maintain staff skills often results in users receiving poorer service, which in turn leads to user dissatisfaction. As we mentioned in chapter 9, technology carries with it two financial challenges—acquiring and upgrading requisite technology and funding staff training.

Certainly training and development go beyond technological issues. Other major areas include training for individuals moving into supervisory positions and keeping staff up-to-date on changing professional standards. In technical services, for example, staying current with cataloging and data management standards is critical.

Professional associations provide excellent training opportunities. Annual conferences often have workshops and other continuing education programs as part of the overall program. Unfortunately, there are few such organizational opportunities for support staff, primarily because there is limited assistance for support staff travel. In addition, their salaries are substantially lower, making it difficult for many to pay for such opportunities on their own. As a result, many support staff rely heavily on distance education opportunities through webinars and videoconferencing. Many such opportunities can provide needed information, though the opportunity to build relationships with colleagues from other institutions is lacking.

In addition to funding struggles, libraries often face the problem of limited staffing. When staff are limited, it becomes difficult to have employees away at conferences and training programs for any length of time. Some institutions won't even give staff time off to attend conferences and training programs even when the staff member is willing to pay all expenses—this practice can discourage staff members from wanting to learn and grow their skills and may understandably result in staff becoming less motivated. Singer and Goodrich (2006) outlined five critical factors for retaining and motivating library staff. The following are principles for a supervisor to exemplify to help employees perform well:

- Focus: employees know what they need to do and what is expected of them
- Involvement: people support most what they help to create
- Development: opportunities for learning and growth are encouraged
- Gratitude: recognition of good performance (formal and informal)
- Accountability: employees are responsible for their performance or lack thereof (p. 62)

PERFORMANCE APPRAISAL

Singer and Goodrich's fifth point regarding accountability directly links to performance appraisal. Performance assessment takes many forms, from ongoing daily review with occasional corrective action to an annual overall assessment. After all, "employees have a right to know what their managers expect from them, and they're entitled to learn how to meet those expectations" (Armstrong and Mitchell, 2008, p. 63). Although you may not be in a supervisory role right away, at some point you likely will be, perhaps first with student employees, so we felt it would be helpful to go through the performance appraisal process. Certainly it is useful information for your own performance.

In terms of corrective action, the supervisor should discuss poor performance as situations arise. Trying to avoid unpleasant interactions regarding performance and letting problems slide only hurts everyone in the long run. Being told that something is amiss during the annual performance review can cause anger, frustration, and poorer performance down the road. Furthermore, other employees will notice the lack of any corrective action, and they are likely to conclude that the supervisor doesn't really care about quality performance. When this happens, they are likely to let their work performance slide as well. By the time this occurs, the supervisor will face a highly complex situation that will be difficult to resolve. Finally, service to users also suffers, and this outcome in turn can lead to a serious lack of user support. Ultimately, the goal is to be as consistent as possible. Standards should not shift from one week to the next or, worse, vary from one employee to another.

Some steps to follow when corrective action is necessary can help make the process as effective as possible. Start by stating the purpose of the session. Even if the situation has the potential for confrontation, speak calmly. Plan on letting the employee talk as much as possible. *Listening* is the key to having a successful session. Too often, there is a tendency to start planning one's response rather than listening and trying to hear what the person is saying. Silence, even a long one, although uncomfortable, serves a good purpose—it lets both parties think about what is taking place. Setting a time limit for the session can defeat the purpose of the session as it may take time to get to the central issue. The employee may be unhappy, upset, and possibly argumentative. Try to end the session on a positive note and, if appropriate, schedule a follow-up session. Sometimes it takes a series of sessions to reach a complete resolution. In any case, it is important to work with your HR department and ask questions throughout the process. This approach is particularly important the first time you are in a supervisory role and need to work through the various steps of the performance appraisal process, especially with corrective action.

Annual performance reviews are events that many people endure and almost never look forward to, much less enjoy. Neither the givers nor the recipients have great faith in

---

▌▌▌ CHECK THIS OUT

There are signs that the performance review may become less of an annual activity. An old article that spells out the pros and cons of even doing the annual appraisal process is "Another Look at Performance Appraisal in Libraries" by G. Edward Evans and Bendict Rugaas (*Journal of Library Administration* 3, no. 2 [1982]: 61–69). The article explored the differences between the U.S. practice of conducting the process and the Nordic countries' lack of such a process.

The signs of the changing views about performance appraisal appeared in Lori Goler, Janelle Gale, and Adam Grant's "Let's Not Kill Performance Evaluations Yet" (*Harvard Business Review* 94, no. 11 [2016]: 90–94). The article reviewed the changing nature of the performance appraisal.

the process or believe that much good will come out of the ordeal. Probably the biggest challenge, and where the difficulty lies, is in the dual nature of the review process. Although most HR departments attempt to keep the review to a single purpose, performance enhancement, the reality is that there is sometimes an unofficial but real link to salary increases. The dual purpose is well documented in the literature but was most clearly articulated by Saul Gellerman (1976). He made the point that essentially the single process attempts to handle behavioral issues (work performance) and administrative issues (compensation and occasional promotions). He further stated that the two purposes are almost diametrically opposed in character. Trying to accomplish both in a single process is a challenge. Almost every employee believes the salary aspect is the dominant factor.

In spite of one's best efforts, there will be times when disciplinary action must take place. Needless to say, such action occurs only after a number of counseling sessions have failed to resolve the issue. Progressive discipline is critical before any move is made toward termination. Giving an employee a chance through agreed-on goals for improvement, including a time line, demonstrates the supervisor's willingness to work with the employee.

The process consists of a series of steps that become progressively more strict and can end with termination. Although institutions employ their own stages of progressive discipline, the stages generally include the following: oral warning (one or more depending on the institution's procedure), counseling session (again one or more), formal reprimand (a copy of the reprimand is placed in the individual's personnel file), suspension with or without pay (the time frame varies), and, finally, if it comes to that point, termination. Most of the time, the process never reaches the termination stage because the parties resolve issues earlier. The sooner you address performance issues, the less likely you will have to go through the stress of a formal grievance procedure.

We hope this chapter has provided you with an overview of key staffing issues that will be valuable to you as an employee and essential to you as a supervisor at any level. Again, we can't stress enough how important it is to know your HR staff and to consult with them and your own supervisor on any issues you may have.

🔒 KEY POINTS TO REMEMBER

- The basics of library personnel management are the same for all types of libraries with only a few variations, most notably in faculty status.
- Academic library staff are expected to fulfill a variety of roles with a limited number of staff, and strong, generic skill sets are important to maintaining the greatest possible flexibility in job assignments.
- Faculty status for librarians is a long-standing issue and is a desired goal at many academic libraries; however, many do not have such status.
- Librarians at libraries with faculty status face the challenge of performing well as a librarian and demonstrating strong research and scholarship skills.
- Support staff members are increasingly being asked to assume duties that were previously librarians' responsibilities as workloads increase and economic times are difficult. Developing and maintaining solid working relationships between support and professional staff lead to quality service.
- Student workers constitute as much as one-fifth of the academic library workforce in most libraries. They may be a challenge to supervise and motivate at times, but they bring a number of benefits that far offset the challenges.

- Understanding the staffing process and working closely with your HR department will make your first supervisory experience less daunting.

REFERENCES

ACRL Association of College and Research Libraries. 2010. *A guideline for the appointment, promotion and tenure of academic librarians.* www.ala.org/acrl/standards/promotiontenure.

ACRL Association of College and Research Libraries. 2011. *Standards for faculty status for academic librarians.* www.ala.org/acrl/standards/standardsfaculty.

Annoyed Librarian (blog). 2016. "A tough lesson to learn." http://lj.libraryjournal.com/blogs/annoyedlibrarian/2016/05/19/a-tough-lesson-to-learn/.

Armstrong, Sharon, and Barbara Mitchell. 2008. *The essential HR handbook.* Franklin Lakes, NJ: Career Press.

Bagshaw, Maria C. 2006. Keep your student workers. *Library Journal* 131, no. 19: 44.

Bodemer, B. B. 2014. They CAN and they SHOULD: Undergraduates providing peer reference and instruction. *College and Research Libraries* 75, no. 2: 162–178.

Bolin, Mary K. 2008. Librarian status at U.S. research universities: Extending the typology. *Journal of Academic Librarianship* 34, no. 5: 416–424.

Bonfield, Brett. 2011. Is the United States training too many librarians or too few? (Part 1). *In the Library with the Lead Pipe.* www.inthelibrarywiththeleadpipe.org/2011/is-the-united-states-training-too-many-librarians-or-too-few-part-1/.

Bryan, Jacalyn E. 2007. The question of faculty status for academic librarians. *Library Review* 56, no. 9: 781–787.

Bureau of Labor Statistics, U.S. Department of Labor. 2016a. "Librarians." *Occupational outlook handbook, 2016–17 edition.* https://www.bls.gov/ooh/education-training-and-library/librarians.htm.

Bureau of Labor Statistics, U.S. Department of Labor. 2016b. "Library technicians and assistants." *Occupational outlook handbook, 2016–17 edition.* https://www.bls.gov/ooh/education-training-and-library/library-technicians-and-assistants.htm.

Buschman, John. 2016. Different, but more similar now: Faculty status. *Journal of Academic Librarianship* 42, no. 4: 476–477.

Christianson, Elin. 1973. *Paraprofessional and nonprofessional staff in special libraries.* New York: Special Libraries Association.

Dewey, Barbara I., and Loretta Parham. 2006. *Achieving diversity: A how-to-do-it manual for librarians.* New York: Neal-Schuman.

Evans, G. Edward, and Bendict Rugaas. 1982. Another look at performance appraisal in libraries. *Journal of Library Administration* 3, no. 2: 61–69.

Gardner, Marilyn. 2007. "New-job regrets: Should you go or stay?" *Arizona Daily Sun,* August 12, D1, D4.

Gellerman, Saul. 1976. *Management of human resources.* New York: Holt Rinehart.

Ghouse, Nikhat, and Jennifer Church-Duran. 2008. And mentoring for all: The KU Libraries' experience. *portal: Libraries and the Academy* 8, no. 4: 373–386.

Goler, Lori, Janelle Gale, and Adam Grant. 2016. Let's not kill performance evaluations yet. *Harvard Business Review* 94, no. 11: 90–94.

Hanna, Kathleen, Ann O'Bryan, and Kevin F. Petsche. 2008. Our excellent adventure: A somewhat irreverent look at how three tenure track librarians prepared their dossiers and lived to tell about it. *College and Research Libraries News* 69, no. 9: 554–556.

Hernon, Peter, Joan Giesecke, and Camila A. Alire. 2008. *Academic librarians as emotionally intelligent leaders.* Westport, CT: Libraries Unlimited.

Kaufman, Paula T. 1992. Professional diversity in libraries. *Library Trends* 41, no. 2: 214–230.

Lane, Liz A., and Barbara Stewart. 1998. The evolution of technical services to serve the digital library. In *Recreating the academic library: Breaking virtual ground,* edited by Cheryl LaGuardia, 151–168. New York: Neal-Schuman.

Mestre, Lori S., and Jessica M. LeCrone. 2015. Elevating the student assistant: An integrated development program for student library assistants. *College and Undergraduate Libraries* 22, no. 1: 1–20.

Murphy, Jo Ann. 2016. Enhancing the student experience: A case study of a library peer mentor program. *College and Undergraduate Libraries* 23, no. 2: 151–167.

Murray-Rust, Catherine. 2005. Should librarians get tenure? Yes, it's critical to their jobs. *Chronicle of Higher Education* (September 30): B10.

Neal, James G. 2005. Raised by wolves: The new generation of feral professionals in the academic library. Paper presented at the ACRL Twelfth National Conference, Minneapolis, Minnesota, April 7–10. www.ala.org/acrl/sites/ala.org.acrl/files/content/conferences/pdf/neal2-05.pdf.

O'Neill, Lindsay. 2015. "The making of an instructional design librarian." *ACRLog* (blog). http://acrlog.org/2015/01/20/the-making-of-an-instructional-design-librarian/.

Shank, John D. 2006. The blended librarian: A job announcement analysis of the newly emerging position of instructional design librarian. *College and Research Libraries* 67, no. 6: 515–524.

Singer, Paula, and Jeanne Goodrich. 2006. Retaining and motivating high-performing employees. *Public Libraries* 45, no. 1: 58–63.

Sweetman, Kimberly B. 2007. *Managing student assistants.* New York: Neal-Schuman.

Triumph, Therese F., and Penny M. Beile. 2015. The trending academic library job market: An analysis of library position announcements from 2011 with comparisons to 1996 and 1988. *College and Research Libraries* 76, no. 6: 716–739.

Walters, William H. 2016. Faculty status of librarians at U.S. research universities. *Journal of Academic Librarianship* 42, no. 2: 161–171.

CHAPTER 14

Career Development

No library or information science school can teach you everything you will need to know to have a successful career. Schools provide course work that creates a solid foundation for starting your career, but it would be unrealistic to expect the school to provide everything you will need to know for a long-term career. Career success is largely dependent on four elements: the quality of basic education, a commitment to mastering the basics, ongoing continuing education and networking, and, perhaps most important, a commitment to lifelong learning.

The immediate years after moving from being a student to being an employed academic librarian can have a considerable influence on your career development. Actions and decisions taken will shape a rewarding and enjoyable working life as well as affect your ability to meet challenges and opportunities that will arise in the future. Thinking about the future has never been as important as it is today. The possibilities are enormous—information skills are transferable skills, and the work is challenging and offers great job satisfaction. Just think about how much higher education and the work environment in general have changed for earlier generations who are still in the workforce.

An interesting perspective on just how quickly your work environment may change and require a host of different skills and knowledge appeared in an article by Mary Madden DeMajo (2008). She recorded the challenges she faced while transitioning from being a public library reference staff member at the New Orleans Public Library to joining the reference staff of Southeastern Louisiana University post-Katrina. Her opening sentence spelled out the issue: "Much has been written about teaching information literacy to library users and about in-service training for library professionals and paraprofessionals, but little has been said about mid-career librarians who must retrain when moving from an environment with only basic technology to one that's technology-rich" (p. 50). More to the point of this chapter, she took it upon herself to go beyond the basic assistance her new employer could reasonably provide, concluding, "I have developed a deep appreciation for both academic and public library environments and for the dynamic, knowledge-fostering components of each; and I continue to renew my commitment to my profession" (p. 53).

In a somewhat similar vein, Susan Kell (2007) wrote,

Deciding what we need to learn is also tough. While professional growth is the hallmark of every good librarian, deciding what is a critical skill to learn can be daunting. . . . Considering that I went back to school to earn a second master's degree in Instructional Technology and am continuing on with coursework toward a doctorate, it might seem that I've got a good handle on keeping current. But coursework is only part of professional growth. (p. 8)

Kell went on to discuss learning opportunities arising from work experience and unexpected events, commenting, "I believe that knowing your shortcomings can help you leverage them to your advantage" (p. 8).

We often start a career with high hopes, expectations, and aspirations. We can dream about where we might be in the years ahead and how our careers will develop. At one time, it was important to get a foot on the ladder of an academic library and move upward. With hard work, one might move up the ladder in a hierarchical structure and remain at that organization for an entire career. Today, people may change jobs more frequently, perhaps expecting to get to the top faster, and they may take career breaks along the way. Some organizations are now flatter and more agile and perhaps support teleworking. There are challenges but also more opportunities.

Planning your career and personal goals will assist you in having a rewarding and successful career. Such a plan needs flexibility, and it should be reviewed occasionally. What appears reasonable today may in a year or two be unrealistic as the field changes. Thinking about your long-term goals now will help as you seek your first academic librarian position.

FROM STUDENT TO ACADEMIC LIBRARIAN

Many students completing their MLS degree will have some work experience in a library as a result of internships, practicums, or part-time or full-time employment. Such work provides the opportunity to gain experience as well as some insight into what a librarian position might be like in a particular library environment.

Applying for your first full-time academic library position will likely be influenced by the size of your student loans, the state of the job market, and geographic or family considerations. Therefore, it may well be a compromise in terms of your ideal; however, if possible, seeking a position that fits into your long-term plan is desirable. It's a good idea to start watching vacancies well in advance of graduation to familiarize yourself with the kinds of jobs being advertised as well as the skills and experience expected for them. You can find vacancies in a number of sources. Discussion lists, websites, professional organizations, and paid advertisements in publications like the *Chronicle of Higher Education* are all good sources. As we will discuss later in this chapter, the academic librarian hiring process takes considerable time, so it's wise to review job advertisements early and start applying before graduation, if possible.

Marketing Yourself with a CV and Cover Letter

In applying for a position, you are essentially marketing yourself. The first step in promoting yourself starts with your curriculum vitae (CV). You likely have a résumé from

---

⟳ TRY THIS

Think about what you do best, what you like doing best, what you do not like doing or avoid doing, what you hope to accomplish from your working life, and what your long-term goals are. Use this review to start a first draft of what your career goals are. This is an important exercise to do throughout your career, and now is a great time to start.

 **CAREER TIP**

Professional Organizations and Conferences

We cannot emphasize enough how important it is to be involved in at least one professional organization during your career. Perhaps you will become involved in several organizations as your goals, interests, and job responsibilities change. We have both found this involvement to be a rewarding and essential aspect of our professional lives.

Most schools of library and information science offer student chapters of some of the major library professional organizations: American Library Association (ALA), Society of American Archivists (SAA), Special Libraries Association (SLA), and so on. Although being a student places numerous demands on your time, becoming involved in these organizations while still a student provides you with achievements for your vita, additional experience, and contacts, not to mention discounted membership fees for these organizations at the national level. Your membership also includes access to the organization's publications, discussion lists, and discounted rates to attend conferences. Many state organizations have similar arrangements for library school students that are particularly valuable if you are seeking employment within the state. In any case, all these opportunities will help you build your professional network.

Greenwell has pointed out many times how her work with professional organizations early in her career helped her develop skills that she later used in the workplace. As an entry-level librarian, you may not have the opportunity to run a meeting or prepare a budget or plan a program. As a volunteer in a professional organization, you can develop and practice these skills in a somewhat low-risk environment. Building these skills is helpful as you take on additional responsibilities at work and perhaps consider job changes. Professional organizations can be a good place to "test out" new skills and grow professionally.

Keep in mind that there are many different kinds of organizations and conferences that may be appropriate for your professional involvement. Certainly there is ALA and its many divisions of interest, such as the Association of College and Research Libraries (ACRL). Some organizations, like the Coalition for Networked Information (CNI), require institutional membership for involvement (CNI is one organization that publishes numerous free reports as well as twice-annual meeting proceedings). A substantial and growing number of SLA members are academic librarians, and the organization offers divisions in diverse subject disciplines (Biomedical and Life Sciences, Business and Finance, Environment and Resource Management, Social Sciences, Transportation, etc.) as well as a general academic division. The Medical Library Association (MLA) and the American Association of Law Libraries (AALL) are valuable for librarians serving those professional fields. Some subject-focused librarians may even become involved in their disciplinary conferences, such as the Modern Language Association (MLA) for literature librarians, the American Educational Research Association (AERA) for education librarians, or the American Society for Engineering Education (ASEE) for engineering librarians.

As for conferences, we previously mentioned the Academic Library Advancement and Development Network (ALADN) conference, which is focused primarily on fund-raising issues in academic libraries. Some other examples of topical conferences of

[CONTINUED ON FOLLOWING PAGE]

[CONTINUED]

interest include the Charleston Conference, which is focused on collections, the Library Assessment Conference, which is affiliated with the Association of Research Libraries, and LOEX, which specializes in information literacy instruction and assessment. Large vendors may offer conferences as well for their software products.

As your career progresses, you may develop an interest in international work, and there are many such opportunities for that as well. Greenwell has served on committees for both the European Conference on Information Literacy (ECIL) and the International Federation of Library Associations and Institutions (IFLA). Both have been very rewarding and inspiring experiences, and, again, these help substantially strengthen your professional network as well as your knowledge base.

previous jobs, and it's a good idea to create a CV as well. Academic institutions almost always prefer the CV when screening applicants for a job. The CV is essentially your academic and career history. By definition, a CV will be longer than a résumé, and that's normal. Later in your career, it can easily surpass ten or more pages. The basic difference between the CV and the résumé is that the CV is intended primarily for an academic audience and will include intellectual accomplishments such as presentations, publications, awards, and professional service in addition to your education and work history. As a recent student, you may not have any of those items to include, and that is common. If you have some achievements in these areas—perhaps you presented a poster session, published a book review, or chaired a student organization—by all means include them.

Because the CV is a record of your achievements, it's important to get into the habit of keeping it current, even if you aren't currently looking for a position. When you present or moderate a conference session, record it. When you serve on a committee, record it. This habit will help you throughout your entire career. The CV is the foundation for job applications, for volunteer work on professional and other committees, and for applications for further study such as grants and scholarships. The CV should be adapted for each of these situations by tailoring information that is relevant for the particular job opportunity, committee, or grant application. When your CV is current, this process will be much easier to do. Keep in mind that, if you are in a tenure-track position or a position with opportunities for promotion, your CV will be part of your dossier to be reviewed by your colleagues, so keeping it current is a good practice to help you be prepared for that experience.

As part of that promotion experience, you may be expected to prepare a CV in a specific format preferred by that institution. Until then, you can be a bit creative in how you organize and categorize your achievements. Common elements on a CV typically include the following:

- Name, address, phone number, e-mail address, and web presence, as applicable.
- Education history, including degrees and any distinctions or awards. If you had a particular focus of study for your MLS and it would be helpful for the particular position, you might state that (for example, "with an emphasis in cataloging and metadata creation" or "with a focus on instructional design theories and strategies"). Conversely, if your area of focus does not relate to the position, you may wish to exclude it.

- Special courses or workshops that developed additional skills, such as languages, computer programming, and so forth.
- Work experience to date. Include all that preceded your current course work—remember that any work with the public, such as at a grocery store, will show communication and team skills, so identify those. When you are writing about work experience, information about preparing résumés might be helpful because those materials usually offer suggestions for action words and specificity (for example, "Provided technical assistance and consultation to two hundred-plus library employees in twelve library locations and set goals and priorities for library technology needs" or "Planned, designed, taught, and assessed instruction sessions for three hundred-plus upper-level students majoring in English literature").
- Presentations and publications regardless of subject because these reflect communication skills. Early on in your career, you may combine these two categories but later separate them when you have more items to include. When you are invited to speak to a group, be sure to indicate that your presentation was "invited."
- Organizational memberships. This list primarily includes library professional organizations, but you might wish to include organizations from your undergraduate career as well as any relevant community organizations.
- Committee or leadership work. You might want to briefly explain these to show your level of involvement (for example, "Coordinated the division's awards program, wrote monthly welcome letters to new members, and managed membership statistics").
- Professional development. You should list any conferences you've attended, as well as workshops, webinars, or other types of continuing education.

💼 CAREER TIP

Marketing Yourself Online

You might wish to create your own website to share some information about your career goals, experience, and links to any relevant publications, presentations, online exhibits, websites, or other work. There are many such platforms to do this.

There are also platforms for professional networking. A popular one at the time of our writing is LinkedIn. Numerous higher education professionals and librarians are on LinkedIn. Greenwell used to trade business cards at professional conferences, but some years ago, she began connecting with new contacts via LinkedIn. A platform like LinkedIn offers more than individual profiles because the site includes numerous discussion groups as well as job postings.

A note about business cards: if you attend professional conferences or networking events as a student, create some business cards for yourself to exchange. You might be surprised at how much we still use them, even though we have phones, LinkedIn, and the like. You might include your name, contact information, where you are a student, your career goal, expected date of graduation, and so forth. This is a great thing to talk about with your mentor if you have one and with your advisor as well as your classmates.

Several years into your library career, you may choose to weed this list a bit, but for now, include anything that seems relevant.
- Awards and honors.

As your career develops, the document will include such items as attendance in professional development courses, papers presented at conferences, publications, professional awards, and, of course, positions held. If you read information about preparing résumés, you will be advised to keep it short, but you do not have that constraint with a CV. At the same time, you don't want to pad your CV with completely irrelevant items. A mentor can provide sound advice on what to include and not include. Throughout the job-seeking process, keep in mind that it's important to match your application documents to the needs of the position.

When applying for a position, you should tailor your CV to reflect the information most relevant to that position. Be honest, but don't embellish your talents. Have a mentor or friend proofread your application documents, and don't be afraid to ask a librarian or instructor you have worked with for advice. Most of the time in this profession, you will find colleagues who want to see new professionals succeed and are generous with their time.

Most employers require that you fill out the institution's online job application form. Some institutions use software to process applications before sending them to the search committee; the software may look for keywords and phrases relevant to the employer's interests, so be sure to read the job description carefully and make sure you address all the specific requirements in your cover letter and CV.

The cover letter is an essential part of the application process. The prospective employer will use it to evaluate your writing skills and to determine your level of interest and qualifications for the position. Writing good cover letters takes time, but good cover letters get attention over those that are clearly generic and used for all sorts of different positions.

 CAREER TIP

Publications and Presentations

Even while you are a student, it isn't too early to consider presenting or publishing. Some of the substantial papers you complete for your course work might be suitable for publication in a state library association journal or other local venue. If your work is outstanding, you might consider submitting it beyond those publications. Greenwell has advised students in the past to approach major papers and projects in a library and information science program with an intent to publish. Even if you choose not to publish them now, you may go back to the work in the future as a starting point for a different publication.

A relatively low-stress opportunity to present your work is a poster session. Many state library organizations (and an increasing number of national and international ones) welcome excellent student work. For a poster session, you will be asked to prepare a large-print poster describing your research in some detail. You will be expected to be available at designated times to answer questions about your research. In addition to gaining some presentation experience and something to include on your CV, you will help build your professional network and reputation.

Don't be concerned if your letter grows to two pages in length; this is not uncommon in academia. Reviewing the posted job description and outlining in your cover letter how you match the required and desired attributes of the position is key to getting an interview. It's important that a cover letter not simply be a list of your accomplishments; rather, you should match your skills and accomplishments to the specific responsibilities of the position. Showing some knowledge about the institution and what excites you about working there can be helpful as well. Your goal is to show that you can do the work they need done, and you can do it well and with enthusiasm.

The Search Committee

Search committees for vetting candidates are part of academic life for almost all higher education professional positions. Two of the most relevant reasons for such committees harken back to the concepts of shared governance and shared decision making that we discussed earlier in this book. Another reason is that staff in the hiring unit have a much sounder understanding of the position's expectations and organizational culture than the appointee would encounter with a person in the Human Resources Department. In chapter 13, we outlined the process for assessing staffing needs and described the elements of a proper job description. The following discussion assumes that such issues were addressed before posting the vacancy. Although you may not be part of a search committee right away in your first academic librarian position, understanding how search committees work is important in the job-seeking process.

Developing a clear committee charge and defining the time line of the search process are important starting points for a search committee. The committee reviews applications and then interviews a small pool of finalists. The interviews will likely happen in two rounds—phone or videoconference interviews with a larger pool and in-person interviews with a smaller pool. At some point, candidate references will be checked. The committee will then prepare a written assessment of each interviewee. The committee will pass these assessments to the person (director or dean, for example) who will make the decision regarding the individual to whom an offer will be made.

The academic hiring process tends to be long and expensive in terms of time and money. Almost all searches move slowly. From the time a position becomes vacant until there is someone again performing the work, a year can easily elapse for a beginning librarian position and longer for a senior library administrator job. If you are interested in applying for academic jobs, it's a good idea to start while still in school because of the lengthy academic hiring process. A variety of factors contribute to the length of the search process:

- A case may need to be made to fill the position because of economic constraints.
- Even in strong financial times, it is good management to consider whether the position is needed with the library's current and future priorities in mind.
- With any job, the specific position responsibilities need to be outlined and described for advertising the position.
- The institution may require a minimum amount of time that the position must be open for applications, and the search committee may choose to extend that time.

- The search committee needs to consider where to advertise the position and for how long. In addition, meeting publication deadlines and allowing a reasonable time for responses to the advertisement will add yet more time.
- Planning search committee meetings can be challenging because of other scheduling issues.
- Scheduling and planning each interview require a fair amount of logistical work that can lengthen the entire process. Prospective candidates will need to meet with multiple groups of people: the search committee, the department, the potential supervisor, the dean or director, the promotion and tenure committee (if applicable), and other interested groups. Organizing all of those meetings with busy people takes time.

We should mention one more time factor that can slow down the process. Sometimes the search committee will make an offer to the top candidate only to learn that the candidate has accepted a position elsewhere or rejects the offer for some reason. Sometimes even the second choice is unavailable. There are several options for the committee: go back to the list of preferable candidates, go back to the overall pool to see if there may be one or two applicants the committee might also interview, or reopen the search. Committee members as well as campus administrators will have strong views about these options. Whatever the decision, the process will get just a little or substantially longer.

Given all this, is it any wonder why the academic hiring process is so unbearably slow? Many first-time job seekers have no idea why things move so slowly and wonder if they should contact the library. Keeping in mind the discussion of the usual time frame for the process may provide some guidance for whether this is a good idea.

Selecting the Pool

Most recruiting efforts usually generate a larger pool of applicants than is feasible to interview. The most common place to begin the sorting process is the cover letter and vita. As we mentioned, how carefully you prepare these documents often decides your chances of getting interviewed.

Some of the factors the committee looks for are whether the person has the required skills, how carefully the material is presented, and whether the person supplied all the required information. Looking at these basic issues will reduce the pool by a substantial number. A further reduction, if necessary, can result from reviewing how many of the desirable skills each applicant possesses. Phone or video interviews can further narrow the pool. Having a final interview pool of three to six people usually produces a candidate suitable for the position. Because the selection process involves a substantial amount of subjectivity, developing sound job success criteria and job specifications will assist in keeping the process as objective as possible.

The Interview

Being interviewed for a position is always somewhat stressful, regardless of how senior a person may be in terms of her career. Being prepared will help reduce the stress. For example, doing some research about the institution, the library, and the surrounding community will give you some background information and a basis for developing questions you can ask when you go to the interview.

Thinking about how to best sell yourself to the prospective employer can also help reduce stress. Draw up a list of potential questions that may be asked and decide how you will answer them. More institutions are starting to provide one question in advance, giving you the opportunity to prepare an answer in depth, but don't expect that approach. The following are some frequently asked questions, regardless of the position:

- What interests you in this position?
- What are some skills you would bring to this job?
- Have you performed the kind of work described in this position before? If so, when, and do you see any significant differences between then and now?
- How do you define service?
- What do you consider to be your strengths?
- What are your weaknesses?
- What do you think your current supervisor would say are your strengths and weaknesses?
- Tell us about a job you've had that you did not like and what it was about that job that caused the dislike.
- Tell us about the job you liked best and why.
- What are your current career plans? Do you see them changing in the next three to five years?

💼 CAREER TIP

"Interviewing" Your Prospective Employer

Although you may not be in a position to be choosy, ideally part of the interview process is about you deciding whether the potential position and employer are a good fit for you. Part of this process is learning more about the job, the institution, your potential coworkers, and even the community itself.

Later in this chapter, we'll include some questions you might ask. In addition to doing your research before the interview and talking with people on campus, you can pick up a lot by observing, though it can be challenging to observe while you're "on" for an interview. As best you can, consider the following:

- How busy is the library?
- Do the desk staff you observe seem friendly, approachable, and happy to be there?
- How new and maintained are the furnishings? How clean is the library?
- Even if the library building is in need of refurbishing, are the computers fairly new?
- What does the rest of the campus look like? How many construction or renovation projects are currently under way?

If your interview schedule allows you to spend some time observing the campus and community, that experience will help you get a sense of the culture and the challenges (and opportunities!) you might have in your potential new position.

Often the interview will begin with a statement such as "tell us something about yourself." One reason for starting this way is that everyone knows interviews are stressful, and starting with something the candidate knows best will help relieve some of the tension. Decide what is and is not appropriate to say. Sometimes minds go blank at the start of an interview, and it is easy to say the first thing that springs to mind. Do your homework about the questions that an employer shouldn't ask and have polite ways to deflect them. Carrying out a mock interview with someone who knows you well and can offer constructive criticism to help adjust your presentation can also ease pre-interview stress.

We devote some space to the interview process because it will come into play not only when applying for a position but also when serving on a search committee. Both instances require an understanding of the process as well as practice to become effective as interviewee or interviewer. What follows applies to both sides of the interview table.

A sound interview process has six important elements. First, there is the need to plan the process. Beyond the obvious, such as time and place, some of the key planning issues are the length of the interview, whom to involve in the interview, the questions to ask, what kinds of tours should be given, and how much time should be devoted to answering candidate questions. As a candidate, you should also plan your questions about the position and institution.

The second element, and perhaps the most critical in a legal sense, is a careful review of the interview questions for their compliance with nondiscrimination laws. This is an area in which HR staff will be of great assistance. You want to have consistency and comparability of information about each candidate. Maintaining consistency in the questions and in the structure of the entire process for all the candidates is critical when it comes time to assess each one and make a final recommendation. Questions must be job related. Asking a few open-ended questions gives candidates an opportunity to respond more fully and demonstrate some of their skills. Some seemingly innocent questions can be problematic, which is all the more reason to work with HR about what is appropriate.

What should you do if you are asked inappropriate questions, and is this likely to happen? Gardner (2007) indicates that it happens more often than you'd expect, especially with medium-sized and small organizations, in part because people are not aware that they are doing anything wrong. In her article she quoted John Petrella, an employment lawyer: "It happens all the time. . . . It's really easy for employers to get in trouble. It's really easy to run afoul of the anti-discrimination laws" (p. D1). The article goes on to address what to do when asked improper questions and offers approaches for you to think about before responding to such questions. First, ask yourself and perhaps the interviewer, "Is this question related to the position I'm applying for?" Remember, the question could be appropriate if it is clearly job related. At the same time, you might want to consider, "Do I really want to work for an organization that asks such questions?" You do have the choice of not answering the question, knowing it might cause you not to get an offer. You can, of course, answer the question and then inquire about the relevance of the question to the position. As an interviewee, you face a reasonable chance of having to deal with this issue at some point in your career. As an interviewer, don't ask inappropriate questions.

The third element is a segment of time in which to give the candidate a clear sense of what the vacant position actually entails as well as an overview of the library's operation and mission. Taking some time to explain the relationship of the library to the campus helps candidates make an informed decision should an offer be made. It is also the time for the candidate to ask questions of the search committee.

The fourth element in the process is the impact of the candidate and the interviewer on each other. Creating a relaxed and friendly atmosphere at the outset helps candidates become less nervous and thus more effective during the formal interview. Tone of voice, eye contact, posture, and gestures influence both parties.

Related to impact is how the interviewer responds to the applicant, which is the fifth element of a sound interview process. Interviewers must be careful to control any nonverbal behavior that may encourage or discourage an applicant in an inappropriate way. For example, not showing an interest in what the candidate is saying will discourage the person from expanding on his thoughts, and this response may well carry over to the remainder of the interview. Anyone with extensive interviewing experience understands just how difficult controlling those behaviors can be at times.

The final element is fair and equitable assessment of the interview data for all the interviewees. Some of the following issues can cause unfair processing:

- Having a preconceived sense of the "right" person for the position
- Using different weights for various attributes by different members of a search committee
- Overusing visual clues about the candidate that are not job related
- Not recognizing "contrast effects"—that is, when a strong candidate follows a very weak candidate, the contrast makes the stronger applicant look even stronger than she may be

 CAREER TIP

Possible Interview Questions to Ask

When you have the opportunity to ask questions, you definitely want to have a number of questions prepared. Ideally you should have a few different questions for each group and individual on your schedule, though some questions are worth asking everyone to get different perspectives. Your questions might pertain to specific job responsibilities, goals for the position, strategic directions for the library and campus, and so forth. Doing your research about the institution and library will help you in framing these questions.

Library science students have often asked Greenwell how they might learn more about the organizational culture of an institution during an interview. This is a challenge, as we have mentioned. Questions like the following might help. These questions might be best asked at a social event or on a tour when you have an opportunity to develop one-on-one rapport with a potential colleague. Some may also work well with a group to encourage participation as well as get further insight about the institution.

- What do you like most about your job?
- What are people talking about most on campus right now?
- What is the perception of the library on campus?
- What do you see as the top priorities for someone in this position? What would the successful candidate need to focus on first?
- What do you value most about the library?
- What have you been working on in the last month?

At the end of a group interview meeting, a good question to ask might be, "What do you like most about [the city]? What should I do while I'm in town?" That's a fun question, and it may also give you some insight about your potential coworkers and the community itself.

- Take some time to research the library and its parent organization ahead of time. Their websites can tell you a great deal about them. Earlier in this book, we discussed using NCES and other tools to find data about the institution and its library.
- Generate a few questions about the library based on your research and your own interests. For suggestions see the sidebar "Career Tip: Possible Interview Questions to Ask."
- If you did not receive a full position description, ask for one as well as for any other information that might be pertinent to the position.
- Spend some time thinking about the answers you might give to questions that are likely to be part of the interview. We listed several of these earlier in the chapter.
- Be certain to know the interviewer's name and its correct pronunciation. It's a good idea to do some research on all the search committee members, if possible. At least knowing their names and position titles is helpful.
- Remember that your body language also reflects your interest and attentiveness.
- Taking time to think before answering complex questions is appropriate— thinking before speaking is always a good idea.
- If you are asked a multipart question, be sure to cover all the parts—asking for clarification or for repetition of a part of such questions is appropriate.
- Asking how any personal or potentially illegal question relates to job performance is appropriate; however, be sure to ask in a nonconfrontational manner because the question may be job related.
- Thank the interviewer(s) for the opportunity to interview for the position.
- Asking about the anticipated time frame for deciding on who will be hired is appropriate.
- To learn from each interview experience, jot down a few post-interview notes about some of the high and low points of the interview.

Even if you decide during the interview process that this is not the position for you, send a follow-up thank-you note to the chair of the search committee, the position supervisor, or the head of human resources (whichever is most appropriate), thanking the person for his time and for giving you an opportunity to meet with him.

ADJUSTING TO THE POSITION

Moving into your first professional position is not easy. Likely you will have great enthusiasm and desire to demonstrate your skills and knowledge. Such zeal is important, but it can generate problems. Yes, everyone wants a team member who is keen, talented, and committed, but sometimes new appointees go over the top in attempting to prove themselves. It is best to remember that there are usually good reasons why the procedures are the way they are, so look and listen and wait a bit before offering your advice as a newcomer. Likely there are newer and better ways to carry out a task—the new graduate should be at the cutting edge of developments—but understand the reasons why things are being done in a certain way before proposing a change.

One challenge of any new job is learning the organization's culture and politics. There will be an organizational chart that shows formal relationships, but the way things are done may be rather different than what the official structure suggests. It takes time to gain a clear understanding of the culture; ignoring the culture can be one of the factors that leads to serious job dissatisfaction.

Although internships and part-time employment provide useful insights into what the field is like, they cannot replicate full-time, day-in and day-out work. Everyone experiences some degree of difference between hopes and reality when starting a new job. First-time librarians experience a much higher difference than do librarians who have several years of experience.

Joanne Oud (2008) wrote about the transition from student to academic librarian. The first year is critical in career planning. A good or great experience will probably lead to a long-term successful career. A very negative experience could lead to a decision to leave the field. Part of what creates this experience is the individual's initial expectations. Oud surveyed 111 new librarians who began work in the spring of 2004, and she received ninety-seven useable responses. Her major themes regarding the individuals' expectations versus reality are worth listing. She drew nine themes from the respondents' answers to an open-ended question about the differences between their expectations and the work:

- More flexibility/independence
- Greater variety of job responsibilities/tasks
- Bureaucracy, slow pace of change
- Negative workplace environment (politics, not collegial)
- Collegial workplace

💼 CAREER TIP

Interview Presentation

In addition to meeting with the usual groups of people (the search committee, the department, your potential supervisor, the dean or director, the promotion and tenure committee if applicable, and other interested groups), you will likely be expected to give a presentation during your on-campus interview. This presentation will be open to library personnel and maybe even to other constituents on campus (for example, if you are interviewing for an education librarian position, faculty from the Education Department will probably be invited).

All candidates will be given a topic for the presentation that will often be extremely broad ("the future of reference services in research libraries," for example) as well as an allotted time for the presentation followed by questions from the audience. Those interviewing you want to see how informed you are about the topic as well as how you manage what can be a fairly stressful public speaking engagement. At the presentation, attendees will have a chance to ask you questions. You'll also have a chance to ask questions.

We can assure you this experience isn't as daunting as it seems as long as you are prepared. As we mentioned with anticipating and preparing for possible interview questions, it's important to practice, ideally with a mentor or friend. Do your research, organize your presentation well, and practice your delivery until you feel comfortable. Think about what questions the audience might ask you, and have some questions ready for the audience.

- Busier/heavier workload
- Faculty and student attitudes to the library
- Difficult school-to-work transition
- Lack of training and time to learn (p. 256)

Oud also asked about the aspects of the job that were most challenging. Not too surprisingly the most difficult aspects were "getting things done," when and how to take the initiative, and learning the organizational culture. Also not surprising was that new librarians with the highest degree of difference between expectations and reality had the lowest job satisfaction.

In her conclusions, Oud (2008) wrote, "First, the results confirmed that most new academic librarians would benefit from more assistance in their adjustment to their new workplace. . . . [I]n many academic libraries the new librarian is left to learn much of the job informally or on his or her own initiative" (p. 263). She went on to suggest, "Given the difficulties reported by new librarians with learning the cultural aspects of their new jobs and workplaces, more effort should be made to develop ways to assist new employees in this critical area of their transition process" (p. 264).

STARTING YOUR CAREER DEVELOPMENT PLAN

After the first several months in your new position, it's a good time to assess your long-term career plans that you first started thinking about while in school. We hope you have found time to read or at least regularly skim some professional journals and keep current with events in higher education. We cannot emphasize enough how valuable it is to regularly scan the *Chronicle of Higher Education*. This only takes a few minutes, and such reading helps you keep current in academic librarianship as well as the broader environment, both of which will be beneficial when it is time to take the next career step. We mentioned earlier how important it is to be involved in professional organizations, and, if you aren't already, this is a good time to start.

👥 FROM THE AUTHORS

Greenwell thinks that looking at the *Chronicle of Higher Education* (www.chronicle.com) every day is such an important habit that she makes it part of the curriculum for her academic libraries course. Students in the class work in groups each week to find a timely article and develop questions concerning that article. Questions might include how the particular topic might affect student graduation rates or faculty workload, or how the library might play a role. Students often comment that this is one of their favorite parts of the course because it helps them see how important it is to pay attention to broader higher education issues and how those need to be on the radar of a good academic librarian. Although some articles require a premium subscription, a fair number are available for free. Another good source of higher education reporting is *Inside Higher Ed* (www.insidehighered.com), and that content is freely available. This is a good habit for you to start now. Check it out!

👥 FROM THE AUTHORS

Both of us have doctoral degrees and have found them to be intellectually satisfying, useful if not essential in securing one or more of our professional positions, and, above all, very useful in working with teaching faculty and campus administrators. Do we believe such degrees are essential for a successful career as an academic librarian? Not at all. Do we believe they can be beneficial to your career? Absolutely.

Mentors

Mentors and role models are an element in developing your career. A mentor can be an asset at any stage in a career, providing advice when requested. A key factor in having a mentor is that the mentor needs to be able to understand the mentee and her goals. A mentor can offer realistic advice and provide a second opinion on a proposed course of action but cannot make decisions on behalf of the person mentored. A mentor is an informed sounding board, serving in the role of advisor, counselor, friend, and supporter. In turn, the person being mentored needs to develop listening skills and to be able to learn from the experience of others, evaluate the offered advice, and understand as well as accept constructive criticism.

Mentors need to be chosen with care, having demonstrated a rapport with you and an interest in you as a new professional. A mentor could be a member of the library school faculty or an experienced practitioner. Some libraries as well as many library professional organizations offer formal mentor match programs, which may be a good way to get started, though many of the most effective mentoring experiences arise almost without either party thinking the relationship is a mentoring one—it just happens. In making a choice, it is important that you respect the would-be mentor, that the two of you have good rapport, and that you both share a level of trust that enables advice to be offered and received with a generous spirit.

Beyond developing a mentoring relationship informally, there are other options for finding a mentor. As we mentioned earlier, some libraries and professional associations have established committees that match people willing to mentor with those seeking a mentor. This approach provides an opportunity to be matched with someone in a different type of library, geographic region, and so on. Some academic libraries have their own internal mentoring program, which could be particularly helpful when navigating promotion and tenure. In a study of mentoring programs for novice tenure-track librarians, Mandi Goodsett and Andrew Walsh (2015) pointed out other benefits as well: "Program benefits also included less tangible effects such as increased understanding of institutional culture and improved communication and time management skills (p. 927)."

Mentors may be asked to provide references and comment on strengths and perhaps weaknesses. They should be able to offer advice about a position that is under consideration

💡 SOMETHING TO PONDER

Do you have a mentor? List the attributes that you think would be helpful for a mentor to have.

and should have a view about its suitability. The mentor's networks may yield advance notice of a post not yet advertised.

As you advance in your professional career, you might consider becoming a mentor yourself. It is a valuable experience because you contribute to the profession and will likely learn something new yourself. Marta Lee (2009) described it well:

> Library schools do not teach everything individuals need to know to be a good librarian; this knowledge often comes from on-the-job experience. Mentoring newly graduated librarians in the workplace is a way to , , , gain valuable knowledge and to become a better librarian. (p. 31)

Self-Assessment of Knowledge and Skills

Conducting a self-assessment is not easy, and a mentor should be able to provide input. Consider the following points:

- Degrees held
- Short courses attended
- Any formal or informal study in progress
- Involvement in professional activities and committee work within the institution, a professional organization, or both
- Work experience
- Level of job satisfaction
- Preferred career direction
- Preferred sector and specialization
- Areas that would not be welcomed at this stage
- Personal strengths—what you do well
- Personal weaknesses—what you do not do well
- Level of commitment to working in the field—is the current institution a long-term career goal or a short-term goal?
- Are there other factors that are important to you? Are there other activities outside work that are important and that influence your professional growth?

The last two factors are particularly important. Long-term intention to stay in the field may not be part of your career development; however, information skills are transferable. Taking personal circumstances into account will result in better decisions. Carrying out a regular self-assessment assists career development at any point in your working life. A preferred move may require the acquisition of new skills or the honing of some that have been dormant. Lifelong learning and the acquisition of new skills are essential for career development. Thus, education and training needs change over time. Some individuals choose the option of earning an additional master's degree in the discipline of their undergraduate degree or a new area of interest. Then there may be a shift to doctoral study to pursue research in a professional subject or academic discipline.

One long-standing question in academic librarianship concerns additional advanced degrees: are they nice or necessary? Clearly the issue is a significant factor in terms of career development. In spite of a great many informal discussions among academic librarians, there has not been very much research on the value of having advanced degrees beyond the MLS. An older article by Mary Grosch and Terry Weech (1991) reported on a study of perceptions of the value of such degrees, and not much has been published in this area recently. Occasionally you see ads that list a second advanced degree as desirable, though you will see that more often in ads for dean or director. Some academic institutions, in an effort to encourage professional growth, will provide an increase in salary when an individual completes another advanced degree.

Probably one of the common benefits of such degrees, from a workplace perspective, is enhanced credibility with teaching faculty outside the library. Having the degree indicates that you have successfully been through and understand the scholarly process. In Gilman and Lindquist's study (2010), librarians with a non-LIS doctorate cited these as the greatest

 CAREER TIP

Professional Involvement and Work-Life Balance

Greenwell has been asked by students and colleagues how she managed to be involved in so many professional activities early in her career. One thing that worked well for her was to stick to a maximum number of professional activities per year. This approach was made much easier, though, because she had flexible supervisors while she was working toward tenure. At the time, her "formula" for professional involvement included one library committee, one university committee, and one state or national committee or board. She also kept in reserve at least one or two more time slots for something amazing that might come along, such as the first time she was asked to serve on a national committee. She felt like setting some limits was good, and, at the same time, she left herself with some flexibility for new opportunities. Although this plan would not work well for everyone, it worked well for her at the beginning of her career.

Along those lines, Greenwell has noticed that there are some librarians who can't seem to say no to any professional opportunity (whether it is serving on a committee, serving on a board, publishing an article, giving a presentation, etc.). Granted, sometimes you may not be in a position to say no, but to some extent, we have choices about where to spend our time professionally. Make choices and set priorities where you can, and you will do better work as a result. Greenwell has seen friends and colleagues not turn down a single professional opportunity, and she has watched them (and their work) suffer for it. At a certain point, you just cannot do all those professional activities along with your job, not to mention having any sort of personal life. We can't emphasize enough how important it is to have a comfortable work-life balance.

Greenwell believes that librarians who do not have any sort of professional plan tend to get scattered all over the place and often end up not doing anything well. Her advice is to have a plan. Think about where you want to go in your career. If writing interests you, think about possible writing projects or opportunities to work with colleagues who are good writers to help you learn more about the process. If you are interested in national board work, start with a small project in the organization, do an outstanding job, and you will probably be asked to do more. Try to fit what you're doing professionally into your own goals as much as you can, and try not to take on too much, especially at the beginning of your career.

advantages to having a doctorate: credibility with the teaching faculty, subject expertise, ability to relate to academic users, and in-depth understanding of the research process. Interestingly, the disadvantages those librarians cited most frequently were perceptions from library colleagues, tension between being both a librarian and a researcher, undervalued subject expertise, and less than satisfactory compensation.

CHANGING VIEWS OF A CAREER

In the past, most people's view of a career was probably one of steady progression from the bottom to the top of an organizational structure. Today's careers are more flexible, but the factors that contribute to the achievement of progress remain the same: having the appropriate qualifications, experience, attitude, and aptitude. Setting career goals helps sharpen the awareness of specific needs and how they can be met.

One way to obtain different kinds of experience is to work from home as a freelancer. Some examples of these experiences include writing, handling research requests, providing marketing and social media support, creating websites and instructional materials, editing, and so forth. Some academic librarians teach online in a library and information science program on an adjunct basis. These opportunities can provide a wider variety of experience as well as more income, though working in this way requires good organization and communication skills and a strong service ethic.

In moving higher up the salary ladder, many academic librarians face the frustration of having to spend a greater percentage of time on managing. Less time is devoted to using their professional knowledge and skills. The balance between the two is often a significant factor in considering whether to apply for a position with a higher salary. Just how much management will it entail? For some people the management aspects of the workplace are not all that attractive, yet they know higher salaries are linked (to varying degrees) to how much management is involved in a position. Giving serious thought to this issue early in your career and making some personal decisions may well save some heartache, stress, and frustration down the road. A final point to make about career goals is that they will change over time. Changes take place in your personal life and the profession, but having goals and knowing your personal values will help you make better decisions when considering a change of post.

Career Breaks

Career breaks benefit both the employee and the employer. Academic librarians may have two options for a break from the daily workplace. Most with faculty status have an opportunity to apply for a sabbatical. The other method is to secure an unpaid leave. The person who enjoys a break comes back refreshed and reinvigorated. Another benefit is that another member of the staff can be offered the opportunity to demonstrate his skills temporarily in a different post.

For the person considering a break either as an unpaid leave or a sabbatical, there is a range of opportunities. Developmental internships or fellowships, such as those organized by the Association of Research Libraries, may be available. Librarians who are eligible for a sabbatical must have a research project to pursue during their time away from the library. Such projects usually must have some linkage or relationship to the individual's present or future position. The project may even be an opportunity to test the waters in a new area of interest.

There may be opportunities to travel abroad at any stage in a career. Travel scholarships for short periods are offered by a number of organizations. Exchanges with professionals in a number of countries around the world can be set up with facilitators through registers that list people seeking an exchange in many types of services. Voluntary service overseas was, at one time, the province of the new graduate, but now as more people take early retirement or a career break, their skills and experience can be of value in other countries.

Breaks for family responsibilities, such as maternity or paternity leave, are part of established employment policies and practices. These breaks help parents enjoy and more fully participate in the early stages of their child's life. A survey about parenthood and professorship conducted by Graves, Xiong, and Park (2008) among tenured and tenure-track librarians showed that the promotion and tenure process does play a role in decisions regarding parenthood. The researchers concluded, in part, "The study has implications for academic libraries and the larger university audience. The message is clear that there is still a sense of discrepancy between parenthood and professor-hood in librarianship" (p. 209).

Work-Life

The management literature demonstrates a continuing concern regarding the pressures being placed on managers and their staffs as organizations strive to cut operating costs. Much has been written about the negative effects of stress that can affect anyone within an organization, regardless of age, gender, or level. Progressing in a career can increase the susceptibility to stress. Learning a new job can mean taking work home and acquiring new knowledge, qualifications, or skills. Being online and always available adds to the pressures of daily life, making it hard to break away from work and creating the feeling of always needing to catch up. In its most serious manifestations, stress can lead to excessive eating, drinking, or smoking. Stress can damage physical and psychological health and reduce the effectiveness of a person's performance, which, in turn, impacts the work of her colleagues. Recognizing the symptoms may be unpalatable to the employee and difficult for the employer. Many universities provide in-house counseling that may be of help.

MOVING FORWARD

Part of moving forward is making your talents known. Success is easier to achieve if others know about you, both within and outside the institution in which you are working. Looking for ways to do your job more effectively and presenting them to a supervisor—at the right time and in the right way—will show initiative, particularly if the thoughts have been developed as part of a team. Becoming known in the profession can come from joining committees, attending meetings, writing in the professional literature, and making thoughtful contributions at conferences.

Membership in a professional association pays dividends. Its journal, publications, and website keep practitioners in touch with news and developments. Selecting appropriate discussion lists and contributing to discussions stimulate professional thinking and allow an exchange of viewpoints and experiences. Meetings provide an opportunity to exchange ideas and make yourself known outside your library. Conferences provide exposure to a wide range of professional activities. Those who travel to the annual professional conference find that it is an exhilarating potpourri of meetings, exhibitors, and enthusiastic librarians and prospective employers.

Keeping in touch with change means that you will need to consult a range of sources regularly. Reading a variety of journals in the profession is essential. Becoming a member of a professional committee develops the essential political skills needed in career development. Giving papers and talks enhances communication skills. Involvement in the activities of international associations extends your network and provides insight into professional practices overseas. No single country has a monopoly on good practice. And for the librarian who cannot travel and is geographically isolated, there are many ways to participate online without leaving your desk.

The direction a career may take will, to an extent, be conditioned by factors outside the control of the individual and will include economic, political, social, and technological change and the state of the labor market. But there is a range of opportunities, and individuals have choices in selecting the direction in which they would prefer to move. Career development depends on staying well informed. We hope that this book has informed you and that it has furthered your desire to refine your career goals and to keep current and stay active within this wonderful profession.

❶ KEY POINTS TO REMEMBER

- Know yourself, both your strengths and weaknesses.
- Have high standards and ethics, both personal and professional, and demonstrate them in your daily work.
- Demonstrate commitment to whatever job you have.
- Cultivate clear thinking and maintain an objective viewpoint.
- Be reliable.
- Be adaptable.
- Cultivate and never lose your sense of humor.
- Understand the way others think.
- Show a concern for others in your professional and personal life.
- Keep at the cutting edge of change.
- Develop good communication and influencing skills.
- Acquire political skills.
- Extend managerial knowledge and know what is best practice in management thinking.
- Ensure that you are working effectively as a member of a team at all stages in your career.
- Know how to make decisions and change them if the situation demands.
- Delegate.
- Maintain control over your own time.
- Recognize mistakes that you have made and learn from them.
- Understand that career development requires an investment of time and money.
- Enjoy the job you are doing—if you don't enjoy the one you are in, find another.
- Believe in yourself.

REFERENCES

DeMajo, Mary Madden. 2008. It's never too late to retool. *American Libraries* 39, no. 10: 50–53.

Gardner, Marilyn. 2007. "Job interviewers: What can they legally ask?" *Arizona Daily Sun,* July 29, D1, D4.

Gilman, Todd, and Thea Lindquist. 2010. Academic/research librarians with subject doctorates: Experiences and perceptions, 1965–2006. *portal: Libraries and the Academy* 10, no. 4. https://doi.org/10.1353/pla.2010.0007.

Goodsett, Mandi, and Andrew Walsh. 2015. Building a strong foundation: Mentoring programs for novice tenure-track librarians in academic libraries. *College and Research Libraries* 76, no. 7: 914–933.

Graves, Stephanie J., Jian Anna Xiong, and Ji-Hye Park. 2008. Parenthood, professorship, and librarianship: Are they mutually exclusive? *Journal of Academic Librarianship* 34, no. 3: 202–210.

Grosch, Mary, and Terry L. Weech. 1991. Perceived value of advanced subject degrees by librarians who hold such degrees. *Library and Information Science Research* 13, no. 2: 173–199.

Kell, Susan E. 2007. Technically speaking: Professional growth is essential for librarians. *Learning Media* 35, no. 2: 8–10.

Lee, Marta. 2009. Growing librarians: Mentorship in an academic library. *Library Leadership and Management* 23, no. 1: 31–37.

Oud, Joanne. 2008. Adjusting to the workplace: Transitions faced by new academic librarians. *College and Research Libraries* 69, no. 3: 252–266.

ABOUT THE AUTHORS

G. Edward Evans, PhD, is a semi-retired, award-winning author and Fulbright Scholar. He holds several graduate degrees in anthropology and library and information science (LIS). Throughout his career, he has been an administrator, researcher, teacher, and writer. As a researcher, he has published in both anthropology and librarianship. He held a Fulbright Fellowship in librarianship as well as a National Science Foundation Fellowship in archaeology. His teaching experience has also been in both fields in the United States and the Nordic countries. Of note, he completed the faculty ladder (assistant to full professor) while teaching at the Graduate School of Librarianship and Information Science at the University of California, Los Angeles. Evans has extensive administrative experience in private academic libraries such as Harvard University and Loyola Marymount University. He retired from full-time work as associate academic vice president for libraries and information resources at Loyola Marymount University. Evans spends his semi-retirement years volunteering at the Museum of Northern Arizona, serving on the Foundation board for the Flagstaff City–Coconino County Library System, and doing professional writing.

Stacey Greenwell, EdD, has served the University of Kentucky Libraries since 2001 in several roles, including associate dean for academic affairs and research, head of the Information Commons, and head of Desktop Support. Recently she began working with the information literacy and assessment department to provide instructional design support, teach, and work on research projects. Dr. Greenwell is a Fellow of the Special Libraries Association and has held numerous leadership roles in the organization including chair of the Information Technology Division and founding chair of the Academic Division. She is a standing committee member for the Education and Training Section of the International Federation of Library Associations and Institutions (IFLA) and is a standing member of the Programme Committee for the European Conference on Information Literacy (ECIL). She is a frequent conference presenter and has taught an academic libraries course for the iSchools at Syracuse University and the University of Kentucky.

ABOUT THE COAUTHOR
OF THE FIRST EDITION

Dr. Camila A. Alire is dean emerita at the University of New Mexico and Colorado State University. Alire received her doctorate in higher education administration from the University of Northern Colorado and her MLS from the University of Denver. She is past president of the American Library Association and ALA/APA (2009–2010), past president (2005–2006) of the Association of College and Research Libraries (ACRL), and past president of REFORMA (the National Association to Promote Library and Information Services to the Spanish Speaking).

ABOUT THE
ADVISORY BOARD

Jim DelRosso is the digital projects coordinator for Cornell University's Hospitality, Labor, and Management Library. He manages two open access digital repositories: DigitalCommons@ILR, which supports the New York State School of Industrial and Labor Relations, and the Scholarly Commons, which supports the School of Hotel Administration. Jim also serves as a scholarly communication, research, and instruction support librarian. He has presented and written on topics related to open access, scholarly communication, and community building and has served on the boards of the Upstate New York Chapter and the Academic Division of the Special Libraries Association.

Catherine Lavallée-Welch has been the director of the Murphy Library at the University of Wisconsin–La Crosse since May 2013. She has experience as an information professional and librarian in the nonprofit, co-op, and higher education sectors in Canada, Europe, and the United States. She has been active in the Special Libraries Association (SLA) since 2000. She's held several offices over the years in SLA and in various state library organizations.

Leslie J. Reynolds is the interim dean of libraries at the University of Colorado Boulder. Her career includes six years as a subject specialist and seventeen years in research library management and administration. She holds baccalaureate and graduate degrees from Drake University and the University of Illinois at Urbana-Champaign. Her research interests involve outreach to library users, library instruction, and management and leadership in libraries.

INDEX

References to notes are indicated by "n" following the page number (e.g. 198n11); references to figures are indicated by *f.*

A

academic freedom, 31, 32–33, 57
academic integration, 71
academic library
    challenges of, 13–17
    classification system for, 2–3
    context for, 1–18
    definition of, 2
    environment of, 12–13
Academic Library Advancement and Development Network (ALADN), 235
accountability, 1, 85, 181–188, 215, 241
accreditation
    about, 173–178
    ceremonial senates and, 113
    curriculum and, 85, 87–89
    distance education and, 98
    information literacy and, 178–181
accreditation boards/agencies, 29–30, 174–177
acquisition procedures, 202–203
active listening, 221
adjunct faculty, 59–60
administrative bloat, 11–12
admissions, 66–69
advanced degrees, 262–264
advocacy, 111, 130–131
African American colleges, 36, 37
ALA Code of Ethics, 221
Albanese, Andrew R., 224
allocation decisions, 201–202
amenities, 10–12
American Association of University Professors (AAUP), 109, 114
American Indian Higher Education Consortium, 37
Americans with Disabilities Act (ADA), 145
Annoyed Librarian, 231
Applegate, Rachel, 213–214

approval plans, 203
archives, 207
Art of War, The (Sun-Tzu), 12
article processing charge (APC), 55
articulated-transfer curriculum, 31
Ascendant Strategy Management Group, 187
assistant professors, 58, 60
associate colleges, 3
associate professors, 58, 60
Association of American Colleges and Universities, 8
Association of American Publishers (AAP), 224
Association of College and Research Libraries (ACRL), 13, 16, 71, 98, 147, 180–181, 188, 232
Association of Governing Boards of Universities and Colleges (AGB), 105
Association of Research Libraries (ARL), 3, 187, 188, 195, 196–198, 200, 213, 233
athletics, 31, 77–79
Atkinson, Ross, 194
Auchter, Dorothy, 215
Austin, Ann, 45
authority, shared governance and, 114

B

baccalaureate colleges, 3
Bacone College, 36
badges, 8–9
Bagshaw, Maria, 240
balance, collection, 200–201
balanced scorecard, 186–187
Beagle, Donald, 157
Beichner, Robert, 50–51
Beile, Penny M., 230
Bell, Steven J., 170–171
benchmarking, 183, 184–185
Bergquist, William, 111

Berry, Leonard L., 182, 185
best-in-class benchmarking, 183
Beyond Bullet Points (Atkinson), 50
Blank, Rebecca, 5–6
blanket orders, 202
"blended librarian" skill set, 170–171
Blumenstyk, Goldie, 9–10, 12
Blurton, C., 159
board responsibilities, 105
boards, governing, 103–107, 123–124
Bok, Derek, 1, 5, 9
Bolin, Mary K., 233
Bonfield, Brett, 231
Boning, Kenneth, 83
Books for College Libraries (ALA), 34
Bowdoin College, 28
Bowen, Howard, 120, 137–138
Bradbury, Danny, 208–209
Bradley, Kevin, 208
Browne, John W., 28
Bryan, Jacalyn, 233
budget cuts, 68
budget process
    about, 124–125
    budget as control device, 125–127
    budget cycle, 127
    budget preparation, 127–129
    presenting and defending requests, 129–132
building program, 146
Burgan, Mary, 50
burnout, 110
Buschman, John, 230
business officer, 235
businesses, partnerships with, 135–136
Butin, Dan, 46
Butler, Pierce, 195

C

California state system, 106
Campos, Paul, 10
campus, concept of, 22
campus facilities, 11, 12
capital budgets, 127
Carbo, Toni, 14, 16
career breaks, 264–265
career counseling, 79
career development
    about, 247–248
    adjusting to positions and, 258–260
    career trajectory and, 248–258
    changing views of career and, 264–265

moving forward, 265–266
    plan for, 260–264
Carey, Ronadin, 202
Cargill, Jennifer, 131
Carlson, Ronald H., 64–65
Carlson, Scott, 214
Carnegie Classification, 4, 213
Carnegie Foundation for the Advancement of
    Teaching, 90
carpet, 144
Carrott, Gregory, 13
Cavanaugh, Joseph, 51
CCC2NAU, 32
Center for Research Libraries (CRL), 197, 205
central reference, 217–218
ceremonial senates, 113
Cevetello, Joseph, 50–51
Cheyney College, 37
chief information officer (CIO), 108
Christianson, Elin, 234
Church-Duran, Jennifer, 233
circulation data, 203–204
circulation services, 218–224
Clark, Burton, 44
Coalition for Networked Information (CNI), 16
Coconino County Community College, 32
Code of Ethics, ALA, 221
Cohen, Daniel, 208
Coleman, John, 7
collaboration, 135–136
collaborative learning groups, 72
collaborative learning spaces, 50–51
collections
    about, 193–194
    assessment of, 203–204
    development of, 194, 198–209
    early donations to, 27
    environmental controls and, 150–151
    facilities and, 142, 143
    funding and, 129, 201–202
    licensing considerations and, 209–210
    management of, 194
    off-site storage, 204–206
    off-site storage of, 156
    past and present practice regarding, 194–196
    policy for, 199–200
    preservation and, 206–209
    purposes of, 194
    World War II and, 196–198
College of William and Mary, 26–27
colleges
    curriculum expansion and, 31

description of, 4
types of, 3
collegial governance, 101–102
Collegiate Learning Assessment (CLA), 85
collegiate sports, 31, 77–79
Commission on the Future of Higher Education
    Report (Spellings Report), 85
committee work, 47–48, 232
Common Core State Standards Initiative, 85
community colleges (CCs), 3, 4–5, 31–32, 34, 106
community engagement, 40–41
compact shelving units, 205
competitive benchmarking, 183
comprehensive universities, 3
conferences, 241, 249–250
confidentiality, 221, 223
confrontational situations, 220–221
Congressional Budget Office (CBO), 6
consolidated libraries, 143
consulting, 46–47
continuing education, 92–95
Cooperative Institutional Research Program
    (CIRP), 65, 75, 79
cooperative storage, 205
copyright, 74, 223–224
Corinthian Colleges, 39
Cornell, 30
corporate model, 107
corporate partnerships, 135–136
cost analysis, 187
costs. *See also* funding
    of degree programs, 92
    of higher education, 10–12
    nonrecurring, 127
    recurring, 127
    student, 67
    of subscriptions, 167–168
    of technology, 167–170
Council for Aid to Education, 85
Council for Higher Education Accreditation
    (CHEA), 174, 176
Council on Library and Information Resources,
    161
councils, 111–112
counterpoint approach, 85
Counting Opinions, 183
cover letters, 252–253
Creswell, John, 53
crime, 152–153
critical success factors (CSFs), 165–166
cross-disciplinary scholarship, 44
curators, 104

curriculum
    about, 83
    continuing education, 92–95
    debating, 86–90
    distance education and, 95–99
    expansion of, 27, 30–31
    general education, 83–86
    modifying, 90–92
Curzon, Susan, 14
customer service, 214–216, 236–237
CV (curriculum vitae), 248, 250–253

D

Dartmouth College, 27–28, 36, 103. *See also*
    Trustees of Dartmouth College v. Woodward
data recovery, 154
database subscriptions. *See* subscriptions
Davidson, Paul, 7
Davis-Kahl, Stephanie, 193
de-acidification, 207
deans, 108
DeBard, Robert, 76–77
debt load, 6
default on loans, 6
deferred maintenance, 144, 155–156
degree programs, 91–92, 93–94
degrees
    badges versus, 8–9
    immediacy versus long-term benefits of, 7–8
    for librarians, 231
    worth of, 7
DeMajo, Mary Madden, 247
departmental politics, 90
departmental reference, 218
deserted library, 213, 214
development officer, 235
developmental approach, 85
Dewey, Melvil, 173
digital records, 207–208
digitization, 193
disabilities, facility planning and, 145
disaster management, 153–155
disciplinary actions, 243
dissertation defense, 54
distance education, 38, 95–99, 241
distributive core, 84
diversity, 60–61, 68–69, 106
divisional reference, 217–219
doctorate-granting universities, 3
document delivery, 222
Doshi, Ameet, 188

Dougherty, Richard, 187-188
due process, 74
Dugan, Robert E., 168
Duncan, Arne, 9
Dunster, President (Harvard), 26
Dupuis, Elizabeth A., 225

E
Eagan, K., 65
education levels
    for librarians, 231
    for staff, 229
EDUCAUSE Center for Analysis and Research
    (ECAR), 50-51
e-learning communities, 96
elective courses, 83
electronic resources
    funding and, 129
    licensing considerations and, 209-210
Elfstrand, Stephen, 202
Eliot, Charles William, 32, 108, 204
embedded librarians, 219, 225
Emberton, John, 166
emergency response plans, 149
emeritus/emerita title, 59
Emory College, 28
Empire State Editions, 55
employability, 8
empowerment approach, 85
endowments, 123-124
energy and utilities expenditures, 121
Engstrom, Cathy, 72
Evans, Luther, 198
extension programs, 35, 41, 46

F
facilities
    about, 141-143
    deferred maintenance and, 155-156
    health, safety, and security and,
        150-155
    library differences and, 143-144
    managing, 148-150
    recruitment and, 66
    renovation planning, 144-148
    trends regarding, 156-157
faculty
    adjunct, 59-60
    curriculum and, 84-85
    diversity and, 60-61

emeritus, 59
    German model and, 31
    job titles for, 58-59
    overview of, 43-44
    part-time, 59-60
    preparation time and, 43, 51-52
    responsibilities of, 44-56
    technology and, 43, 45, 50-51
    tenure and, 57-60
    workloads for, 230
fair use, 223-224
Fairburn, Linden, 225
Farmington Plan, 34, 196, 197, 198
Federal Student Loan Repayment Program,
    Calendar Year 2009, 39
fees, student, 10-11, 67
finances, higher education, 119-121. *See also* costs;
    funding
financial aid, 66-67, 69-70, 121
fines, 134, 220
Fisher, James L., 105
floor coverings, 144
Fordham University Press, 55
for-profit education, 38-40
foundations, 122-123, 132, 134, 136
Fox, Robert, 188
Framework for Information Literacy for Higher
    Education, 181
fraternities, 76-77
freelancers, 264
Friends of the Library groups, 134
full professors, 58, 60
full-time equivalent (FTE), 210
functional senates, 112-113
funding. *See also* costs
    about, 119
    accountability and, 181
    budget process and, 124-132
    challenges of, 10-12
    collections and, 201-202
    early challenges for, 26, 28
    early sources of, 27
    endowments and, 123-124
    federal, 110
    grants and research and, 121-123
    higher education finances and, 119-121
    income generation and, 132-137
    planning and budgeting and, 137-138
    research grants for, 60
    student costs and, 67
fund-raising, 133, 134-136, 235
Furco, Andrew, 41

G

gap reduction, 182
Gardner, Marilyn, 256
Gasman, Marybeth, 68
Gellerman, Saul, 243
general education, 83–86
general reference, 217–218
German model, 31, 52–53
Ghouse, Nikhat, 233
G.I. (Government Issue) Bill of Rights, 34, 195
gifts in kind, 133
Gilman, Daniel Coit, 54
Gilman, Todd, 263–264
Ginsberg, Benjamin, 11–12
Goodrich, Geanne, 241
Goodsett, Mandi, 261
governance
    about, 101–102
    administration and, 107–111
    concluding thoughts on, 114–116
    guidelines and, 103–107
    role of state and, 102–103
    "those who do" and, 111–114
governing boards, 103–107, 123–124
grade inflation, 9
graduation, 79
grants, 121–123, 136
Graves, Stephanie J., 265
Greek letter organizations, 76–77
Grosch, Mary, 263

H

Harper, William Rainey, 31
Harvard, 25–26, 32
Harvard, John, 26
Haveman, Robert, 9
health, facilities and, 150
Hensley, Merinda Kaye, 193
heritage approach, 85
Hewitt, Joseph, 187
higher education
    in 20th century, 34–41
    costs of, 10–12
    English influence on, 22–23
    in Europe, 20–24
    French influence on, 21–22
    future of, 5–12
    German influence on, 23
    historic roots of, 19–20
    history of in U.S., 24–32
    income and, 64–65

institutions of, 2–5
    Italian influence on, 21
    natural laws of, 137–138
    student thoughts on, 64–65
    wars and, 32–34
Higher Education Act (1965), 34
Higher Education Research Institute at the
        University of California, Los Angeles
        (UCLA), 65
Hijleh, Renee, 202
hiring freezes, 35, 128, 168
Hirshon, Arnold, 215
Hispanic Association of Colleges and Universities
        (HACU), 37–38
historically black colleges and universities
        (HBCUs), 36, 37
Holder, Sara, 143
holistic planning model, 166
Holt, Glen, 128–129, 135–136
horizontal study, 183
hours of operation, 143–144, 148
housekeeping, 149
Hughes, Julia, 49
Human Relations Area Files (HRAF), 34
human resources (HR) officers, 235–236
humidity, 150–151
hybrid courses, 51

I

in loco parentis concept, 28
income generation, 132–137
incremental budgets, 130
independent study requests/projects, 48–49
industry benchmarking, 183
influential senates, 113
information and communication technology (ICT)
    description of, 159–160
    scholarly communication and, 160–161
    staff for, 235
information commons, 157, 159
information literacy, 178–181
Information Literacy Standards for Higher
        Education, 181
information technology, funding and, 121
insect problems, 206
instructional services, 219
instructors, 59
instrumental approach, 85
insurance, 149–150
integrated library systems (ILSs), 163, 166,
        168–170, 203–204, 235

integrative learning theory, 84
intellectual honesty, 74
intellectual property, 52, 122
interlibrary loan (ILL), 222
internal benchmarking, 183
Internet. *See also* information and communication
    technology (ICT); technology
    development and growth of, 38
    for-profit education and, 39
    scholarly communication and, 56
intersession, 95
interview presentations, 259
interviews, 253, 254–258

J

Jaeger, Audrey, 45, 47–48
job descriptions, 239
job seeking process, 248–258
job specifications, 239
job success criteria, 239
job titles, 58–59, 234
Johns Hopkins University, 31
Johns Hopkins University Press, 54
Johnson, Gerald W., 23
Johnstone, Bruce, 119
joint-use services, 148
Joliet Junior College, 31
journal subscriptions. *See* subscriptions
junior colleges (JCs). *See* community colleges (CCs)
Juran, Joseph, 186
"just in case" versus "just in time" collecting, 198

K

Kaplan, Robert, 186
Kaske, Neal, 179–180
Kaufman, Paula T., 229
Kell, Susan, 247–248
Kell, Thomas, 13
Kerr, Clark, 23
Kilgour, Frederick, 35
King, C. Judson, 115–116
King, John B., 8
Kirch, Claire, 55
Kissler, Gerald, 111

L

ladder appointments, 58, 60
land-grant institutions/schools, 29, 32, 37, 46
Lane, Liz, 229–230

Lannon, Amber, 143
"Last Lecture" (Pausch), 45
Latin American Cooperative Acquisitions Program
    (LACAP), 197
Leadership in Energy and Environmental Design
    (LEED) standards, 121, 147
Lean Six Sigma, 186
learning communities, 72
lecturers, 59
Lee, Marta, 262
legacy students, 68–69
Leuzinger, Julie, 216
Levi, Yaniv, 208
Lewis, David, 14
liberal education, 85–86
LibPAS, 183
LibQUAL+, 182–184
LibQUAL+ Lite, 183
librarians
    faculty status for, 231–233
    job market for, 230–231
    status of on campus, 230
"library as place," 157
Library Associates, 134
Library Bill of Rights (ALA), 221
library instruction, 219
library liaison services, 224–225
Library of Congress (LC), 196, 197
library societies, 29
library spaces, trends in, 142, 156–157
library technician, 234
library value, 188
LibSat, 183
licensing considerations, 209–210
life-long learning. *See* continuing education
Lincoln College, 37
Lindquist, Thea, 263–264
listening skills, 221, 242
living-learning communities (LLCs), 72, 76
lobbying, 130–131
Lowenstein, M., 84

M

maintenance, deferred, 155–156
marketing yourself, 248–253
Martell, Charles, 213
master's colleges and universities, 3
Maynard, Meleah, 41
McCarty, J. P., 206
McChesney, Christopher S., 64–65
Meaning of General Education, The (Miller), 85

Measuring Information Service Outcomes (MISO), 183

mentors, 261–262

Meraz, Gloria, 130–131

Merkley, Cari, 217

Miami University of Ohio, 28

micromanagement, 107

Midwest Inter-Library Corporation (MILC), 197

Miles, Dennis B., 217

Miller, Gary, 85

Mills, Michael R., 103

Minor, James T., 112–114

mold, 206

Moorman, John, 219

Moor's Indian Charity School, 36

Morrill Act (1862), 29, 32, 46

Morrill Act (1890), 37

Morris, Libby, 47

Mortenson, Thomas, 6

Murphy, Sarah, 186

Murray-Rust, Catherine, 231

N

naming opportunities, 26

National Association of College and University Business Officers (NACUBO), 123, 183

National Center for Education Statistics (NCES), 64, 120

National Collegiate Athletic Association (NCAA), 76–77

National Program for Acquisitions and Cataloging (NPAC), 197–198

National Union Catalog, 196

Native American tribal colleges, 36–37

Neal, James G., 130, 231

needs assessment, 199

new degree programs, 91–92

nonrecurring costs, 127

Norton, David, 186

O

Oakleaf, Megan, 179–180

Oberlin, 28

Occupational Outlook Handbook (OOH), 234

off-site storage, 156, 204–206

Ohio College Association, 35

Oldenburg, Ray, 157

"one shot," 219

Online Computer Library Center (OCLC), 35

online courses and materials, 40, 97

online learning, 51–52

online services, 216

open access (OA) publishing movement, 56, 193

Open Content Alliance, 16

open education resources (OERs), 193

open source software, 169

"open to all" concept, 35, 63, 76

operating budgets, 126–127

operations research, 187

organizational culture, 13

orientation, 239–240

other full-time staff, 235–237

Oud, Joanne, 259–260

outsourcing, 170

overhead, 121

overseers, 104

Oxford/Cambridge model, 22–23

P

paralibrarian, 234

paraprofessional, 234

Parasuraman, A., 182, 185

Park, Ji-Hye, 265

Parker, Wyman, 35

part-time faculty, 59–60

Pausch, Randy, 44–45

peer review, 55–56

Pembroke State College, 36

Petrella, John, 256

Pew Research Center, 7

Philadelphia College of Apothecaries, 27

Pittendrigh, Adele, 86

PL-480 (Public Law 480) effort, 197

plagiarism, 74

planned giving, 135

planning and budgeting, 137–138

Pogue, Korolyn, 51–52

postsecondary education, overview of U.S., 1–2

power, types of, 114–115

Pratt, Darrin, 54–55

presentation software, 50

presentations, 252

preservation, 206–209

presidents

    expectations of, 110

    governance and, 104

    library and, 110–111

    role of, 108–109

    tenure of, 110

President's Commission report (1947), 34

professional organizations, 249–250, 265–266

professors, 58, 60
program and planning budgeting systems (PPBSs), 130
prohibited books, 27
public relations (PR) officer, 236
publications, 252

Q
quality management, 185
Quinn, Brian, 182, 209

R
radio frequency identification (RFID) chips, 151
RAND Corporation, 85
recruitment
    staffing and, 239
    of students, 66-69
recurring costs, 127
reference services, 216-219
regents, 104, 106
relationship-based services, 215
remote storage. *See* off-site storage
renovation planning, 144-148
research
    crossover, 44
    faculty and, 52-56
    funding and, 121-123
research universities, 3
Reserve Officers' Training Corps (ROTC), 33
reserve services, 222-224
responsibility center management (RCM), 130
retention
    of staff, 240
    of students, 9, 71-73
Rhodes, Frank, 86
risk management, 149-150
Robb, Robert, 7
Rodwell, John, 225
Rose Bowl, 31
Rosovsky, Henry, 53
Rossiter, Marsha, 92, 94
Ruffalo Noel Levitz, 79
Ryan, Susan, 217
Ryland, John, 195

S
sabbatical, 264-265
Sacks, Casey, 76-77
safety and security, 150-155

salaries
    controlling costs of, 167-168
    differentials in, 236
    funding and, 120, 129
    grants and, 121
    performance appraisals and, 243
Saunders, Laura, 179
Schachter, Debbie, 215
Schlosser, Melanie, 224
Schmidt, Karen, 193
scholarly communication, 54, 160-161, 193-194
scholarly publishing, 55-56
Scholarly Publishing and Academic Resources
    Coalition (SPARC), 16
Schumann, David W., 49
Seaman, Scott, 204
search committees, 253-254
security audits, 151, 152
security systems, 151-152
selection, staffing and, 239
selection resources, 200
Self, Jim, 186
self-assessment, 262-264
Seltzer, Rena, 48
senates, 111-114
service and outreach, 40-41, 45-48
service desks, combined, 216-217
service hours, 143-144, 148
service learning, 46
services
    about, 213-214
    circulation, 218-224
    customer, 214-216
    instructional, 219
    library liaison, 224-225
    reference, 216-219
    reserve, 222-224
Shaman, Susan, 67
Shank, John, 170-171
Shapiro, Bernard, 89
Shapiro, Daniel B., 67
shared governance, 101-102, 112, 114-116
Shumaker, David, 225
Singer, Paul, 241
Sinwell, Carol A. Pender, 31
Six Sigma, 186
"smart" classrooms, 50, 159
Smeeding, Timothy, 9
Smith, Dan, 88
Smith, Kenneth, 178-179
Smith, Lynn, 130
Smith, Mark, 219-220

Smith, Virginia, 86
Sobrero, Patricia, 96
social agenda approach, 85
social integration, 71, 75
social mobility, 9
socioeconomic gap, 9–10
"soft" money, 121
Sorcinelli, Mary Dean, 45
SPEC Kits, ARL, 188
special collections, 207
special-focus institutions, 3
sponsorships, 135–136
staff and staffing
    about, 229–231
    development for, 240–241
    librarians, 231–233
    other full-time staff, 235–237
    performance appraisals and, 241–243
    process for, 238–241
    student employees, 237–238
    support staff, 234
    training and, 170, 240–241
standing orders, 202
Stanley, Christine A., 61
state, role of, 102–103, 110
Sternberg, Robert J., 46
Stoddard, Solomon, 27
storage
    cooperative, 205
    off-site, 156, 204–206
stress, 265
student debt, 5–7, 39
student discipline, 73–74
student employees, 6, 69–70, 237–238, 240
student government, 75
student groups, 75–77
student libraries, 29
student services, 73–75
student work teams, 238
students
    collegiate sports and, 77–79
    diversity and, 68–69
    financial aid and, 69–70
    graduation and, 79
    on higher education, 64–65
    legacy, 68–69
    overview of, 63–64
    recruitment and admissions of, 66–69
    retention of, 71–73
    student groups and, 75–77
    student services and, 73–75
study skills, 71

subscriptions, 35, 56, 68, 91, 103, 127, 131, 167–168, 193, 202, 209
subverted senates, 114
summer schools, 95
Sun-Tzu, 12
supervisory responsibilities, 229
support groups, 134–135
support staff, 234

T
teaching, faculty and, 48–52
teaching and learning centers (TLCs), 49, 50
teaching assistants (TAs), 58–59
teaching methods, 49–50
Teaching Online (Ko and Rossen), 50
technology
    about, 159–163
    academic libraries and, 163
    controlling costs of, 167–170
    distance education and, 98
    facilities and, 145
    faculty and, 43, 45, 50–51
    future directions for, 170–171
    influence of, 35–36, 38
    long-term planning for, 164–167
    merging services with, 168
    staff training and, 170
    training and, 241
technology-enabled active learning (TEAL)
    classrooms, 50
temperature, 150–151
tenure, 57–60, 232–233, 265
textbooks, online materials and, 40
thefts, 151–152
thesis defense, 54
third places, 157
Thornton, Courtney, 45, 47–48
Tierney, William, 112
time management, 71
Tinto, Vincent, 72
Todaro, Julie, 219–220
Toews, Michelle, 44
training, staff, 170, 240–241
transaction-based services, 215
transparency, increased demands for, 1
travel scholarships, 265
tribal colleges, 3, 36–37
Triumph, Therese F., 230
trustees, 104, 106
Trustees of Dartmouth College v. Woodward, 27–28, 103, 104

tuition
  discounts to, 66–67
  increases in, 10–11, 119–120
  out-of-state, 67, 119

U
Udermann, Brian, 52
university (term), 21
University of Chicago, 31
University of Northern Arizona, 32
University of Virginia, 27
University of Wisconsin, 30–31, 41
University Press of Kentucky, 55
university presses (UPs), 54–55
U.S. Department of Education (USDE),
    174, 176
U.S. Department of Education's National Center
    for Education Statistics (Institute of
    Education Sciences [IES]), 2
USA PATRIOT Act, 221
user base, funding and, 131
user studies, 188

V
value engineering, 144
valuing approach, 85–86
Van de Vord, Rebecca, 51–52
vanity publishing, 55
vertical study, 183
visitors, 104
volunteerism, 46
Vultaggio, Julie, 68

W
Wagner, Ralph, 198
Walsh, Andrew, 261
Walters, William H., 233

water damage, 153–154
Watson, Mark, 209
Webster, Daniel, 28
Weech, Terry, 263
weeding, 204
Wehmeyer, Susan, 215
Weingand, Darlene E., 215–216
Wesleyan College, 28
West Point Military Academy, 27
Wheelock, John, 27–28
White, Lydia, 186
Wilberforce University, 37
Wildavsky, Aaron, 130
Wilensky, Rona, 73
Williams, Gordon, 193
Williams, Karen, 224–225
Willis, Alfred, 186
wills and trusts, 135
"Wisconsin idea," 31, 41, 46
work analysis, 187–188
work-life balance, 263, 264–265
workloads, 230
work-study employment, 6, 69–70. *See also* student
    employees
World War II, 195, 196–198

X
Xiong, Jian Anna, 265

Y
Yale, Elihu, 26
Yazedjian, Ani, 44

Z
Zeithaml, Valarie A., 182, 185
Zemsky, Robert, 67
zero-based budgeting (ZBB), 130